MUSIC EVERY DAY

Transforming the Elementary Classroom

Carol P. Richardson
University of Michigan

Betty W. Atterbury

Boston Burr Ridge, IL Dubuque, IA Madison, WI New York San Francisco St. Louis Bangkok Bogotá
Caracas Lisbon London Madrid Mexico City Milan New Delhi Seoul Singapore Sydney Taipei Toronto

McGraw-Hill Higher Education

A Division of The ***McGraw-Hill*** *Companies*

MUSIC EVERY DAY: TRANSFORMING THE ELEMENTARY CLASSROOM
Published by McGraw-Hill, an imprint of The McGraw-Hill Companies, Inc., 1221 Avenue of the Americas, New York, NY 10020.

This book is printed on acid-free paper.

1 2 3 4 5 6 7 8 9 0 QPD/QPD 0 9 8 7 6 5 4 3 2 1 0

ISBN 0-07-052396-7

Editorial director: *Phillip A. Butcher*
Senior sponsoring editor: *Chris Freitag*
Developmental editor: *JoElaine Retzler*
Marketing manager: *David Patterson*
Project manager: *Craig S. Leonard*
Production supervisor: *Michael McCormick*
Senior designer: *Kiera Cunningham*
Supplement coordinator: *Rose Range*
New Media project manager: *Kimberly Stark*
Photo researcher: *Keri Johnson*
Cover illustration: *Paul Turnbaugh*
Interior design: *Z Graphics*
Compositor: *A-R Editions, Inc.*
Typeface: *10/12 Times Roman*
Printer: *Quebecor Printing Book Group/Dubuque*

Library of Congress Cataloging-in Publication Data

Richardson, Carol P.
Music every day / Carol P. Richardson, Betty W. Atterbury.
p. cm.
ISBN 0-07-052396-7 (alk. paper)
1. School music—Instruction and study. 2. Music—Instruction and study. I. Atterbury, Betty Wilson. II. Title.

MT1 .R535 2001
372.87—dc21 00-033924

www.mhhe.com

This book is dedicated
to the memory of
Betty Wilson Atterbury
1937–1998

C.P.R.

Brief Contents

Contents

Music Fundamentals for Creating Music 331

Enables you to experience the role of composer as you create your own rap and blues songs. Adds the high E to your recorder repertoire.

Creating Music with Children 349

Enables you to plan and lead group composition activities that integrate with other areas of the elementary school curriculum. Builds your recorder skill through playing harmony.

13 *Life in the Classroom* 369

Introduces you to "real world" situations through a series of case study activities that require you to take on the role of the teacher-protagonist.

Preface

APPROACH

Music Every Day: Transforming the Elementary Classroom represents a vision for the musical preparation of prospective elementary teachers that is radically different from anything that has been published to date. The basis of this vision is a belief that all humans are musical beings and that all prospective elementary classroom teachers bring with them a background in music just as they do in reading, math, and language. The aim of this text is to produce elementary classroom teachers who believe that music is an important part of children's daily classroom lives and who have the confidence and ability to make this vision of human musicality a reality.

An important aspect of creating confidence in prospective teachers is ensuring that their understanding of music is thorough and related clearly to their future as classroom teachers. Instead of overpowering elementary education majors with all there is to know about music fundamentals, this text presents a sequential, paced approach to learning that leads students from experience to iconic representation to musical symbol. Different facets of notation are discussed then reviewed and integrated in a spiral manner throughout the text. The same approach is taken with the development of recorder playing skills. Each successive chapter introduces a new note on the recorder while offering a variety of recorder literature to reinforce and integrate the learnings from previous chapters.

This text is unlike any other fundamentals/classroom methods text for two reasons. First, the adult musical learners are taught through materials and experiences appropriate for adult musical tastes, rather than through "kiddie" music. Second, and perhaps more important, this text aims to teach classroom teachers how to integrate music into the elementary curriculum—not how to be music teachers. This is accomplished through a format of paired chapters: the first chapter of the pair addresses the musical fundamentals required for singing, listening, moving, playing, and composing through the use of materials and experiences appropriate for adult tastes; the second chapter of the pair demonstrates how to apply these learnings to enhance the elementary curriculum.

Our emphasis in this text is that music is important in the daily lives of children. The power of the musical experience lies in its transcendent quality that allows the child to gain personal musical insights and cultural understandings that are unavailable elsewhere in the curriculum. The present educational system occasionally provides time for children to have these important musical experiences—when led by a music specialist. In order for elementary teachers to understand the importance of music in the classroom day, they must experience valid musical encounters in their own teacher education coursework. This text enables methods courses to engage students in mastering the necessary knowledge base while simultaneously encountering the power of the musical experience.

AUDIENCE

Because the paired chapters alternate between fundamentals for adult learners and "how to teach these to children," this text can meet the needs of both the one-semester combined music fundamentals/elementary music methods course and the two-semester sequence where fundamentals and methods are taught separately. In both cases, students only need to purchase one textbook. Because of the innovative combination of music fundamentals with teaching approaches found in this text, it can serve a wide variety of students. Apart from its obvious use as a methods text for nonmajors, this text is a valuable resource for graduate music education courses because of its focus on integrating music in the elementary curriculum.

CONTENT/ORGANIZATION

This text addresses the educational realities of today's schools such as cooperative learning, creative and critical thinking, gender issues, multiculturalism, and integrated learning. Students become involved immediately in the challenging realities and joys of elementary teaching through case studies, cooperative group experiences, and teaching scripts. Although the individual teaching-related chapters focus on single musical behaviors, through the use of teaching scripts prospective teachers experience an ever-widening spiral of model lessons that incorporates the musical behaviors discussed in each successive chapter. The teaching scripts show pre-service teachers that many avenues to musical integration are available. The lesson scripts also provide models of lesson planning as well as effective questioning.

One current emphasis in education is a thrust toward inclusion of handicapped learners in regular classrooms. This "regular education initiative" or "total inclusion" policy means that all teachers must be prepared to educate a vast range of learners within one class. Each of the chapters dealing with making music with children includes a section that addresses practical ways to tailor musical experiences to meet the needs of the special learners in the classroom.

Case studies form an integral part of this text, as they are a powerful and effective way to experience the delights and dilemmas of the day-to-day professional life of the elementary teacher. Each teaching application chapter begins with a case study portraying a classroom teacher who meets a dilemma related to the chapter content. The case study is followed by cooperative learning tasks that give undergraduates an opportunity to reflect on the experiences of the fictional classroom teacher featured in the case. Cooperative learning experiences are essential in contemporary teacher preparation if undergraduates are to become comfortable and familiar with this important instructional strategy.

The materials in this book are clearly marked for use in a variety of settings. In addition to case studies, teaching scripts, and cooperative discussion questions, each chapter includes content that students can read before coming to class. In-class activities provide opportunities for students to work cooperatively with a partner or in small groups. Further practice sections allow students to synthesize chapter learnings and can be used as in-class activities or homework assignments.

Chapter 1 takes the reader into the life of a classroom teacher and a music teacher through case studies that give the reader a glimpse of the complexity of teaching and the rewards for teachers that children share as they experience music. This chapter presents both a rationale for including music in the school day and ways to achieve musical integration. Also addressed are the challenges of exploring music from outside one's own musical culture and the ways that gender impacts on classroom instruction.

Chapters 2 and 3 introduce the music fundamentals of rhythm and pitch required for confident singing as well as introducing three notes on the recorder. Chapter 2 focuses on reading rhythms. Chapter 3 enables the adult learner to experiment with her or his singing voice while reading pitch notation.

Chapter 4 is the first of the "how to teach" chapters, focusing on ways to select and teach a wide variety of songs to children of various ability levels. Included are suggested song materials from many musical cultures, ways to help special needs singers, and the national standards for singing.

Chapter 5 introduces adult learners to the fundamentals of music listening, including recognition of musical form, timbre, and texture. A wide range of music listening examples (available on the accompanying compact disc) is used to teach two- and three-part form, theme and variations, and timbre differences.

Chapter 6 shows students how to use their newly acquired music listening skills to enhance other areas of the elementary curriculum such as social studies and writing. Included here are ways to nurture thinking skills in music listening experiences, a case study focusing on integrating science and music, and the national standards for music listening.

Chapter 7 expands on the rhythm reading skills from previous chapters by showing adult learners how to play a wide array of classroom instruments, including keyboard and guitar. Students learn how to conduct a round and accompany a listening example.

Chapter 8 introduces ways to integrate instrument playing skills throughout the elementary curriculum for both primary and intermediate students. The teaching scripts in this chapter illustrate integrative lessons on categorizing sounds, alternative ways of producing sounds, improvising, adding sound to stories and poems, the science of sound, and enhancing a haiku poem with instruments. The national standards for playing instruments are also introduced.

Chapter 9 reviews the fundamental rhythmic concepts from previous chapters while enhancing the adult learner's movement skills. Basic movement concepts are introduced along with folk dances from various world traditions.

Chapter 10 enables adult learners to integrate movement experiences into lessons from a range of curricular areas, including language arts, social studies, science, and the visual arts.

Chapter 11 assists the adult learners in further developing their rhythmic and notation skills and in experiencing the role of composer by creating their own rap and blues songs.

Chapter 12 acquaints students with planning and leading group composition activities that integrate with other areas of the elementary curriculum such as science and language arts. This chapter also addresses evaluation of student creations and outlines the national standards for composition.

Chapter 13 ("Life in the Classroom") completes the text by returning to the context of the classroom. This chapter introduces students to the real world through a series of case study activities in which the student is allowed to take on the role of the protagonist. The eight cases in this chapter cover the various professional relationships involved in teaching: teacher-student, teacher-teacher, teacher-parent, and teacher-administrator.

ACKNOWLEDGMENTS

I would like to thank the following people for their assistance in bringing this book to life:

The McGraw-Hill team of Cynthia Ward, Chris Freitag, and Joey Retzler for their unfailing support of this project.

The reviewers, whose comments on the manuscript were of great help to us as we refined the book: Nancy H. Barry, *Auburn University;* Sara B. Bidner, *Southeastern Louisiana University;* Lynn Brinkmeyer, *Eastern Washington University;* Joi Freed-Garrod, *Simon Fraser University, British Columbia;* Steven N. Kelly, *University of Nebraska;* Marie C. Miller, *Emporia State University;* Richard Rose, *Miami-Dade Community College;* Margaret Schmidt, *St. Cloud State University;* Sheila Schonbrun, *City College of New York;* and David G. Tovey, *Ohio State University, Mansfield.*

The children of King School, and Mrs. Susan Lake, for graciously allowing us to use their photos.

The students in MUED 342 whose photos appear in this text.

Bob Atterbury for the illustrations that appear in the text and for always being there for my friend Betty.

My loves, Ian, Julia, and Gregory Richardson.

C.P.R.

Music in the Elementary School Day

INTRODUCTION

The opening materials in this chapter are designed to give you a glimpse into the lives of teachers and help you to understand some of the challenges and joys of the career you have chosen. The case studies you will read throughout this text place you in an elementary classroom and provide insight on a teacher's thoughts and intentions. Guiding the learning of a group of children for an entire year or more is a challenging and delightful career choice and one that will give you joy and satisfaction. The authors of this text expect that you will have an engaging time working your way through this enculturation process as you move from the role of student to that of teacher.

THE CLASSROOM TEACHER

Ms. Reema is seated in front of her first grade students, who are all sitting on the floor in three rows. She holds up a picture book and says, "Today's story is about some insects that were friends and a lot of different animals as well. Let's find out what one friend did for another." She holds the book up so that all of her pupils can see the pages as she reads "Grasshopper to the Rescue," a Georgian story translated from the Russian by Bonnie Carey (New York: William Morrow, 1979).

"A grasshopper once made friends with an ant. They became as close as brothers and set out together on a journey. Along the way they came to a river, and the grasshopper said to the ant, 'I will jump across. What about you, brother ant?' "

" 'I'll jump across, too!' said the ant."

"The grasshopper went 'boing' and jumped across to the other side. But the ant went 'phht' and fell into the water. The river began carrying the poor ant away."

" 'Brother grasshopper,' begged the ant, 'please help get me out of the water!' "

"The grasshopper jumped 'boing-boing' up to a pig and asked, 'Pig, give me some bristles! I will weave a rope out of your bristles, toss the rope into the water, and pull out my friend the ant!' "

"The pig said, 'Feed me some acorns. Then you can take as many of my bristles as you like.' "

This cumulative story details how the grasshopper went from the pig to a number of sources to beg for items to fulfill a growing list of conditions: a tree for acorns, a raven for quiet, a hen for a fresh egg, a barn for some grain, a mouse to stop gnawing on the barn, a cat to stop chasing the mouse, a cow for some milk, and a field for some green grass.

When the story is finished, Ms. Reema asks, "What does this story tell us about friendship?" Several hands shoot into the air, and the teacher calls on Jordan.

"I think it tells us that friends help each other," says Jordan.

"Who can tell me how the grasshopper helped the ant?" asks Ms. Reema. This time almost all the students have their hands in the air, and Ms. Reema calls on Lauren.

"The grasshopper worked hard to get all the things he needed to get the pig bristles for the rope," explains Lauren.

"Yes," says Ms. Reema. "He was very patient, wasn't he? He did whatever was needed to save his friend, even though it took him a long time and he had to convince all those different animals and things to give him what he needed to help the ant."

She picks up a pile of small posterboard cards with pictures and labels of each of the speakers from the story and says, "Let's see if we can put these cards into the right order. Which character was the first one that the grasshopper asked for help?" Several children shout out "Pig!" and Ms. Reema places the pig picture and label into the far left pockets of the pocket board behind her. After all the cards and labels are correctly placed, Ms. Reema says, "Let's reread the story now and see if we remembered the order correctly. But before we do that, who would like to go to the music room and borrow a xylophone from Mr. Cole so the grasshopper can have his own music each time he goes to another animal?"

Ms. Reema chooses Gregory and says, "Gregory, you have waited patiently each time you put your hand up this morning, and you did not shout out without being called on. You may choose one friend to go to Mr. Cole's room with you." Gregory chooses Max, and Ms. Reema says, "Tell Mr. Cole why we want to borrow an instrument so he will let you choose mallets that will make a grasshopper sound." While Gregory and Max scurry off to the music room, Ms. Reema continues, "While we're waiting for the instrument to play a grasshopper song, let's move our sound box over here and decide on a sound for all of the other animals in the story."

The teacher bends over and slides a large cardboard box across to the front of the room. The box is filled to overflowing with a variety of percussion instruments. She names each of the animals and calls on individual children to select an instrument for a single animal. In turn, each selected child comes up to the box, peers in and takes an instrument. Ms. Reema then asks the pupils who have instruments to come to the front of the room and line up in the correct order. She takes each of the word label cards out of the pocket board and tapes it to the shirt of the appropriate child.

Gregory and Max return with the xylophone and two wood mallets. Ms. Reema continues, "Now that we have a xylophone for our grasshopper song, how do you think the song should sound? We want to make it sound like a grasshopper flying through the air. Let's close our eyes and see the grasshopper move each time we say 'boing.' I am going to draw one name from our 'turn envelope' and that person will compose our grasshopper melody today."

Ms. Reema pulls a slip of paper from an envelope on top of the piano and announces, "Ellen is our composer today. Let's all listen carefully while Ellen experiments with making grasshopper sounds. Nod your head when you like what you hear."

Ellen comes up to the front of the room, takes the wood mallets from Ms. Reema, and seats herself on the floor in front of the xylophone. Ellen then begins to experiment with the sounds made by the wood mallets on the xylophone's wood resonator bars. The class listens intently, nodding their heads in approval when they hear sounds they especially like.

After a few minutes, Ms. Reema says, "I think we are all ready to reread this picture book together and add the animal sounds and a song for the grasshopper." Ms. Reema reads the story again, cueing each of the instrumentalists when it is time to play a particular animal's sound. At the end of the story, Ms. Reema says, "Children, that was a wonderful performance! It was so good that I think we should share it at a morning meeting. I will talk to the teacher–leader for this week and see which day will be our turn to share a story."

Daniel puts his hand in the air, and Ms. Reema calls on him. "Could we do it again, please, and let different people play the instruments this time?" he asks.

"That's a great idea, Daniel," says Ms. Reema, as she glances at the clock. "But we have to move to gym class right now. We'll work on the story again this afternoon." Ms. Reema walks to the doorway and says, "Line leader and all children in row three may line up."

THE MUSIC TEACHER

Mrs. Lockner meets her kindergarten class at the door and says, "As you walk in to music this morning to this steady beat, will you walk as quietly as possible and find a place to sit on the floor? Be sure you make a good choice about where you sit." The children tiptoe softly to the front of the room and sit down. Once they are seated, they notice an alligator puppet, and several children independently begin to warm up their voices with glissandos in the head register.

Mrs. Lockner follows the last child and picks up the puppet. She says to the children, "Wilbur had a wonderful weekend. He and his mother went to a park, and they saw lots of animals and birds. Wilbur wants to share the sounds he heard with you." Mrs. Lockner then has the children imitate her puppet sounds of birds, baby chicks, kittens, and puppies. After each sound, she asks the children to identify the animal.

The teacher then picks up her recorder and begins to play the tune of "Old MacDonald." The children listen intently. By the time she has begun the second phrase, almost every hand is waving and the children cannot contain themselves. Several volunteer the name of the song before she has a chance to ask, so she asks, "Who would like to choose the first animal?" As the students begin to sing about baby chicks, Mrs. Lockner puts down her recorder and begins to pat her knees softly to the pulse. The children immediately follow her motion and continue to sing. After several verses, the teacher says, "We are going to learn another song about animals today. I want you to listen very carefully and see if you can remember the names of all the animals I sing about." She sings the first three verses of "Barnyard Song."

When she finishes, the teacher asks the children, "Who can tell me the names of the animals?" She calls on three different children and then tells them to listen again and watch her music stand. As she sings each verse, she turns over the corresponding picture of the cat, the hen, and the duck. "Now I want you to sing this song with me." She sings the words "Ready Sing" on the initial pitch; the class watches the music stand and sings the song. Mrs. Lockner smiles and exclaims enthusiastically, "That was really fine singing, and you changed the name of the animal each time. This song is a really neat one because we can make up new verses using the names of other animals."

Mrs. Lockner asks, "Who can think of a good animal to add to this song?" Mandy raises her hand and offers "pig!" The class tries that verse and then Mrs. Lockner suggests they add movement to their song. "I want everyone to stand and look at me by the time I count to three." The children move quickly and Mrs. Lockner counts quietly. "Now let's try out a song with the three verses we already know and the pig verse. As we sing the sound that the animal makes, I want you to move like that animal." The children do a good job of being cats, hens, ducks, and pigs.

Mrs. Lockner says, "Now we can only add one more animal today. What will it be?" Julia raises her hand and asks, "Can we sing about snakes?" Mrs. Lockner smiles and looks at the class. "Well, what kind of a sound will we make?" The children all hiss at her. They begin the song again; and, when they get to the snake verse, the children are all on their bellies in an instant and begin wiggling all over the floor. As Mrs. Lockner finishes singing the song alone, she looks at the children, who are still wiggling with pleasure all around the music room. Not one child is singing—they are too busy moving like snakes! She thinks with a slight amount of panic, "Now how are we going to get back on track?" She stops singing, claps her hands three times, and almost all the children stop moving. "Time to come back to our singing places, children." Most of the children stop moving, stand up, and begin to move back to where they were sitting. Four children are still flat on the floor, and Mrs. Lockner touches each one lightly on the head and says, "The magic wand has changed all the snakes back into children." The stragglers get up and move to join the class.

"Now I want to see if we can remember how to sing our new song because we forgot it when we got to the snake verse. I am going to leave the three pictures on the stand, and, as we sing these verses together, let's all find the steady beat in this song." Mrs. Lockner starts the class singing with the correct pitch and immediately begins to model the pulse by patting her knees. The children all try to imitate her movements, and she notes with pleasure that only three children—Samantha, Kim U., and T.J.—are not yet keeping the pulse. While she is singing the third verse, she stands, moves toward the tape recorder, and notes this information in her class book.

As the song ends, she says "You all are doing a very fine job of keeping the steady beat in our music class today. I have two different pieces of music for us to listen to together. As soon as you think you feel the beat, tap it softly with one finger in the palm of your other hand. First, let's practice what we're going to do." She models the movement, and the children imitate her. She then asks the class to close their eyes while she plays a forty-five-second excerpt from "The Washington Post March." She observes the class carefully and notes that the same three children are having difficulty in this part of the lesson. "You were very good listeners in that music, class. Let's try the second piece. Listen very carefully as the music starts and try to find the steady beat." She plays less than a minute of "Winter" from Vivaldi's *The Four Seasons*.

"How do you think that these two pieces were different, children?" The responses of the children include comments about parades, ball games, TV shows, and dancing. Mrs. Lockner looks at the clock in the back of the room and says, "Our music time is almost over for today. Let's all put a steady beat in our fingertips and put them on our shoulders. Would the line leader walk to the door with our steady beat?" When the line leader, T.J., begins to move, she says, "Anyone who is wearing blue may line up next." She continues to keep the beat until the entire class is lined up and moving out the door, following their teacher back to their own classroom.

Cooperative Questions to Discuss

1. How do these scenarios fit with your memory of your experiences in elementary school?
2. What was the purpose of each of these teachers? How were the lessons similar? How were they different?

WHAT IS MUSIC?

We all recognize music when we hear it. It does not matter what *kind* of music it is. The radio, TV, or CD player may be playing sounds that can be categorized as rap or country or Christian or pop or classical. The second word that follows all these terms is *music!* To take the sounds we recognize and define them in words other than these general classifications is a difficult task because music and language are two very different ways that human beings express themselves.

One definition of music is that it is organized sound. Rain on the roof, the babble of a brook and the noise of traffic are unorganized. In contrast, musical sounds have intention. Someone has decided the order of the sounds—those sounds that occur together and those that occur separately—and what instruments or voices will play or sing the music. The composer makes these decisions in an attempt to share feelings that cannot be expressed in other ways. He/she is also trying to engage the listener in responding with feelings of his or her own. This interaction between music and the listener is called an **aesthetic experience.**

The ability of all human beings to engage in aesthetic experiences is one that even young infants demonstrate. Infants respond to adults singing to them with pleasure, and the effects of soothing songs and lullabies are known to parents in most cultures. While the sounds that infants make are often categorized as prespeech sounds, these same sounds are also premusic sounds. Parents who respond to their infants with musical sounds are providing the foundation for the development of young singers and lovers of music.

Toddlers and preschoolers also respond to music with aesthetic feelings. They cannot name their feelings, but their spontaneous movements and dances to sounds, their own songs about their everyday lives, and their clear enjoyment of music indicate the importance of this aspect of human experience.

Music, then, is a distinct form of expression that exists in all cultures and can be nurtured from early ages in all human beings. Some of the music that youngsters are exposed to will provide an immediate aesthetic response such as the songs that Barney™ and the Cookie Monster™ sing. But as children grow older they will discard this "early" music and discover other types that appeal to them. The music that these same children hear their parents listen to or their church organist play, or that they hear while watching Disney's *Fantasia* or a performance of Tchaikovsky's *The Nutcracker* may be music they listen to for the rest of their lives.

WHO IS A MUSICIAN?

Because of the constant interaction we all have with music produced by professionals, it is hard to imagine that ordinary people who lack conservatory training as well as children at all ages can be musicians. The child who makes up a song about grasshoppers after seeing them in a field and hearing a story about them is practicing the behaviors of a musician. The adult learner who composes a song using three pitches on a recorder is doing the same thing. Learners—at all ages—have musical understanding and are able to express their musicality in unique ways.

Regardless of age, the beginner in music who engages in singing and playing and moving is building a foundation of musical experiences that will provide a platform for further growth. The foundation of "making music" is essential. Jean Piaget[1] described the cognitive growth and development of children and emphasized that young children learn best through imitation and active participation. Abstract reasoning in symbol systems is a development that occurs much later and one that depends on prior concrete experiences. For this reason, learning musical notation is dependent on first actually experiencing music.

Jerome Bruner has also underlined the development of cognitive growth over time. His three modes of representation include the following:

1. Enactive—the learner manipulates the environment and gains knowledge of it through sensory contact.
2. Iconic—the learner represents this sensory contact in some form that looks like the experience.
3. Symbolic—the learner represents the experience in universally understood symbols.[2]

Both of these theorists support the development of musical understanding through initial concrete experiences with actual music. The authors of this text believe that this idea applies to learners at all ages. Musical expression does not depend on knowledge of the musical symbol system. The ability to produce and experience pleasurable musical sounds is available to novices of any age.

WHY DO WE HAVE SPECIAL MUSIC TEACHERS?

The first recognized music teacher was a man named Lowell Mason, who taught children in Hawes School in Boston in 1838. Mason was sure that young children could be taught to sing and read music, and he believed that this should take place in the setting where all children were—not just in private music schools. He taught without pay and successfully demonstrated to the school committee at the end of the year that indeed children could read and sing music. The establishment of public school music teachers—teachers who were trained as both musicians and educators—took a long time and occurred during the period when universal and compulsory education for children was slowly gaining favor in the United States.

Lowell Mason and all the other early music education pioneers believed that music was an essential part of young children's development. In North America, where the ideal of equal opportunity is espoused, the teaching of music by trained musicians/educators provides students with a background in music that is not dependent on their parent's income or the community they live in. This "music equal opportunity" is illustrated to parents and taxpayers in the annual or biannual musical programs their children present, the concerts performed by young instrumentalists and singers, and the pep and marching bands at athletic events. In fact, these performances have become cultural expectations, and they are ways for children not only to learn about music but also to learn about contributing to a group effort and producing a product that is greater than their own individual part. Music class instruction and the preparation for public presentations provide opportunities for students to become engaged in the aesthetic experience.

Music teachers teach the same children throughout their elementary school years while their classroom teacher colleagues typically see a group of children for only one year. Elementary music teachers are experts in the structure of music and know how to introduce and develop a seven-year curriculum wherein children from Kindergarten through sixth grade develop music skills and knowledge at their own rate of development. Part of the music teacher's job is to develop a curriculum that guides the students in focusing on early concrete experiences and relating those experiences to later abstract understandings.

The music curriculum is based on the structure of music, which is usually described by terms that are collectively called **musical elements.** These elements include melody, harmony, rhythm, dynamics (loud and soft), form (parts of music), timbre or tone color (sounds of different instruments and/or voices), and tempo (fast and slow). Teachers of young children focus on one musical element at a time, such as tempo, and plan activities wherein the children will sing, play instruments, move, and listen to songs and music that is fast or slow and then both. In the primary grades, building the foundation is important, and the vocabulary used includes words that are familiar to children—fast and slow. In later years, these same children will learn the musical vocabulary and will be able to discuss, describe, and classify the music they experience or compose using this vocabulary.

In response to the Goals 2000 legislation, music teachers have developed a document that provides nationwide guidance for music curriculum development. This document is titled *National Standards for Arts Education* (Reston: Music Educators National Conference, 1994). Throughout this text, you will find selected parts of this document that relate to chapter content on teaching music to children. These excerpts describe how teachers can evaluate whether children have learned music through musical behaviors such as singing, listening, and composing.

WHY INCLUDE MUSIC IN YOUR DAY?

When children begin school, their experiences are organized by adults into blocks of time that are labeled art, mathematics, music, physical education, reading, science, and social studies. Some blocks are much longer and occur daily. This organization indicates to children and parents that the information being taught at that time is important. Those blocks that occur once or twice a week for a short time are perceived as less important. But the children know better!

Children recognize that what they do in art and music—the so-called special classes —is enjoyable and fulfilling. They question the classroom teacher in the morning to find out if they have a "special" that day; and, if they do not, they are disappointed. Why does this universal response occur in elementary classrooms? It is because the types of activities that children participate in during these subjects result in aesthetic experiences! They are learning through doing and are responding not only with their bodies but with their emotions.

Preschool children can express themselves at any time of the day by making up a song or dance about their lives. Imagine their disappointment upon entering school at age five, where this form of expression is suddenly restricted to a once- or twice-a-week short block of time called music. It is essential for complete child growth and development that the classroom teacher includes making music on a daily basis. As a classroom teacher, you will become an expert on individual children over the course of a year. You will also be an expert in how to teach reading, science, math, and social studies. This text will enable you to become confident in finding ways to incorporate musical experiences into your classroom on a daily basis. You will expand how you teach and enable children to more naturally develop musically.

Including music every day will make your classroom one where both cognitive and aesthetic growth occur. Some of the music content you include may be directly related to what your children are learning in their music class. At other times, you may wish to include experiences that relate to the content of other subjects. The integration of two or more subjects is a way to enhance and broaden children's learning, and this text will provide you with many opportunities to prepare for this type of classroom teaching.

If you teach in an elementary school that does not have a music teacher, you will be responsible for this important part of children's growth. You can use the specific music textbooks that are published by either McGraw-Hill (Share the Music Series) or Silver Burdett/Ginn. Each of these two publishers has a series of music texts for grades K–8, and they also produce a set of CDs for each grade level. These books are clearly sequenced, beautifully illustrated, and very teacher-friendly. The teacher editions of these books are designed to be used by both classroom and music teachers.

The most important aspect in incorporating music into your classroom is your own attitude. Whatever feelings you may have about music or your own musical ability, you know that children enjoy making music. At the conclusion of this course, you will be more confident about your own ability to incorporate music into your classroom. All that will remain will be to combine your confident attitude with the children's delight in making music and explore the many ways that you can enhance your classroom teaching by integrating music every day.

INCLUDING MUSIC IN YOUR DAILY PLANNING

The basic premise of the authors of this text is that music is a central component of the elementary school curriculum. Throughout the following chapters you will experience numerous examples of ways in which you can make music an integral part of your teaching, although not in the same way that the music teacher would. As the classroom teacher, you will find that integrating music in your daily curriculum will involve ingenuity, creativity, and good planning. More important, however, will be your disposition to provide opportunities to enable your students to come alive through musical activities.

Music has always been part of the traditional elementary curriculum, often included by state mandate. In fact, elementary classroom teachers in many states have music teaching as part of their official job description, whether or not there is a specialist music teacher on the staff. Because of this, music has often been integrated into classroom teachers' lessons through other subject areas. For example, the teacher preparing a unit on the Civil War might include a song from that era in her plans. But the concept of curricular integration has broadened to mean more than simply fitting a special subject, such as music, into the rest of the elementary curriculum.

Proponents of curricular integration argue that, because the elementary curriculum is compartmentalized into separate segments (subject areas of art, language arts, mathematics, music, physical education, science, and social studies), students need help in making connections between subject areas as they build knowledge and understanding in each area. A curriculum based on rote memorization of facts, drill and practice, and other lower-level thinking skills gives students a store of raw materials but fails to provide a place in which to use these materials in meaningful ways. An integrated curriculum, on the other hand, relates the various subject matter areas to each other and to the child's own life. Proponents of curricular integration[3] argue that the goal is to produce an insightful child who is able to explain ideas in her or his own words, apply conceptual understanding in real life situations, and transfer learnings from one situation to another.

Just how one should remove the barriers between subject areas of the elementary curriculum is a matter of opinion, and many approaches have been taken. One approach to curricular integration that exemplifies teaching for insight is the whole language approach to the teaching of reading and writing. Rather than having children memorize lists of sight words, complete series of sequential phonics exercises, and read basal reading texts, whole language teachers depend on children's literature, children's own stories and poems written in invented spelling, and in-class collaborative writing activities with peers. While there are as many interpretations of "whole language" as there are practitioners of it, all agree that the students' levels of motivation and involvement in this learner-directed approach make it especially appealing. Researchers have found that children's disposition toward learning is positively influenced in the whole language classroom.[4]

Approaches to integrating areas of the curriculum other than reading and writing include project organization, thematic units or cycles, and topic webs. Each of these terms denotes ways of providing young learners with in-depth involvement in learning and provides further ways for learners to make connections between disparate subject areas. Topics may range from seeds to myths to types of work, but the underlying principle is the same—integrating many areas of learning and making them meaningful to learners.

An effective way to include music in your classroom is as an enhancement for another portion of the elementary curriculum. For example, you might plan a lesson on punctuation and use a musical example that has definite sections to illustrate your point. Other lessons could include the application of concepts, such as repetition, pattern, and symmetry, that are shared by poetry, visual art, and music.

In your other curriculum courses you will learn how to include integration activities in the teaching/learning process. Throughout this text you will have the opportunity to learn specific ways to integrate music into your lesson plans. The authors are confident that you will not only learn the principles of integration of music throughout the curriculum, but you will have your own creativity sparked to find even better and more interesting ways to make music part of your daily classroom routine.

EXPLORING MUSIC FROM AROUND THE WORLD

Many of the songs and listening examples that you will encounter in this text originate in cultures outside of North America. Many appear in languages other than English. Learning this type of song or listening to this type of musical example may appear initially to be a challenge. You may be tempted to skip over the "world music" examples both now and later in your own classroom. The authors suggest that to do so would limit your musical experience to the familiar and leave you and your students with a narrow view of our musical world. Stretching yourself to move outside of your "music comfort zone" will help you to realize just how easy it is to sing songs from musical cultures and languages besides your own. It will also give you the confidence to demonstrate music risk-taking for your students.

TEACHER FEELINGS AND CLASSROOM REALITIES

As you begin your teacher training courses, you bring with you a certain set of feelings and impressions about what to expect in the role of teacher. This may be your first methods class, or you may have already taken a number of such classes. In either case, you have spent more than twelve years watching teaching on the student's side of the desk. It is now your turn to step behind the desk and try out the role of teacher. As you do this, you may experience a wide variety of emotions that range from fear and frustration to comfort and confidence. This is to be expected, and you can feel certain that these emotions are a normal part of being a teacher.

Perhaps the most frightening feeling for all of us as we take on this role is the initial feeling of inadequacy, which is the burden of all beginning teachers no matter what their discipline. You may feel that there is an almost endless list of skills and understandings that you need to master in order to get ready for student teaching, and you may wonder if you will be able to achieve competence in all of them.

Some of the most important skills you will learn are in the areas of classroom management and instructional planning. Classroom management is the result of good planning. The two topics are really inseparable. Effective teachers give precise directions, provide children with a sense of security, and impart a sense of purpose. You establish a sense of security through the use of carefully worded directions and consistent explanations and behavior.

In this text you will find many teaching scripts and lesson plans that include both content and descriptions of ways to manage groups of children in varied activities. These scripts, plans, and cooperative activities are designed to help you develop your own abilities as a teacher. Understanding and practicing the transitions that occur in every lesson will also contribute to your sense of competence as a teacher. These teaching skills will be illustrated throughout the text as you learn how to incorporate music into your daily classroom life.

Very little attention, if any, has been given to the topic of gender in elementary school instruction. Children clearly demonstrate unspoken but clear sex segregation in their informal choices such as lunchroom seating and playground games. This whole set of unwritten rules governing male and female behavior has been called "the second curriculum" by one researcher.[5] All teachers need to be aware of this powerful influence on children's behavior and learning as well as the subtle ways in which they can foster cooperation and interaction between genders in their classes.

Even more important than how you manage groups of children are the behaviors you engage in throughout your instructional day. Researchers have found that teachers treat children differently on the basis of their gender. As noted in a major report,

> *whether one looks at preschool classrooms or university lecture halls, at female teachers or male teachers, research spanning the past twenty years consistently reveals that males receive more teacher attention than do females. There is also a tendency beginning at the preschool level for schools to choose classroom activities that will appeal more to boys' interests and to select presentation formats in which boys excel or are encouraged more than girls.*[6]

As a future teacher, you will need to monitor your own actions and expectations regarding gender in your classroom. For example, do you typically call on girls more often than boys? Are the activities in your lessons selected because one gender will like them? Is the pace kept quick so as not to lose the attention of one group? Do you typically use one gender group to determine whether learning has occurred?

Although many teachers often use gender as the basis for classroom management of transitions (moving from one activity to another, taking turns, or moving from classroom to lunchroom), there are other effective ways to divide children into manageable groups. Instead of having boys and girls line up separately, you can use eye, hair or clothing color, shoe type (lace up, high tops, sandals, boots), birthday months, or first letters of names. When you begin teaching, you must be aware of the signals you send to children in your responses to them, your lesson planning, and your classroom management routines.

THE TASK AHEAD

You will be responsible for creating an optimal learning environment for all your students, including those labeled exceptional due to their learning, behavioral, or physical disabilities. You may teach in a school where there are multi-grade or composite classrooms with students from several grade levels in the same class. You will be expected to know which children in your class are aural, visual, and kinesthetic learners and to include students' learning styles and cognitive strategies in your teaching approach. You will need to identify and make special instructional provision for children labeled at-risk of failure for reasons beyond your control, such as poverty, abuse, or parental problems. In short, you face an enormous task as a classroom teacher, and not all of the issues are merely ones related to instruction. Physical safety in the school is an issue that one cannot overlook, and, although many states are enforcing stronger penalties for students found in possession of weapons, the atmosphere of doubt and uncertainty that pervades many schools is troubling.

No single course will address all these areas of concern, nor will you be expected to achieve expertise in these areas overnight. It is important to remember, however, that achieving competence and excellence as a teacher depends on your commitment to yourself and the children you will be teaching. Deciding how much you want to put into becoming the very best teacher you are capable of becoming, and then putting in the appropriate amount of effort, will serve both you and your future students well.

INTRODUCTION TO THE FOLLOWING CHAPTERS

The following chapters will lead you through a variety of materials that are designed to do two things. First, they will enhance your musical skills in singing, listening, moving, playing instruments, composing, and reading music. Second, they will show you how to use your musical skills to include music-making activities in your daily classroom routine.

The chapters are paired around the various skills, with chapter 3 focusing on your singing skills and chapter 4 showing you how to lead your class in singing activities. In the musical skills chapters, you will be addressed as an adult music learner, and materials appropriate for your level of musical understanding will be included. In the second chapter of the pair, the focus is on pedagogical issues for you as the classroom teacher.

Each of these teaching chapters begins with a case study that lets you understand the role of the teacher and is followed by cooperative in-class activities. The chapters also include one or more teaching scripts that are provided for you to practice with your peers, roommates, and children. You will also find a rationale section that explains reasons for including the various types of activities in your lesson plans. Each chapter contains sections that explain the musical content, methods, and materials appropriate for various grade levels.

As you can see from this brief description, in your role as learner you will be actively involved in discussion, cooperative activities, practice teaching using scripted lessons, and self-evaluation through videotaped teaching segments. As in this introductory chapter, you will be expected to jump into the role of teacher through both case studies and actual teaching episodes. Each chapter will provide you with the kinds of information and procedural help that can make this one of the most engrossing classes of your college career.

NOTES

[1] Jean Piaget, *Origins of Intelligence in Children* (New York: Norton, 1963).

[2] Jerome Bruner, *The Process of Education* (New York: Vintage Books, 1963), p. 33.

[3] David N. Perkins, "Educating for Insight," *Educational Leadership* 44, no. 2 (1991), pp. 4–8.

[4] K. L. Dahl and Penny A. Freppon, "A Comparison of Inner-City Children's Interpretations of Reading and Writing Instruction in Skills-Based and Whole Language Classrooms," *Reading Research Quarterly* 30 (1995), pp. 50–74.

[5] R. Best, *We've All Got Scars: What Boys and Girls Learn in Elementary School* (Bloomington: Indiana University Press), p. 18.

[6] *How Schools Shortchange Girls: The AAUW Report* (Washington, D.C.: AAUW Educational Foundation and the National Education Association, 1992), p. 60.

Rhythm Fundamentals for Confident Singing

What you will be able to do by the end of this chapter

- *Find the steady* ***pulse*** *in rhymes and music*
- *Read rhythm notation that subdivides the pulse*
- *Read rhythms using stick notation and rhythm syllables*
- *Organize sounds and silences into* ***metrical*** *groups*
- *Read actual rhythm notation*
- *Play three notes on the recorder*

BEGINNING TO LEARN RHYTHM

The system for writing down sounds that we now call music notation evolved slowly over hundreds of years. It took a long time for humans to devise an effective way to describe sounds and silences that had so many different attributes. The music notation we now use is a type of shorthand system that describes the length and pitch of sounds and whether the sounds occur at the same time, as well as other ideas, such as volume and speed. This system is a way to organize all these meanings. As you may already know, the note symbols that we use to represent sound indicate two ideas simultaneously—**pitch** and **duration.** Pitch and duration attributes are often differentiated in initial music notation learning because this approach clarifies the two characteristics found in one symbol.

In chapters 2 and 3, we will introduce each of these two important aspects of notation separately. If you have prior musical experience, you should be able to master this material very quickly. But if your prior music education was not extensive, you will need to spend more time with this material. Understanding the notation system is one step in the process of becoming a confident teacher who will be able to share the joy of music with children.

CHAPTER GOALS

In this chapter you will become acquainted with the rhythm symbols most commonly used in music; and, through activities, you will receive a systematic introduction to rhythm fundamentals. By participating in these experiences, you will become a confident rhythm reader and will therefore be prepared to move to the second part of music notation reading, which uses the musical staff to specify the sound or pitch.

The beginning experiences in this chapter use a simplified form of notation called stick notation. This approach assists learners in becoming proficient rhythm readers. In addition, you will learn a system of **rhythm syllables** that will help you read rhythm more accurately. Subsequent experiences then move to the use of actual rhythm notation.

All of the rhythm fundamentals introduced in this chapter are used in the recorder units, which begin on p. 28. These units will reinforce your rhythm reading, but the rhythm fundamentals are introduced very slowly. Learning to play an instrument and learning to read a new symbol system are two very difficult tasks to combine, and we want you to be successful at both!

EXPERIENCES WITH THE STEADY BEAT

To begin, listen to **"Galway Hornpipe"** (track 1) and move your finger or foot to the music. With any luck, your foot or finger found a steady feeling, called the **pulse** or the **steady beat.** Most music contains this steady feeling, and it is the basis for the organization and understanding of sound as well as the way that we write music notation. The speed of the steady beat determines the **tempo** of the music. A composition with a slow steady beat has a slow tempo, and a composition with a fast steady beat has a fast tempo. There can be variations of tempo within a composition as well.

Now, listen to **"'Til There Was You"** (track 2) and move your finger or foot to the music to show the steady beat. Note whether this is faster or slower than the tempo of "Galway Hornpipe." Now listen to two pieces from your personal CD collection and tap the steady beat. Bring one of your selections to class to share with your peers.

After you have listened to these pieces of music, try each of the following activities so that you will be prepared to do them with your classmates.

ACTIVITY Say each of the following rhymes and softly tap the steady beat. Be careful not to tap on every word! The accent marks over the words will help you find the steady pulse.

/ / / /
Way down South where bananas grow,
/ / / /
A grasshopper stepped on an elephant's toe.
/ / / /
The elephant said, with tears in his eyes,
/ / / /
"Pick on somebody your own size."

/ / / /
One potato, two potato, three potato, four.
/ / / /
Five potato, six potato, seven potato, more.

/ / / /
Froggy Boggy tried to jump
/ / / /
On a stone and got a bump.
/ / / /
It made his eyes wink and frown
/ / / /
and turned his nose upside down.

Now, see if you can find the pulse in the following rhymes. As you say them, tap the steady feeling on your knee.

Ours is not to reason why,
Ours is but to do or die.

Acka backa soda cracker, acka backa boo,
Acka back soda cracker, out goes you.

Ooga wooga dumb dumb,
Ooga wooga doo.
Mish mash, Ho hum,
I love you!

Lickety split, bibbity bop,
Turkey's down the back.
Pick him up, give 'im a chop,
Throw him in the sack!

Sninkle, prinkle, poppity crew,
Ocean's broken, hullabaloo!

Aloysius Allen, Stephanie Green.
He thinks he's the smartest,
She thinks she's the queen!

One, two, three, four five. Once I caught a fish alive.
Six, seven, eight, nine, ten. Then I let it go again.

All riddles are blues
And all blues are sad
And I'm only mentioning
*Some blues I've had**

**(Maya Angelou, "A Good Woman Feeling Bad." Stanza 5.* The Complete Collected Poems of Maya Angelou, *p. 184 [N.Y.: Random House, 1994]). From SHAKER, WHY DON'T YOU SING by Maya Angelou, Copyright © 1983 by Maya Angelou. Reprinted by permission of Random House, Inc.*

PULSE AND RHYTHM

Now return to the Froggy Boggy rhyme and, while saying the rhyme, tap or clap every sound or syllable in the poem. You are now clapping the **rhythm** of the poem. There are many more taps for the rhythm than there are for the pulse. Try to tap the pulse with your foot and tap the rhythm of the poem with your hand. It will help if you first begin tapping the steady feeling and then, after a few beats, begin to say and tap the rhyme. Practice all the above rhymes in this manner.

ACTIVITY Return to each of the above rhymes and, while everyone is saying the poem, have half of the class clap the rhythm and the other half clap the pulse. Try a second time with the actions reversed. Next, have the entire class tap the pulse and say and clap the rhyme.

SUBDIVIDING THE BEAT

As you say and tap the following lines, listen carefully to where you say one sound on each beat and where you say two sounds.

Ours is not to reason why,
Ours is but to do or die.

The underlined words below were spoken and tapped with only one sound on each beat.

Ours is not to reason <u>why</u>,
Ours is but to do or <u>die</u>.

When the beat is divided into two equal sounds, we can use simple or stick notation to show this difference. (⊓)

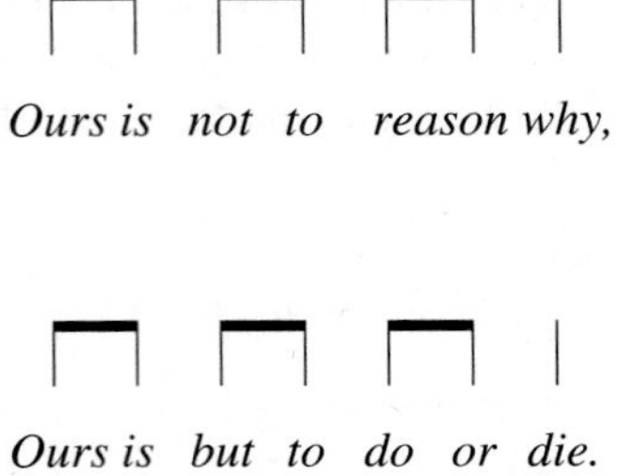
Ours is not to reason why,
Ours is but to do or die.

Here is the first part of the Froggy Boggy rhyme with stick notation inserted over the first two words. Write the stick notation over the rest of the poem.

Froggy Boggy tried to jump

On a stone and got a bump.

There are rhythm syllables that you can use with these symbols that assist in learning to read musical notation. When the sound receives one beat the syllable is "ta." When there are two sounds on the beat, use "ti-ti." Here is an example of stick notation and syllables used together.

ti - ti ti - ti ti - ti ta

Ours is not to reason why,

ti - ti ti - ti ti - ti ta

Ours is but to do or die.

ti - ti ti - ti ti - ti ta

Froggy Boggy tried to jump

ti - ti ti - ti ti - ti ta

On a stone and got a bump.

Now say the following rhyme and tap the steady pulse to discover which words receive one tap. After you have tried this, underline the words that receive one tap or pulse.

One, two, three, four, five. Once I caught a fish alive.

Six, seven, eight, nine, ten. Then I let it go again.

Did you underline "one," "two," "five," "six," "seven," and "ten"? If not, erase what you underlined and repeat the exercise to see if you can say the rhyme and tap one pulse on only these words. Next, write the stick notation over the rhyme and the rhythm syllables under the rhyme.

ACTIVITY Compare your stick notation and rhythm syllables with a partner. Practice saying the rhyme, tapping the beat, and clapping the rhythm of the text.

Here is another poem to say. Tap a steady pulse and underline the words or parts of words where the pulse is strongest.

Ooga wooga dumb dumb,
Ooga wooga doo.
Mish mash, Ho hum,
I love you!

Did you discover that you needed an extra beat at the end of this rhyme's second line to make it work? This extra beat or rest is notated with the following sign: (𝄽). As you read the rhyme again, tap the steady pulse and say the words. Make sure you have a beat with no sound at the end of the second line.

Now write the stick notation and rhythm syllables for this poem. The stick notation and rhythm syllables have been inserted for the second line.

Ooga wooga dumb dumb,

ti - ti ti - ti ta

⊓ ⊓ | 𝄽

Ooga wooga doo.

Mish mash, Ho hum,

I love you!

ACTIVITY In class, compare your stick notation and syllables with a partner. Next, with your partner, say the following rhyme, tap the steady beat, and decide how to write the stick notation above and rhythm syllables under the following rhyme.

Star light, star bright, first star I see to-night,

I wish I may, I wish I might, have the wish I wish to-night.

You can also read stick notation without rhymes. The following activities will enable you to become secure with the rhythm symbols.

ACTIVITY With a partner or in a small group, tap a steady beat and use the rhythm syllables (ti-ti, ta) to say the patterns in set one of figure 2.1. Do not stop at the end of a line but move your eyes right down to the next line!

Figure 2.1

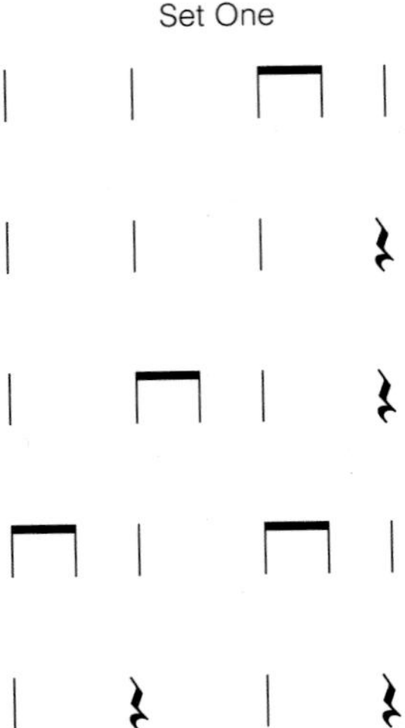

ACTIVITY Now try a partner quiz where one partner says the rhythm syllables for one line in set one and the other partner decides which line was spoken. If you have no difficulty with this exercise, try this harder version: one partner claps the rhythm of a line and does not say the syllables aloud while the other partner decides which line was performed. Continue in this partner practice with rhythm sets two, three, and four of figure 2.2.

Figure 2.2

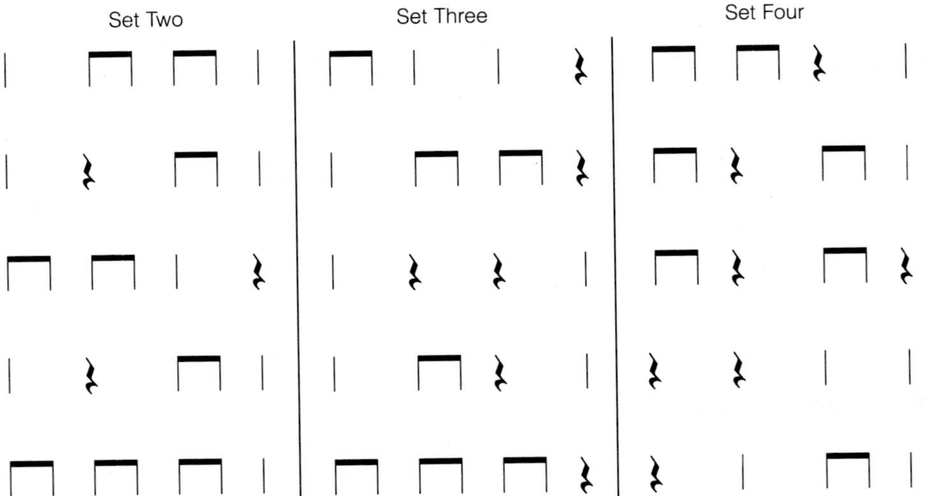

FURTHER SUBDIVISIONS OF THE BEAT

As you have learned in the above exercises, the beat can be subdivided into two equal sounds. In addition, other subdivisions are possible. Say the following words and divide the beat into three sounds of equal length. As you do so, tap one steady beat for each word.

pineapple, blackberry, strawberry pie

Say the following words and divide the beat into four sounds of equal length. Tap one steady beat for each word.

boysenberry, huckleberry, elderberry pie.

The stick notation that is used for subdivisions of three and four is shown below.

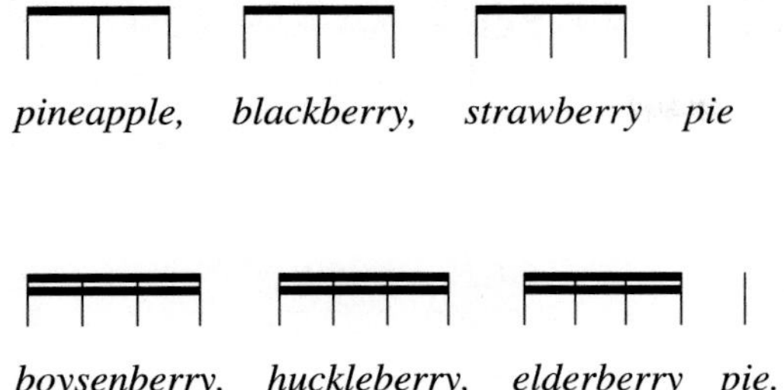
pineapple, blackberry, strawberry pie
boysenberry, huckleberry, elderberry pie.

The rhythm syllables that are used for subdivisions of three and four are tri-o-la and ti-ri-ti-ri, respectively. The stick notation and rhythm syllables that are used for subdivisions of three and four are shown below.

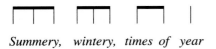

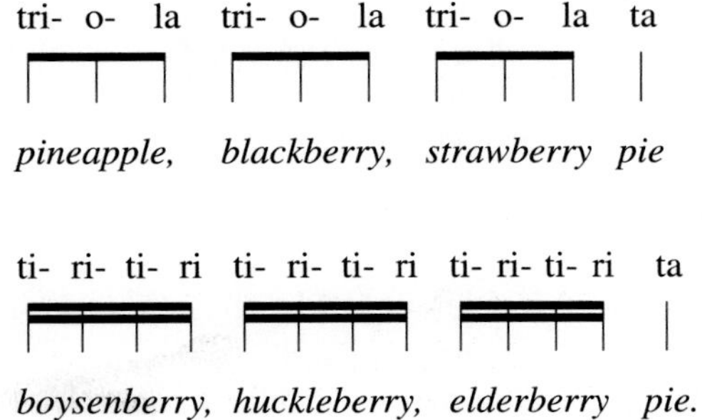
tri- o- la tri- o- la tri- o- la ta
pineapple, blackberry, strawberry pie
ti- ri- ti- ri ti- ri- ti- ri ti- ri- ti- ri ta
boysenberry, huckleberry, elderberry pie.

Write the stick notation for the following nonsense rhymes. The notation for the first line is provided.

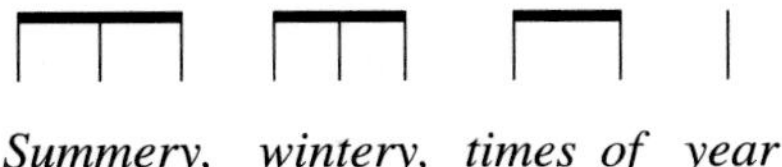

Summery, wintery, times of year

Isn't it wonderful you are here.

Kookaburra likes to eat a lot.

Avocados shouldn't be eaten hot.

 **ACTIVITY** Compare your rhythm notation for the preceding four lines with a partner.

Now use your understanding of the different ways of subdividing the beat and write your first and last name using stick notation. Use one beat for your first name and one or two beats for your last name.

For example:

Carol Richardson Betty Atterbury

Your Name: ______________________________

Your Rhythm: ______________________________

ACTIVITY When the class instructor calls on you, speak your name in rhythm. The instructor will put the entire class rhythm on the board using stick notation, and then the entire class will speak the rhythms together.

ORGANIZING RHYTHM

When you are in class looking at all of the rhythms of your names together, it will be very apparent why a system has evolved to organize different durations into groups. This grouping occurs through putting together sets of beats of equal length. The steady beat in music is most often organized in sets of two or four (**duple**) or three (**triple**). Sets of two, three, or four beats are separated by lines into groups called measures or bars. When beats are organized in this way, the first beat (in sets of two and three) and the first and third (in sets of four) are slightly stressed.

A single **bar line** looks like this |. Two bar lines define a **measure** ||. The measure is the space between the two bar lines.

Figure 2.3 presents a set of rhythms for you to organize in sets of four beats. Remember that when the beat is subdivided into two, three, or four sounds, there is still only one beat. Also remember that the rest that you used above stands for one beat also.

Figure 2.3 Stick Notation to Organize

ACTIVITY With your instructor, organize the class name rhythm collection into sets of two, then three and four by placing a bar line between each set. As you speak the rhythms, slightly stress the first beat of each measure.

At the beginning of notated songs, such as those on page 85 in chapter four, there is a number and note that looks something like a fraction. This is a **meter signature,** and it indicates how the beats in the song are organized. The top number tells you how many beats will be in every measure of the song and usually it ranges from two to six. On the bottom you will see a note that indicates which note receives one beat.

Meter Signatures Using Quarter Note as One Beat

ORGANIZING RHYTHM AND METER

Figure 2.4 presents a single rhythm that is organized in a meter of two, three, or four beats per measure. Note the **double bar** at the end of each example. The double bar means "the end."

Organize the rhythms in figure 2.5 into sets of two, three, and four as indicated by the meter signature at the beginning of each line. Be sure to count the beats and use a double bar at the end of each line of rhythm.

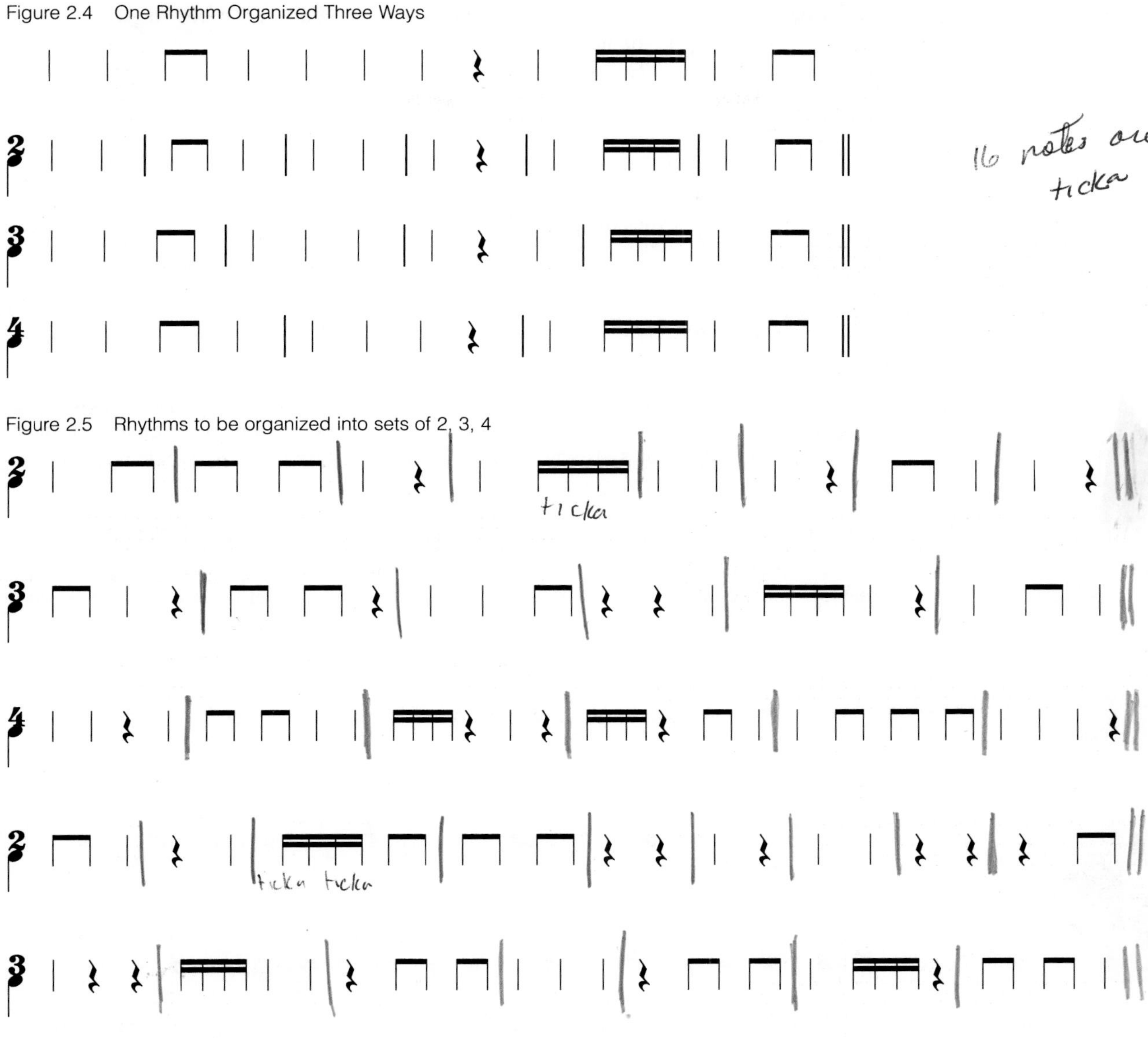

Figure 2.4 One Rhythm Organized Three Ways

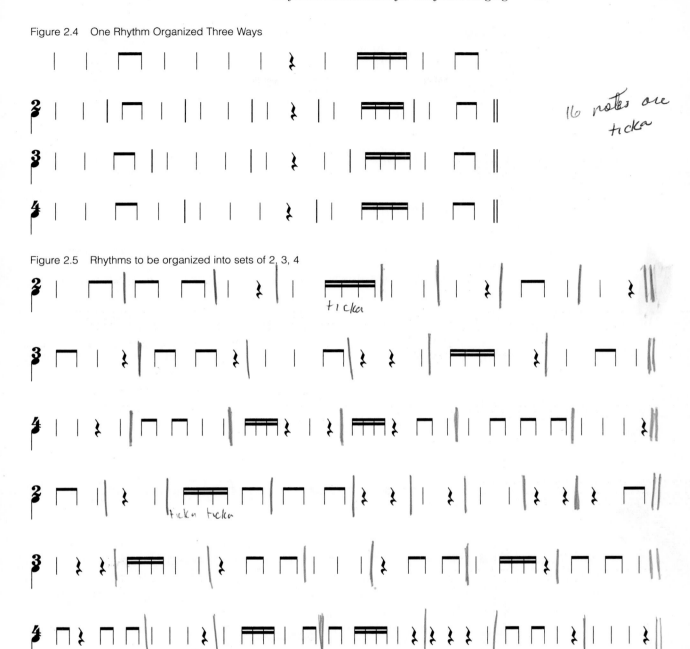

Figure 2.5 Rhythms to be organized into sets of 2, 3, 4

ACTIVITY Compare how you organized the rhythms in figure 2.5 with a partner. Tap the steady beat, and say the rhythms using rhythm syllables.

ADDING NOTEHEADS

When heads are added to stick notation, the result is the set of symbols used in music notation. Notes consist of two parts—**noteheads,** which can be filled in or empty (● ○), and **stems,** which are the lines attached to the noteheads. Combinations of these two basic ideas, along with **dots** following the notes, provide a variety of ways to indicate the duration and relative speed of sounds.

Here are the actual notes for the stick notation we have used thus far: (♩ ♫ ♬♬). The names of these notes are:

Quarter ♩

Eighth ♫

Sixteenth ♬♬

There are three types of rests that correspond to the three types of notes. They are:

Quarter 𝄽
Eighth 𝄾
Sixteenth 𝄿

Noteheads that are empty signify longer sounds. The note with a stem and an empty notehead is called a half note (𝅗𝅥). It has the same duration as two quarter notes. The empty notehead with no stem is a whole note (𝅝) and has the same duration as four quarter notes. These two notes also have corresponding rests (half rest 𝄼, whole rest 𝄻).

USING NOTES OF VARIED DURATIONS

Examine the rhythms in figure 2.6 and decide what number to put on top of the meter signature. You can discover this number by counting the number of beats in each measure.

Figure 2.6

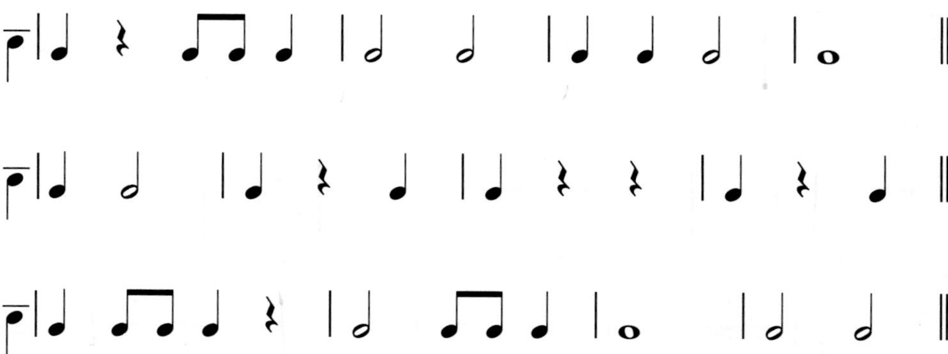

The eighth and sixteenth notes you have used so far have been joined (♫ ♬♬), but these notes can also be written separately.

♫ = ♪♪ ♬♬ = 𝅘𝅥𝅯𝅘𝅥𝅯𝅘𝅥𝅯𝅘𝅥𝅯

Figure 2.7 presents a rhythm with eighth and sixteenth notes written two different ways. When you say each of the two lines with syllables or clap it, the sound will be the same.

Figure 2.7

Figure 2.8 Chart of Notes and Rests

	Note		Rest
Whole			
Half			
Quarter			
Eighth		Set of 2	
Sixteenth		Set of 4	

READING RHYTHMS

Figure 2.9 presents six rhythms that use standard notation. First, write rhythm syllables under the notes. Next, write an accent mark at the beginning of each beat, tap the beat slowly, and say the syllables. Finally, tap the beat again, saying and clapping the rhythms.

Figure 2.9 Rhythms to Read

TIES AND DOTS

One way to represent a longer duration in music is to use the half note and the whole note. Another way is to combine two notes together with a symbol called a **tie** ( ). When two notes are connected by a tie, the second note is not sounded. The first note is extended through the duration of the second. For example, see figure 2.10.

Figure 2.10

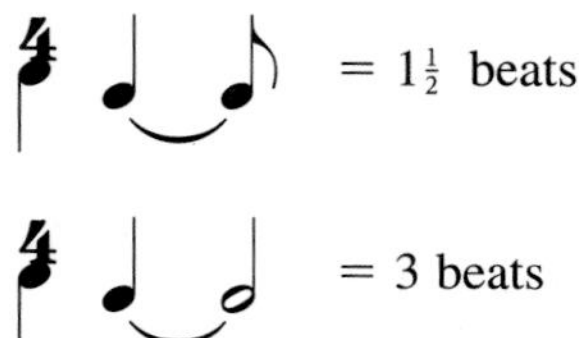

Figure 2.11 presents some rhythms with tied notes for you to practice. The last two lines are more difficult because one eighth note is tied to a quarter. To make the exercise less difficult, write the rhythm syllables under the notes, and say the syllables in your head.

Figure 2.11

The sounds that you clapped and said in figure 2.11 can be written another way using dots. When a dot is placed after a musical note, the note's duration is extended by one half of its original value. In figure 2.12 the rhythms from figure 2.11 are written using dots. Although the rhythms in figure 2.12 appear to be different from those in figure 2.11, they will sound the same.

Figure 2.12

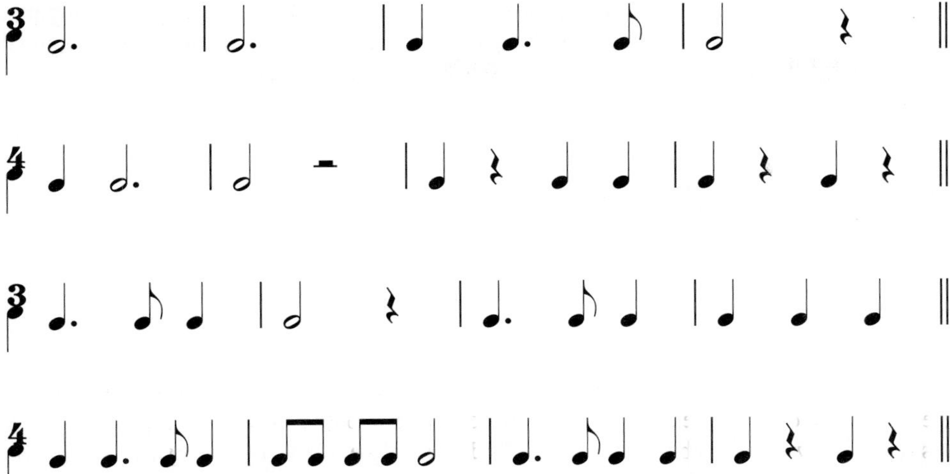

A difficult rhythm to master is a dotted eighth note followed by a sixteenth (♪.♬). If you write the rhythm syllables underneath each of the notes, you will be able to understand where each duration sounds (figure 2.13).

Figure 2.13

ti - ri - ti - ri = ti - ri or ti - ri

Figure 2.14 presents additional rhythms to practice. First, write rhythm syllables beneath the notes. Next, establish a steady beat with your foot and say the rhythms without stopping the beat.

Figure 2.14 Rhythms Using Dotted Notes

ACTIVITY Compare the rhythm syllables you wrote under the notation in figure 2.14 with a partner. Practice the rhythms with a partner before the entire class claps the rhythms together.

COMPOUND METER

Another frequently used meter signature is 6/♪. The basic pulse in this meter is the same as a dotted quarter note.

In this meter (and others that have ♪ on the bottom), there is a way to use beats with subdivisions of three. All of the meter signatures you have used thus far have had a quarter note on the bottom, and the basic pulse has been divided into two or four equal parts. Such meter is known as **simple** meter. When divided into three parts, the meter is known as **compound** meter. Figure 2.15 presents several compound meter signatures and examples of measures of rhythm. Write the rhythm syllables under each line. Next, practice the rhythms using the method learned earlier in the chapter.

Figure 2.15 Compound Meter Signatures and Rhythms

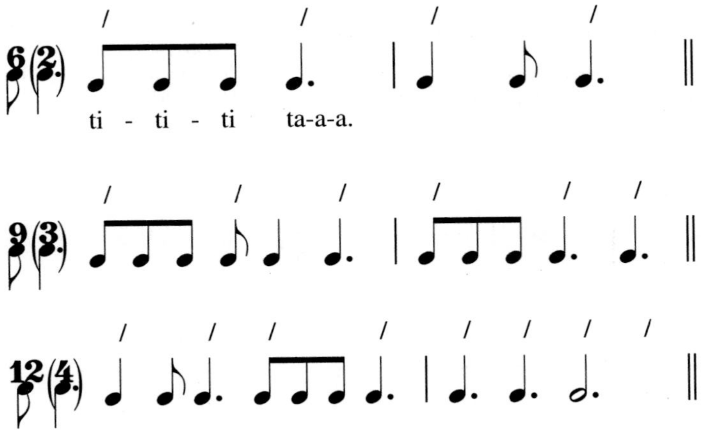

ACTIVITY Compare your rhythm syllables with those of a partner. Practice the compound rhythms together in class.

Sets of three eighth notes in compound meter can also be changed with the addition of dots ( ). This rhythm provides yet another way to have variety in music durations. Figure 2.16 presents compound rhythms for you to practice. First, write the rhythm syllables beneath the notes. Next, insert the accent signs that show where each beat begins. The first line has been completed for you.

Figure 2.16 Compound Rhythms

ACTIVITY Compare your rhythm syllables with those of a partner. Take turns with one partner clapping the beat and the other partner clapping the rhythm pattern. When you are proficient in clapping the rhythms, one partner should clap a line while the other partner decides which line was clapped.

SYNCOPATION

Another way to provide interest and variety in music is to change the stress from the usual place of right after the bar line or on beats one and three (in 4/♩). Composers often decide to move the stress to an unaccented part of the pulse or of the measure. The resulting sound is called **syncopation.** Figure 2.17 presents several examples of syncopated rhythms. Write the rhythm syllables under each of the three examples and try saying them. The syncopated measures are marked with an *.

Figure 2.17 Syncopated Rhythms

ACTIVITY Practice the syncopated rhythm patterns presented in figure 2.18. Write the rhythm syllables under the notation in each example. Compare what you wrote with a partner and practice the rhythms together.

Figure 2.18 More Syncopated Rhythms

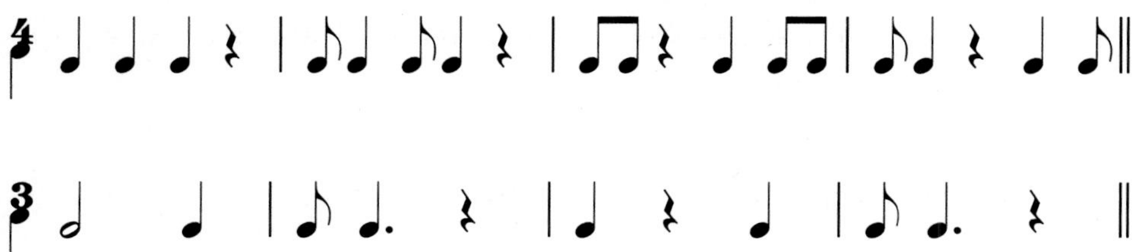

Figure 2.18 *continued*

ANACRUSIS—PICKUP

Often songs begin with an incomplete measure of rhythm known as an **anacrusis** or pickup. You will find that the last measure of a song with a pickup balances the first by containing only the number of beats needed to complete the first measure. For example, a song with a pickup measure in 4/♩ containing a quarter note must have a final measure with only three beats. Figure 2.19 presents two examples of pickup measures with correct final measures. Insert notes and rests in the final measure of each of the remaining six examples in figure 2.19 to complete the pickup.

Figure 2.19 Pickup Measures

ACTIVITY Compare your final measures in figure 2.19 with a partner. Explain why you used the notes and rests that you wrote.

MORE COMPLICATED RHYTHMS

Some of the songs you will be learning in this text use more complicated rhythms. These involve different combinations of sixteenth notes, and some use dotted rhythms as well. If you use the knowledge you have already acquired in this chapter, these rhythms are not difficult to master, and they add interest and flavor to music. Figure 2.20 presents several more complicated rhythm patterns. Note how each is a different arrangement of eighth and sixteenth notes.

Figure 2.20 More Complicated Rhythms

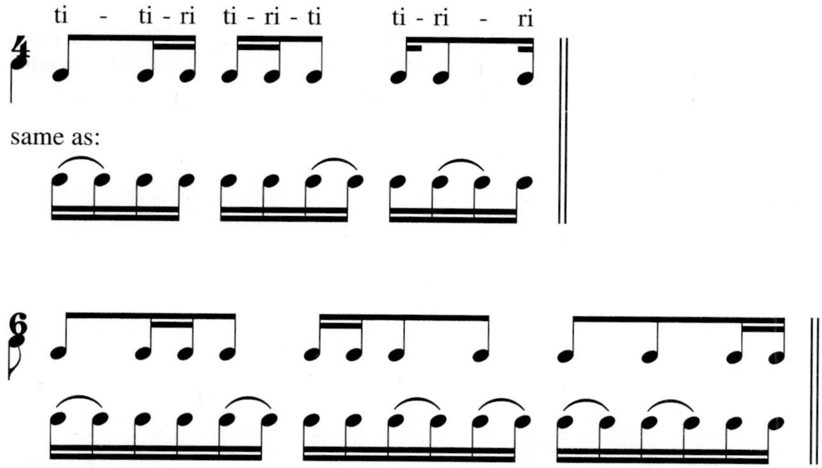

Practice the rhythms found in figure 2.21. Write the rhythm syllables under the notation in each example. Next, mark the places where each beat falls. The first example has been completed for you.

Figure 2.21 Rhythm Practice

Figure 2.21 *continued*

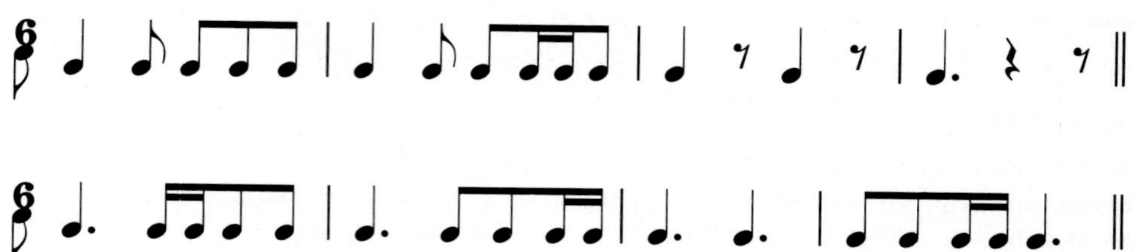

ACTIVITY Compare your rhythm syllables in figure 2.21 with a partner and practice the rhythms together, taking turns to keep the beat and clap the patterns.

TRIPLETS

The last rhythm introduced in this chapter is a way to subdivide the beat into three parts when a meter is used with a quarter note on the bottom. This rhythm is called a **triplet** (figure 2.22). Figure 2.23 presents several rhythms to practice that include triplets. Each of the three sounds in each triplet should be of equal length.

Figure 2.22 Triplet Rhythm Syllables

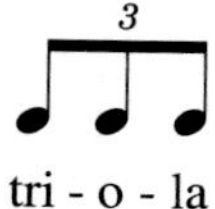

Figure 2.23 Rhythms Using Triplets

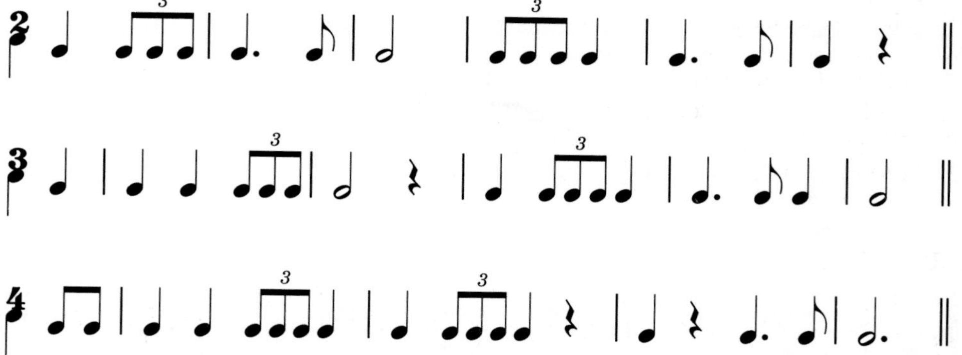

PLAYING RECORDER

Whether you have never played a recorder or you are an experienced player, take time now to examine your recorder and find out how it works. Your soprano recorder may be made of plastic or wood, and it has several parts—the head joint, the middle joint, and the foot joint. Some plastic recorders have a single piece that replaces the middle and foot joints. If you can, take your recorder apart and look inside. If your recorder has a head joint, try playing that part alone. What kind of sound did you hear? Reassemble your recorder. Carefully align the parts of the instrument correctly: the wind way should align with the holes in the middle joint, and the foot joint should be off-set to accommodate the shorter length of your right-hand little finger.

After you play the recorder, you should dry the interior of the middle joint either by using a swab or by pulling a soft cloth through the part. If you have a three-joint recorder, make sure that the holes of the foot joint are slightly out of line with the holes of the middle joint. This placement will help your right-hand pinkie reach the lowest note, C.

Hold the recorder with your left hand at the top and your right hand below it. Explore the different sounds you can make by blowing, humming, and breathing into the little slot at the top of the mouthpiece, which is called the wind way. See how many sound effects you can make and how many **dynamic** levels you can produce.

To make a variety of pitches sound, make sure that your left-hand thumb is completely covering the single hole under the instrument. Press the ball of your thumb squarely over the hole without pressing too tightly. Check the finger placement of each hole to make sure you've covered the hole. Now experiment with creating sounds.

You will notice that the more holes you have covered, the lower the resulting pitch that you can produce. Covering the holes effectively lengthens the middle joint: the longer the pipe, the lower the sound produced. Conversely, if you uncover holes, you shorten the pipe, which raises the pitch. Experiment with making lower and higher sounds. Remember to swab out your instrument before putting it away.

BEGINNING TO PLAY THE RECORDER

The recorder is an instrument that is often used in classrooms. If your school has a music specialist, he or she may begin teaching this instrument in class as early as the third grade. If your school does not have a music specialist, you may want to add recorder playing as a valuable daily experience.

The recorder is a viable instrument to learn during this course—you will be able to use it in your own classroom to establish the starting pitch for songs. This use of the recorder will ensure that the sounds you have children sing are within their proper vocal range. Recorders are available in both plastic and wooden models: the plastic models are easy to care for and can be purchased at a very moderate cost; the wooden models are more expensive and need more care, but they produce a better sound.

There are only six rules to follow when learning to play the recorder.

1. Blow easily (breathe into the instrument).
2. Use the left hand on the top three holes.
3. Blow softly (breathe into the instrument).
4. Cover each hole completely.
5. Blow gently (breathe into the instrument).
6. Release air with the tongue whispering "too."

FIRST PITCH: B

The first pitch you will learn on the recorder is B. You finger this pitch as shown in figure 2.24, with your left thumb covering the back hole and your left first finger covering the top hole on the front of the recorder.

Figure 2.24 Fingering for B

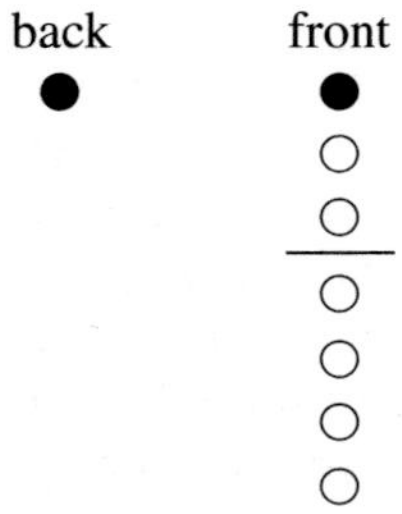

back	front
●	●
	○
	○
	———
	○
	○
	○
	○

On the staves in figure 2.25 you will find repeated quarter notes and rests. When you play the lines in figures 2.25, 2.26, and 2.27, separate each pitch by using your tongue to block the air hole after each sound. You can pretend to say "tah" to start each individual pitch.

Figure 2.25 Playing B

Figure 2.26 Playing Longer Sounds

Figure 2.27 Playing Notes and Observing Rests

ANOTHER PITCH: A

The next pitch you will learn is A. This pitch is lower than B. The fingering for this note is shown in figure 2.28. You use the two fingers you used for "B" and add the middle finger of your left hand over the second hole.

Figure 2.28 Fingering for A

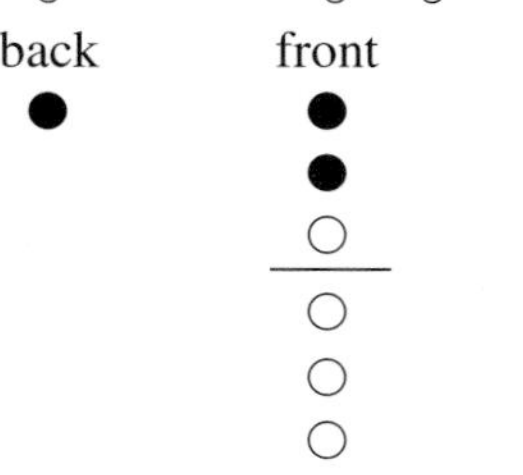

Figure 2.29 Playing A

Figure 2.30 Playing Whole Notes and Observing a Whole Rest

Figure 2.31 Combining Two Pitches with Whole and Half Notes

Figure 2.32 Combining Two Pitches with Whole, Half, and Quarter Notes

You may have already noticed that the lines (stems) placed on half and quarter notes in the preceding figures change direction for the notes A and B. This change in direction is purely for ease of printing and has no other meaning or significance. When notes are written on or above the middle line of a staff, the stem lines are drawn downward on the left side of the note heads. When the note head is placed below the middle line, the stem points up on the right side of the note head.

MORE PRACTICE WITH B AND A

Figure 2.33 presents additional opportunities to practice playing the pitches of B and A.

Figure 2.33 More Practice with B and A

ANOTHER PITCH: G

The third pitch you will learn in this section is G. You use the fingers as used for playing A, except you now place your left third finger on the next hole on the recorder. This new pitch is lower than A.

Figure 2.34 Fingering for G

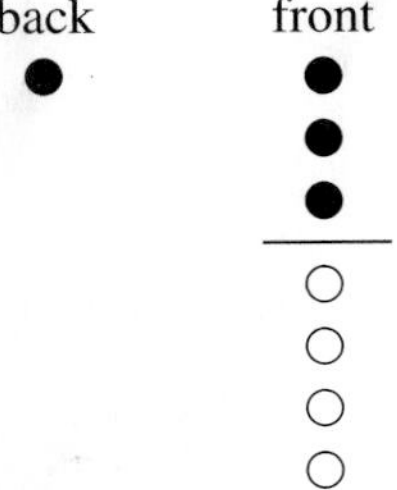

Figure 2.35 presents two examples for you to play that demonstrate the pitches of B, A, and G in the same piece of music.

Figure 2.35 Combining the Pitches of B, A, and G

PLAYING SKIPS

You play a **skip** when you play a B and then a G without playing the A. Figures 2.36 and 2.37 present examples of skips that you can play.

Figure 2.36 Playing Skips

Figure 2.37 More Practice Playing Skips

CHILDREN'S SONGS USING THREE PITCHES

The three children's songs in figure 2.38 ("Suo Gan," "Au Clair De La Lune," and "Merrily We Roll Along") are composed of the three pitches B, A, and G. Practice playing these three songs on your recorder.

Figure 2.38 Three Children's Songs Using B, A, and G

Suo Gan

Welsh Folk Song

Su - o Gan do not weep, Su - o Gan go to sleep.
Su - o Gan Moth-er's near, Su - o Gan have no fear.

Figure 2.38 *continued*

Au Clair De La Lune

French Folk Song

Prê - te - moi ta plu - me pour é - crire un mot.

Merrily We Roll Along

Traditional

Mer - ri - ly we roll a - long, roll a - long, roll a - long.

Mer - ri - ly we roll a - long o'er the deep blue sea.

FOR YOUR OWN COMPOSITIONS

On the following four blank staves, write your own compositions that use the pitches B, A, and G.

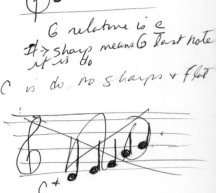

Diatonic scale
D is do with one sharp

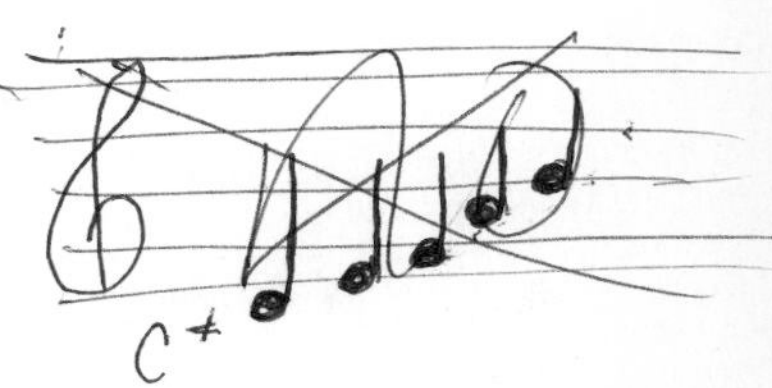

G relative is e
→ sharp means G last note it is do
C is do no sharps + flat

C relative minor a

Solfege Do Re Mi
1 2 3

Key signature with 1 flat is F and it is always a b

FURTHER PRACTICE

In the space below, prepare a mystery rhythm exercise for class. Write four lines of rhythms using the patterns you have learned. Write all your lines in the same meter, and write four measures in each line. Be ready to say and/or clap one line and have a partner or small group decide which of the rhythms you performed.

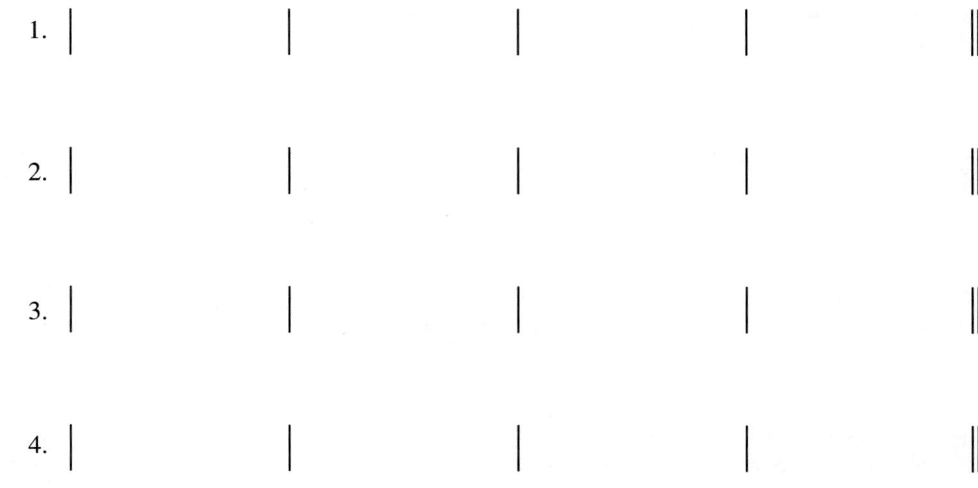

Figure 2.39 Further Practice Organizing Rhythms in Meter

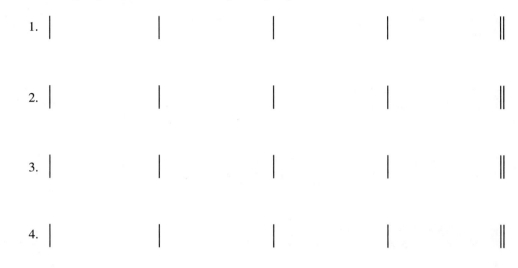

Figure 2.39 *continued*

Figure 2.40 Further Practice with Complicated Rhythms

Fill in the missing note or rest.

Circle any incorrect measures.

Pitch Fundamentals for Confident Singing

What you will be able to do by the end of this chapter

- *Sing confidently using your natural singing voice*
- *Move your voice from speech to song*
- *Use hand signs that assist in singing*
- *Sing music notated with icons*
- *Identify different styles of singing*
- *Read simple music notation for pitch*
- *Play more difficult rhythms and simple duets on the soprano recorder*

THE JOY OF SINGING

As adults, many of us are often less confident about singing alone than we were as children. When we were young we would often break into spontaneous song about our everyday lives or play or imaginary friends. But as we grew into adulthood, we became constrained out of fear that others would think us strange if we walked along singing our hearts out. Even now, if we sometimes let our adult facades slip and we hum or whistle a bit, people around us often respond to the sound by saying, "You must be happy today!" This response is a recognition that musical sounds communicate their own nonverbal meaning, and this meaning is understood across the human experience. Singing is such a valuable part of who we are because we can experience joy and pleasure and a multitude of other unnamed feelings as we sing alone or with others.

One purpose of this text is to enable you to be a confident participant in music making. Your first musical participation in this chapter will involve your vocal instrument—the ready-to-use singing voice that you carry around with you all day. Singing in class with others will help you develop security as a singer and support your individual development as a confident performer.

Confident singers are not extraordinary people by any means. They are simply people who can open their mouths and produce a musical sound that pleases them. Confident singers understand that singing is not a skill reserved for one room of a school or one department of a university. Confident singers are sure that singing, like breathing and talking and walking, is an important part of being human.

An important aspect of developing singing confidence is to understand that the sounds of the singers you hear on the radio or MTV are sounds that have been carefully engineered in recording studios. They are not the natural sounds that originally came from the performer's mouth. It is impossible for anyone to replicate these electronically modified singing sounds, and we should not begin to try to do so.

Gaining comfort with your own unique voice is the first step to becoming a confident singer. Acceptance of your own singing voice comes as a result of one thing only—singing! Singing is not a skill that can be read about or studied in a textbook; it must be experienced daily. Once you discover how much fun singing is, you will not want to stop and you will be ready to use your singing voice everywhere you go.

CHAPTER GOALS

The goal of this chapter is to enable you to learn to sing confidently and expressively. The authors recognize that singing is frightening for some people and fun or satisfying for others. This chapter is designed to boost your singing skill as well as your confidence. Through class activities you will learn to support and control your voice so that you can produce changes of pitch. Some other changes will be of intensity or dynamics, the degrees of loudness and softness, and the gradations between these. Other changes will be of speed or tempo and still others will involve trying different styles of singing such as folk, gospel, jazz, and many others. You will learn musical skills that will support continual vocal development.

One aspect of becoming a confident singer is learning how to interpret the symbol system that is used to represent pitches. This notational system has developed over many centuries, and it is the result of successive attempts to find a way to write symbols that will be interpreted by readers as sound. The route that you will take to understanding musical notation will involve further musical participation through singing and through playing the recorder.

The sequence of musical experiences contained in this chapter has been designed to enable you to enjoy the delight of singing and playing music. We want you to become secure in the belief that singing is a valuable part of living and that it is equally important for adults and children.

VOCAL PRODUCTION BASICS: SPEAKING VS. SINGING VOICE

Often, adults believe they cannot sing because instead of using their singing voice, they are actually using their speaking voice. Finding one's singing voice is something that happens during early childhood, as mothers sing to their infants and engage in vocal play. Early childhood education programs stress singing development; and through a variety of activities, children have regular, consistent opportunities to discover and experiment with their young singing voices. However, many children still do not gain the requisite skills for confident singing. Perhaps you were one of those children who did not get the kind of specific instruction you needed during your elementary years, and you have yet to realize your potential as a confident singer. If so, the process of singing that you will experience in this course will enable you to develop your singing potential.

The human voice is an amazing instrument. It can produce spoken sounds as well as sung pitches, and it is capable of expressing a wide variety of emotions. Each voice is distinctive, with its own timbre or tone color, among many other characteristics. Speaking voices can be high or low pitched, mellifluous or squeaky, mellow or strident, smooth or raspy, and many gradations in between. Singing voices are also as various in character as the people who produce them. In addition to the voice's character, another factor governing how it sounds is the way the owner uses it. Learning how the voice works and how to use your own singing voice comfortably are basic goals for this course that you will begin to realize in this chapter.

HOW THE VOICE WORKS

As you read the following description, try to visualize and be aware of where these body parts are in your own vocal instrument. There are five steps in the vocal process that result in the production of singing tone.

1. The brain and neurological system send commands to and receive messages from the body, resulting in muscular responses that control various aspects of the vocal process.
2. The muscles and organs of breathing (trachea, lungs, bronchi, diaphragm, ribs, abdominal and back muscles) act in coordination to control the inhaling and emission of air.
3. The larynx, or voice box, consists of folds, muscles, ligaments, and cartilages that coordinate airflow, resulting in vibrating vocal folds and a fundamental buzzing sound.
4. The combined resonance cavities (throat, mouth, and nose) provide acoustical secondary vibrators for enhancing the fundamental buzzing sound. They amplify the sound, giving it space in which to grow and change character from a simple buzz to a pitched tone.
5. The organs of speech (tongue, jaw, cheeks, teeth, lips, hard and soft palates, and dental ridges) coordinate in producing all of the sounds normally associated with speech.[1]

EXPLORING YOUR VOICE

As you explore the following activities, you may notice that you have more than one type of vocal quality. The higher and lighter sounds are referred to as the head voice; heavier and lower sounds, the chest voice. There is a break between these two voices or registers. The break might sound like an empty place where no sound is produced, or you may actually feel or hear your voice shift from one register to the other.

Record yourself as you speak each of these exercises. Listen to the recording and analyze what you hear. Come to class ready to discuss your findings.

1. Get a sense of your natural speaking voice by saying "OK," "Hello there!" and "Sure!" Did your voice sound low, high, or somewhere in between? Can you distinguish whether you were using your head voice or chest voice when you spoke each of the words?
2. Think about a funny joke that you heard recently, and work up to a good laugh. Note whether the laugh is lower or higher than the pitch of your speaking range.
3. Think about the last time you took a long afternoon nap, and work up to a yawn. What kind of sound did you make? Describe the pitch level of the yawn.
4. Choose any paragraph in this text and read it aloud three different ways. First, use your normal speaking voice but pretend you are on the stage and want the people in the back row to hear you. Second, read the paragraph in your high-pitched speaking voice, as if you were still five years old. Third, pretend you have smoked cigarettes for forty years, and read the words as loudly and harshly as you can. Note the different sensations that each of these voices produces in your throat, head, and chest.

FINDING YOUR OWN SINGING VOICE

To begin to find your singing voice, speak the following rhyme in your normal speaking pitch:

Aloysius Allen, Stephanie Green.
He thinks he's the smartest,
She thinks she's the queen!

Now say the rhyme again and use a lot of inflection (i.e., make your speaking voice go up and down in pitch).

Look at the rhyme printed on the next page and say it again; this time speak the words in a single pitch that is comfortable. The graphics that are placed above the words are called icons. When the line of the icon ascends, allow your voice to slide upward to a higher speaking pitch; when the line descends, let your voice slide down to a lower pitch.

Aloysius Allen, Stephanie Green.

He thinks he's the smartest,

She thinks she's the queen!

You may have noticed that your speaking voice has a variety of pitch levels within its range and that it takes just a little bit of effort to change the inflection of your speaking voice. In addition to the pitch level of your speaking voice, you can also change the dynamic level. Musicians use the term **dynamics** to refer to the loudness or softness of sound—its intensity. While loud and soft are the more global terms used for differences in dynamic level, musicians also use much finer gradations in dynamic changes and have developed symbols to indicate these changes. The term **crescendo,** which is represented by the symbol $<$, indicates that the loudness of a sound should be gradually increased. Conversely, **decrescendo,** which is represented by the symbol $>$, indicates that a sound should be gradually decreased.

Speak the following rhyme on a single pitch, following the symbols for crescendo and decrescendo.

Ours is not to reason why,

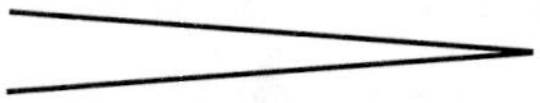

Ours is but to do or die!

To begin to explore your singing voice, read the rhyme again but instead of beginning on a speaking pitch, choose a comfortably low singing pitch and sing both lines of the rhyme on this pitch.

Ours is not to reason why,

Ours is but to do or die!

Now, starting on a comfortably low singing pitch, sing the rhyme again. The icons indicate where you should raise or lower the pitch of your singing. Practice singing the rhyme until you are comfortable with following the icons.

Ours is not to reason why,

Ours is but to do or die!

Your singing voice may be well developed or this may be the first time you have really explored its potential. Whatever your level of comfort, your singing voice is as unique as your fingerprint and is much more versatile. Throughout this text you will find activities that will both help you gain experience in using your singing voice and expand your understanding of music fundamentals.

SPEECH TO SONG

Many people do not realize that when we speak and when we sing we do not use the same part of our vocal mechanism. A simple way to discover this important idea is to say the following rhymes, lightly touching your fingers to the front of your throat as you speak. If you leave your hand in place and then sing the words on one pitch, you will feel a difference in the vibrations that are being produced by your vocal mechanism.

Soft Snow
I walked abroad in a snowy day;
I ask'd the soft snow with me to play:
She play'd & she melted in all her prime,
And the winter call'd it a dreadful crime.
—William Blake

First Fig
My candle burns at both ends
It will not last the night;
But ah, my foes, and oh, my friends
It gives a lovely light.
—Edna St. Vincent Millay

A Good Woman Feeling Bad
All riddles are blues
And all blues are sad
And I'm only mentioning
Some blues I've had
—Maya Angelou

Try each of the rhymes again, but this time alternate speaking and singing lines. Keep your hand on your throat to monitor the differences between your speaking and singing voices. Move your singing voice around to different pitches as you experiment.

ACTIVITY In groups of four, select one rhyme and choose two lines for you to sing. Speak the other lines in unison. Have two members of the group sing one line and change their singing pitch at least once. The other two group members should sing the second line in a similar manner. After you have finished experimenting as a group, draw iconic representations of the ways your singing voices moved during the exercise. Share your rhyme and icons with the class.

ACTIVITY In pairs, select one rhyme and choose one line that both of you will speak together. Divide the other lines with your partner and make decisions about changing your voices from high to low within each line. After you have experimented with the rhyme, draw iconic representations of the ways you moved your singing voices. Share your rhyme and icons with the class.

MOVING YOUR SINGING VOICE ON TWO PITCHES

As you have just discovered, the two vocal productions of speaking and singing are very different, indeed. Finding and using your singing voice is not "magic" but rather the result of careful thinking, practicing, listening, and comparing the results of these two different ways to use your voice.

ACTIVITY The next step in the process of becoming a confident singer is to use your singing voice to produce two sounds that are found in the folk music of many cultures. Musicians describe these pitches with the musical syllable names of "sol" and "mi." You probably know these sounds as the first two sounds of the children's song, "This Old Man." The sound of "this" is a sol and is represented by the following hand sign:

Figure 3.1 Hand Sign for Sol

Drawing by Robert M. Atterbury

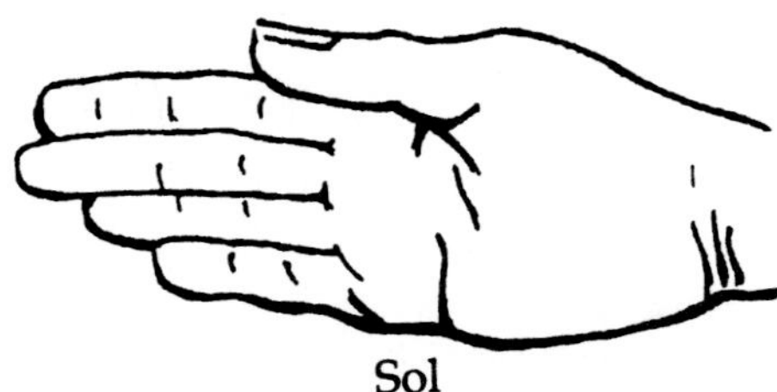

The sound of "old" is a mi and is represented by the following hand sign:

Figure 3.2 Hand Sign for Mi

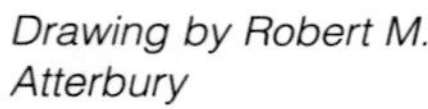
Drawing by Robert M. Atterbury

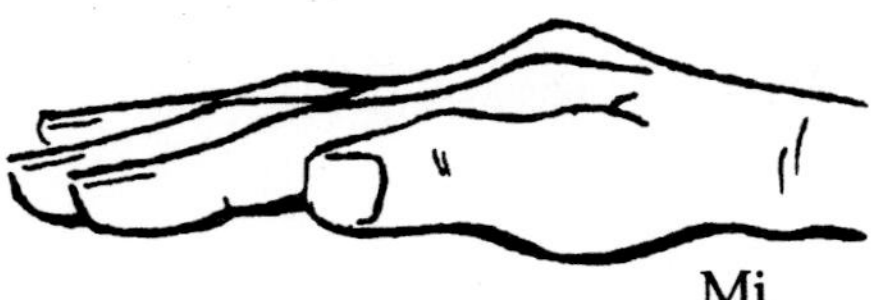

For this activity we will take a short poem and use the lines underneath the poem as a guide to our singing.

```
      I had a little pig
Sol   -  -  -       -
Mi              - -
      S  S  S MM  S

      I fed him in a trough,
S     - -  -        -
M               -   -

      He got so fat
S     -   -  -  -

      His tail dropped off.
S     -  -
M              -        -
```

So I got me a hammer,
S - - - - -
M - -

And I got me a nail,
S - - - - -
M -

And I made my little pig
S - - - - -
M - -

A brand-new tail.
S -
M - - -

ACTIVITY Choose one of the rhymes found earlier in this chapter. Work in pairs or groups of no more than three or four people and make up your own sol-and-mi song. Be sure to write the sols and mis that you decide on so you can sing your song to your classmates.

Another way to show the two sounds we have used so far is to use two lines and draw note heads which will initially just appear as filled-in circles. Figure 3.3 shows how the first line of the poem would look.

Figure 3.3 Notation for Two Pitches, Using Lines

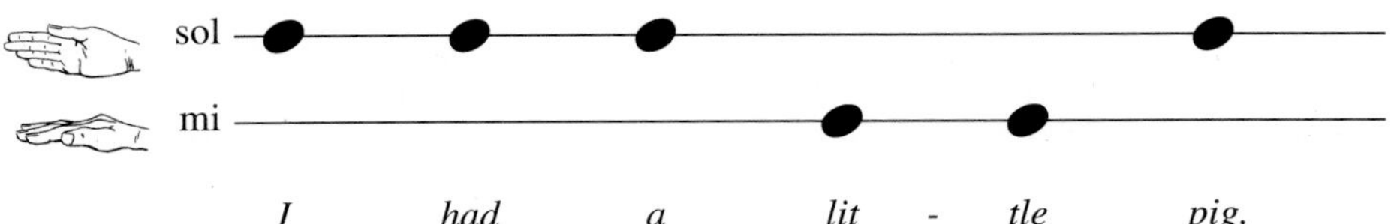

ACTIVITY Go back to the previous activity and notate your sols and mis on a two-line staff using note heads as illustrated in figure 3.3. Practice your song using the hand signs for sol and mi.

MOVING THESE TWO NOTES TO SPACES

The two sounds that you just sang and read using two lines can also be notated using the spaces between the lines. Figure 3.4 presents the first line of the little pig poem with the space notation.

Figure 3.4 Notation for Two Pitches, Using Spaces

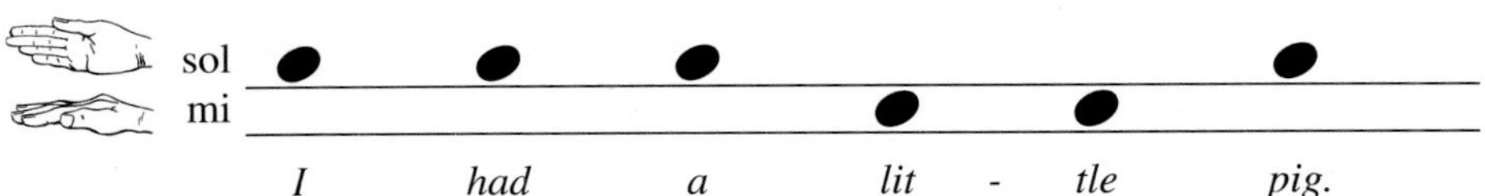

ADDING ANOTHER PITCH

The next singing sound that we will add is the syllable "la." When you sing "This Old Man," you sing many sols and mis with the phrase "This old man, he played one." When you sing the next word, "he," you sing a la. As you can see from the following icon, the pitch la is directly above sol.

Drawings by Robert M. Atterbury

Figure 3.5 Hand Signs for La, Sol, and Mi

When we are using two lines and note heads, la will be placed directly above sol, on either the next line or the next space. If we changed the contour of the first line of "I Had a Little Pig" to use three pitches, it might look like figure 3.6 or figure 3.7.

Figure 3.6 Notation for Three Pitches, Using Lines

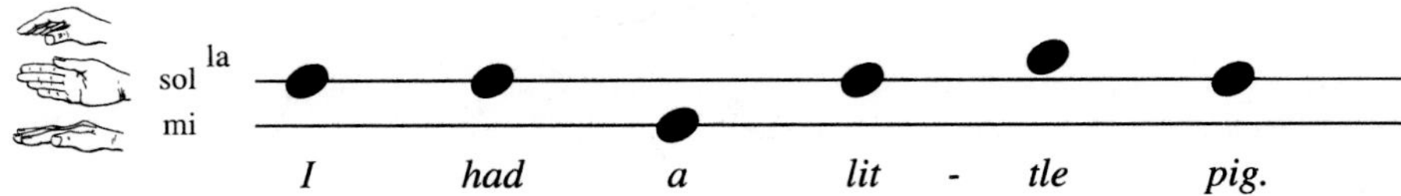

Figure 3.7 Notation for Three Pitches, Using Spaces

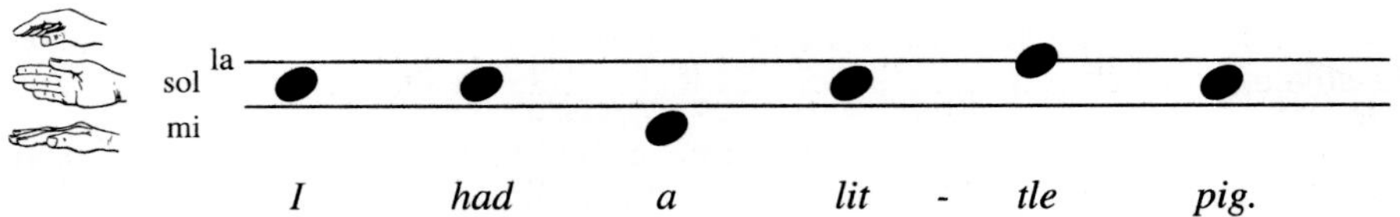

PREPARING TO SING THREE PITCHES

ACTIVITY Practice the three pitches in figure 3.8 in the following manner:
1) look at the notation and practice the hand signs silently
2) move your hand and practice singing the pitches with the syllable names.

Figure 3.8 Pitches and Hand Signs for "Winter Moon," by Langston Hughes

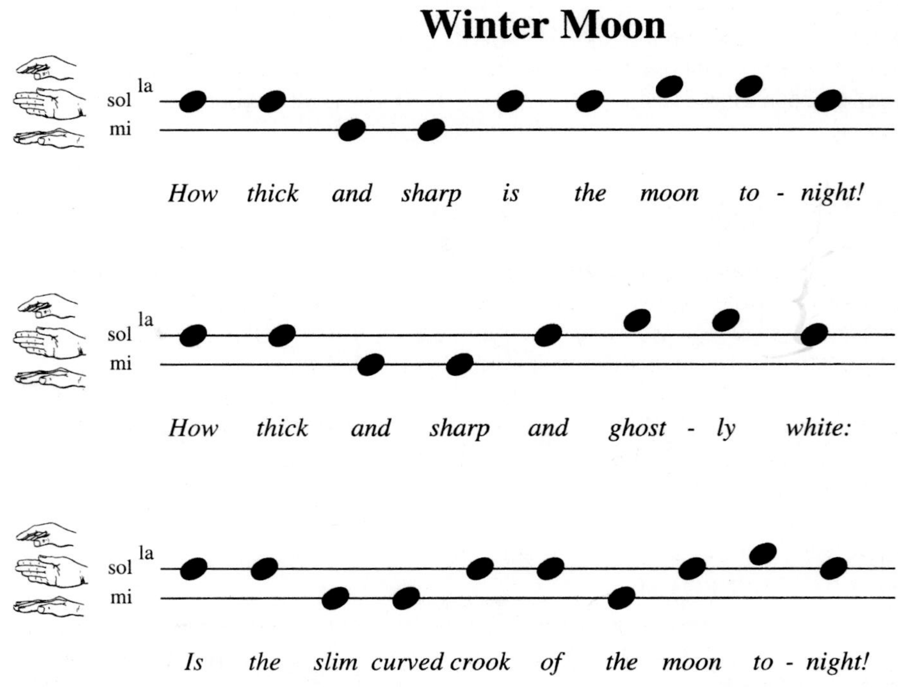

Now look at the two-line notation in figure 3.8 again and this time practice reading the pitches while singing the words and using hand signs. Take your time and be prepared to do it several times before you're comfortable.

In figure 3.9 is a different melody for a song. Practice it first by saying only the syllables and making the hand signs. Then try singing the pitches while showing the hand signs. Finally, try to sing the words on the correct pitches while showing the correct hand signs.

Figure 3.9 More Practice with Three Pitches

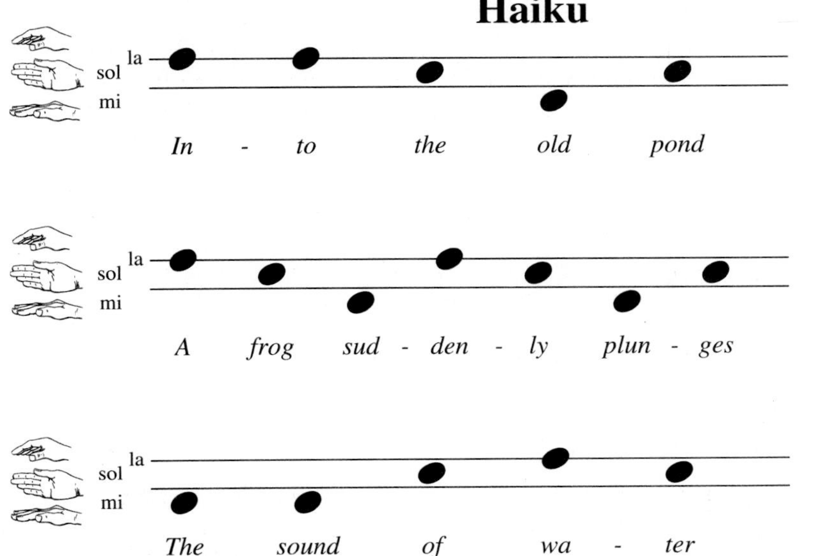

ACTIVITY Select a different rhyme from earlier in this chapter and create a three-note song with a partner. Write down your syllable letter names above the words of the rhyme. Practice your song using the three hand signs and share it with another set of your classmates. If you finish before others in the class, try singing some different combinations of these three syllables and using your hand signs. Have your partner echo what you sing.

USING THE STAFF

In most music, the symbols of duration and pitch are printed using more than the two lines that were presented earlier in this chapter. Music notation is written on a five-line staff that has a sign at the beginning that indicates whether the notation placed on the staff is of a high or low sound. These two symbols are called clefs.

The treble clef indicates that music notation is of a relatively high pitch and can be sung by females or children. Music notation written on this staff can be played on the recorder, violin, trumpet, and flute. The treble clef is also called the G clef because the ending of the clef circles the line of the staff that is called "G."

Figure 3.10 Staff with G Clef and the Female Vocal Range

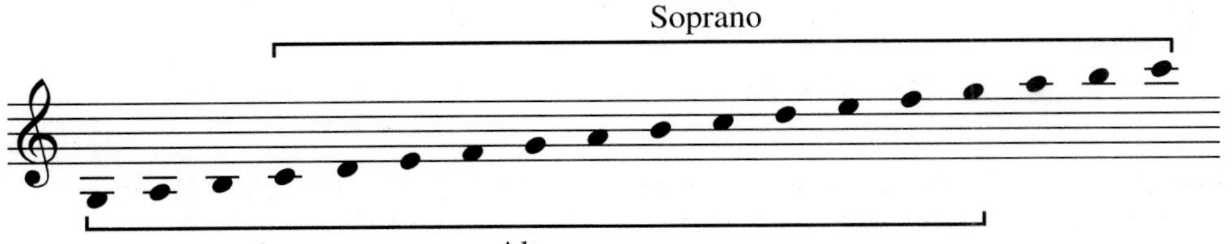

The bass or F clef indicates that the music notation is within the singing range of adult males or the playing range of tubas and double bass or bass violin. The bass clef is sometimes called the F clef because the two dots beside the clef denote the "F" line on that staff.

Figure 3.11 Staff with F Clef and the Male Vocal Range

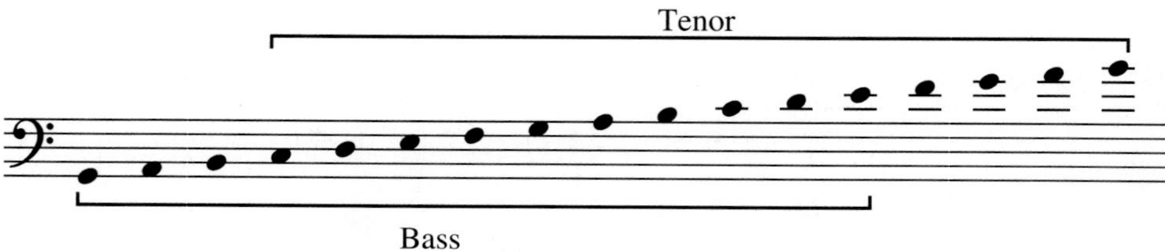

The lines and spaces of the staff are labeled with the alphabetical letters A to G, as shown in figure 3.12. For now, you will only be reading the treble clef as you begin to read the pitch and rhythm notation you have mastered so far in this chapter.

Figure 3.12 Letter Names of the Lines and Spaces of the G and F Staves

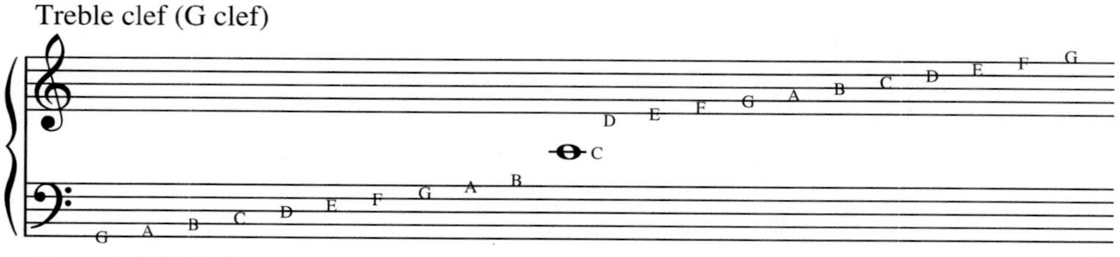

READING PITCH AND RHYTHM NOTATION

The next step in learning to read music is to put pitch and rhythm symbols together on a staff. First review the following rhyme:

> *Ours is not to reason why,*
> *Ours is but to do or die!*

You can perform this rhyme three different ways. First, say it and softly tap the steady beat (see figure 3.13). Second, sing the pitches as shown on the two lines or spaces (see figure 3.14). Third, say the rhythm syllables that go with the stick notation shown (see figure 3.15). Figure 3.15 presents the rhyme as it is notated on the treble staff.

Figure 3.13 Stick Notation and Rhythm Syllables

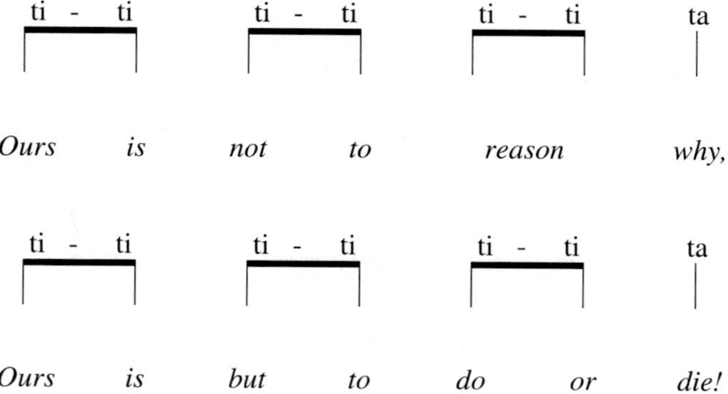

Figure 3.14 Notation for Three Pitches, Using Lines and Spaces

Figure 3.15 Notation on the Treble Staff

Figure 3.16 presents other songs that use sol, mi, and la.

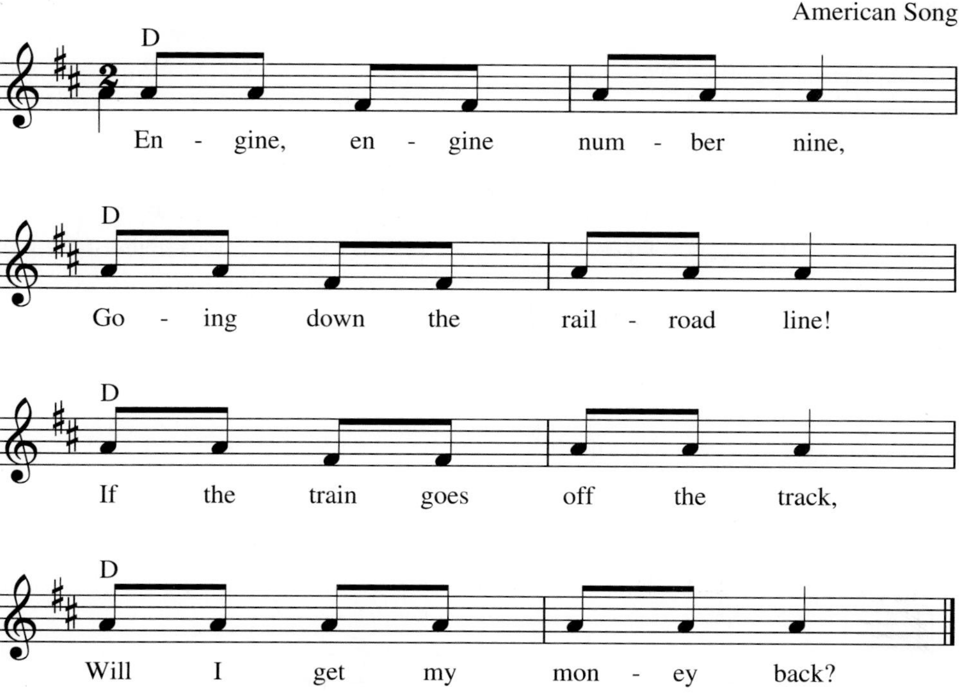

Figure 3.16 *continued*

Pease Porridge Hot

English Nursery Rhyme

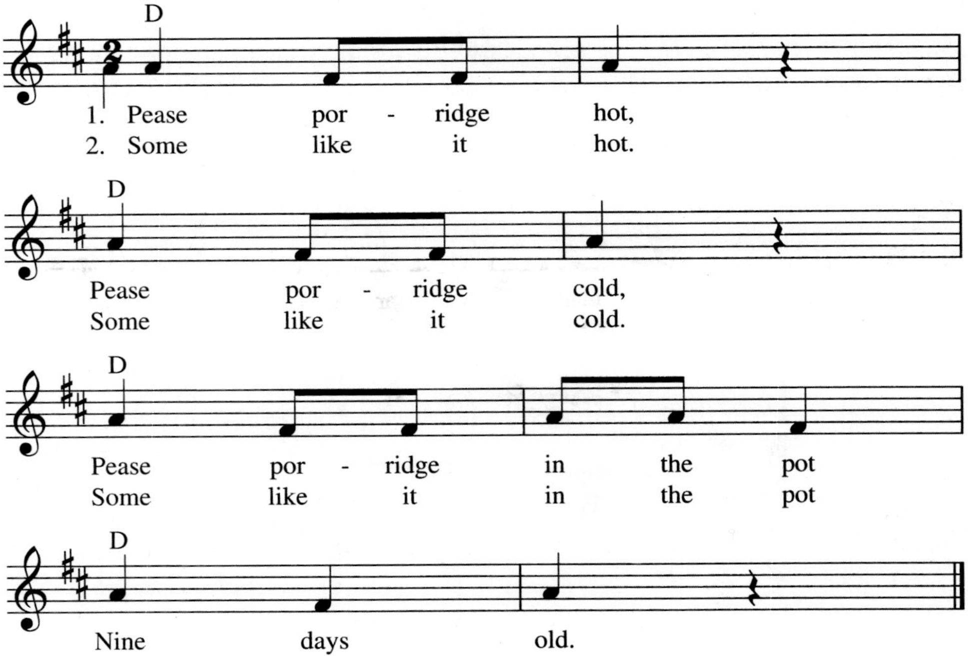

D
1. Pease por - ridge hot,
2. Some like it hot.
D
Pease por - ridge cold,
Some like it cold.
D
Pease por - ridge in the pot
Some like it in the pot
D
Nine days old.

See-Saw

American Song

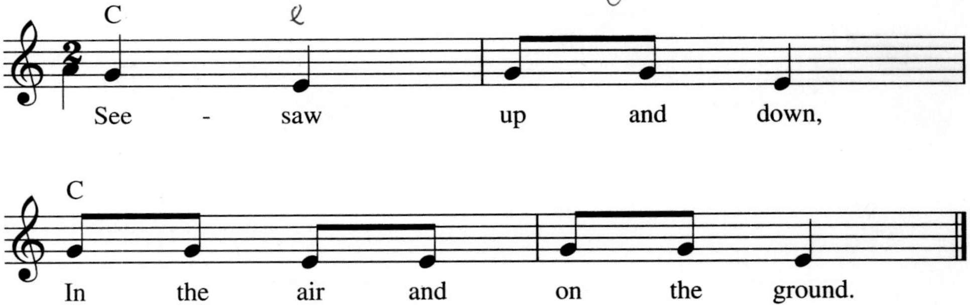

C
See - saw up and down,
C
In the air and on the ground.

Bye, Bye Baby-O

American Song

E
Bye, bye, ba - by - o,
E
Off to dream - land you must go.

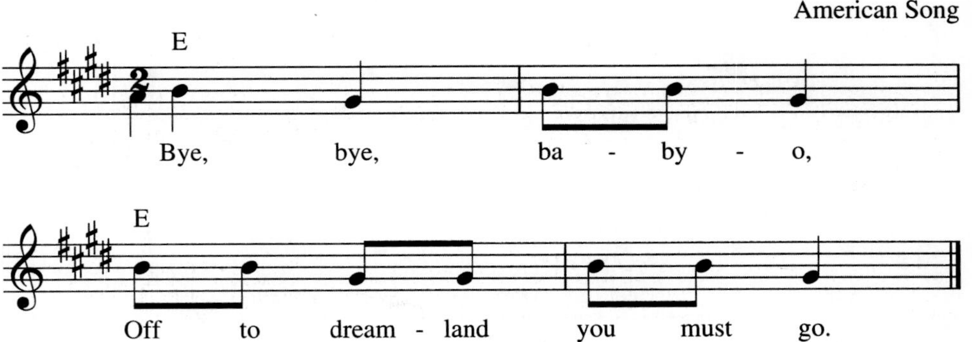

Figure 3.16 *continued*

Tinker, Tailor

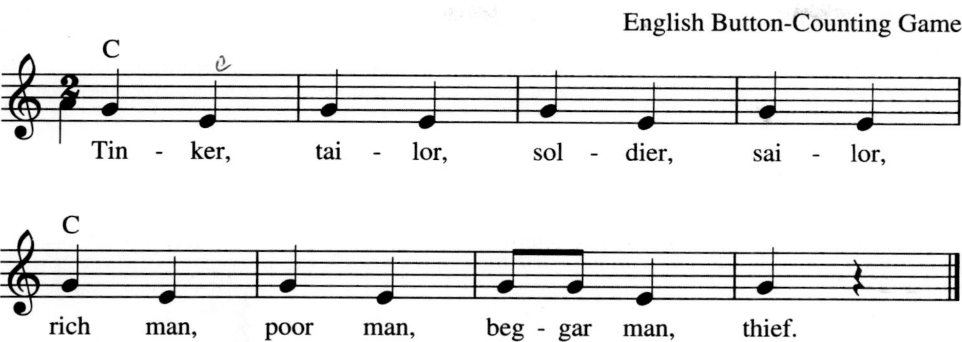

Doggie, Doggie

Little Tommy Tucker

Figure 3.16 *continued*

Lucy Locket

American Song

Rain, Rain, Go Away

Traditional Children's Song

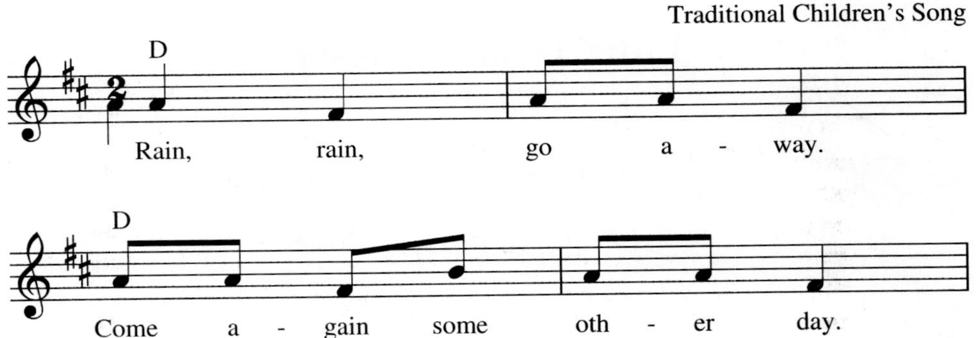

Figure 3.16 *continued*

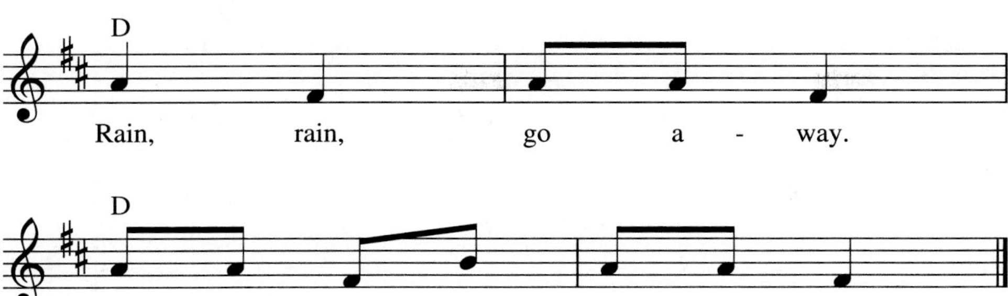

D
Rain, rain, go a - way.
D
Lit - tle chil - dren want to play.

ADDING MORE SINGING SYLLABLES

ACTIVITY The next two syllables that you will learn to sing and sign are "re" and "do." When you sing "This Old Man" and you get to "rolling home," you will be singing the pitches mi, re, and do. The hand signs for re and do are shown in figure 3.17.

Figure 3.17 I Eat My Peas with Honey, with Do on a Line

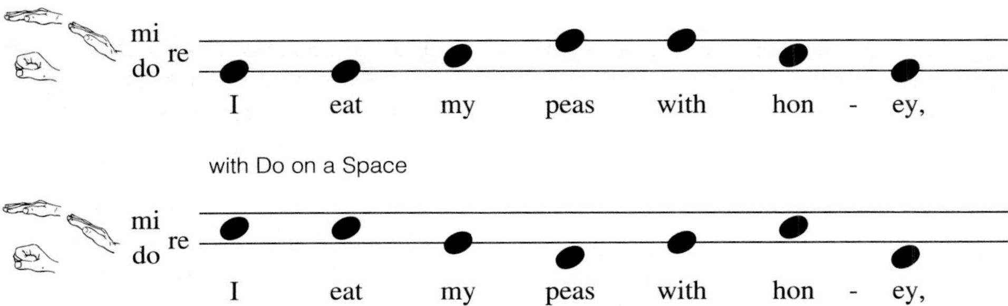

Now practice singing these two new sounds as they appear on the simplified staves in figure 3.17.

ACTIVITY With a partner create some melodies which are combinations of do and re. Write them out in iconic notation, practice them together, and then share your new tunes with another set of partners.

Figure 3.18 presents simple notation for "I Eat My Peas with Honey," a song that uses sol, la, mi, re, and do. First, practice the hand signs for the syllables and then sing the syllables with the hand signs. After that, sing the song with the text. Then sing the song using the simplified notation found in figure 3.18 and on a complete staff as found in figure 3.19.

Figure 3.18 Simple Notation

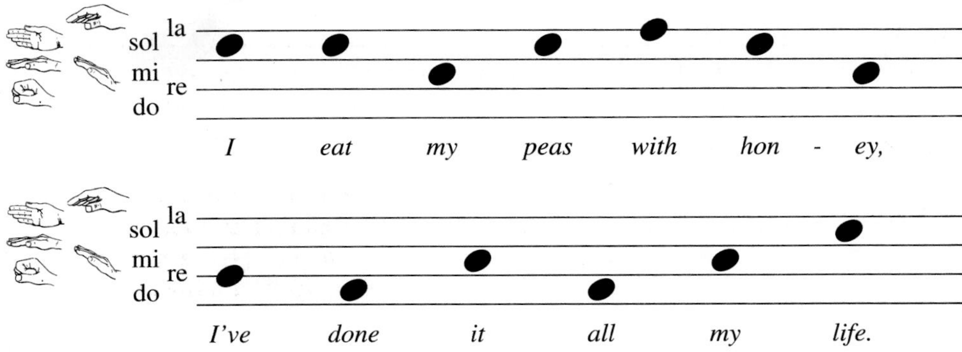

Figure 3.18 *continued*

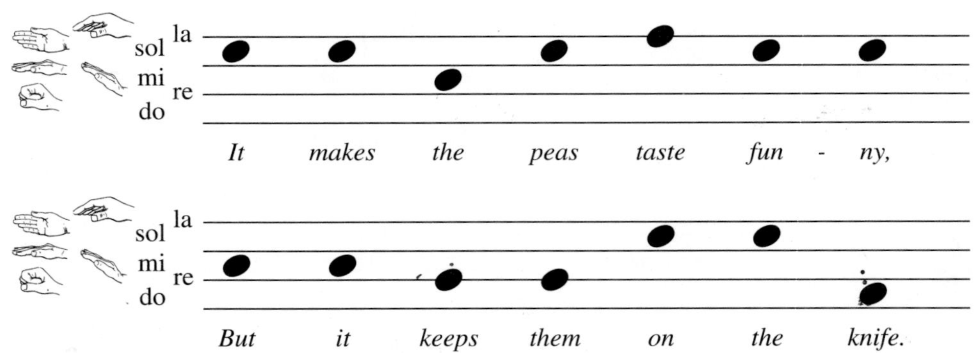

Figure 3.19 Treble Staff Notation

Figure 3.20 presents five songs that include sol, la, mi, re, and do.

Figure 3.20 Songs Using Sol, La, Mi, Re, and Do

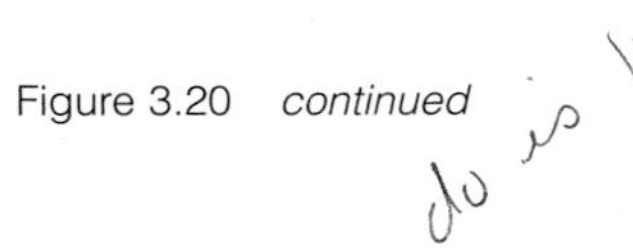

Figure 3.20 *continued*

Oh, Susanna

Stephen Foster | Stephen Foster

I __ come from Al - a - bam-a with my ban-jo on my knee. I'm __
I __ had a dream the oth-er night, when ev'-ry-thing was still. I __

going to Loui - si - an - a, my __ true love for to see. It __
thought I saw Su - san - na a - com-ing down the hill. The __

rained all night the day I left, the weath-er it was dry, The __
buck-wheat cake was in her mouth, the tear was in her eye. Says __

sun so hot I froze to death, Su - san - na, don't you cry.
I, "I'm com - ing from the South, Su - san - na, don't you cry."

I Have a Car

American Camp Song

I have a car, it's made of tin. No-bod-y knows what shape it's in. It

has four wheels and a rum-ble seat. Hear us chug-ging down the street. Honk

honk rat-tle rat-tle rat-tle crash beep beep. Honk honk rat-tle rat-tle rat-tle

A7 D

crash beep beep. Honk honk rat-tle rat-tle rat-tle crash beep beep. Honk honk.

Figure 3.20 *continued*

Button, You Must Wander
American Singing Game
F
C7
F
But - ton, you must wan - der, wan - der, wan - der,
F
C7
F
But - ton, you must wan - der ev' - ry - where.
B♭
F
B♭
F
Bright eyes will find you, sharp eyes will find you.
F
C7
F
But - ton, you must wan - der ev' - ry - where.

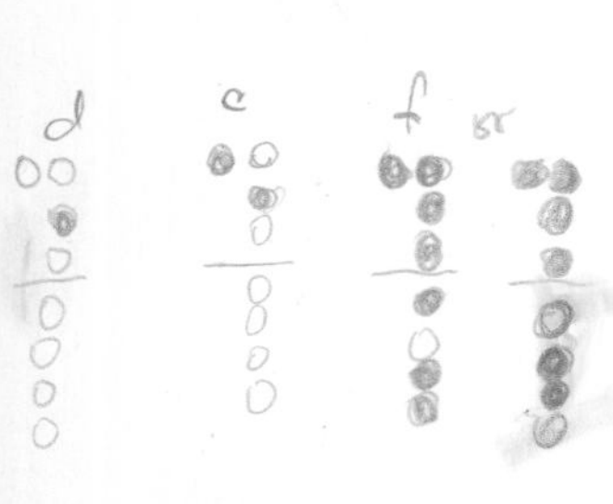

Built My Lady a Fine Brick House
Texas Folk Song
D
A7
Built my la-dy a fine brick house, Built it in a gar-den; I
D
A7
D
put her in but she jumped out, So fare thee well my dar - lin'!

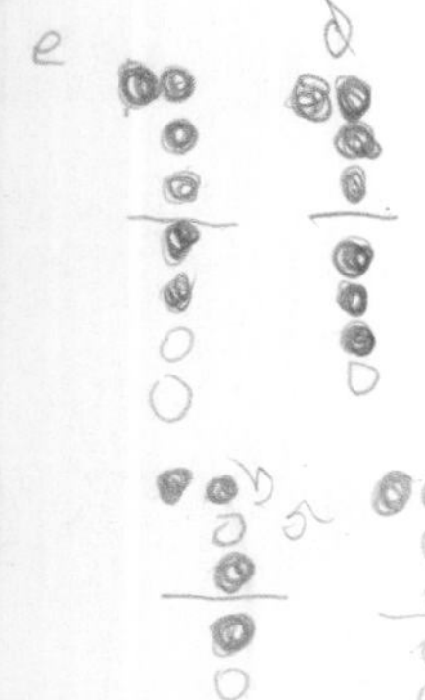

SINGING THE COMPLETE SCALE WITH HAND SIGNS

The last two syllables that you will learn are "fa" and "ti." The hand signs for these syllables are shown in figure 3.21.

Figure 3.21 Hand Signs for Ti and Fa

Drawings by Robert M. Atterbury

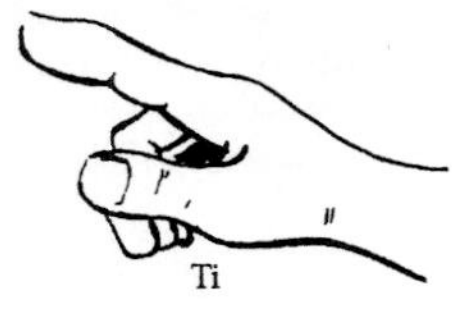
Ti

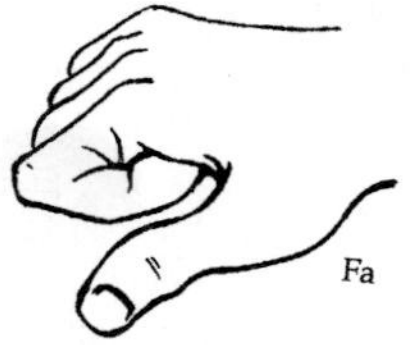
Fa

You can now sing, with hand signs, all of the pitches in a **major scale,** or the set of eight sounds from low do to high do. Figure 3.22 presents the C major scale. You will notice that the first two pitches are printed under the staff. The line that goes through the first note, C, is called a **ledger line.** A ledger line is simply a way of extending the staff and making it possible to write, sing, or play additional sounds without using the grand staff, which is composed of both treble and bass staves.

Figure 3.22 C Major Scale

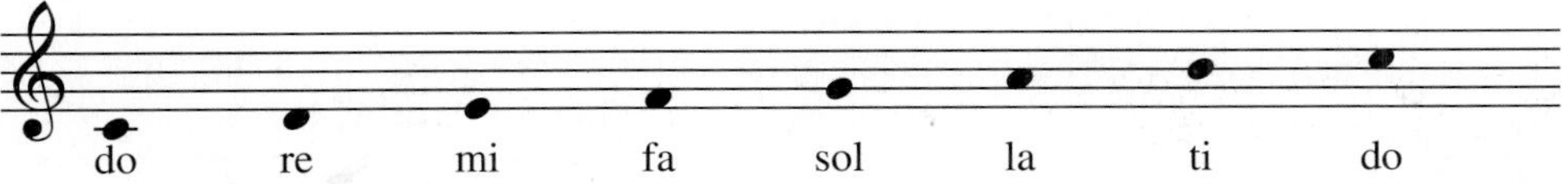

Figure 3.23 presents two songs that use all eight pitches in the major scale.

Figure 3.23 Two Songs That Use the Major Scale

Figure 3.23 *continued*

3. Oh, the ladies of the palace of the court of King Carraticus are just passing by.

4. Oh, the faces of the . . .

5. Oh, the noses of the . . .

6. Oh, the powder on the . . .

7. If you want to take a photo of the . . .

Spoken at end:
It's too late! They just passed by!

READING THE SYMBOLS FOR DYNAMIC CHANGES

One important way that music exhibits variety is through the many contrasts of intensity or dynamics. The letter symbols used to indicate dynamic levels are abbreviations for Italian words referring to loud, soft, and many other possible gradations of volume. The table below provides a reference list of the abbreviations and terms for musical dynamics.

Abbreviation		Term	Meaning
p		piano	soft
mp		mezzo piano	medium soft
f		forte	loud
mf		mezzo forte	medium loud
pp		pianissimo	very soft
ff		fortissimo	very loud
cres.	(crescendo hairpin)	crescendo	gradually getting louder
decres.	(decrescendo hairpin)	decrescendo	gradually getting softer

As you sing the song "Go Down Moses" in figure 3.24, make your voice reflect the dynamic markings. Notice that there are no dynamic markings in the last line of the piece. Decide which dynamic markings will make the song end most expressively.

Figure 3.24

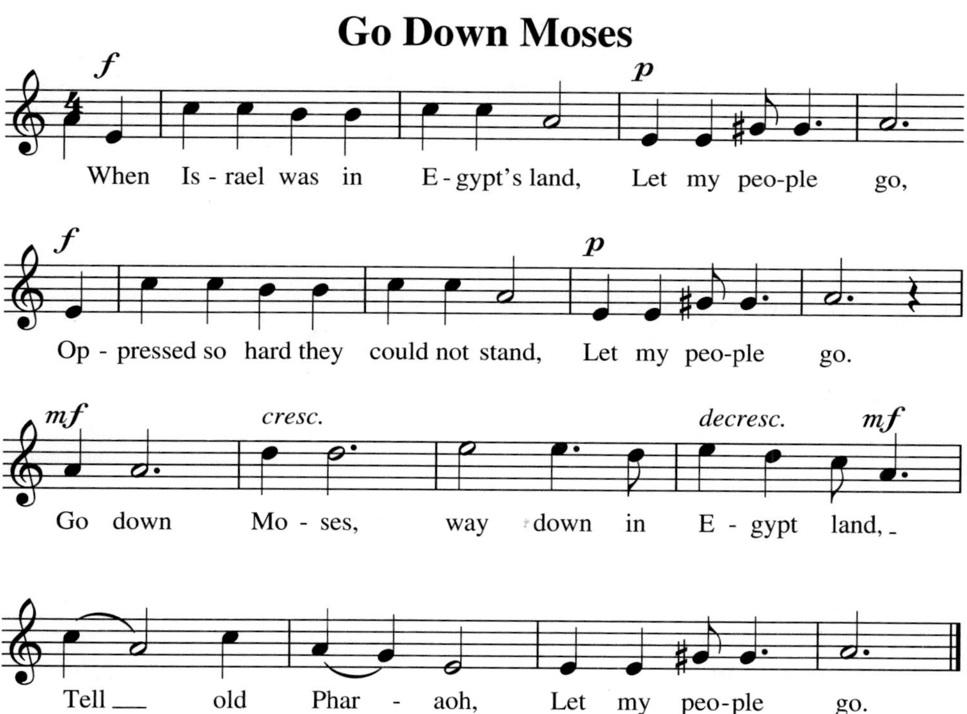
Go Down Moses
f
p
When Is - rael was in E - gypt's land, Let my peo-ple go,
f
p
Op - pressed so hard they could not stand, Let my peo-ple go.
mf
cresc.
decresc.
mf
Go down Mo - ses, way down in E - gypt land, -
Tell __ old Phar - aoh, Let my peo-ple go.

VOCAL DIFFERENCES IN ADULT SINGERS

In the singing you have experienced in this class, you may have noticed clear differences in how your classmates sound. Some may be able to sing only a few pitches and others may be able to sing every sound in every song. Still others may be using their speaking voice part or all of the time. This wide variety is due to the vast contrast in individual vocal development. As you continue to use this text you will gain more facility in singing and will begin to notice changes in your own singing ability.

There are many different types of singers. You are probably most familiar with the professional singers you hear on TV, radio, or recordings. Singing voices are often trained to sing particular styles of music. For example, folk singers often use their "natural" singing voices. They open their mouths and use a clear, pure sound without any modification through manipulation of the interior of the mouth, throat, or vocal mechanism. The example from the CD listed on the following page illustrates just one example of an adult folk singer.

"Coal Quay Market Song," CD track #3

Singers of classical music, such as opera or art songs, have a much more trained sound: their voices seem louder, more resonant, and they seem capable of producing much longer notes, more dynamic contrasts, and smoother singing. They are also trained to produce **vibrato.** Vibrato is the fluctuation of a single pitch that is usually heard when the singer is holding a note for a length of time.

"Pie Jesu" from *Requiem* by John Rutter, CD track #4

A contrasting style of singing can be found in Broadway musicals, where the singers "belt" the notes by using a more forced singing style that is both louder and more strident than the classically trained sound. Belting developed in the days before lavalier microphones, when the performer needed to project her or his voice over the pit orchestra into the audience.

"Some People" from *Gypsy,* CD track #5

Right now your natural singing voice may not sound like any one of these particular styles. In fact, you may think that it doesn't sound like much of anything at all! With a little regular practice you will soon be singing freely, using your natural voice and experimenting with the distinctive sounds that only you can make. The following activities will help you explore the sound and feeling of your own voice from the inside out, as both a singer and a listener.

EXPLORING YOUR OWN SINGING VOICE

"Try to Remember" from *The Fantasticks,* CD track #6

As you listen to "Try to Remember," pay attention to the wide range of pitches in this song. There is a big distance between the lowest note and the highest note. Use a comfortable starting pitch and sing the song yourself following the notation in figure 3.25. While you are singing, pay attention to the way your voice sounds and how it feels when you produce the different pitches.

Figure 3.25

Try to Remember

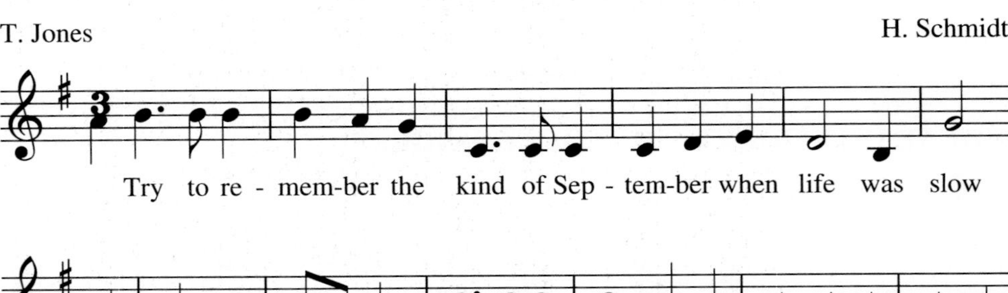

and oh, so mel-low._ Try to re - mem-ber the kind of Sep - tem-ber

Figure 3.25 *continued*

when grass was green and grain was yel-low._ Try to re - mem-ber

the kind of Sep - tem-ber when you were a ten-der and cal-low fel-low._

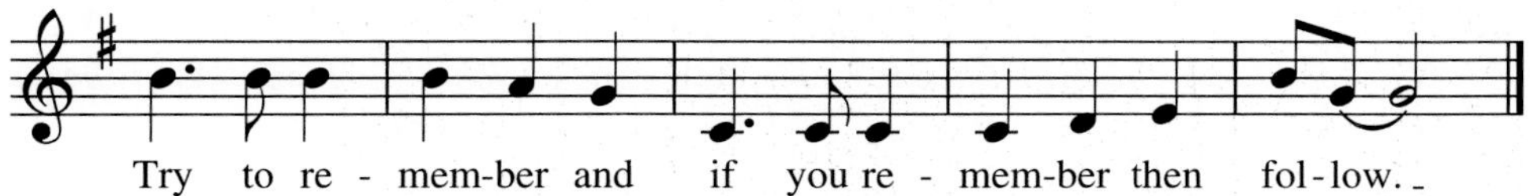
Try to re - mem-ber and if you re - mem-ber then fol-low._

Questions to ask yourself:

1. What was the easiest part to sing?
2. Where in the melody were you happiest with the sound of your voice?
3. Were there any pitches that felt too high or too low?
4. Where did you take a breath in the song?
5. If you were to sing the song again right now, what would you try to do differently with your voice to make it sound better?

There are some essential elements of comfortable singing that you can incorporate into your performance. The first is the positioning of your body. The singing instrument requires a lot of internal space for extra air in the lungs. You must hold yourself so that your lung capacity can be maximized.

Try the following exercise. Sitting up straight in your chair, raise your shoulders so that they are almost even with your ears. You now have no neck! Rotate your shoulders back and down to a comfortable position. You may feel as if you have just grown a few inches—your spine is probably straighter and more elongated than before. Another way to check that your body is in the correct position for maximum lung capacity is to lift a few strands of hair from the top of your head. Pull them (gently!) up in the air as if you were hung by your hair from the ceiling. Notice how your spine feels—straight, rather elongated. Drop your hair and return your arms to your sides. Your body is now in position to use as a singing musical instrument. Your shoulders should have no tension.

The following exercise will enable you to concentrate on the correct breathing needed for singing. Take a sip of air and note where your body expands. Let the air out and try again. This time take a sip and consciously use the muscle just below your rib cage to push out and expand your middle. All the breathing activity should focus on your middle, not your shoulders. Take a few more sips this way and see how slowly you can release all the air. This kind of breath is often called a preparatory breath and it truly prepares you to make a well-supported singing sound.

Try singing "Try to Remember" once again. This time use the correct singing posture and the preparatory breath. Pay close attention to the places you had difficulty before, and see how this time it is different. Discuss your findings with a partner.

ACTIVITY Figure 3.26 presents the staff notation for "Kum Ba Yah." This song is simpler than "Try to Remember" and is much easier to sing. It uses fewer notes and the range is smaller. With a partner, sing "Kum Ba Yah" together and answer the following questions.

Figure 3.26

Kum Bah Yah
African-American Spiritual
C F C
Kum ba yah my Lord, Kum ba yah. Kum ba
G7 C F
yah my Lord, Kum ba yah. Kum ba yah my Lord, Kum ba
C F C G7 C
yah, Oh, Lord, Kum ba yah.

1. How could you add dynamics to make this song sound more musical?
2. How would you describe the characteristics of your singing voice?
3. How would you describe the characteristics of your partner's singing voice?

LONGER SONGS IN MUSIC NOTATION

Figures 3.27–40 present fifteen songs, many of which are familiar. They range from patriotic tunes to spirituals.

Figure 3.27

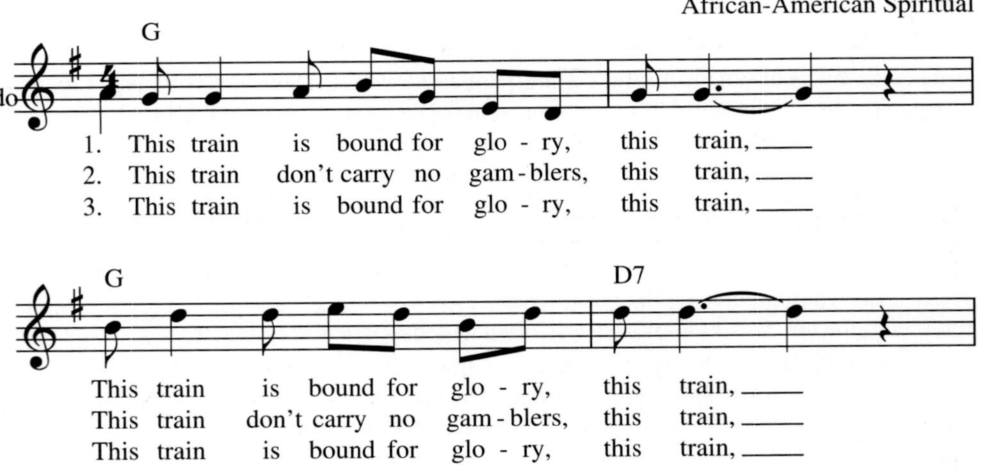
This Train
African-American Spiritual
G
do
1. This train is bound for glo - ry, this train,
2. This train don't carry no gam - blers, this train,
3. This train is bound for glo - ry, this train,
G D7
This train is bound for glo - ry, this train,
This train don't carry no gam - blers, this train,
This train is bound for glo - ry, this train,

Figure 3.27 *continued*

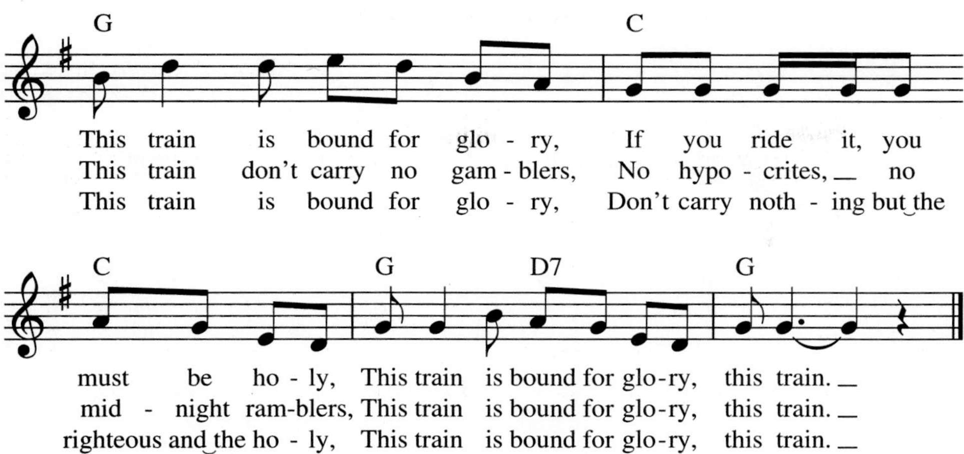
G
C
This train is bound for glo - ry, If you ride it, you
This train don't carry no gam - blers, No hypo - crites, no
This train is bound for glo - ry, Don't carry noth - ing but the
C
G
D7
G
must be ho - ly, This train is bound for glo-ry, this train.
mid - night ram-blers, This train is bound for glo-ry, this train.
righteous and the ho - ly, This train is bound for glo-ry, this train.

Figure 3.28

Waltzing Matilda

Adapted from A. "Banjo" Paterson
Adapted by Marie Cowan
Verse
E♭
B♭
Cm
A♭
do
1. Once a jol - ly swag - man camp'd by a bil - la - bong,
2. Down came a jum - buck to drink at that bil - la - bong,
3. Up came the stock - man, mount - ed on his thor-ough-bred,
4. Up jumped the swag - man, sprang in - to the bil - la - bong,
E♭
B♭7
Un - der the shade of a coo - li - bah tree, And he
Up jumped the swag - man and grabbed him with glee, And he
Down came the troop - ers, one, two, three.
"You'll nev - er catch me a - live," said he, And his
E♭
B♭
Cm
A♭
sang as he watched and wait - ed till his bil - ly boiled,
sang as he shoved that jum - buck in his tuck - er - bag,
"Who's that jol - ly jum - buck you've got in your tuck - er - bag?"
ghost may be heard as you pass by that bil - la - bong,
E♭
B♭7
E♭
"You'll come a - waltz - ing Ma - til - da with me."

Figure 3.28 *continued*

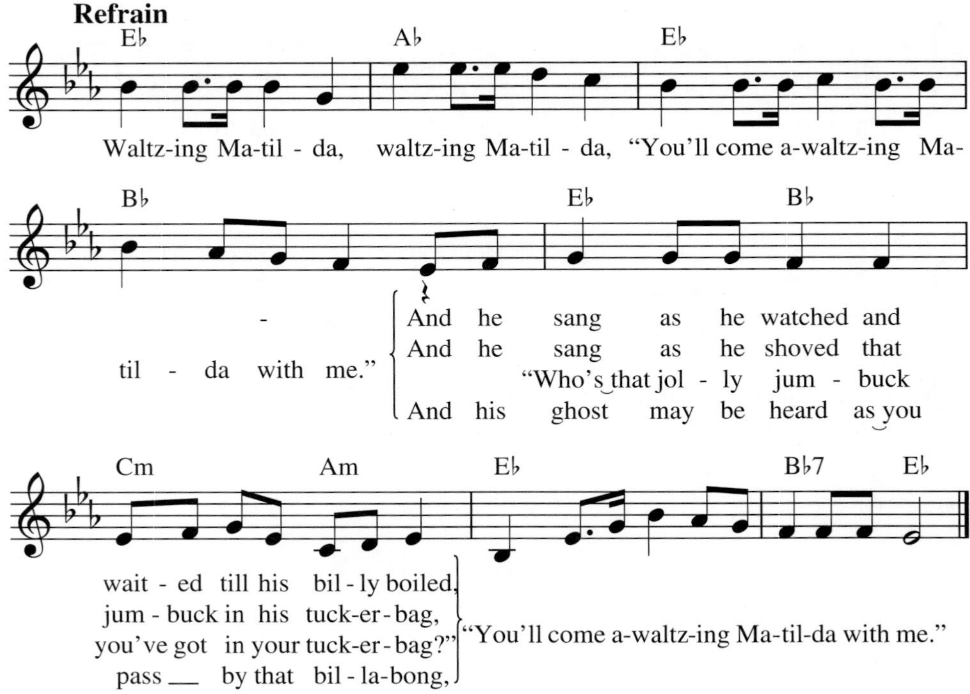

Figure 3.29

You're a Grand Old Flag

George M. Cohan George M. Cohan

Figure 3.29 *continued*

D7 Gm C7
Where there's nev - er a boast or brag;
F C C7
But should auld ac - quaint - ance be for - got,
Gm C7 F
Keep your eye on the grand old flag.

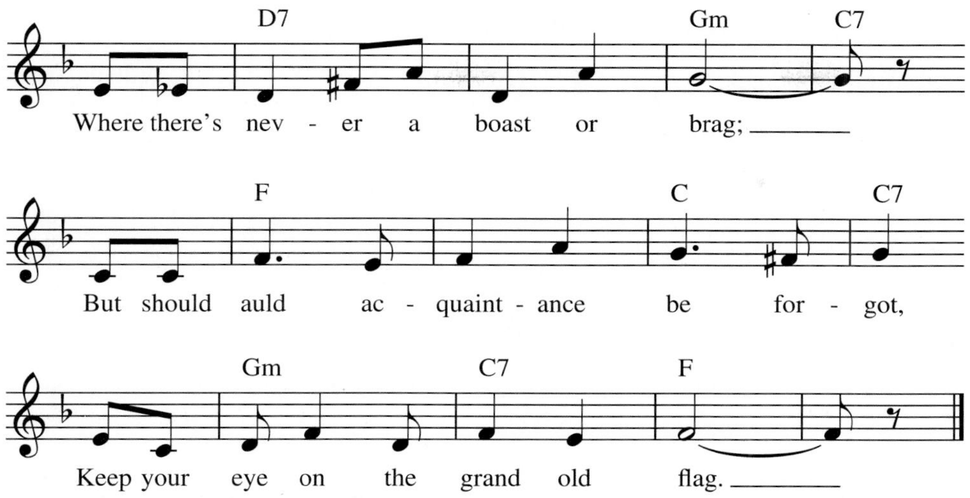

Figure 3.30

America

Samuel F. Smith Henry Carey

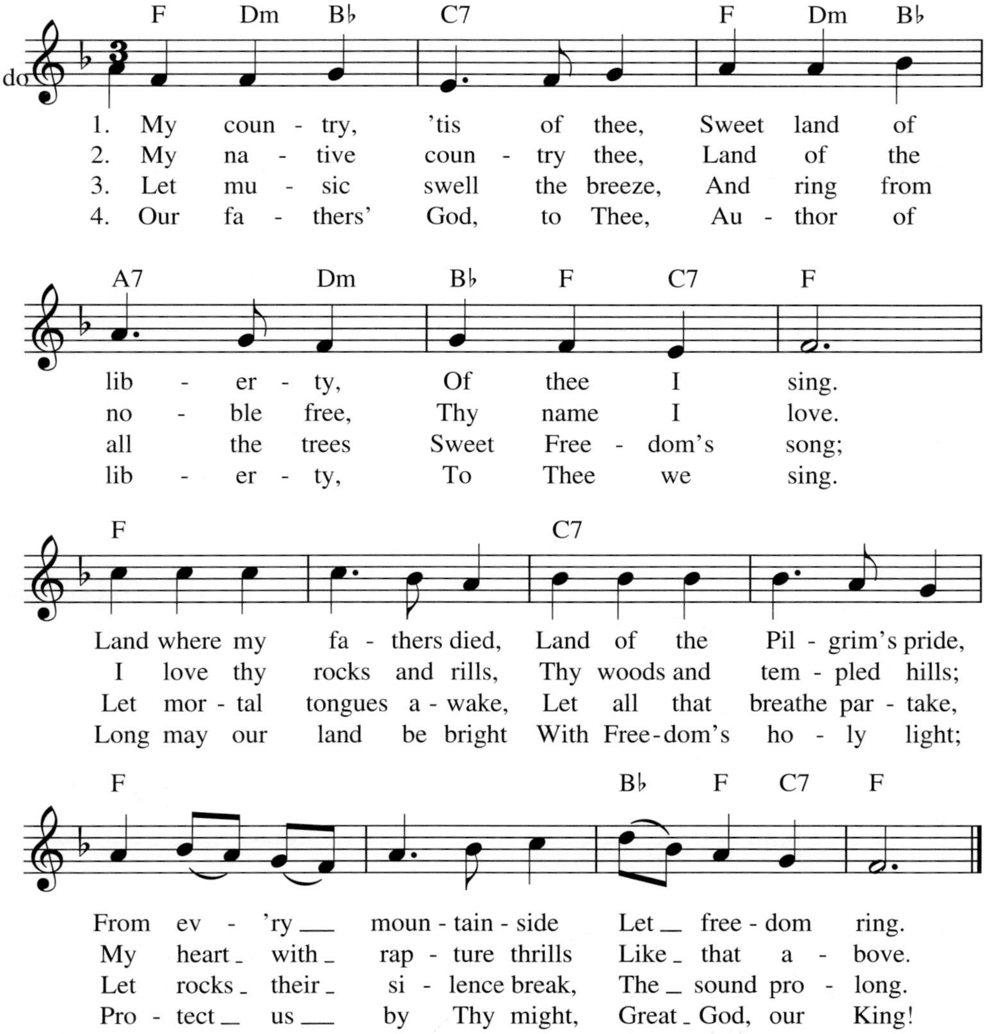

F Dm B♭ C7 F Dm B♭
do
1. My coun - try, 'tis of thee, Sweet land of
2. My na - tive coun - try thee, Land of the
3. Let mu - sic swell the breeze, And ring from
4. Our fa - thers' God, to Thee, Au - thor of
A7 Dm B♭ F C7 F
lib - er - ty, Of thee I sing.
no - ble free, Thy name I love.
all the trees Sweet Free - dom's song;
lib - er - ty, To Thee we sing.
F C7
Land where my fa - thers died, Land of the Pil - grim's pride,
I love thy rocks and rills, Thy woods and tem - pled hills;
Let mor - tal tongues a - wake, Let all that breathe par - take,
Long may our land be bright With Free-dom's ho - ly light;
F B♭ F C7 F
From ev - 'ry moun - tain - side Let free - dom ring.
My heart with rap - ture thrills Like that a - bove.
Let rocks their si - lence break, The sound pro - long.
Pro - tect us by Thy might, Great God, our King!

Figure 3.31

Battle Hymn of the Republic

Figure 3.32

Home on the Range

Figure 3.32 *continued*

B♭ F C7 F
cour - ag-ing word, And the skies are not cloud-y all day.
Chorus
F C7 F G7 C7
Home, home on the range, Where the deer and the an - te-lope play; Where
F B♭ F C7 F
sel-dom is heard a dis-cour-ag-ing word, and the skies are not cloud-y all day.

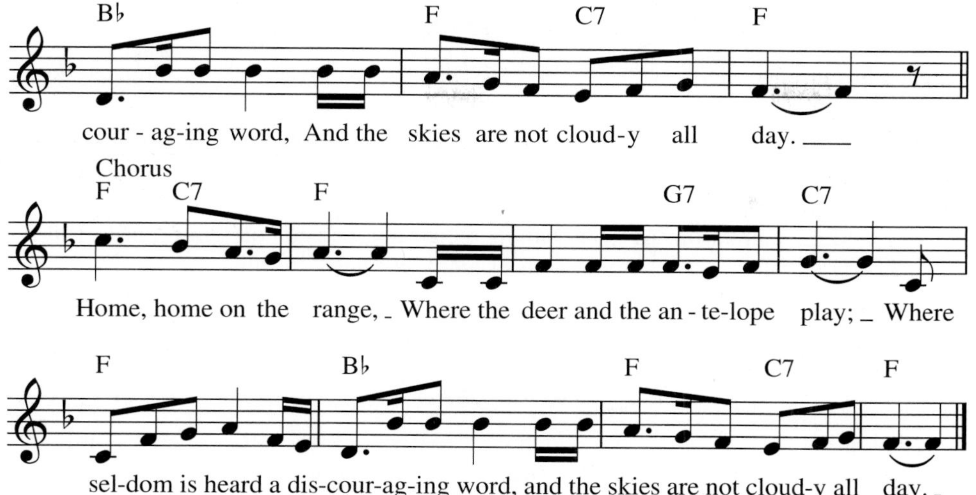

Figure 3.33

Swing Low, Sweet Chariot

African-American Spiritual

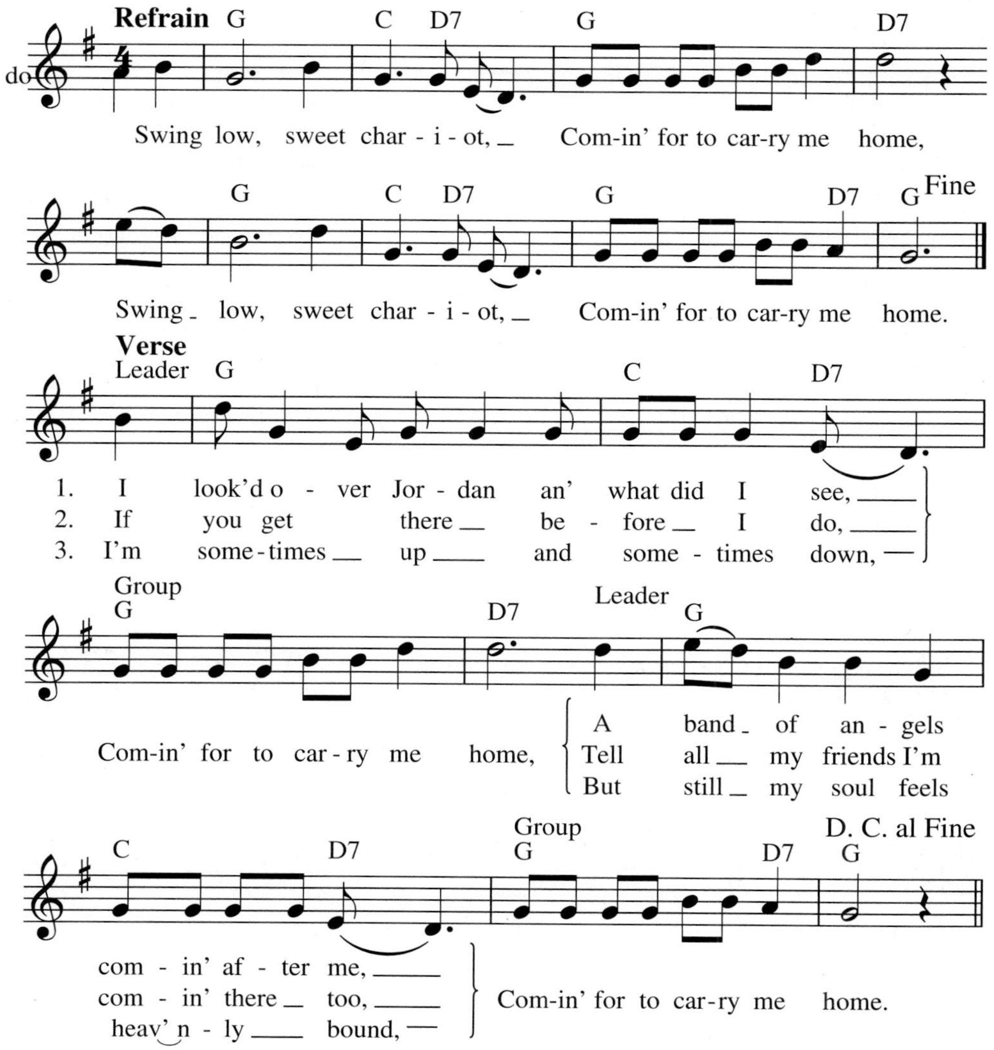

Refrain G C D7 G D7
do
Swing low, sweet char - i - ot, Com-in' for to car-ry me home,
G C D7 G D7 G Fine
Swing low, sweet char - i - ot, Com-in' for to car-ry me home.
Verse
Leader G C D7
1. I look'd o - ver Jor - dan an' what did I see,
2. If you get there be - fore I do,
3. I'm some-times up and some - times down,
Group
G D7 Leader G
Com-in' for to car - ry me home,
A band of an - gels
Tell all my friends I'm
But still my soul feels
C D7 Group G D7 G D. C. al Fine
com - in' af - ter me,
com - in' there too,
heav'n - ly bound,
Com-in' for to car-ry me home.

Figure 3.34

Oh, Susanna
Stephen Foster
Stephen Foster
Verse
F
C
do
1. I ___ come from Al - a - bam-a with my ban-jo on my knee. I'm _
2. I ___ had a dream the oth-er night, when ev-'ry-thing was still. I ___
F
C
F
going to Lou' - si - an - a, my ___ true love for to see. It ___
thought I saw Su - san - na a - com-ing down the hill. The _
F
C
rained all night the day I left, the weath-er it was dry, The _
buck-wheat cake was in her mouth, the tear was in her eye. Says _
F
C
F
sun so hot I froze to death, Su - san - na, don't you cry.
I, "I'm com - ing from the South, Su - san - na, don't you cry."
Refrain
B♭
F
C
Oh, Su - san - na, oh, don't you cry for me. I ___
F
C
F
come from Al - a - bam - a with my ban - jo on my knee.

Figure 3.35

Old Texas

Oklahoma Cowboy song

do
F
1. I'm going to leave old Tex - as
2. They've plowed and fenced my cat - tle
3. I've roped and tied the dog - ies
4. I'm gonna turn my back on the Tex - as
5. Say "A - di - os" to the friends I
C7
now, They've got no use
range, And the peo - ple there
small, And lis - tened for
sky, We'll ride a - way,
know, I'll hit the trail
B♭ F
for the long - horn cow.
are all so strange.
the coy - o - te's call.
old Paint and I.
for Mex - i - co.

Figure 3.36

Every Night

Appalachian Folk Song

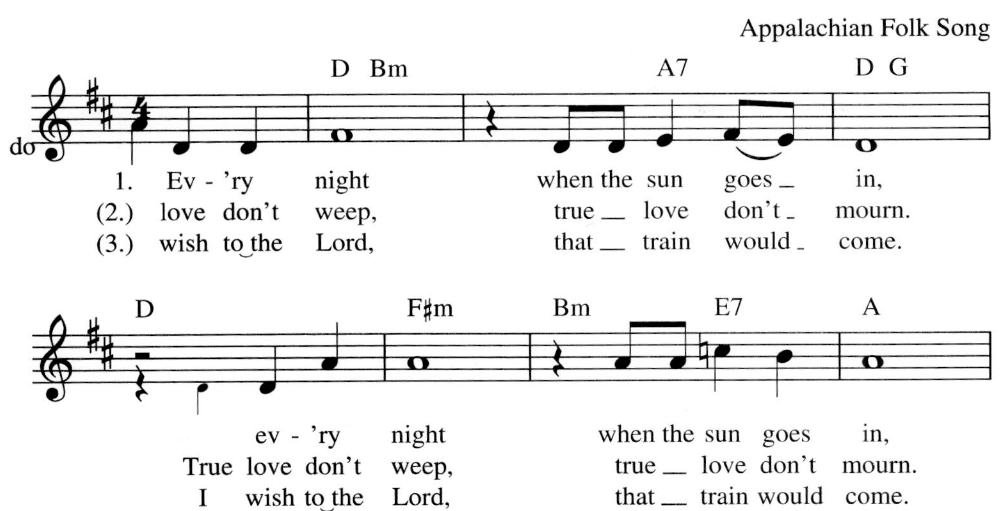
do
D Bm A7 D G
1. Ev - 'ry night when the sun goes in,
(2.) love don't weep, true love don't mourn.
(3.) wish to the Lord, that train would come.
D F♯m Bm E7 A
ev - 'ry night when the sun goes in,
True love don't weep, true love don't mourn.
I wish to the Lord, that train would come.

Figure 3.36 *continued*

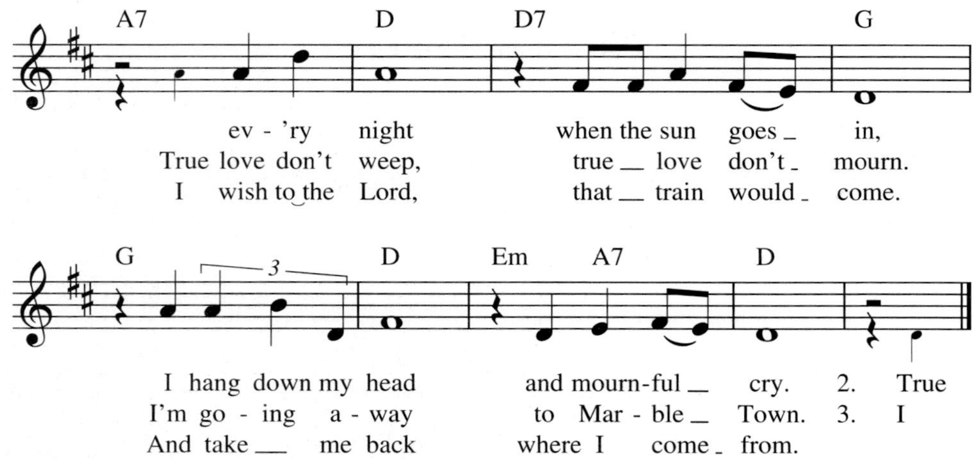
A7
D
D7
G
ev - 'ry night when the sun goes in,
True love don't weep, true love don't mourn.
I wish to the Lord, that train would come.
G
3
D
Em
A7
D
I hang down my head and mourn-ful cry. 2. True
I'm go - ing a - way to Mar - ble Town. 3. I
And take me back where I come from.

Figure 3.37

The Water Is Wide
Folk Song from England
(C7)
F
B♭
F
1. The wa - ter is wide, I can-not get o'er,
F
C7
And nei - ther have I wings to fly.
C7
F
Dm
Oh, go and get me some lit - tle boat
Dm
B♭
F
C7
F
To car - ry o'er my true love and I.

Figure 3.38

Now Let Me Fly
African-American Spiritual
Refrain
F
do
Now let me fly, Now let me fly,
Bb F C F
End
(Fine)
Now let me fly way up high, Way in the mid-dle of the air.
Verse
F
Way down yon - der in the mid - dle of the field,
F C F
See me work - ing at the char - iot wheel.
F
Not so par - tic' - lar 'bout work - ing at the wheel,
Go to the beginning and sing to the End
(Da capo al Fine)
F C F
But I just want to see how the char - iot feels.

Figure 3.39

Figure 3.40

PLAYING RECORDER

USING THREE NOTES IN DIFFERENT RHYTHMS, HARMONY, AND SONGS

As you begin to practice the new material in each chapter of the text, we encourage you to first review the recorder section in the previous chapter. In this way, you will improve much faster! The recorder exercises in this chapter do not include a new note but rather opportunities for you to practice eighth notes and dotted half notes, in addition to the other notation you used in chapter 3. In lines 9–10 of figure 3.41 you will notice that the two staves are joined together. This type of writing implies that the two lines are to be played together. Since you cannot do that alone, you need to practice each line at home. When you come to class, your instructor will lead you in playing these two lines which will then be in **harmony**.

Figure 3.41

Figure 3.41 *continued*

In figure 3.42 you will find five more children's songs for further recorder practice.

Figure 3.42

Fais Do-Do

Fais do - do co - las mon p'tit frère Fais do - do ma - man est en bas

Fais do - do pa - pa est en haut Quand il vien - dra tu- au-ras des gâ - teaux.

Hot Cross Buns

Hot cross buns, Hot cross buns. One a pen-ny, Two a pen-ny, Hot cross buns.

Ridin' in the Buggy

American Folk Song

Closet Key

I have lost the clos - et key in my la - dy's gar - den.

I have lost the clos - et key in my la - dy's gar - den.

Figure 3.42 *continued*

Long-Legged Sailor
Did you ev - er ev - er ev - er in your long - leg - ged life,
No I nev - er nev - er nev - er in my long - leg - ged life

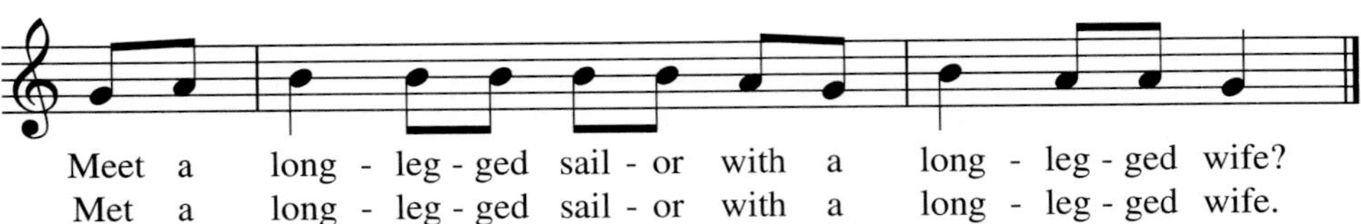
Meet a long - leg - ged sail - or with a long - leg - ged wife?
Met a long - leg - ged sail - or with a long - leg - ged wife.

In figure 3.43 are two recorder songs for you to complete, using the notes you have learned to play. After you have written the missing notes, practice each piece so you can play it in class.

Figure 3.43 Recorder Songs to Complete

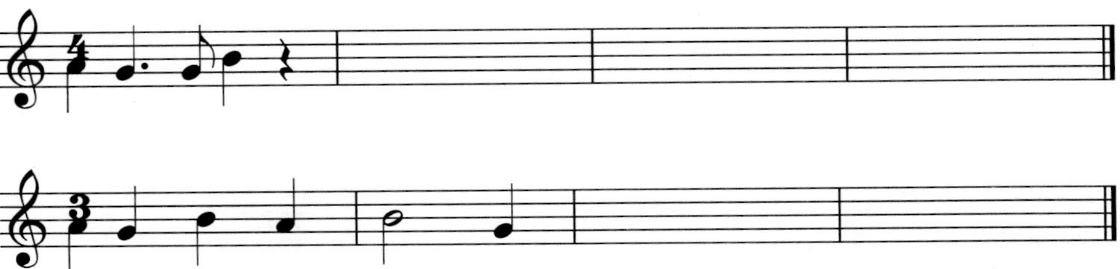

COMPOSE YOUR OWN THREE-NOTE SONGS

On the following staves, write your own song using the three notes you have learned thus far. Use as many rhythms and rests as necessary to make your melody interesting to listen to. Also try to use repeated notes, steps, and skips. Choose some places where you will change the volume or dynamics and use at least two different dynamic changes.

FOR YOUR OWN COMPOSITIONS

FURTHER PRACTICE

1. Compose your own five-note melody that uses any combination of the pitches do, re, mi, sol, and la. Your melody should contain four measures in $\frac{3}{4}$ or $\frac{4}{4}$. Write it down in musical notation and practice singing it with hand signs. Come to class prepared to teach your melody to a classmate.

2. Prepare a mystery melody excerpt for class. Play different combinations of the three notes you have learned and find a combination that sounds like the beginning of a song you know. One example would be the opening measures of "Mary Had a Little Lamb" (see figure 3.44). Play the sounds rhythmically so that your classmates will be able to guess the name of your mystery melody.

Figure 3.44

Mary Had a Little Lamb
Mar - y had a lit - tle lamb,

3. Write the correct syllable names (sol, mi, and la) under the pitches in figure 3.45.

Figure 3.45 Syllable Name Practice

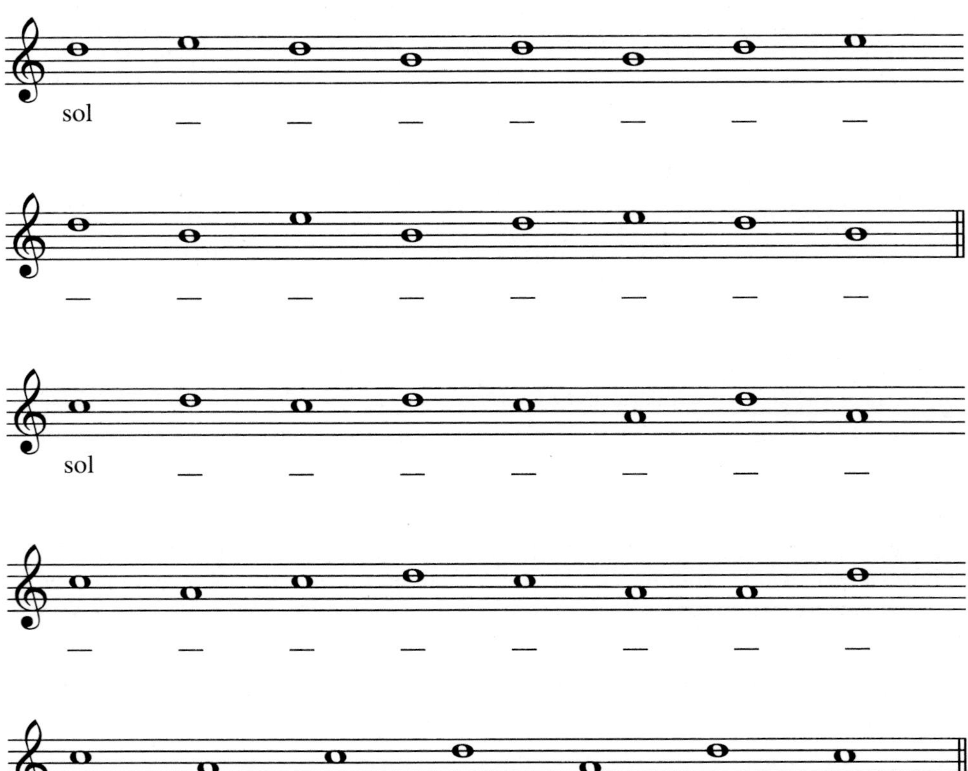

Write the correct syllable names (sol, mi, la, re, and do) under the pitches in figure 3.46.

Figure 3.46 Further Syllable Name Practice

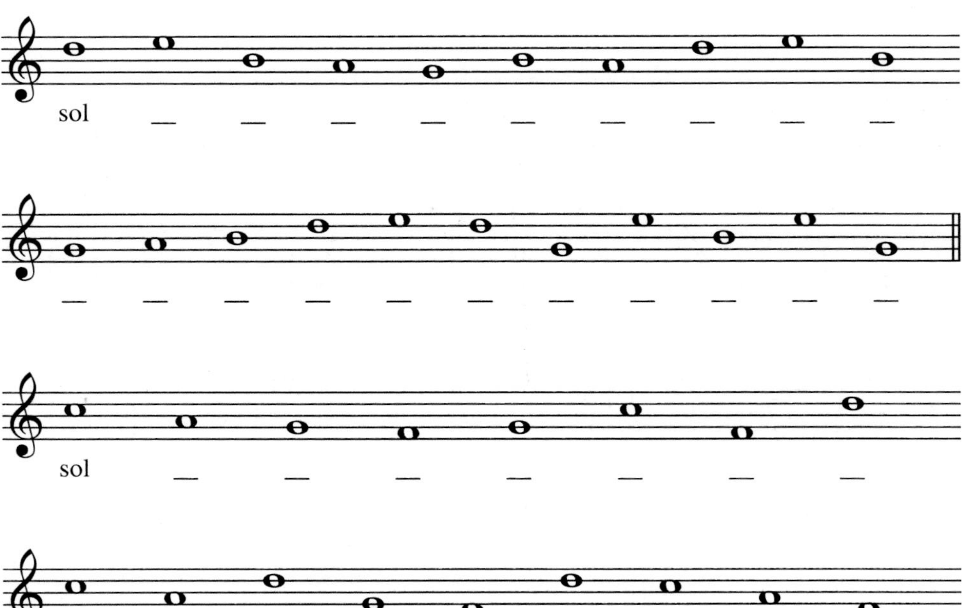

Draw note heads on the staves for the pitch syllables given in figure 3.47.

Figure 3.47 Note Head Practice

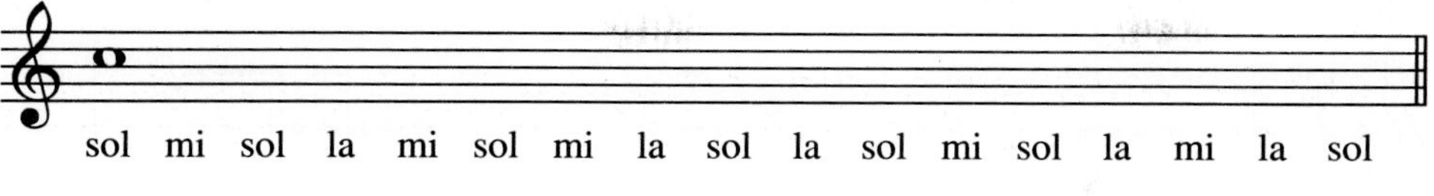

4. Practice reading the stick notation in figure 3.48. Say the rhythm syllables and clap them.

Figure 3.48 Rhythm Reading Practice

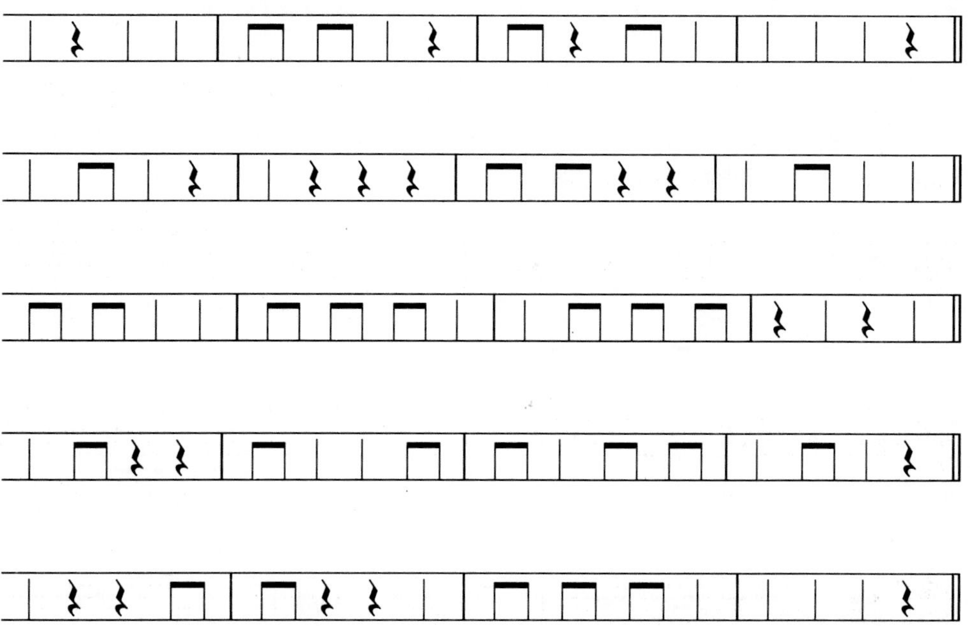

5. Insert bar lines in each of the twelve staves in figure 3.49 to divide the notes into correct metrical sets. Note the meter indicated at the beginning of each staff.

Figure 3.49 Meter Practice

NOTES

[1]Clifton Ware, *Adventures in Singing* (New York: McGraw-Hill, 1995), pp. 6–7.

Singing with Children

4

What you will be able to do by the end of this chapter

- *Model good singing technique for children*
- *Make singing activities part of the classroom routine*
- *Teach a song using the rote and whole song methods*
- *Use recordings to enhance classroom singing*
- *Develop a lesson plan that includes singing*
- *Choose songs for both primary and intermediate grades that children will enjoy*
- *Play a new pitch on the recorder*

THE SINGING CLASSROOM

The natural act of singing is a satisfying human activity that is an essential element of being alive. For young children, singing is a natural way of expressing themselves. Young children will often sing snippets of melody and text while they engage in other activities such as walking down the street with their parents or playing quietly on their own. Song just seems to pour out of younger children; but as they grow older many children lose this magical source of personal music making. In the midst of constant pressure to learn new facts and skills in all areas of the elementary curriculum, older children simply do not have time to putter around in the classroom, exploring the world through imaginative play and spontaneous song as they did in the early primary years.

By the time they are in intermediate grades, children still love to sing, but the conditions for their music making through song need to be provided each day. When you include singing as a daily activity in your classroom, you create an atmosphere where students can sing for the pure joy of it. The experience of singing with others regularly can enhance your students' singing skills as well as their sense of common purpose with their classmates, adding new meaning to the concept of classroom community. Providing daily experiences with singing is an ideal way for your students to learn the power of group effort and cooperation. The contribution of each individual's voice to group sound is a unique attribute of classroom singing, and the process—as well as the product—can be most satisfying for the entire class.

Teachers who understand the interrelatedness of all subject matter recognize singing as a way to illustrate and illuminate curriculum areas and enhance student learning. Classroom experiences across several literacy skills areas (writing, reading, editing, revising, evaluating) can be enriched by reading and writing song texts. Through singing experiences that involve the language and music of other cultures, children's classroom learning about these cultures is enhanced. The richness of the adult world of work explored in social studies can be further revealed when children learn songs of real workers on the job: women grinding flour, postal workers canceling stamps, or mariners raising sails. Singing is a natural extension of daily curriculum content that can enhance student learning and provide additional motivation and interest in classroom experiences.

But most important of all, singing with your class contributes to children's understanding of music and their own musical culture. In some cultures, past and present, learning to sing is an essential part of acculturation. No matter what culture, all children need the opportunity to expand their innate capacity to respond to the affective power of music. This capacity needs to be developed in order for students to have a complete education. It is as important for all children to learn to use their natural instruments—their singing voices—as it is to learn any other skill.

The purpose of this chapter is to show you how to make singing a natural part of your daily classroom activities, whether you teach a primary or intermediate class.

CHAPTER GOALS

In this chapter you will practice using your singing and recorder skills in the role of classroom teacher of both primary and intermediate children. You will learn to incorporate your own singing voice into daily classroom routine and be a confident and powerful singing model for your students. You will also learn many ways to nurture the singing development of your students.

One important aspect of singing with your students is understanding how children best learn a song. In this chapter you will learn the different ways to teach a song to children of all ages and how to write this process in effective lesson plans. In addition, you will also learn many appropriate songs to use with younger and older children. The songs in this chapter are songs that children love to sing! This chapter will also teach you how to choose songs that will interest and challenge children at all age levels.

The sequence of information and activities in this chapter has been designed to enable you to become more confident about your ability to lead children in singing. We want you to understand that you must sing with the children you teach because singing is such an important aspect of being a human being that it must be part of children's daily classroom life.

CASE STUDY

It is Thursday afternoon in April and Mr. Jones is introducing a social studies unit to his multi-age class of third and fourth graders. He has a new bulletin board that displays a copy of the school picture of every child in the class. When they came in this morning, the students clustered around it and had lots of comments about their own pictures as well as those of their friends.

Mr. Jones walks over to the bulletin board and holds up a piece of paper that reads, "What are our Customs and Traditions?" As he pins it on the board above the pictures, he asks, "What are the customs and traditions in our class this year?"

Students look at him with interest but no one raises a hand. He continues to allow thinking time and waits in silence. Finally, one child tentatively raises her hand. As Mr. Jones nods, Maria says, "Do you mean the order that we do our work?"

The teacher says, "Maria is coming close to the idea."

Other hands begin to move into the air and Mr. Jones begins calling on children. Their contributions include the days and times of their special classes such as art, music, and physical education, how their day is usually organized, when they sing, and the procedures for lunch and recess.

"Who would like to look up custom and tradition in the dictionary?" Mr. Jones asks. Lots of hands are waving and he assigns Sarah and Jake the task of finding the two definitions. "As Sarah and Jake are working, I want the rest of us to begin a list of customs and traditions. Turn to this week's partner and see if both of you can write a list with three or four of your own families' customs or traditions."

While the children discuss their ideas, Sarah and Jake bring their definitions to Mr. Jones. He asks the class to pause for a moment, listen carefully to what their researchers have found, and use the findings as they make their lists. "After you finish your list, I want you and your partner to write your customs or traditions somewhere on the long piece of paper on the back wall. Then, as each of you think of more, you can add them throughout the week." The sounds of discussion continue while some children move to the back of the room and use the color markers that are on a nearby table to write their family customs.

After all the children have finished their partner discussions and some are still writing in the back, Mr. Jones turns on his tape recorder and the sounds of a male voice singing "Old Dan Tucker" begin to fill the classroom, softly at first. As the children begin to focus their attention on the music, Mr. Jones turns up the volume. After the song is finished, he asks the children "Can anyone describe how this song is like any other song we know?"

Several children raise their hands and Timmy answers, "It tells about a person in the old times."

"What songs have we learned this year that are like 'Old Dan Tucker?' "

The children contribute several titles, including "Old Joe Clark."

"Which song would you like to begin with today?" asks the teacher, and the clamor of children calling out their favorites is heard, with about equal members naming each song. "Well, today we'll choose alphabetically, so we'll begin with Dan, not Joe. Here is our starting pitch." Mr. Jones picks up his recorder, plays an F and sings "one, two, ready, sing." Most of the class joins in enthusiastically but three boys on one side of the room look at each other and do not sing with the class. Mr. Jones notices the looks and the nonparticipation and decides to approach this minor mutiny in an oblique way.

"As we sing the last verse and refrain again, I'd like you to move into your cooperative group seating and then we'll sing one verse of 'Old Joe Clark' together. After that we'll have different groups sing the rest of the verses and we'll all sing the refrain." The children continue singing and move to their new seating positions. The group that contains two of the nonsinging boys sings their verse but the sound is very thin.

After all the verses are finished, Mr. Jones asks the children, "How did our song sound when we had fewer people singing each verse?"

A number of hands begin to wave and Andrea yells out, "Liam and Isaac weren't singing in their group!" The teacher looks at Andrea intently; she says softly, "Sorry."

Mr. Jones asks the class, "Why do you think someone would decide not to sing with us?"

Children look around and shrug their shoulders but a few hands go up. As Mr. Jones looks at different children they contribute several reasons. "Maybe they don't feel well."

"Perhaps someone feels they don't have a good voice."

"Maybe they don't like the song anymore."

Mr. Jones looks at Liam and Isaac. "Was anyone right?"

Liam nods and says "Well, we tried singing that great song that you taught us yesterday about the Spanish cat ("Don Gato") on the bus going home. My big brother told us to shut up, and he told me when we got off the bus that we couldn't sing right so why did we keep trying."

Mr. Jones looks at Liam and then at the class. He moves to the back wall and motions to the long piece of paper listing customs and traditions. He begins, "We have just begun to explore our family differences. Have we found that everyone in this class has the same family customs and traditions? Don't we all have different abilities, too? I wonder if there are people with different abilities in other subjects besides singing?"

He looks at the class and asks, "What do you folks think?"

The children look back at him intently. Andrea raises her hand and says, "Well, I still have a lot of problems with multiplication and division. I'm not as good as Liam in math but I don't stop trying."

Mr. Jones sees some nods of understanding and other children raise their hands. He calls on Tyrone who says the same about reading and then Kristen, who says the same about writing cursive.

Mr. Jones decides it is time to bring this part of the day to closure. "Well, everyone has a different ability in every subject. You all come to school to learn how to improve your skills in each of the things we do here, and singing is a part of our day. We'll each improve as we practice and I hope all of you will join in as we learn a new song."

Mr. Jones motions to the long sheet of paper on the back wall. "We have begun to collect our family customs and traditions. Very soon, I am going to ask you to bring in an article made by someone in your family, or you can demonstrate something you have learned in your family. That is one way we will share customs and traditions. Another way is by learning songs that are traditions in our country. We already know quite a few and I have a new one for you today. How is this song like the other two we just sang?" He picks up his recorder, plays a G and begins to sing "Clementine."

Cooperative Questions to Discuss

1. Should Mr. Jones have spent this much time on a few children who were not singing?
2. How else could Mr. Jones have handled the minor mutiny?
3. Does anything about this case study make you uncomfortable?
4. What are some other ways that Mr. Jones could have directed the class to discuss individual abilities?

HOW CHILDREN LEARN TO SING

Young children begin school with a variety of experiences that affect all of their initial learning. Their readiness to learn to read is influenced by the presence or absence of over thousands of hours of language interactions as infants, toddlers, and preschoolers. This early exposure to the language of their culture is the basis for understanding that the spoken word can be transmitted in the written form. In a similar manner, the presence or absence of carefully structured musical experiences affects the young child's development as a singer.

Parents usually respond to their infant's beginning sound production by speaking back to the infant, but some parents respond to these initial sounds by imitating the infant's exact pitches and making singing sounds. Parents who understand that these vocalizations are the basis for both singing and speaking provide continual speech and singing feedback to their infants. One set of such parents is described in an interesting 1987 research study by Kelly and Sutton-Smith.[1] The study focused on the singing development of three different infants from birth to age two years. The infants, all first-born females of similar socioeconomic status, were observed by the researchers once a week for the first two years of their lives. Of particular interest was the difference in the musical backgrounds of the parents and the degree of their musical interactions with their infants. One set of parents was professional musicians, the second set of parents was not professionally trained but was musically oriented, and the third set of parents was not musical. At eight months, the child of professional musicians could sing a three-note contour. The child of the musically oriented parents could not sing the same contour until age fifteen months. The third child had inaccurate pitch at age two years, and her singing tone was more speech than song. The report describes the types of continual vocal interactions that the parents of the first child initiated with her and the lack of similar experiences for the other two children in the study.

Young children whose parents realize the importance of early experiences in development and provide these experiences for their children will show far more singing ability than children without such rich musical exposure. As the young toddler develops the ability to speak, the singing toddler begins to sing parts of familiar songs, sometimes making up words or parts they do not remember and sometimes putting parts of different songs together. The singing toddler may sing parts of the tune correctly and may sometimes sing above or below the pitch as well. The toddler and preschool years are characterized by periods of vocal experimentation and vocal creativity. Young children will often create their own songs about their independent play that describe their own actions. They may also incorporate parts of familiar songs such as "e-i, e-i, o" from "Old MacDonald."

When these youngsters begin public school, they may sing on pitch and know many of the songs that are sung in class. Some of their classmates will be children whose parents did not understand the importance of responding musically to their children's initial babbling sounds and who have not been sung to throughout their first five years of life.

These children may have tried to imitate the singing they heard on television, videos, and compact discs. Unfortunately, music sung by adults is rarely sung at a pitch that children can easily sing so their attempts at singing along may sound like droning. Other children may have had some nursery school background and be at a stage of correctly matching pitches for parts of "The Wheels on the Bus" while speaking the rest of the song.

The wide variety of singing backgrounds and levels of development contribute to the diversity of sounds that Kindergarten teachers will hear when they begin to sing with their classes. Sung by Kindergartners, "Old MacDonald" and "The Wheels on the Bus" may sound like the same song, and sometimes they may sound pretty strange. The first two years of school are a time to provide the readiness for singing that may not have been part of a child's home life. These experiences will include many speaking and singing contrasts, a steady diet of interesting songs, and a continual stress on how each of our singing voices has its own distinct sound.

Children's distinct sounds are apparent in older grades as well. Elementary school children vary greatly in physical development and often boys and girls in fifth and sixth grade have growth spurts that affect not only their outward appearance but also their vocal production. Boys' voices change the most radically, with embarrassing breaks and squeaks in their speaking voices that signal the vocal deepening to come. This vocal change so greatly affects the young male's singing voice that some boys prefer not to try singing at all. As with all aspects of child development, no two boys proceed through this vocal change in the same manner. It is important that boys understand what is happening to their bodies and their vocal mechanisms.

In addition, it is important that young males' interactions with significant adults be supportive. Teachers should recognize the beginnings of vocal change and let the boys know that they notice. Teachers and parents all need to speak of this change with excitement and in a positive way. Such discussions will help intermediate boys advance into this sometimes embarrassing part of growing older with an emphasis on celebrating the changes, not wishing for them to disappear. In classroom unison singing the lowering voice will be very obvious to the rest of the class and you need to emphasize how neat and exciting it is to have this new sound in your class.

NURTURING CHILDREN'S SINGING SKILLS

You will be the most important musical influence in your students' daily experience; therefore, it is essential that you demonstrate musical competence, enjoyment, and leadership whenever you lead a musical activity. Your competence and comfort as a singer will enable you to lead classroom singing, and the vocal model you produce will be more important to the class's development of vocal tone than anything you can tell them about singing. You should use your clearest, purest singing tone, without any vibrato. Researchers have found that when teachers use vibrato in their singing voices, children have more trouble matching the pitch than when the same teachers sang with a "straight" sound. You should sing freely—with enthusiasm and commitment—each time you lead a song in your class.

No matter what opinion you have about the sound of your own singing voice, you must hide any hints of self-consciousness and let your whole face and body work together to communicate complete commitment to the song you are singing. So much of teaching involves taking on a role such as mentor, coach, disciplinarian, and parent: singing allows you to assume the role of competent performer, and whatever success you have in projecting singing confidence and competence will be picked up by each student and magnified in his or her own singing. When you demonstrate good singing posture, proper breathing technique, and a clear, focused tone in your own singing, it is much easier for your students to learn to sing correctly. In a similar manner, your students will emulate your delight in the joyous act of singing. Once you have experienced the unfettered feeling that is created by a group of children singing together, you will seek ways to include singing throughout the school day.

PITCH MATCHING

There are many ways to involve children in singing activities that can actually improve their singing skills, at both the primary and intermediate levels. You can engage children in pitch matching activities at any time during the school day simply by singing an activity rather than speaking it. Examples include such routine classroom tasks as calling the role or collecting milk money. Instead of calling the child's name, sing his or her name on two different pitches and ask the child to answer you on the same pitches. Young children find it easy to sing the sol–mi pattern, while older students with more singing experience could echo a wider variety of pitch patterns. Another avenue for call-response echoing of pitches is when moving lines of children from place to place. Younger classes can also be taught to sing a daily good morning or good-bye to you on a particular set of pitches, such as

Good-bye, second grade:
sol mi sol sol mi

Good-bye Mistress Featherbrain!
sol sol mi la sol sol mi

You can also incorporate pitch matching into other call-response activities such as reciting math facts or spelling words aloud. Another way to include singing is to have children sing their lines when acting out stories. Simply give them a starting pitch and let them move up or down the scale, including as many notes as they want. This can expand their singing range while encouraging their creativity in improvising melodies.

TONAL MEMORY

An important aspect of teaching children how to sing is the development of memory for sound, called **tonal memory.** Some children have an ability to remember musical sounds more easily than others and there will be a variety of developmental levels in any one class. There are many ways to improve this important aspect of singing in the normal classroom day. The simplest is to listen carefully to the individual responses as you use the pitch matching exercises described above. When you know which children can remember a single pitch, increase the number of tones you sing to them by one more. You can continue to expand the number of sounds you use as children demonstrate that they are able to remember what you have sung and reproduce the pitches correctly.

An enticing way to develop children's tonal memory is to introduce a song without its title. Without naming the song, ask your students to raise their hands if they can identify the song. Then play the beginning of the song, or the entire song if needed, on your recorder. You will find that with repeated practice, your students will become more careful listeners and that with some songs, hands will shoot up after you have played only a few sounds.

Playing the recorder for your students is also an effective way to increase their tonal memory. The lesson plan below will provide you with an understanding of how to enhance tonal memory.

TONAL MEMORY LESSON PLAN: PRIMARY

I. **Learning Outcome or Objective:** Students will be able to identify mystery melodies.
Entry ability: Students are able to sing the songs in the lesson.
Exit ability: Students are able to identify songs when performed on the recorder.

II. **Lesson Evaluation or Assessment Procedures:** Teacher will note those students unable to identify the melodies.

III. **Materials and Board/Space Preparation:** Recorder and song notation.

IV. **Teaching Procedures:**

A. Setting the Stage: Teacher asks children to clear their desks.

B. Developing the Lesson:
Step 1: Play the beginning of "Suo Gan" (below).
Transition question: Raise your hands if you can identify the song.
Step 2: Sing the song with your students. Use the recorder to give the starting pitch.
Transition question: Listen carefully to the next song and raise your hand when you recognize it.
Step 3: Play the beginning of "Good News" and give the same direction as above. When the song is identified, sing the song with your class. Start the song by singing the first pitch as "One, two, ready, sing."
Transition question: Who can identify the next song?
Step 4: Continue as above with either of the following mystery tunes: "Bingo," "Engine, Engine Number Nine."

C. Concluding the Lesson: Praise the class for careful listening, if appropriate.

Figure 4.1

Suo Gan

Welsh Folk Song

Su - o Gan do not weep, Su - o Gan go to sleep.

Su - o Gan moth-er's near, Su - o Gan have no fear.

Good News

Good news, the cha-riot's com-in', Good news, the cha-riot's com-in', Good

news, the cha-riot's com-in', And I don't want you to leave-a me be - hind.

Engine, Engine Number Nine

American Song

En-gine, en-gine num-ber nine, Go-ing down the rail-road line!

If the train goes off the track, Will I get my mon-ey back?

Figure 4.1 *continued*

Bingo

There was a farm-er had a dog, And Bin-go was his name-o. B-I - N-G-O,

B - I - N - G - O, B - I - N - G - O, And Bin-go was his name-o.

ACTIVITY With a partner or in a small group, generate a list of ways that pitch matching can be included in the school day at both primary and intermediate levels.

ACTIVITY With a partner or in a small group, discuss the lesson plan format used above and compare it to formats you have used in other methods classes.

SINGING WITH YOUNGER CHILDREN

There is no way to generalize about the kinds of singing skills that younger children will bring to your classroom, for in a single primary class you will find vast contrasts in singing ability. Some singers will demonstrate the unique child vocal quality that can be described as "light" or "clear," and others may have a heavy, forced sound. These contrasts are the result of the vocal models that children have imitated during their preschool singing experiences. Children who are hearing-impaired or developmentally delayed may also have speaking and singing voices that show very little contrast in inflection. In any one class, some children will sing on pitch and in a wide range, some will sing within a restricted range of only a few notes, and some will sing or chant on one or two pitches. Others might have a really good range but are not able to match pitches with other singers. Still others may not be singing at all but only speaking song texts. Despite the wide contrasts of mental and singing ability evident in primary classes, you can enhance each child's singing skill through well-chosen and carefully monitored daily singing activities.

It is important to understand that most children in Kindergarten and grades one, two, and three are not able to sing a wide range of notes the way adults can. Your singing range is probably at least ten pitches from your lowest to your highest note, but most young children have a singing range of approximately six notes, from the B below middle C to the G or A above it.

Figure 4.2 Young Children's Singing Range

Any song you want to teach primary-age children should have most of its pitches in the range presented in figure 4.2, as these are easiest for young children to sing successfully. Unfortunately, many of the songbooks written for young children during the past thirty or so years have not taken this information to heart and the result is that, in many instances, primary teachers try to teach interesting songs that are out of the typical vocal range of their students. In order to choose songs that are appropriate for this age group, you must consider the range and reject those songs with a majority of notes either higher or lower than this ideal.

Another consideration when choosing song materials for primary-age students is the appropriateness of the text. The text should be rich in imagery and be able to stand alone as poetry appropriate for young children. It should have content that children find humorous or enjoyable and be enhanced by its musical setting. Children enjoy the challenge of singing in languages other than English because the vowels and consonants of foreign languages produce unusual combinations of sounds that children find delightful. You should always provide the class with a translation to further their understanding of the song. No matter what the language, it is important that *you* like the song, for you will be singing it many times. You will have difficulty modeling enthusiasm if you do not like the song, even if it does enhance another part of your curriculum. The song should also be fairly short and contain repetition of text and/or melody. Folk music is one genre that often meets both the musical and the textual criteria outlined here, and you will find it a rich source of repertoire for inclusion across a wide variety of curricular areas.

SUGGESTED PRIMARY SONG LITERATURE

Figures 4.3–29 present thirty simple songs that are appropriate for use with primary-age pupils.

Figure 4.3

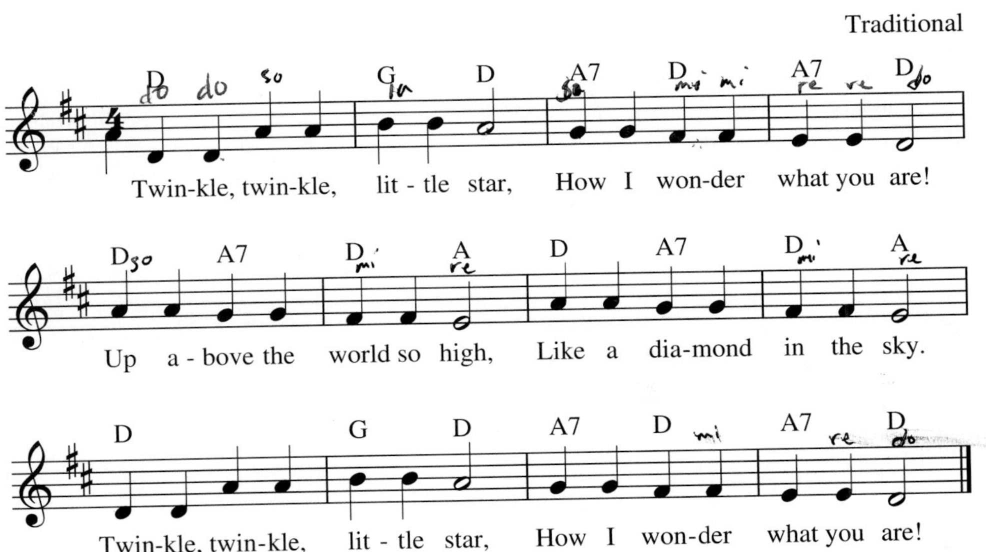

Figure 4.4

Bluebird, Bluebird

Figure 4.5

Barnyard Song

Kentucky Mountain Song

2. I had a hen and the hen pleased me.
   I fed my hen under yonder tree.
   Hen goes chimmy chuck, chimmy chuck,
   Cat goes fiddle-i-fee.

3. I had a duck and the duck pleased me.
   I fed my duck under yonder tree.
   Duck goes quack, quack,
   Hen goes chimmy chuck, chimmy chuck,
   Cat goes fiddle-i-fee.

4. I had a goose . . .
   Goose goes hissy, hissy . . .

5. I had a sheep . . .
   Sheep goes baa, baa . . .

6. I had a cow . . .
   Cow goes moo, moo . . .

7. I had a horse . . .
   Horse goes neigh, neigh . . .

Figure 4.6

This Little Light of Mine

Figure 4.7

Eency Weency Spider

Traditional
F C7 F
Een - cy, ween - cy spi - der went up the wa - ter spout;
F C7 F
Down came the rain and washed the spi - der out.
F C7 F
Then came the sun and dried up all the rain, and the
F C7 F
een - cy, ween - cy spi - der went up the spout a - gain.

Figure 4.8

Dipidu

Translated by Joan Gilbert Van
Folk Song from Uganda
Good-day, good - day to you, Good-day, O dip - i - du,
Good-day, good - day to you, Good-day, O dip - i - du.
Dip, dip, dip - i - du, Dip - i - du, O dip - i - du.
Dip, dip, dip, dip, dip - i - du, Dip - i - du, O dip - i - du.

Figure 4.9

Sakura

Japanese Folk Song

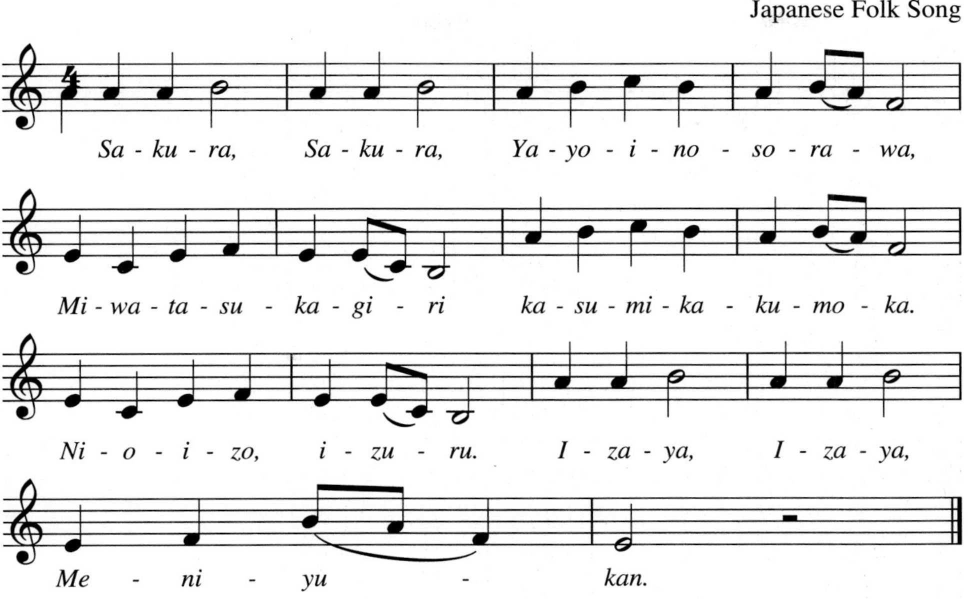
Sa - ku - ra, Sa - ku - ra, Ya - yo - i - no - so - ra - wa,
Mi - wa - ta - su - ka - gi - ri ka - su - mi - ka - ku - mo - ka.
Ni - o - i - zo, i - zu - ru. I - za - ya, I - za - ya,
Me - ni - yu - kan.

Figure 4.10

Tinga Layo

Translated by Merrill Staton

West Indies Calypso Song

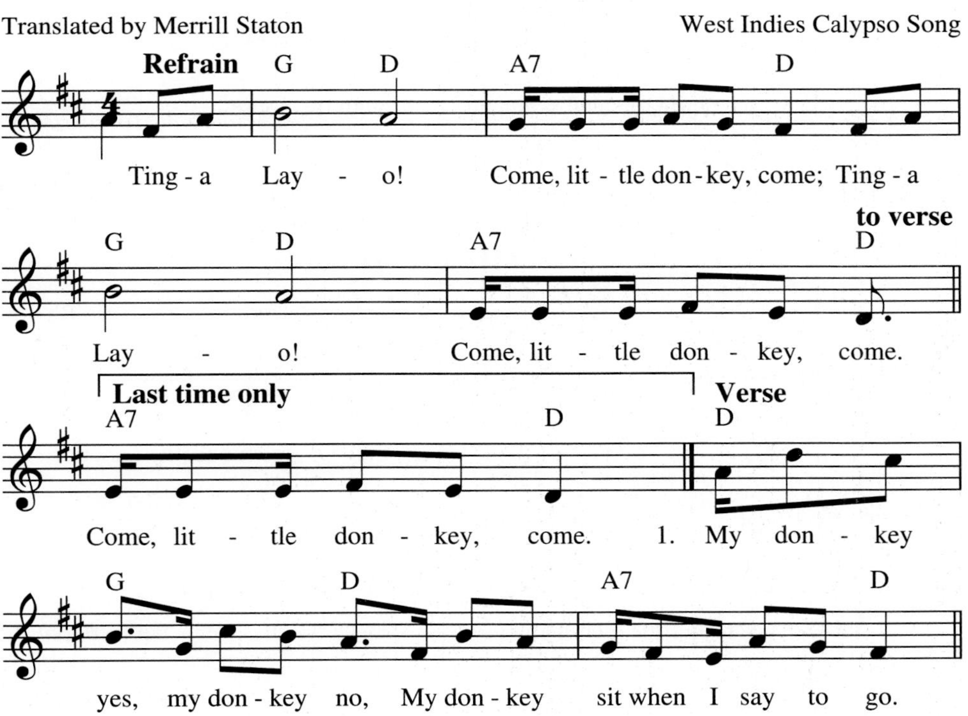
Refrain
G D A7 D
Ting - a Lay - o! Come, lit - tle don - key, come; Ting - a
G D A7 D
to verse
Lay - o! Come, lit - tle don - key, come.
Last time only
A7 D
Come, lit - tle don - key, come.
Verse
D
1. My don - key
G D A7 D
yes, my don - key no, My don - key sit when I say to go.

2. My donkey haw, my donkey gee,
   My donkey don't do a thing for me.
   Refrain

3. My donkey balk, my donkey bray,
   My donkey won't hear a thing I say.
   Refrain

Figure 4.11

The Old Gray Cat

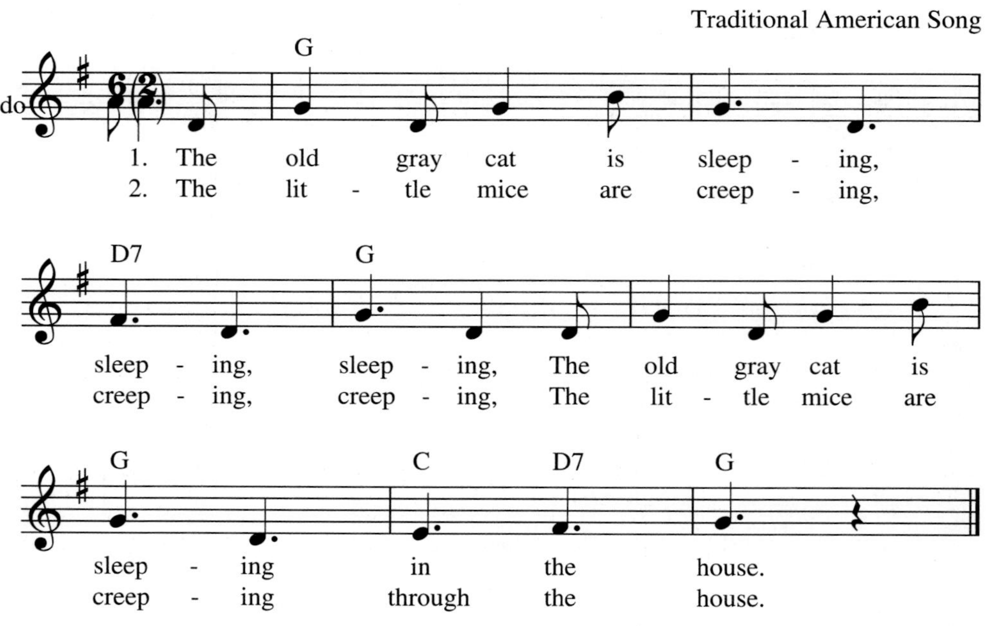

3. The little mice are nibbling . . . in the house.
4. The little mice are sleeping . . . in the house.
5. The old gray cat comes creeping . . . through the house.
6. The little mice all scamper . . . through the house.

Figure 4.12

Sally Go 'round the Sun

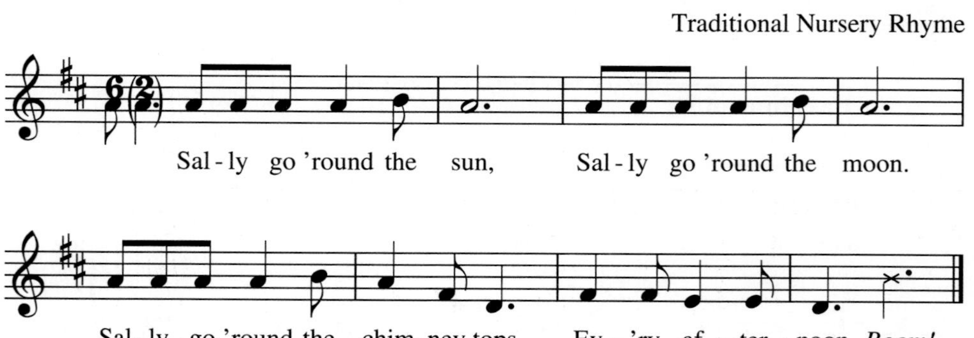

Figure 4.13

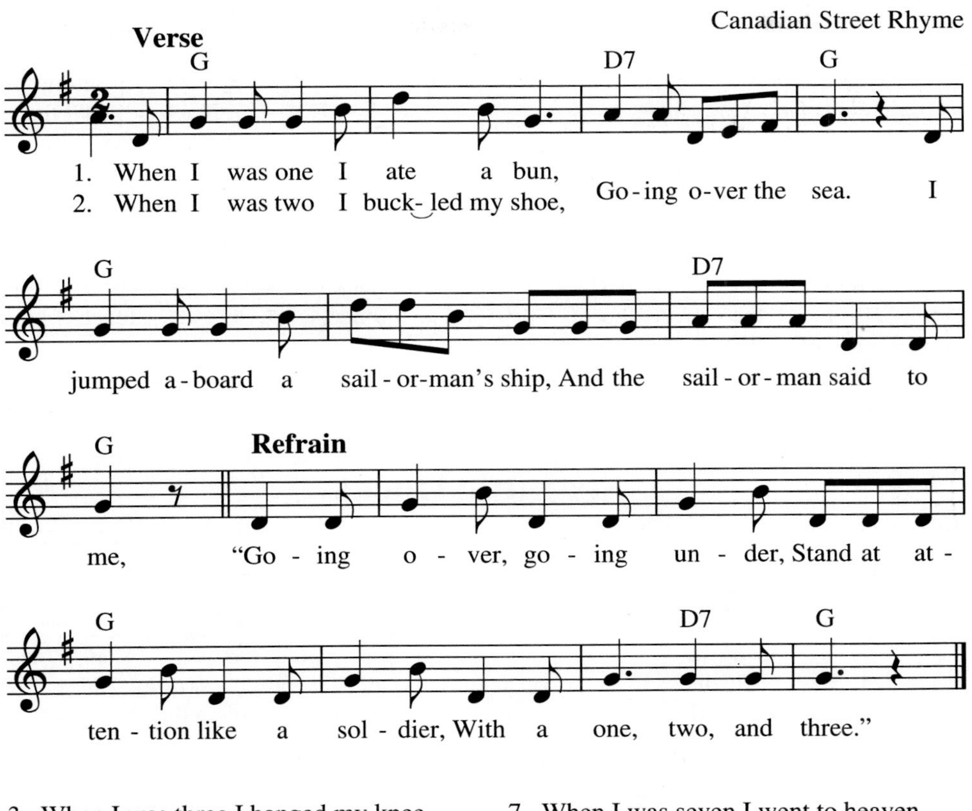
Going over the Sea
Canadian Street Rhyme
Verse
G D7 G
1. When I was one I ate a bun,
2. When I was two I buck-led my shoe,
Go-ing o-ver the sea. I
G D7
jumped a-board a sail-or-man's ship, And the sail-or-man said to
G Refrain
me, "Go-ing o-ver, go-ing un-der, Stand at at-
G D7 G
ten-tion like a sol-dier, With a one, two, and three."

3. When I was three I banged my knee, . . .

4. When I was four I shut the door, . . .

5. When I was five I learned to jive, . . .

6. When I was six I picked up sticks, . . .

7. When I was seven I went to heaven, . . .

8. When I was eight I learned to skate, . . .

9. When I was nine I climbed a vine, . . .

10. When I was ten I caught a hen, . . .

Figure 4.14

Miss Mary Mack

African-American Singing Game

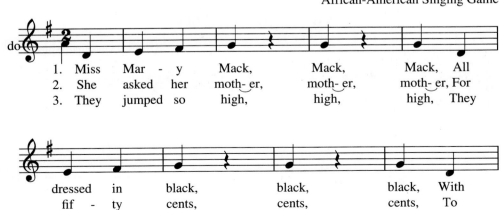

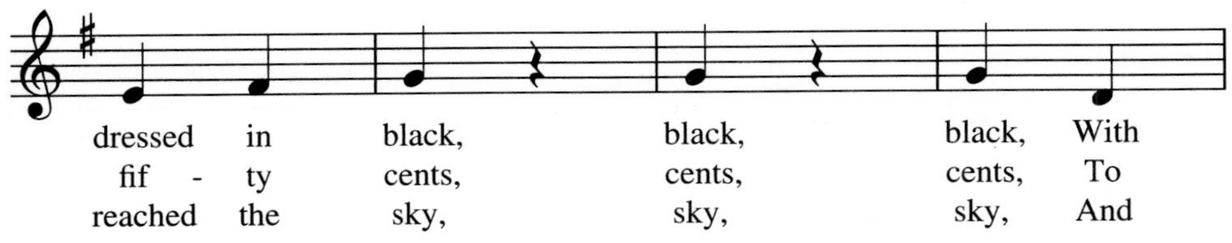
do
1. Miss Mar-y Mack, Mack, Mack, All
2. She asked her moth-er, moth-er, moth-er, For
3. They jumped so high, high, high, They
dressed in black, black, black, With
fif-ty cents, cents, cents, To
reached the sky, sky, sky, And

Figure 4.14 *continued*

sil - ver but - tons, but - tons, but - tons, All
see the cows, cows, cows, Jump
nev- er came back, back, back, 'Til the
down her back, back, back.
o- ver the fence, fence, fence.
Fourth of Ju - ly, lie, lie!

Figure 4.15

Six Little Ducks

Traditional American

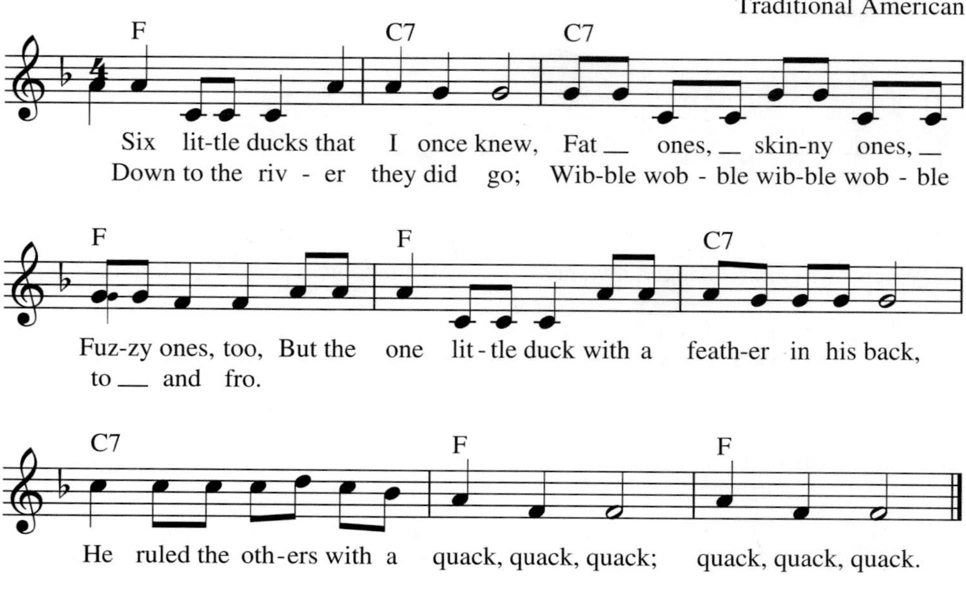
F C7 C7
Six lit-tle ducks that I once knew, Fat ones, skin-ny ones,
Down to the riv - er they did go; Wib-ble wob - ble wib-ble wob - ble
F F C7
Fuz-zy ones, too, But the one lit-tle duck with a feath-er in his back,
to and fro.
C7 F F
He ruled the oth-ers with a quack, quack, quack; quack, quack, quack.

Figure 4.16

All Night, All Day

African-American Spiritual

G
All night, all day
C D7
An - gels watch-ing o - ver me, my Lord.

Figure 4.16 *continued*

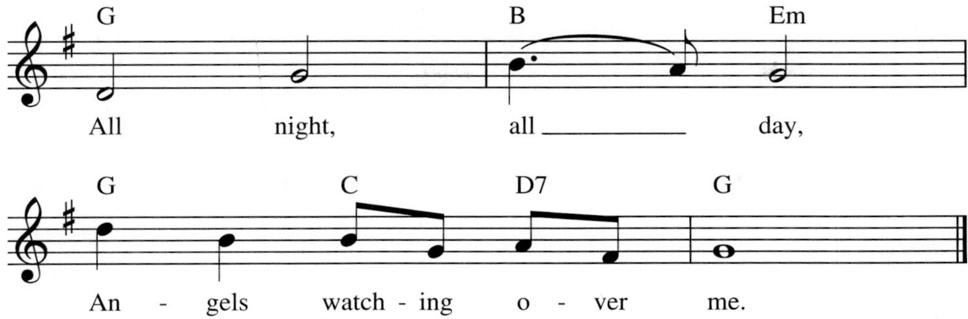

Figure 4.17

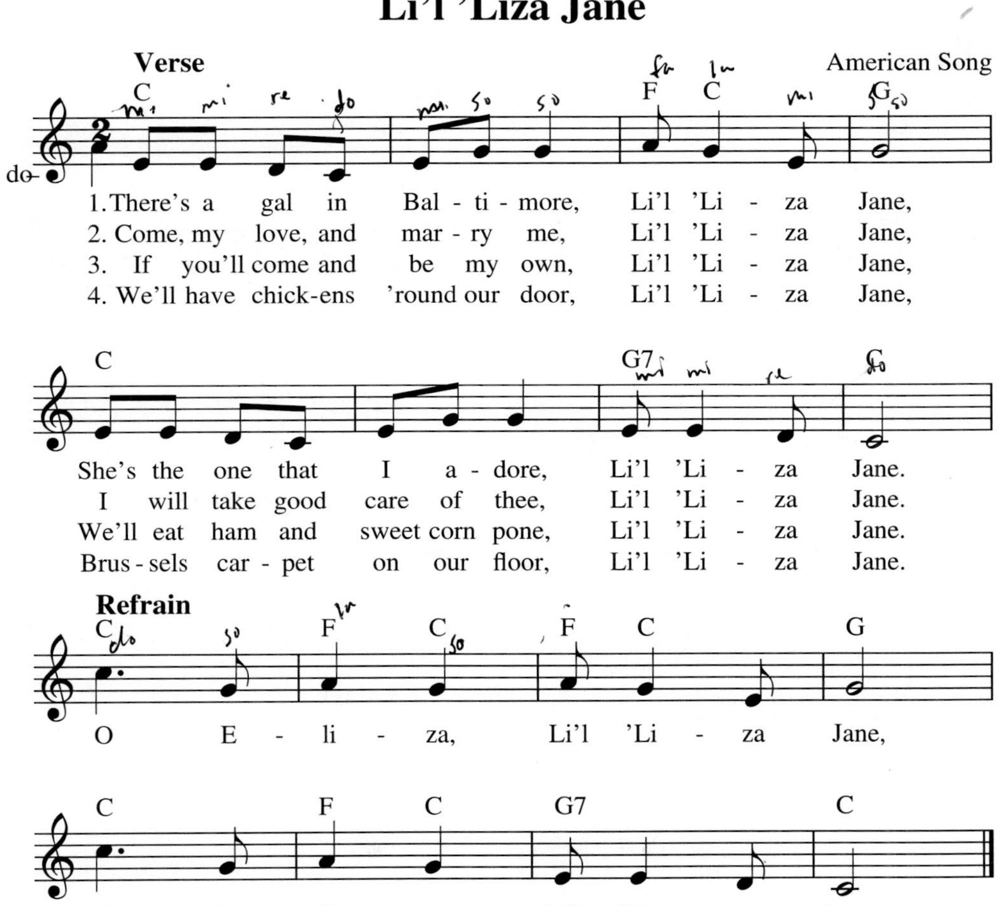

Figure 4.18

Saraspondа
Dutch Spinning Song
C G7 C
do
Sa - ra - spon-da, Sa - ra-spon-da, Sa - ra - spon-da, Ret-set-set! Sa - ra -
C G7 C
spon - da, Sa - ra - spon - da, Sa - ra - spon - da, Ret - set - set!
F C F C
Ah - do - ray - oh! Ah - do - ray-boom-day - oh! Ah -
G7 C G7 C
do - ray - boom-day, Ret - set - set! Ah - say - pa - say - oh!

Figure 4.19

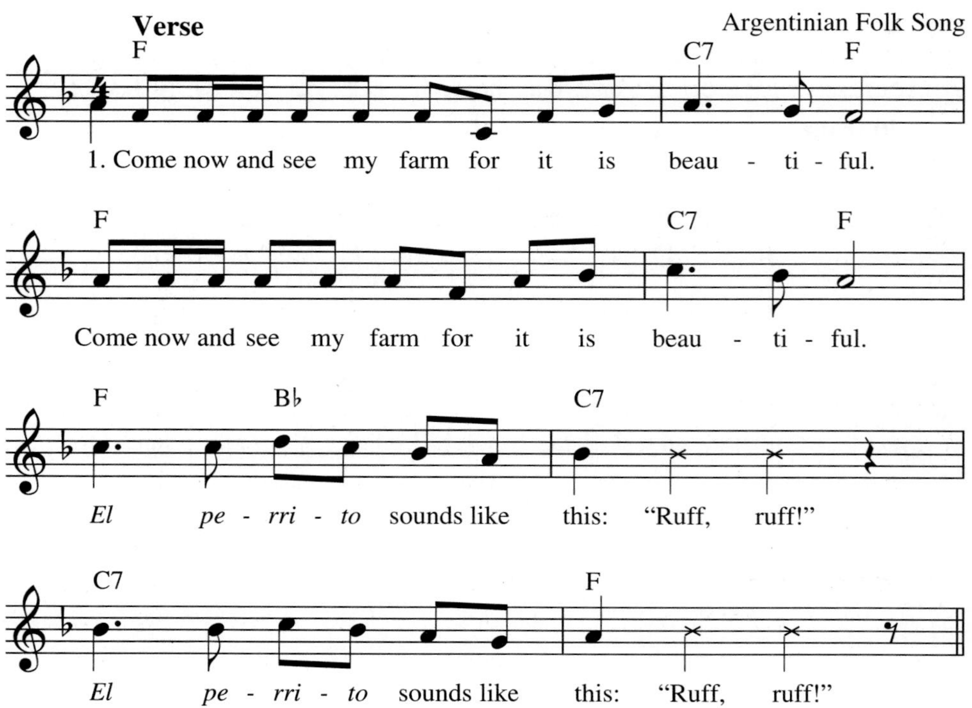
Mi Chacra
Verse
Argentinian Folk Song
F C7 F
1. Come now and see my farm for it is beau - ti - ful.
F C7 F
Come now and see my farm for it is beau - ti - ful.
F B♭ C7
El pe - rri - to sounds like this: "Ruff, ruff!"
C7 F
El pe - rri - to sounds like this: "Ruff, ruff!"

Figure 4.19 *continued*

Refrain
F
B♭
C7
Bi - en - vi - ni-dos, bi - en - ve - ni-dos, ve - nid, ve - nid, ve - nid.
C7
F
Bi - en - ve - ni-dos, bi - en - ve - ni-dos, ve - nid, ve - nid, ve - nid.

2. Come now and see my farm . . .
   El gatito . . . "Meow!"
3. Come now and see my farm . . .
   El patito . . . "Quack, quack!"
4. Come now and see my farm . . .
   El burrito . . . "Hee-haw!"
5. Come now and see my farm . . .
   El chanchito . . . "Oink, oink!"

Figure 4.20

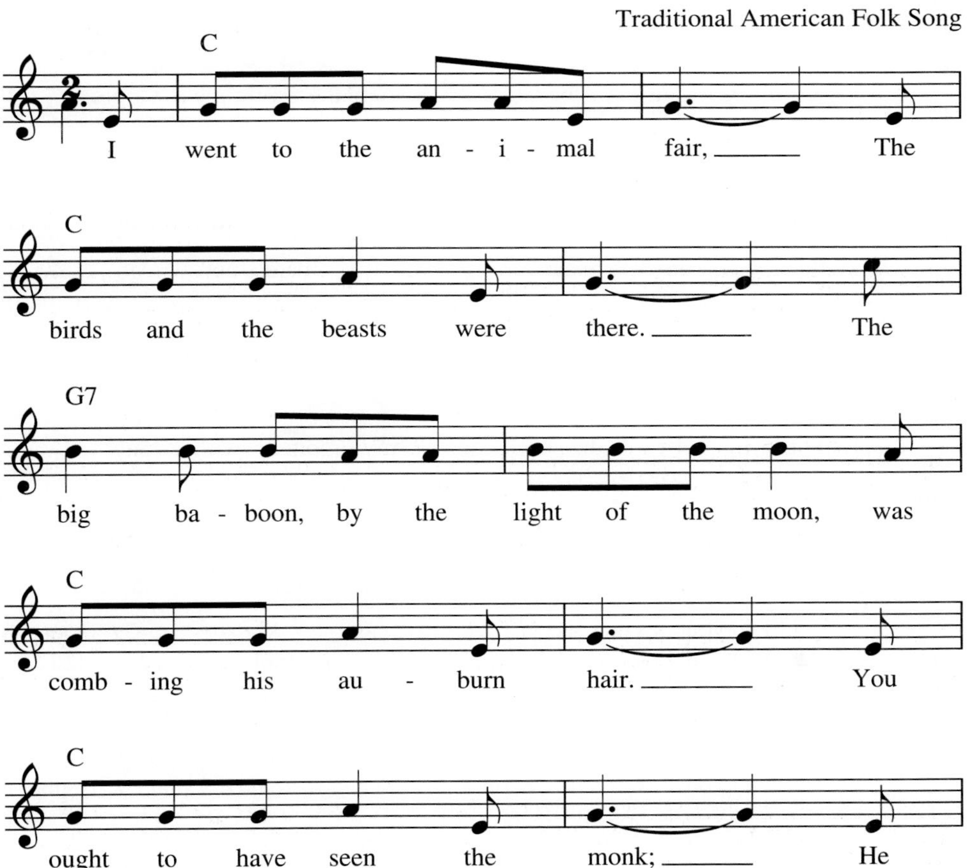
Animal Fair
Traditional American Folk Song
C
I went to the an - i - mal fair, The
C
birds and the beasts were there. The
G7
big ba - boon, by the light of the moon, was
C
comb - ing his au - burn hair. You
C
ought to have seen the monk; He

Figure 4.20 *continued*

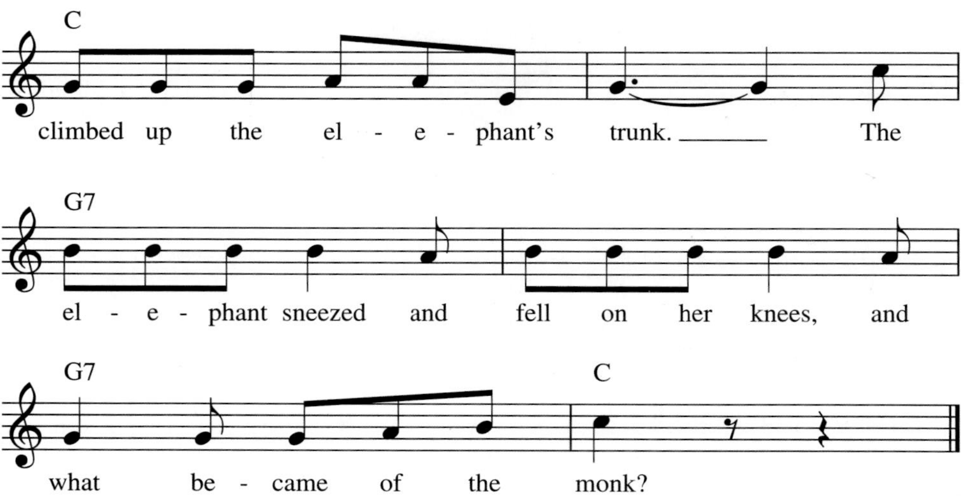
C
climbed up the el - e - phant's trunk. The
G7
el - e - phant sneezed and fell on her knees, and
G7
C
what be - came of the monk?

Figure 4.21

Down by the Bay
American Folk Song
G
D7
Down by the bay, where the wa-ter-mel-ons grow,
D7
G
Back to my home I dare not go,
G
C
G
For if I do my moth-er will say,
G
1. "Did you ev - er see a goose kiss - ing a moose,
2. "Did you ev - er see a whale with a pol - ka dot tail,
3. "Did you ev - er see a fly wear - ing a tie,
4. "Did you ev - er see a bear comb - ing his hair,
5. "Did you ev - er see llamas eat - ing their pa-ja-mas,
6. "Did you ev - er have a time when you could-n't make a rhyme,
1.–5.
6.
D7
G
D7
G
Down by the bay?" Down by the bay."

Figure 4.22

Old Joe Clark
Refrain
American Folk Song
F
C7
'Round and 'round, Old Joe Clark, 'Round and 'round I say;
F
Fine
'Round and 'round, Old Joe Clark, I have-n't long to stay.
Verse
F
1. Old Joe Clark, he had a house Six - teen sto - ries high:
2. I went down to old Joe's house, Nev-er been there be - fore;
D.C. al Fine
F
C7 F C7
Ev - 'ry sto - ry in that house was full of chick-en pie.
He slept on the feath - er bed And I slept on the floor.

Figure 4.23

Mama Paquita
Translated by Merrill Staton
Brazilian Carnival Song
C
1. Ma - ma Pa - qui - ta, Ma - ma Pa - qui - ta,
2. Ma - ma Pa - qui - ta, Ma - ma Pa - qui - ta,
C
G7
Ma - ma Pa - qui - ta has no mon - ey for pa - pa - yas;
Ma - ma Pa - qui - ta has no mon - ey for pa - ja - mas;
G7
Can't buy pa - pa - yas, can't buy ba - nan - as;
Can't buy pa - ja - mas, can't buy som - bre - ros;

Figure 4.23 *continued*

G7
C
She can - not buy pa-pa - yas or ba - nan - as. No, ma - ma - ma -
She can - not buy pa - ja - mas or som - bre - ros. No, ma - ma - ma -
C
ma, Ma - ma Pa - qui - ta, Ma - ma Pa - qui - ta,
ma, Ma - ma Pa - qui - ta, Ma - ma Pa - qui - ta,
C
G7
Ma - ma Pa - qui - ta will not have a ripe pa - pa - ya;
Ma - ma Pa - qui - ta will not have the fine pa - ja - mas;
G7
No ripe pa - pa - ya, no ripe ba - nan - a,
No fine pa - ja - mas, no fine som - bre - ros,
G7
C
So go to Car - ni - val to laugh and dance and sing.

English translation reprinted by permission of Merrill Staton.

Figure 4.24

Kye Kye Kule

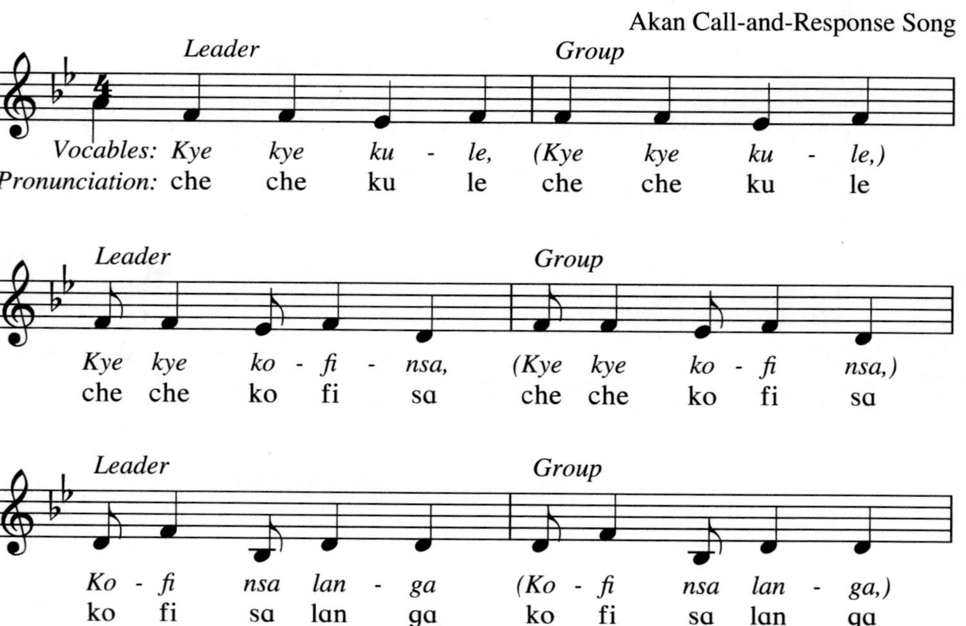
Akan Call-and-Response Song
Leader
Group
Vocables: Kye kye ku - le, (Kye kye ku - le,)
Pronunciation: che che ku le che che ku le
Leader
Group
Kye kye ko - fi - nsa, (Kye kye ko - fi nsa,)
che che ko fi sa che che ko fi sa
Leader
Group
Ko - fi nsa lan - ga (Ko - fi nsa lan - ga,)
ko fi sa lan ga ko fi sa lan ga

Figure 4.24 *continued*

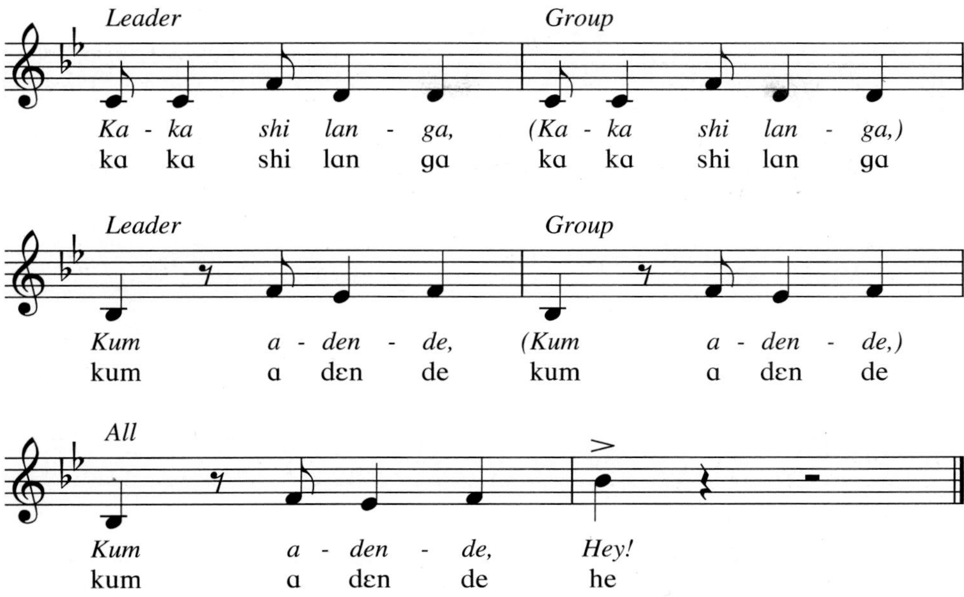

Figure 4.25

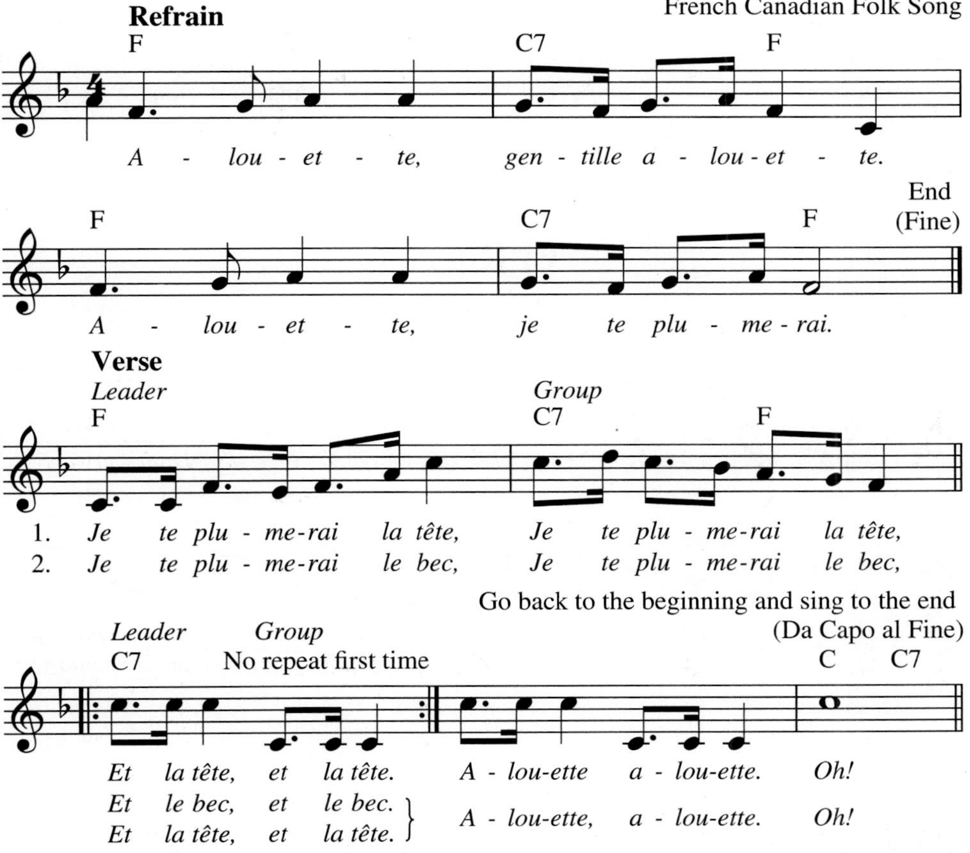

Figure 4.26

Frère Jacques

French Folk Song
F
do
French: Frè - re Jac - ques, Frè - re Jac - ques,
English: Are you sleep - ing, are you sleep - ing,
F
Dor - mez - vous, dor - mez - vous?
Broth - er John, Broth - er John?
F
Son - nez les ma - ti - nes, son - nez les ma - ti - nes,
Morn-ing bells are ring - ing, morn-ing bells are ring - ing,
F
Din, din, don, din, din, don.
Ding, ding, dong, ding, ding, dong.

Figure 4.27

El Rorro

Traditional Mexican
A la ru - ru - ru, chi - qui - to ni - ño, Duer-ma - se
ya mi Je - su - si - to.
Ca-da an - i - mal y pá - ja -
All the an - i - mals are stand-ing

Figure 4.27 *continued*

ro. Tier-na-men-te guar-da be-bé que-ri-do. A la ru-
near. Ten-der-ly ___ guard-ing ba-by small and dear. A la ru-
ru-ru, chi-qui-to ni-ño, Duer-ma-se ya mi Je-su-si-to. ___
ru-ru, ah Ba-by, dear one, Oh, lit-tle Je-su, sleep_ my son. ___

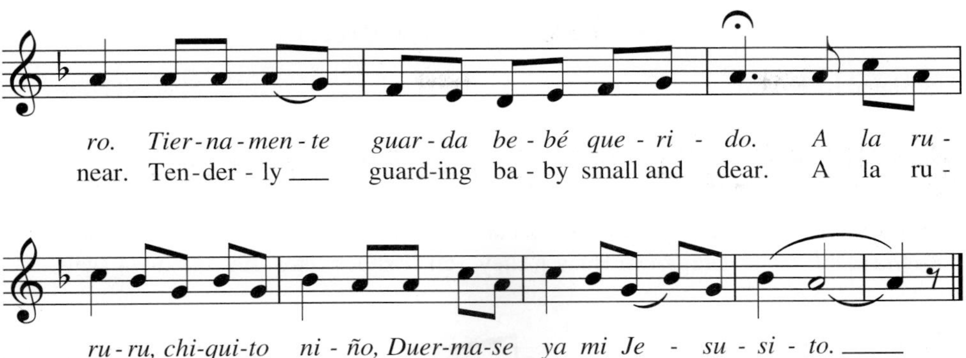

Figure 4.28

Skinnamarink

Tin Pan Alley Song

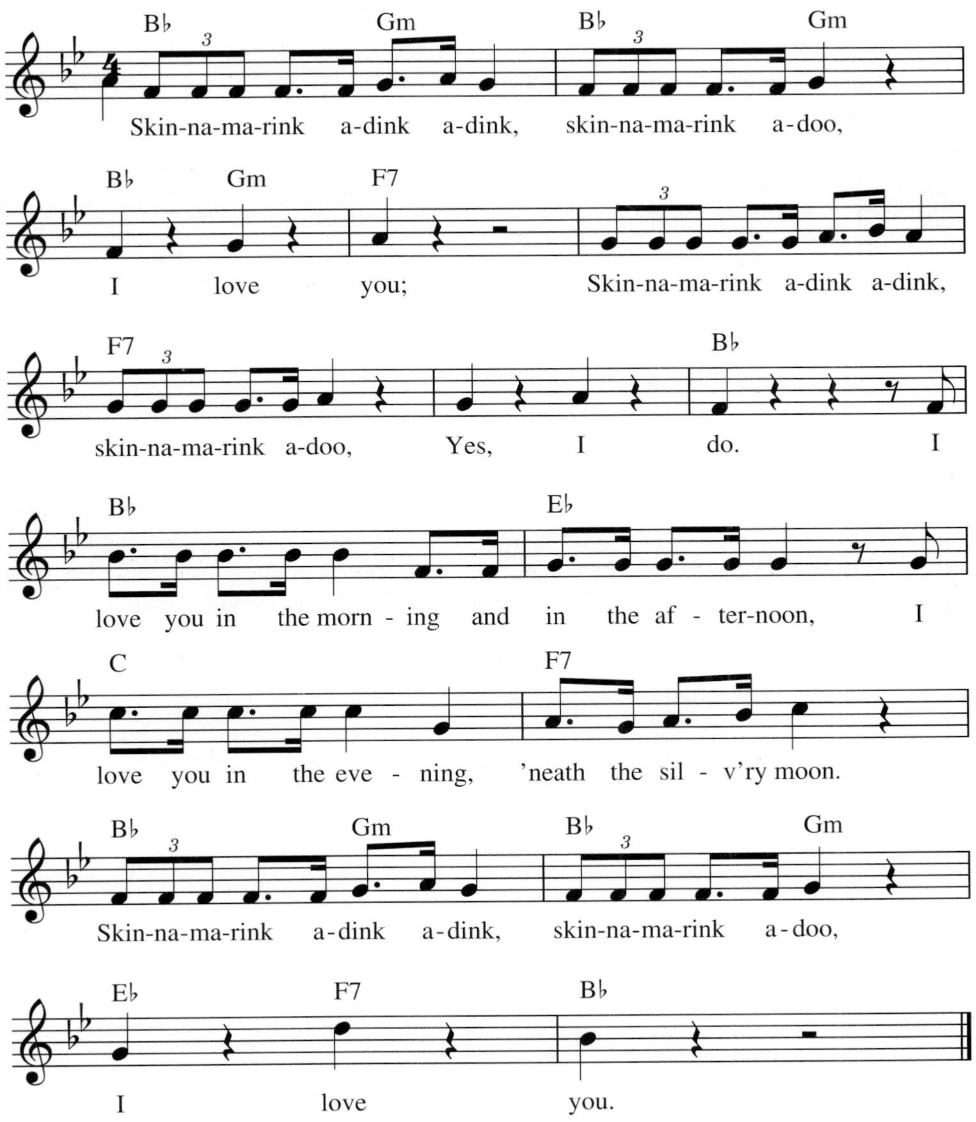

B♭ Gm B♭ Gm
Skin-na-ma-rink a-dink a-dink, skin-na-ma-rink a-doo,
B♭ Gm F7
I love you; Skin-na-ma-rink a-dink a-dink,
F7 B♭
skin-na-ma-rink a-doo, Yes, I do. I
B♭ E♭
love you in the morn-ing and in the af-ter-noon, I
C F7
love you in the eve-ning, 'neath the sil-v'ry moon.
B♭ Gm B♭ Gm
Skin-na-ma-rink a-dink a-dink, skin-na-ma-rink a-doo,
E♭ F7 B♭
I love you.

Figure 4.29

A la puerta del cielo
Translated by R.M.A.
Spanish Folk Song
Spanish: A la puer - ta del cie - lo ven - der za - pa - tos
English: At the gate of Heav'n they sell shoes for the an - gels
Pa - ra los an - ge - li - los que an - dar des - cal - zos,
For the lit - tle an - gels who walk a - round bare - foot
Duér - me - te ni - ño duér - me - te ni - ño
Slum - ber my lit - tle one slum - ber my lit - tle one.
Duér - me - te ni - ño a - rru, a - rru.
Slum - ber my lit - tle one, a - rru, a - rru.

SONG TEACHING: THE ROTE SONG METHOD

The rote method is a most effective way to teach songs to younger children because it does not rely on the printed word. The rote technique helps children remember short segments of both text and melody and provides the practice necessary to learn the whole song. This process was described by developmental theorist Jean Piaget as the assimilation and accommodation of new information.[2] The rote process of song teaching outlined in the following script requires the teacher to sing a short segment of the music (usually two measures) while pointing to herself or himself. Then the teacher points to the students when it is their turn to echo the line. By simply pointing to one's self or to students, a teacher can teach an entire song without speaking. If necessary, the teacher can sing again those lines of text and music that the children did not echo correctly.

PRIMARY TEACHING SCRIPT: THE ROTE SONG METHOD

Figure 4.30

Kaeru no Uta (Frog's Song)

Ka - e - ru - no u - ta ga Ki - ko - e - te ku - ru - yo

Gwa! Gwa! Gwa! Gwa! Ge-ro ge-ro ge-ro ge-ro gwa gwa gwa!

Today I have a new song to teach you. I'd like each of you to listen very carefully as I sing it. Remember the rule about listening to music: You must open your ears and seal your lips. I'd like you to be able to tell me something about the song when I'm finished. Sing whole song.

Who can tell me something about this song? Call on one child, give appropriate response, then continue.

This song is in Japanese, and tells about the song that the frog sings. I'm going to sing it again, and this time see if you can hear the part where the frogs sing their song. Sing the entire song.

Raise your hand if you can tell me the words where the frog sings. Call on a few children, give appropriate responses, then continue.

I want to sing the song to you one more time, because it will help you learn it much more easily. While I sing it this time, see if you can hear the part where the frog sings. Show me thumbs up when I get to the part where the frog sings. Sing the song to the end and put your thumb up at "gwa!" at the end.

Now we're going to learn the song together. I will sing one part and when I finish, I want you to sing that part with me. Teacher sings first two measures. Teacher indicates to class that they are to sing by singing "1 – 2 – ready, sing" on the initial pitch and motions for the class to join in. Teacher and class sing two measures.

Now I want you to listen to the next part of the song. Teacher sings next two measures. Teacher indicates to class when they are to sing by singing "1 – 2 – ready, sing" on the initial pitch of the third measure and motions for the class to join in.

Now we're going to sing both parts together. Teacher sings "1 – 2 – ready, sing" on initial pitch and sings both phrases together.

Now listen carefully to the third part of the song, where the frog starts its song. Teacher sings next two measures, pointing to self while singing and indicates to class that they should echo by pointing to them immediately at the end of the two measures. After they echo, teacher then sings the last two measures while pointing to self, and indicating to class to echo at the end of the two measures. Then teacher points to self and sings the last four measures, indicating at the end that the class should echo.

Now we're going to sing all four parts of the song from the beginning. 1 – 2 – ready, sing. Class sings entire song; teacher continues.

Can someone put up his or her hand and tell me how we sounded? Teacher takes a few responses, then asks:

How can we make it sound better if we sing it one more time? Teacher solicits a few answers, reiterating what individuals have said, then leads class in final attempt with "1 – 2 – ready, sing."

That was good singing today, class. It sounded so nice that we'll be able to sing it at the morning meeting when we discuss what has happened with your polliwog collection project.

The following lesson plan format summarizes the steps used in the rote song teaching script.

ROTE SONG LESSON PLAN: PRIMARY

I. Learning Outcome or Objective: Students will be able to sing a new song.
Entry ability: Students are able to sing five pitches—C to G—with reasonable accuracy.
Exit ability: Students will be able to sing "Frog Song" ("Kaeru no Uta") with reasonable accuracy.

II. Lesson Evaluation or Assessment Procedures: Teacher will note those students unable to sing the song accurately. Were their problems with pitch or with the Japanese text?

III. Materials and Board/Space Preparation: Notation for "Kaeru no Uta"

IV. Teaching Procedures:

A. Setting the Stage: Review listening rules.

B. Developing the lesson:
Step 1: Introduce new song with focus question. Sing the whole song. Take comments. Tell students it is in Japanese and is about a frog singing.
Transition question: See if you can hear the part where the frogs sing.
Step 2: Sing whole song again. Ask children to identify what the frog sings. Take responses from a few children.
Transition statement: Put thumbs up when you hear the frog's singing part.
Step 3: Sing whole song again. Observe class to see which children can recognize the frog's song part.
Step 4: Teach first two measures, pointing to self when singing and to class when they are to echo. After first two measures are secure, teach measures three and four in the same way. Then sing first four measures and have class echo. Repeat procedure for final four measures.

C. Concluding the Lesson: Ask for volunteers to comment on how singing sounded. Take their comments and have class try singing whole song again. Give specific praise, based on the sound of the singing. Explain how song will be part of primary meeting time discussion.

SINGING WITH OLDER CHILDREN

By the time they reach intermediate grades, most children have had enough singing experience to form opinions about their own vocal abilities and to know where they stand in relation to the singing prowess of their classmates. While many of the children will have expanded vocal ranges of ten notes from middle C upward (figure 4.31), some will not have found their singing voices. They may also have strong feelings about singing as a classroom activity, and you may find that some have developed negative attitudes that prevent them from participating fully in classroom singing. Those students who have not learned to match pitch successfully may avoid singing activities completely, using such tactics as mouthing words and pretending to sing. These students are actually living in fear that someone will hear their "horrible voices."

Figure 4.31 Expanded Vocal Range of Older Children

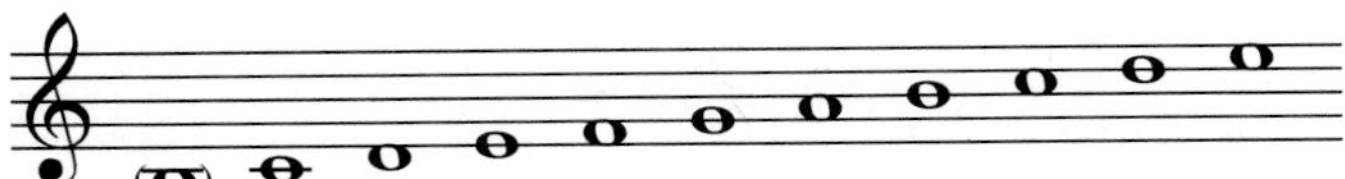

Your intermediate class may include students whose voices wander occasionally, those who sing slightly under pitch, and those who continue to use their chest register rather than head voice. Sometimes boys refuse to sing in their head voices for fear of "sounding like a girl." Or they try to hasten the onset of voice change by singing in chest register and not moving up to head voice, even though their voices are still capable of high notes. Some students may continue to sing in their speaking voices, particularly if they are developmentally delayed or physically impaired. No matter what condition his or her vocal development is in, each intermediate child deserves the joy of participating in daily classroom singing activities. It is up to you to provide your students with singing experiences that will enhance the level of their singing competence.

Children in grades four, five, and six need song literature that is interesting—both musically and textually. Songs that have a greater range (distance from the lowest to the highest note), more than one voice, a melody with a good mix of steps and skips, fairly complex rhythmic patterns, a quick or changing tempo, and changing dynamic levels are more popular with children of this age level. Texts that tell an unusual or silly story or require tongue-twisting to pronounce are also popular with this age group. Intermediate students are fascinated with deciphering and creating code, and you can take advantage of this by introducing songs with more complex non-English texts. Folk songs are a great source of musical and textual variety, and they can help older students experience the musical variety present in other cultures.

SUGGESTED INTERMEDIATE SONG LITERATURE

Figures 4.32–52 present twenty-two songs that are appropriate for use with intermediate pupils. Another song that can be added to this group is "Waltzing Matilda" (figure 3.28, page 61).

Figure 4.32

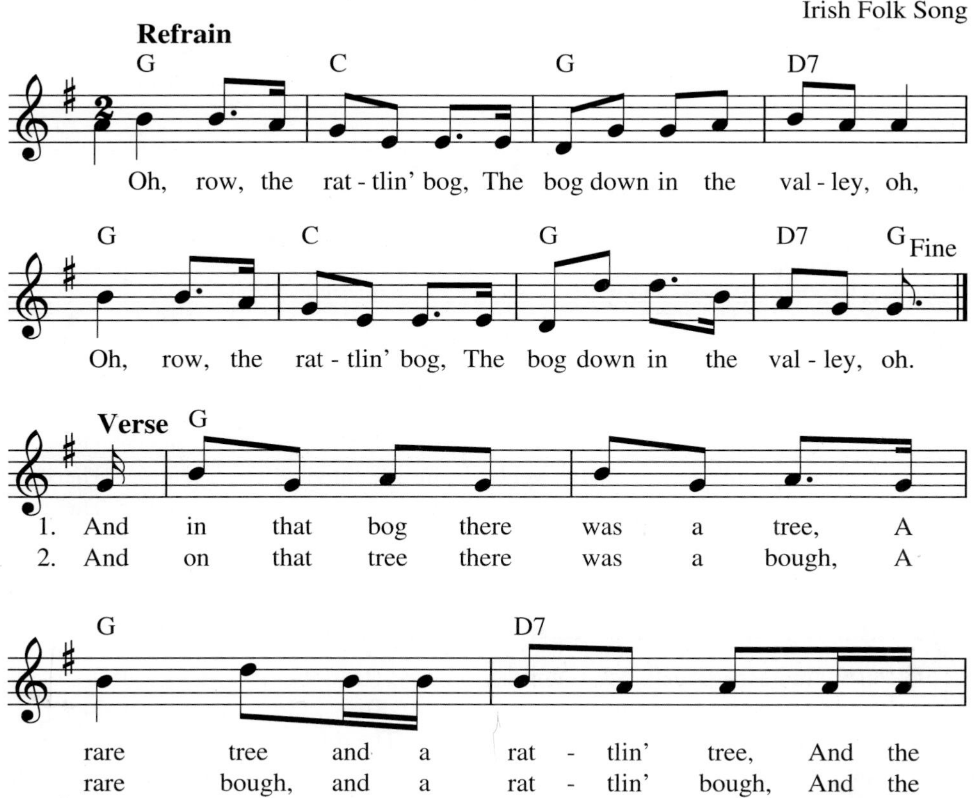

Figure 4.32 *continued*

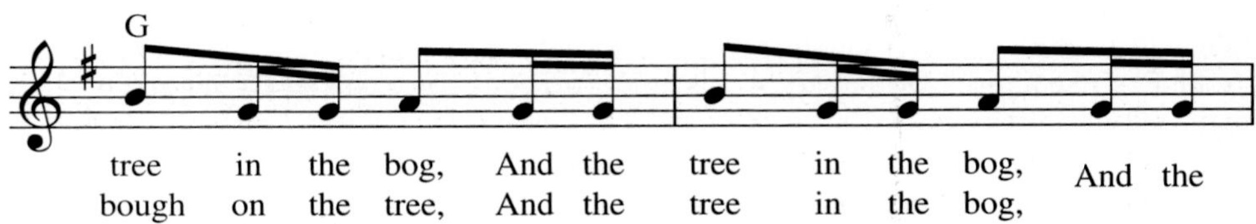
G
tree in the bog, And the tree in the bog, And the
bough on the tree, And the tree in the bog,

D.C. (Last time al Fine)
G
D7
G
bog down in the val - ley, oh.

3. Now on that bough there was a branch,
   A rare branch, and a rattlin' branch,
   And the branch on the bough,
   And the bough on the tree,
   And the tree in the bog,
   And the bog down in the valley, oh.
   Refrain

4. Now on the branch there was a nest,
   A rare nest, and a rattlin' nest
   And the nest on the branch,
   And the branch on the bough,
   And the bough on the tree,
   And the tree in the bog,
   And the bog down in the valley, oh.
   Refrain

5. Now in the nest there was a bird,
   A rare bird, and a rattlin' bird,
   And the bird in the nest,
   And the nest on the branch . . .
   Refrain

6. And on that bird there was a tail . . .
   Refrain

Figure 4.33

One More River

Nineteenth Century College Song

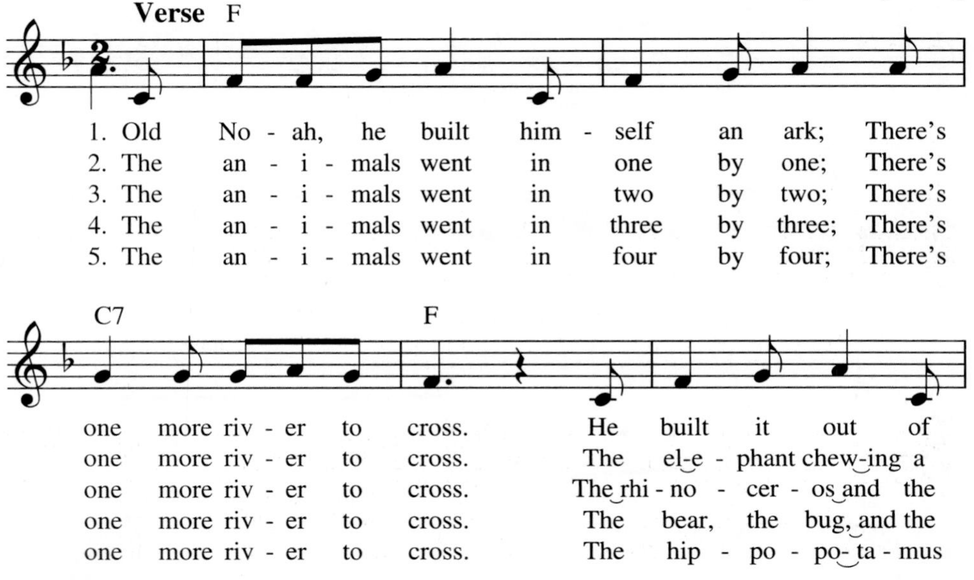
Verse F
1. Old No - ah, he built him - self an ark; There's
2. The an - i - mals went in one by one; There's
3. The an - i - mals went in two by two; There's
4. The an - i - mals went in three by three; There's
5. The an - i - mals went in four by four; There's
C7
F
one more riv - er to cross. He built it out of
one more riv - er to cross. The el-e - phant chew-ing a
one more riv - er to cross. The rhi - no - cer - os and the
one more riv - er to cross. The bear, the bug, and the
one more riv - er to cross. The hip - po - po-ta - mus

Figure 4.33 *continued*

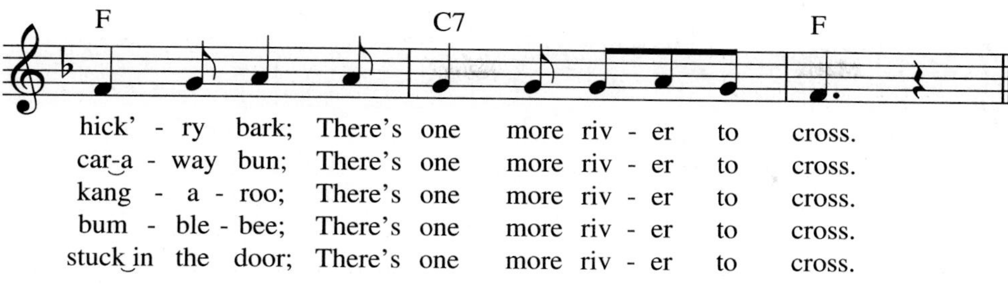
F C7 F
hick' - ry bark; There's one more riv - er to cross.
car‿a - way bun; There's one more riv - er to cross.
kang - a - roo; There's one more riv - er to cross.
bum - ble - bee; There's one more riv - er to cross.
stuck‿in the door; There's one more riv - er to cross.

Refrain
B♭ F
There's one more riv - er, And
C7 F B♭
that wide riv - er is Jor - dan, There's one more
F C7 F
riv - er, There's one more riv - er to cross.

6. The animals went in five by five;
   There's one more river to cross.
   "It's raining," said Noah, "so look alive!"
   There's one more river to cross.
   Refrain

7. The animals went in six by six; . . .
   The monkeys were up
   to monkey tricks . . .
   Refrain

8. The animals went in sev'n by sev'n; . . .
   The rabbit said, "I wish I had driv'n." . . .
   Refrain

9. The animals went in eight by eight; . . .
   "That's 'nuff," said Noah,
   and slammed the gate! . . .
   Refrain

10. And as they talked of this and that; . . .
    The ark, it bumped on Ararat; . . .
    Refrain

Figure 4.34

Amazing Grace

John Newton Early American Melody

G C
1. A - maz - ing grace, how sweet the
2. 'Twas grace that taught my heart to
G D7
sound, That saved a wretch like me!
fear, And grace my fears re - lieved;

Figure 4.34 *continued*

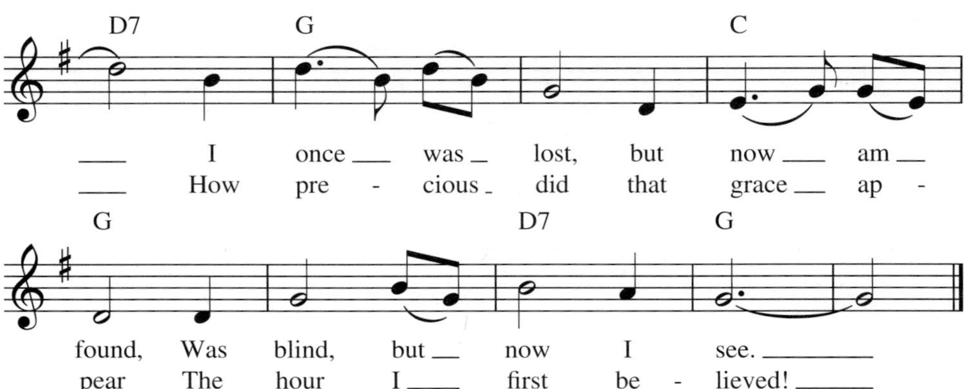

3. Through many dangers, toils, and snares,
I have already come;
'Tis grace has brought me safe thus far,
And grace will lead me home.

4. The Lord has promised good to me,
His word my hope secures;
He will my shield and portion be
As long as life endures.

Figure 4.35

Erie Canal

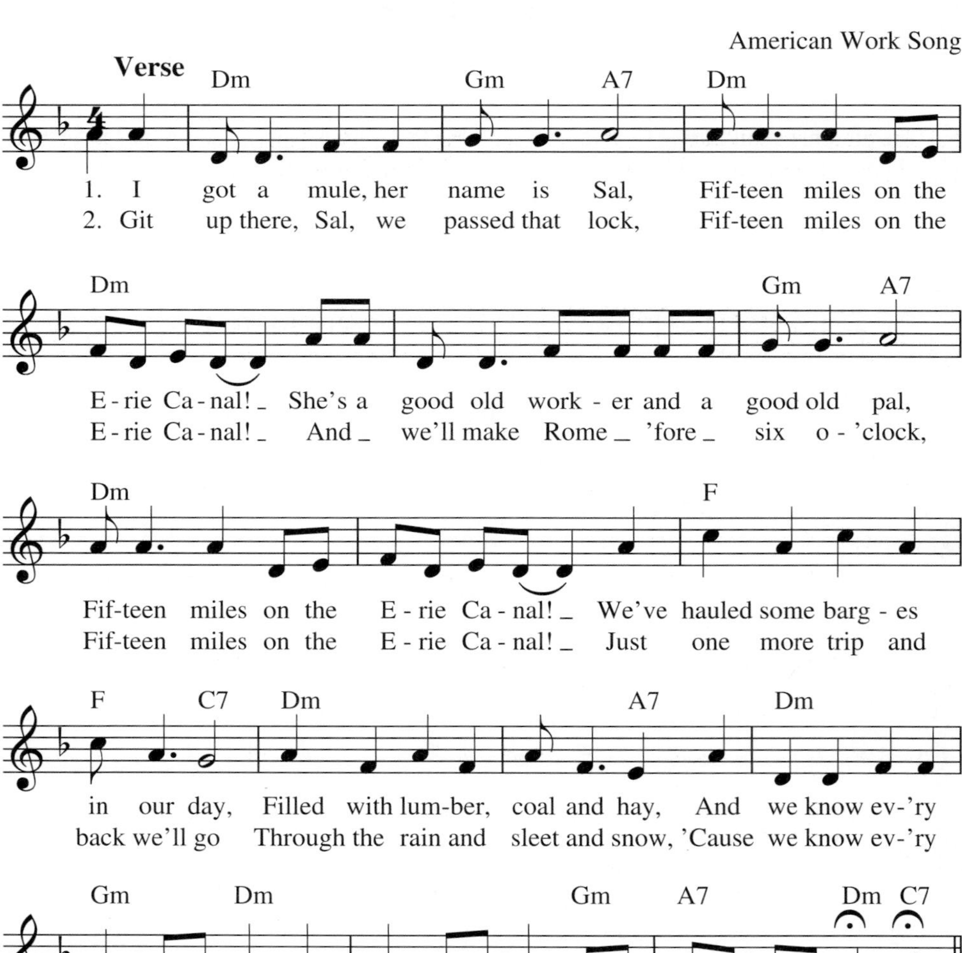

Figure 4.35 *continued*

Figure 4.36

Figure 4.37

Simple Gifts
Shaker Song
G
do
'Tis the gift to be sim-ple, 'tis the gift to be free, 'Tis the
D
gift to come down where we ought to be. And
G
when we find our - selves in the place just right, 'Twill
D
G
be in the val - ley of love and de - light.
G
When true sim - plic - i - ty is gained, To
G
D
bow and to bend we shan't be a - shamed. To
G
turn, turn will be our de - light, 'Til by
D
G
turn - ing, turn - ing we come 'round right.

Figure 4.38

Funga Alafia

Western African Welcome Dance

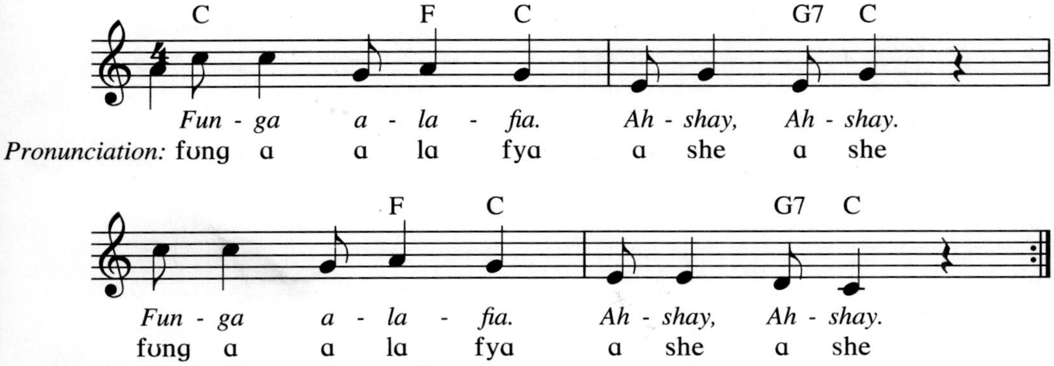

C F C G7 C

Fun - ga a - la - fia. Ah - shay, Ah - shay.

Pronunciation: fʊng a a la fya a she a she

F C G7 C

Fun - ga a - la - fia. Ah - shay, Ah - shay.

fʊng a a la fya a she a she

Figure 4.39

We Shall Overcome

American Freedom Song

C F C F C
1. We shall o - ver - come,
We shall o - ver - come,
2. We'll walk hand in hand,
We'll walk hand in hand,
G Am D7 G
We shall o - ver - come some day; Oh,
We'll walk hand in hand some day; Oh,
C F C F G7 C
deep in my heart I do be - lieve,
deep in my heart I do be - lieve,
C F G7 C
We shall o - ver - come some day.
We'll walk hand in hand some day.

3. We are not afraid,
We are not afraid,
We are not afraid today.
Oh, deep in my heart I do believe,
We are not afraid today.

4. We shall brothers be,
We shall brothers be,
We shall brothers be some day.
Oh, deep in my heart I do believe,
We shall brothers be some day.

5. Truth shall make us free,
Truth shall make us free,
Truth shall make us free some day.
Oh, deep in my heart I do believe,
Truth shall make us free some day.

Figure 4.40

Battle Hymn of the Republic

Figure 4.41

The Star-Spangled Banner

Francis Scott Key — Attributed to J. S. Smith

Figure 4.41 *continued*

F F7 B♭ E♭ G7 Cm C7
there. Oh, say, does that_ Star-Span-gled Ban - ner_ yet_
stream; 'Tis the Star-Span - gled_ Ban - ner, oh, long may_ it_
trust." And the Star-Span - gled_ Ban - ner in tri - umph_ shall_
B♭ F F7 B♭ F B♭ GmC7 B♭ F7 B♭
wave_ O'er the land_ of the free and the home of the brave?
wave_ O'er the land_ of the free and the home of the brave!
wave_ O'er the land_ of the free and the home of the brave!

Figure 4.42

Day-O

Jamaican Folk Song
Adapted by Carol P. Richardson

Day-o_ me say day - o_ Day-light come and me wan' go home.

Three hand, four hand, five hand bunch!_ Day-light come and me wan' go home.

I for-got to eat my lunch!_ Day-light come and me wan' go home.

Figure 4.43

La Cucaracha

Traditional Mexican

Verse
Spanish: *U - na cu - ca-ra-cha pin - ta, Le di-jo a u-na co-lo - ra - do.*
English: There's a spot-ted cu-ca - ra - cha, It's a red-dish cu-ca - ra - cha.
Vá - mo-nos pa-ra mi tie - rra, A pa-sar la tem-po - ra - da.
When it comes in - to our kit - chen, We're to send it on va - ca - tion.

Figure 4.43 *continued*

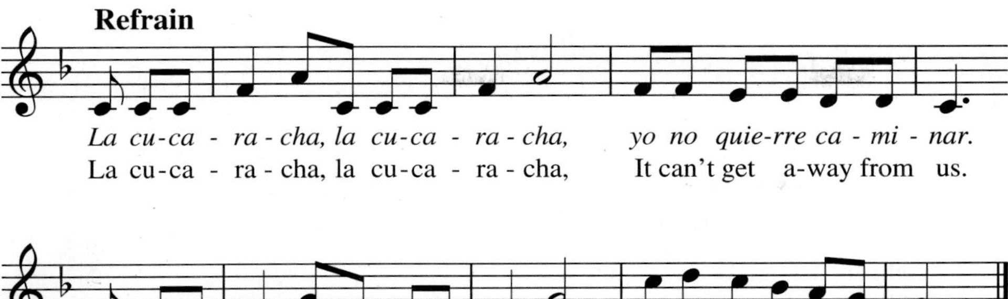
Refrain
La cu-ca - ra - cha, la cu-ca - ra - cha, yo no quie-rre ca - mi - nar.
La cu-ca - ra - cha, la cu-ca - ra - cha, It can't get a-way from us.

Por-que no tie - na, por-que le fal - ta, Di-ne - ro pa-ra gas - tar.
La cu-ca - ra - cha, la cu-ca - ra - cha, It will nev-er get a - way.

Figure 4.44

When I First Came to This Land

Oscar Brand

Oscar Brand

Verse
C F C F C G7 C
1.–5. When I first came to this land, I was not a wealth-y man.
C F C F G C
Then I built my - self a shack. I did what I could.
Then I bought my - self a cow. I did what I could.
Then I bought my - self a horse. I did what I could.
Then I got my - self a wife. I did what I could.
Then I got my - self a son. I did what I could.
Repeat these four measures for additional lines in verses 2–5
F C G7 C
I called my shack Break - my - back.
I called my cow No - milk - now,
I called my horse Lame - of - course,
I called my wife Joy - of-my life.
I told my son My work's done.
Refrain
C F C F G7 C
Still the land was sweet and good, I did what I could.

Figure 4.45

Scarborough Fair

English Folk Song

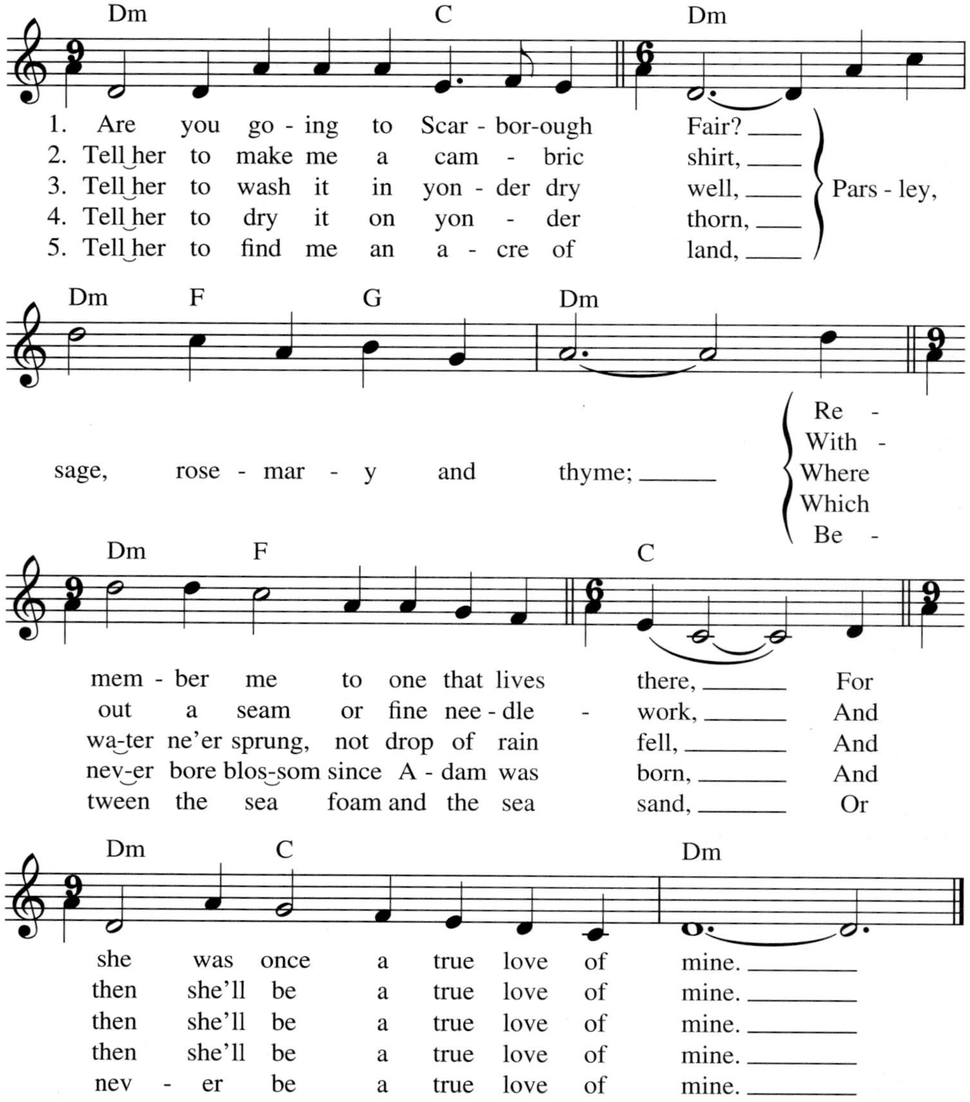

Dm C Dm
1. Are you go - ing to Scar - bor-ough Fair?
2. Tell her to make me a cam - bric shirt,
3. Tell her to wash it in yon - der dry well,
4. Tell her to dry it on yon - der thorn,
5. Tell her to find me an a - cre of land,
Pars - ley,
Dm F G Dm
sage, rose - mar - y and thyme;
Re - / With - / Where / Which / Be -
Dm F C
mem - ber me to one that lives there, For
out a seam or fine nee - dle - work, And
wa-ter ne'er sprung, not drop of rain fell, And
nev-er bore blos-som since A - dam was born, And
tween the sea foam and the sea sand, Or
Dm C Dm
she was once a true love of mine.
then she'll be a true love of mine.
then she'll be a true love of mine.
then she'll be a true love of mine.
nev - er be a true love of mine.

Figure 4.46

Joshua Fit the Battle of Jericho

African-American Spiritual

Refrain
Dm Swing it
A7 Dm
do
Josh-ua fit the bat-tle of Jer-i - cho, Jer-i - cho, Jer-i - cho.
Last time to Coda
Dm A7 Dm
Josh-ua fit the bat-tle of Jer-i - cho and the walls came tum-blin' down.

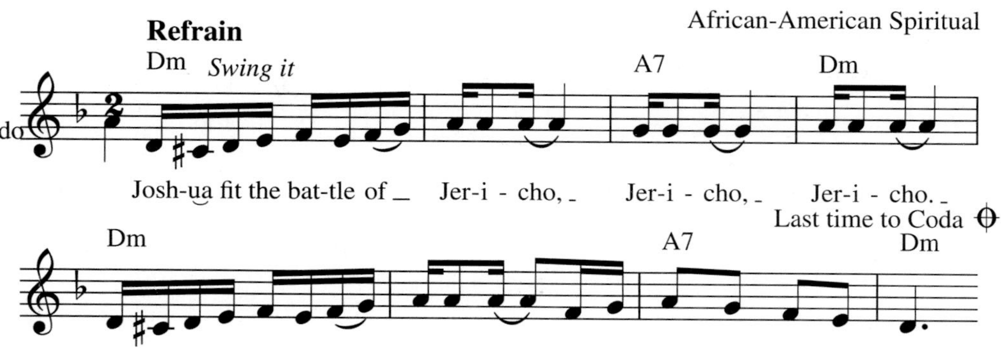

Figure 4.46 *continued*

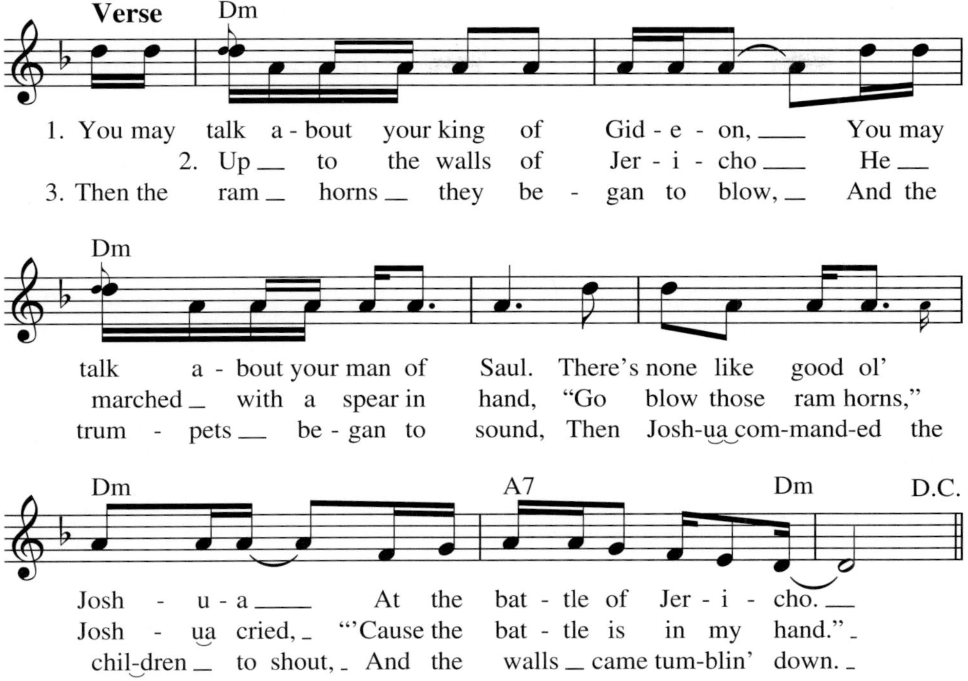

Figure 4.47

John B. Sails

Folk Song from the Bahama Islands

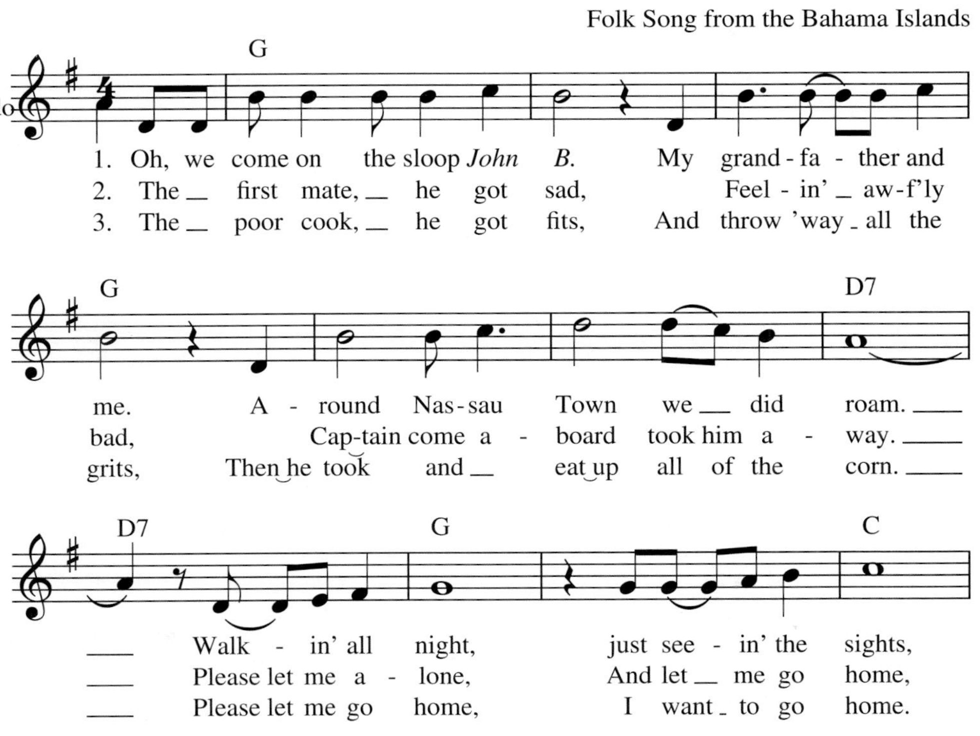

Figure 4.47 *continued*

C G D7 G
Well, I feel so break - up, I want _ to go home.
Well, I feel so break - up, I want _ to go home.
Well, this is the worst _ trip Since I ______ was born.
Refrain
G
So hoist up the *John B.* sails, See how the main-s'l
G D7
set. Send for the Cap-t'n a - shore, Let _ me go home.
G C
Please let _ me go home, I want _ to go home. Well, _ I
G D7 G
feel so break _ up, I want _ to go home.

Figure 4.48

Hava Nagila

Israeli Folk Song

E7 Am E7
Ha-va na-gi-la, Ha-va na-gi-la, Ha-va na-gi-la, ve - nis-m' cha.
Am E7
Ha-va na-gi-la, Ha-va na-gi-la, Ha-va na-gi-la, ve - nis-m' cha.
E7 Dm
Ha-va ne - ra - ne - na, Ha-va ne - ra - ne - na, Ha - va ne-ra - ne - na,

Figure 4.48 *continued*

E7
Dm
ve-nis-m' cha, Ha-va ne-ra-ne-na, Ha-va ne-ra-ne-na, Ha-va ne-ra-ne-na,
E7
Am
ve-nis-m' cha, U - ru, U-ru a-chim, U-ru a-chim b'-lev sa-me-ach,
E7
U-ru, a-chim b'-lev sa-me-ach, U-ru a-chim b'-lev sa-me-ach,
E7
Am
U-ru a-chim b'-lev sa-me-ach, U-ru a-chim, U-ru a-chim b' lev sa-me - ach.

Figure 4.49

Dry Bones

African-American Spiritual

do
C
G7
E - ze-kiel cried, "Them dry bones!" E - ze-kiel cried, "Them
C
G7
dry bones!" E - ze-kiel cried, "Them dry bones," Now hear the Word of the
1.
2.
C
C
Lord. E - Lord!" The foot bone con-nect-ed to the leg bone, The
C♯
D
leg bone con-nect-ed to the knee bone, The knee bone con-nect-ed to the

Figure 4.49 *continued*

D♯
hip - bone, The hip - bone con-nect - ed to the back - bone, The
E
F
back-bone con-nect-ed to the shoul-der bone, The shoul-der bone con-nect-ed to the
F♯
neck bone, The neck bone con-nect - ed to the jaw - bone, The
G
G
D7
G
jaw-bone con-nect-ed to the head bone, Now hear the Word of the Lord.
G
Them bones, them bones gon - na walk a - round, Them
D7
G
bones, them bones gon-na walk a-round, Them bones, them bones gon-na
G
D7
G
walk a - round, Now hear the word of the Lord.

Figure 4.50

Siyahamba

African Folk Song

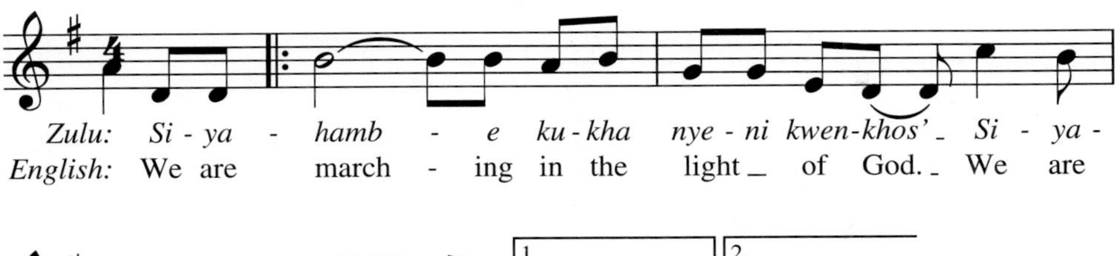

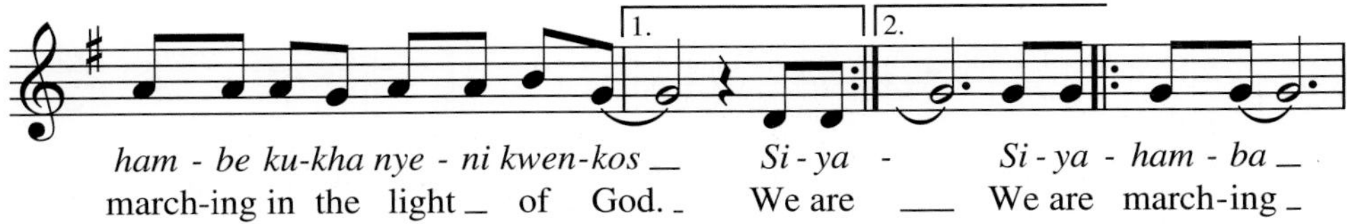

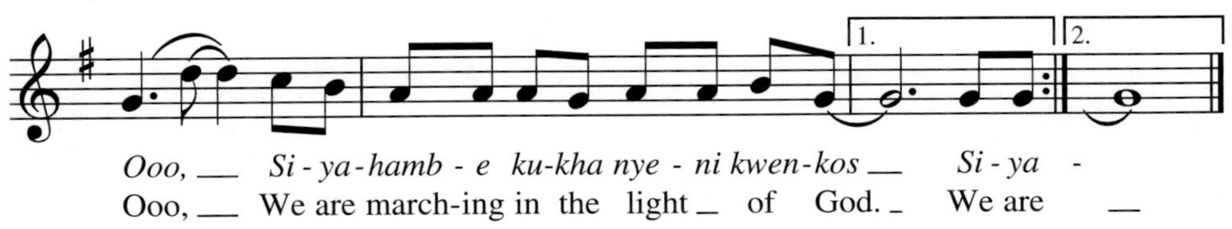

Figure 4.51

Arirang

Korean Folk Song

Figure 4.52

Tzena, Tzena, Tzena, by Issachar Miron, English lyrics by Mitchell Parish, with one line altered by Pete Seeger.

SONG TEACHING: THE WHOLE SONG METHOD

Teaching a whole song at one time is another option for teaching singing in your classroom. Instead of singing bits of the song at a time, you ask the class to listen as you sing the whole song several times. Then you lead them in listening carefully for specific features and answering questions about those features. The whole song method can be used successfully with primary children if the song contains a great deal of repetition of both text and melody. This method is particularly suitable for intermediate grades where children are able to read the song text from either a page or an overhead transparency.

INTERMEDIATE TEACHING SCRIPT: THE WHOLE SONG METHOD

I found a Japanese folk song that will fit well with our dramatization of the Japanese myth "Momotaro, the Peach Boy." It's called "Kaeru no Uta," and it means frog song. The first two lines mean "I can hear the song of the frog." The second two lines sound like the frog's singing. See if you can hear the difference between these two parts of this little song. Teacher sings whole song, then continues.

Raise your hand if you could hear the difference between the two parts of this song. Can someone describe how the two parts were different? Solicit one or two answers.

I'm going to sing "Kaeru no Uta" again, and this time I'd like you to see if you can memorize the words to the frog's song as I sing it. When I've finished I'll ask you to tell me the words of the frog's song. Teacher sings song again.

Who can tell me the words to the frog's song? After a successful response, teacher continues.

Let's look at the screen and sing the whole song together. Teacher sings "1 – 2 – ready, sing" and points to each word on the transparency as the class sings.

That was a good first attempt. I think we need to go over the words again so let's read them together as I point. Teacher leads class through text, pointing to each word on the transparency, correcting any pronunciation as needed.

Now that we're all a little more familiar with the text, let's try to sing the whole song again. Teacher gives "1 – 2 – ready, sing" but this time does not point to each word.

Now let's test how well we've learned this song. I'm going to switch off the overhead and see if we can sing the song without any help. I'd like you to listen carefully while you're singing and be able to tell me what you think of how you sound. Teacher sings "1 – 2 – ready, sing" and leads whole song.

How did we do? Teacher solicits a few responses.

I think we can try it again and this time make it sound a little more like frogs when we get to the frog's part. Teacher sings "1 – 2 – ready, sing" and leads the whole song.

What did you do with your voice that time to make it sound more like frogs? Teacher solicits answers from a few students.

What else can we do to make more of a contrast between the two parts of this song? Teacher solicits answers, then tries suggestions.

You did a great job today, class. You've worked hard to make this song sound like frogs singing. Our next task is to figure out where we'd like to put this song in our dramatization of the Peach Boy story. We'll work on that after lunch today in language arts time.

WHOLE SONG LESSON PLAN: INTERMEDIATE

I. Learning Outcome or Objective: Students will learn a new song.
Entry ability: Students can follow words and staff notation.
Exit ability: Students will be able to sing "Frog Song" ("Kaeru no Uta") from memory with reasonable accuracy.

II. Lesson Evaluation Procedures: Teacher will note who is singing accurately and who has problems following the notation on the overhead.

III. Teaching Procedures:

A. Setting the Stage: Introduce song as example of Japanese song to use with Momotaro story dramatization. Give translation.

B. Developing the Lesson:
Step 1: Introduce new song with focus question. Sing the whole song, then see how many could hear the difference between the two parts.
Transition: See if you can memorize the words to the frog's song as I sing it.
Step 2: Sing whole song again. Take responses to your question from a few children.
Transition: Let's look at the screen and sing the whole song together.

Step 3: Sing whole song again with children as you point to words on transparency.
Transition: I think we need to go over the words together.
Step 4: Have children read words aloud with you as you point to overhead transparency, correcting pronunciation as you go.
Transition: Now that we're all a little more familiar with the text, let's try to sing the whole song again.
Step 5: Lead children through singing whole song again without pointing to each word. Repeat without transparency.
Transition: I'd like you to listen carefully while you're singing and tell me what you think of how you sound.
Step 6: Take responses, then ask for suggestions about how to make it sound more like frogs this time. Lead class in singing it again.

C. **Concluding the Lesson:** Give specific praise, based on the sound of the singing. Explain how song will be part of afternoon's language arts activity.

TEACHING STUDENTS TO SING IN HARMONY

One aspect of singing that clearly differentiates younger and older children is the ability of intermediate age students to sing harmony. The challenge and satisfaction gained in this type of singing creates both intrinsic motivation for continued musical learning as well as aesthetic pleasure. The easiest type of two-part singing for children who are in third grade or older is the singing of **partner songs.** Partner songs are songs that complement each other and can be sung at exactly the same time. A list of these songs appears below.

The first step in teaching a class to sing partner songs would be to have the children learn each song independently. The next step in the process will be for the class to sing one song while the teacher sings the other. When these two steps are achieved, then the class should be divided and challenged to sing both songs simultaneously. One example of two songs that work well are "All Night, All Day" (figure 4.16, p. 94) and "Swing Low, Sweet Chariot" (figure 3.35, p. 65). Partner songs are the easiest way for children to learn to sing harmonically because each of the songs is different both melodically and textually from its partner.

PARTNER SONGS

Figures 4.53, 4.54, 4.56, and 4.57 present four pairs of partner songs. Figure 4.55 presents three songs that can be sung at the same time. Figures 4.58, 4.59, and 4.60 present three songs each of which is composed of parts that can be sung together as partner songs.

Figure 4.53

Ezekiel Saw the Wheel

African-American Spiritual

Figure 4.53 *continued*

Now Let Me Fly

Figure 4.54

Three Blind Mice

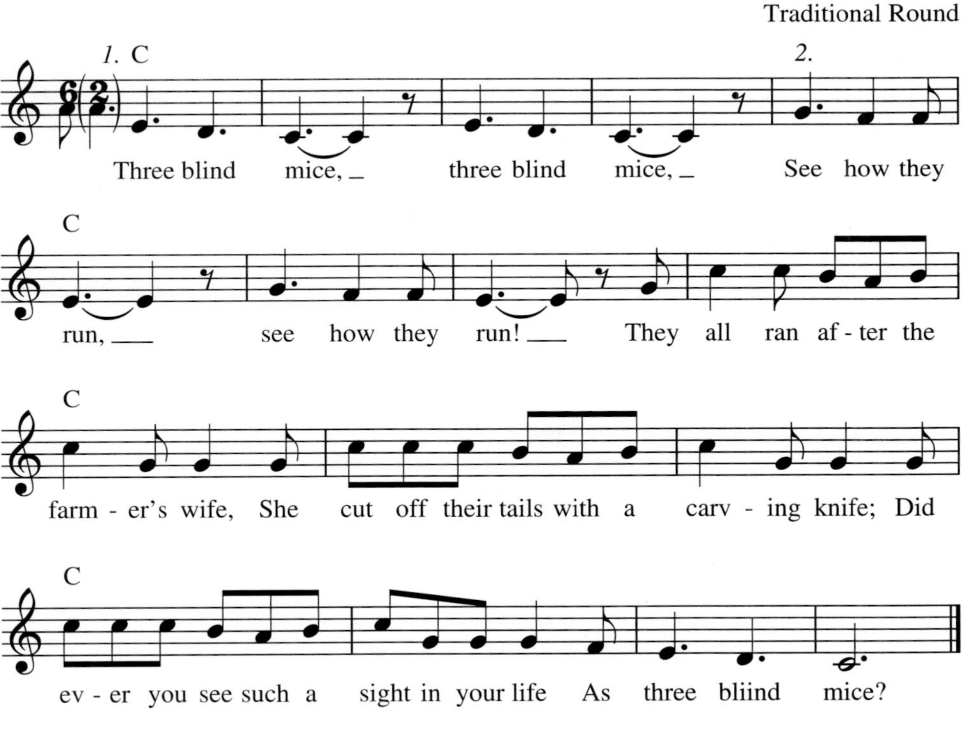

farm - er's wife, She cut off their tails with a carv - ing knife; Did

ev - er you see such a sight in your life As three bliind mice?

Row, Row, Row Your Boat

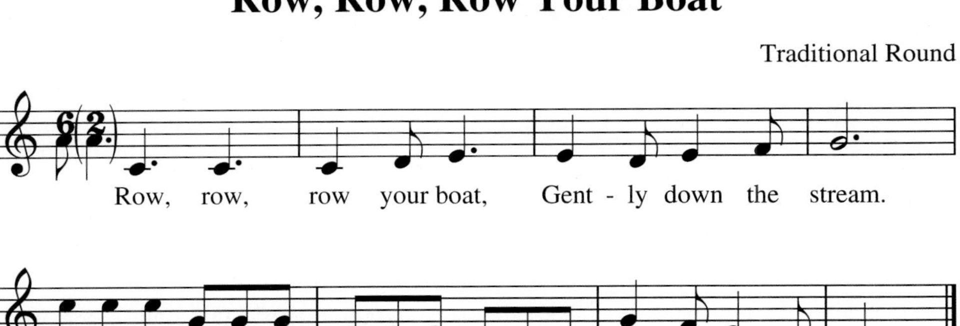

Traditional Round
run, ___ see how they run! ___ They all ran af - ter the
Row, row, row your boat, Gent - ly down the stream.
Mer-ri - ly, mer-ri - ly, mer-ri - ly, mer-ri - ly, Life is but a dream.

Figure 4.55

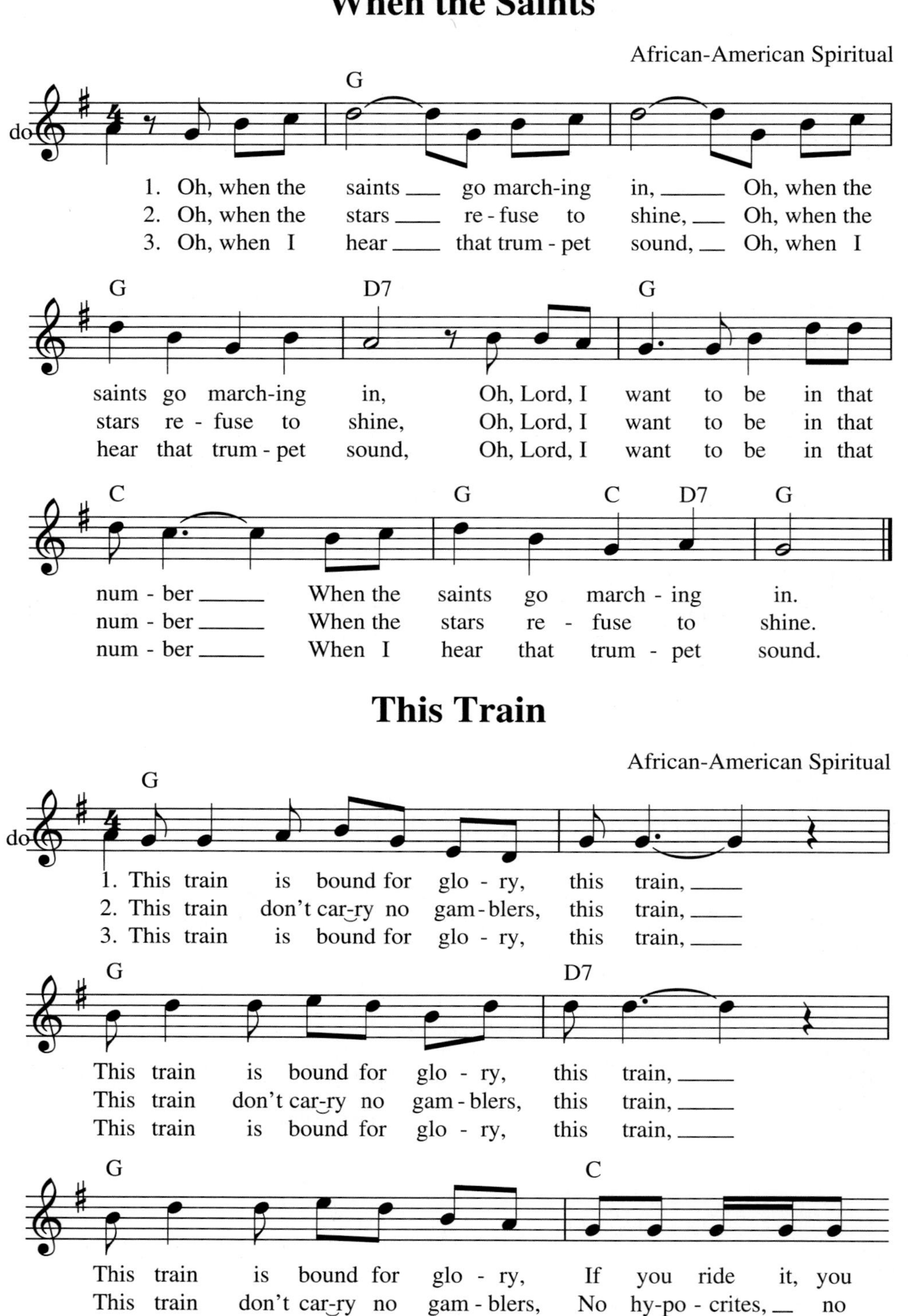
When the Saints
African-American Spiritual
do
G
1. Oh, when the saints ___ go march-ing in, ___ Oh, when the
2. Oh, when the stars ___ re-fuse to shine, ___ Oh, when the
3. Oh, when I hear ___ that trum-pet sound, ___ Oh, when I
G D7 G
saints go march-ing in, Oh, Lord, I want to be in that
stars re-fuse to shine, Oh, Lord, I want to be in that
hear that trum-pet sound, Oh, Lord, I want to be in that
C G C D7 G
num-ber ___ When the saints go march-ing in.
num-ber ___ When the stars re-fuse to shine.
num-ber ___ When I hear that trum-pet sound.
This Train
African-American Spiritual
do
G
1. This train is bound for glo-ry, this train, ___
2. This train don't car-ry no gam-blers, this train, ___
3. This train is bound for glo-ry, this train, ___
G D7
This train is bound for glo-ry, this train, ___
This train don't car-ry no gam-blers, this train, ___
This train is bound for glo-ry, this train, ___
G C
This train is bound for glo-ry, If you ride it, you
This train don't car-ry no gam-blers, No hy-po-crites, ___ no
This train is bound for glo-ry, Don't car-ry noth-ing but the
C G D7 G
must be ho-ly, This train is bound for glo-ry, this train. ___
mid-night ram-blers, This train is bound for glo-ry, this train. ___
righ-teous and the ho-ly, This train is bound for glo-ry, this train. ___

Figure 4.55 *continued*

Good Night, Ladies
Traditional
Good night, la-dies! Good night, la-dies!
Good night, la-dies! We're going to leave you now.
Mer - ri - ly we roll a - long, roll a - long, roll a - long.
Mer - ri - ly we roll a - long, o'er the deep blue sea.

Figure 4.56

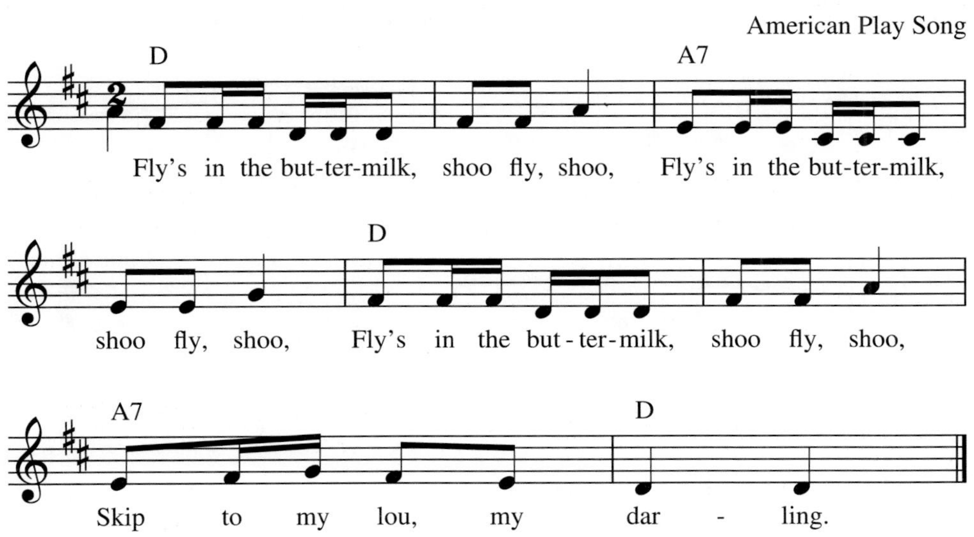
Skip to My Lou
American Play Song
D
A7
Fly's in the but-ter-milk, shoo fly, shoo, Fly's in the but-ter-milk,
D
shoo fly, shoo, Fly's in the but - ter-milk, shoo fly, shoo,
A7
D
Skip to my lou, my dar - ling.

Figure 4.56 *continued*

Figure 4.57

Viva L'Amour

College Song
F Bb C7 F C7
Let ev-'ry good fel-low now join in a song, Vi-va la com-pa-
F Bb C7 F C7 F
gnie, Suc-cess to each oth-er and pass it a-long, Vi-va la com-pa - gnie!
F Bb C7 F
Vi-va la vi-va la vi-va l'a-mour, Vi-va la vi-va la vi-va l'a-mour,
F Bb C7 F
Vi-va l'a-mour, vi-va l'a-mour, Vi-va la com-pa - gnie!

Down the River

American River Chantey

do
F Bb F
The riv-er is up and the chan-nel is deep, The wind is stead-y and

C7 F Bb F C7 F
strong. Oh, won't we have a jol-ly good time, As we go sail-ing a-long.

F Bb C7 F
Down the riv-er, Oh, down the riv-er, Oh, down the riv-er we go.

F Bb C7 F
Down the riv-er, Oh, down the riv-er, Oh, down the O - hi - o!

Figure 4.58

Dobbin, Dobbin

Dutch Tune

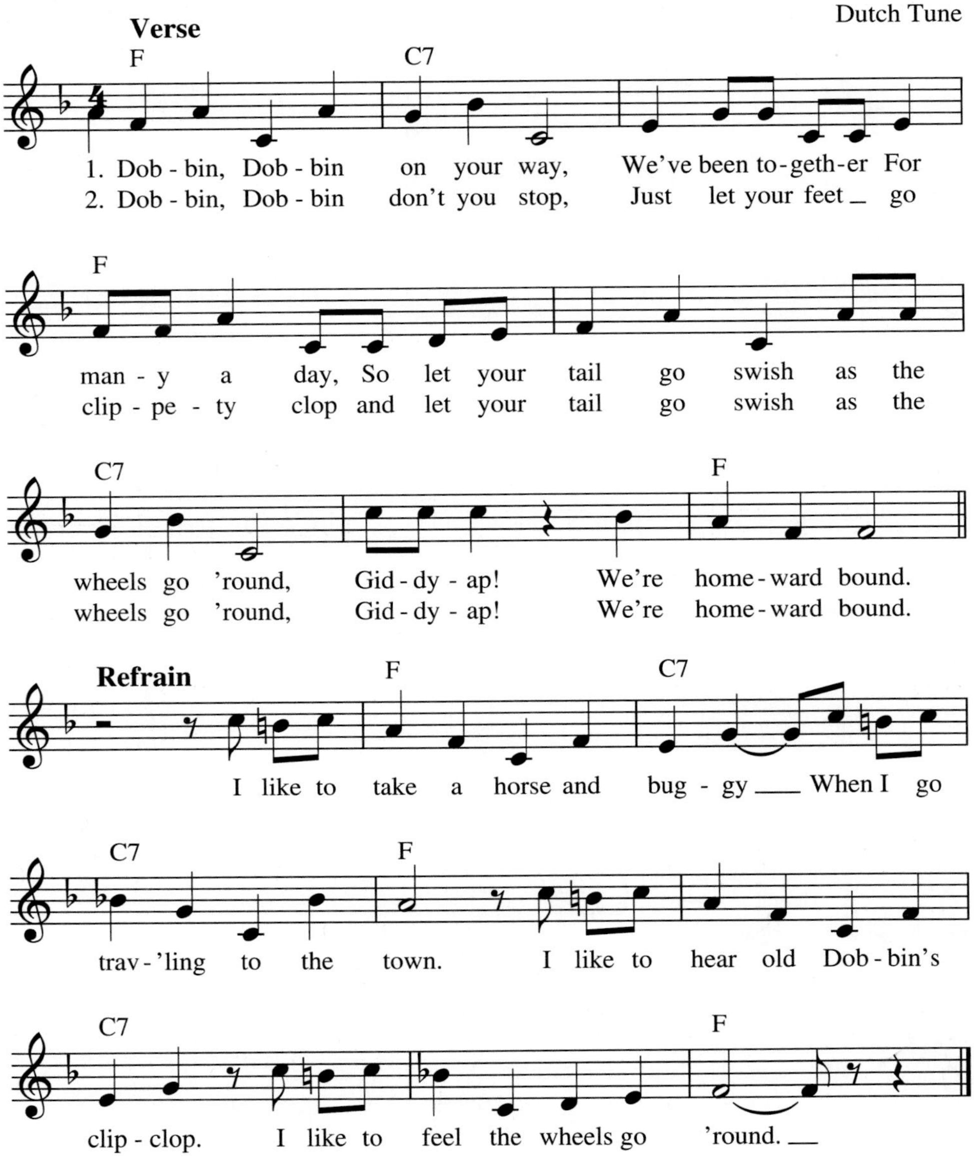

Verse
F
C7
1. Dob - bin, Dob - bin on your way, We've been to-geth-er For
2. Dob - bin, Dob - bin don't you stop, Just let your feet _ go
F
man - y a day, So let your tail go swish as the
clip - pe - ty clop and let your tail go swish as the
C7
F
wheels go 'round, Gid - dy - ap! We're home - ward bound.
wheels go 'round, Gid - dy - ap! We're home - ward bound.
Refrain
F
C7
I like to take a horse and bug - gy ___ When I go
C7
F
trav - 'ling to the town. I like to hear old Dob - bin's
C7
F
clip - clop. I like to feel the wheels go 'round. ___

Figure 4.59

Tina Singu

Folk Song from Lesotho

Verse
Ti - na sing - u le - lu - vu - tae - o wat-sha, wat-sha, wat-sha ti - na.
Ti - na sing - u le - lu - vu - tae - o wat-sha, wat-sha, wat-sha.

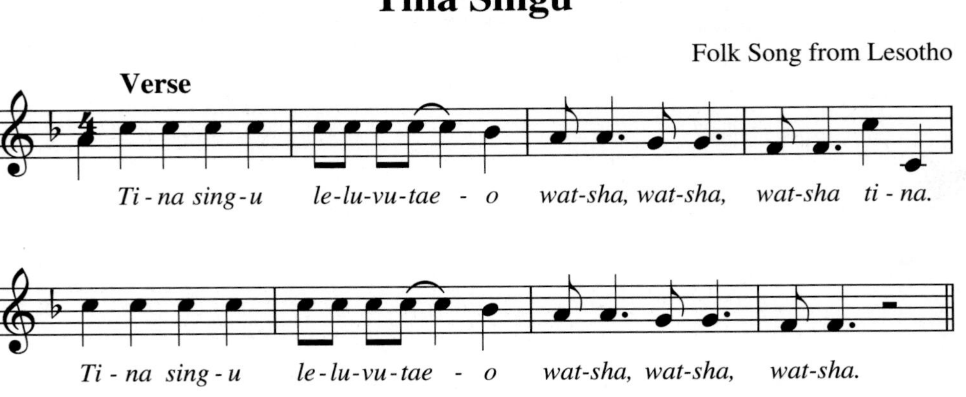

Figure 4.59 *continued*

Refrain
Wat-sha, ___ wat-sha, ___ wat-sha, wat-sha, wat-sha. ___
Wat-sha, ___ wat-sha, ___ wat-sha, wat-sha, wat-sha. ___

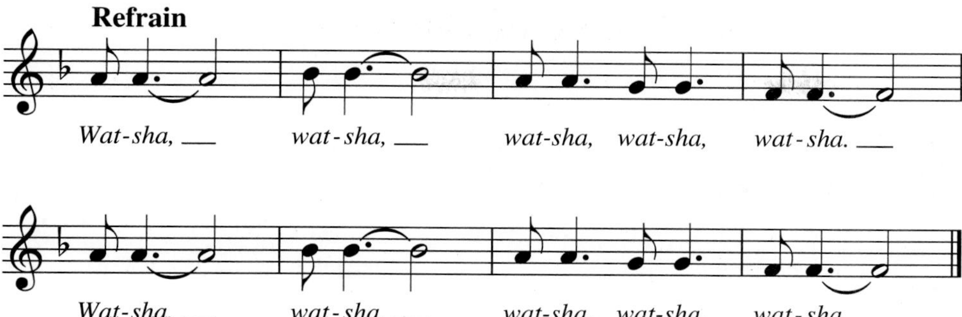

Figure 4.60

One Bottle of Pop

Traditional

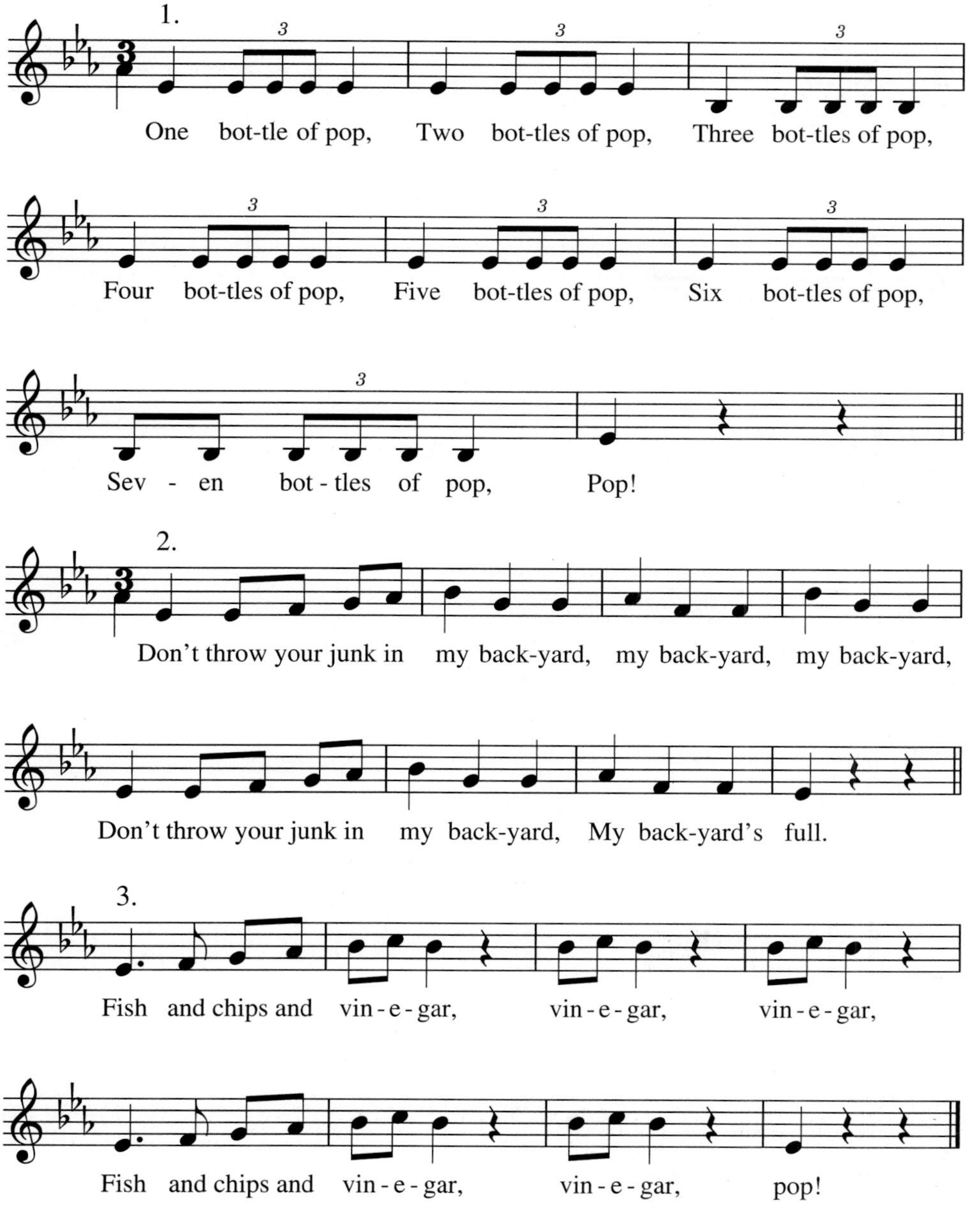

1.
One bot-tle of pop, Two bot-tles of pop, Three bot-tles of pop,
Four bot-tles of pop, Five bot-tles of pop, Six bot-tles of pop,
Sev - en bot - tles of pop, Pop!
2.
Don't throw your junk in my back-yard, my back-yard, my back-yard,
Don't throw your junk in my back-yard, My back-yard's full.
3.
Fish and chips and vin - e - gar, vin - e - gar, vin - e - gar,
Fish and chips and vin - e - gar, vin - e - gar, pop!

LESSON PLANNING ACTIVITY Directions: You plan to use the song "Little Red Caboose" (figure 4.61) in a unit on transportation, but first you need to teach it to your primary class. Fill in the lesson plan form below, based on the examples given in the text.

Figure 4.61

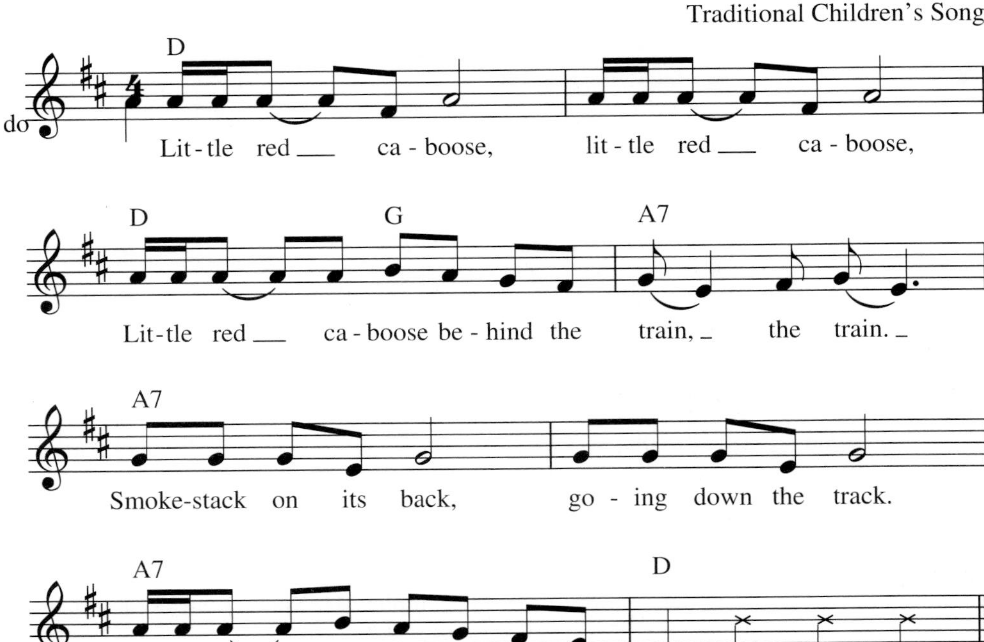
Little Red Caboose
Traditional Children's Song
D
do
Lit-tle red ___ ca - boose, lit - tle red ___ ca - boose,
D G A7
Lit-tle red ___ ca - boose be - hind the train, _ the train. _
A7
Smoke-stack on its back, go - ing down the track.
A7 D
Lit-tle red ___ ca - boose be - hind the train. Woo - woo - woo!

I. Learning Outcome or Objective:

Entry level:

Exit level:

II. Lesson Evaluation or Assessment Procedures:

III. Materials and Board/Space Preparation:

IV. Teaching Procedures:

A. Setting the Stage:

B. Developing the Lesson:

Step 1:

Transition question:

Step 2:

Transition question:

Step 3:

Transition question:

Step 4:

Transition question:

C. Concluding the Lesson:

GREAT HITS FOR YOUR CLASSROOM

The following list of songs is organized into three levels (K–2, 3–4, and 5–6). These are songs that children love to sing.

Level	Songs
K–2	Old MacDonald (Figure 4.62)
	The Farmer in the Dell (Figure 4.63)
	Little Red Caboose (See Figure 4.61)
	Michael Finnigan (Figure 4.64)
	One Little Elephant (Figure 4.65)
	Kye Kye Kule (See Figure 4.26)
	Three Pirates (Figure 4.66)
Grades 3–4	America the Beautiful (Figure 4.67)
	Dipidu (See Figure 4.8)
	One More River (See Figure 4.37)
	Old Dan Tucker (Figure 4.68)
	Oh, Won't You Sit Down? (Figure 4.69)
	Day-O (See Figure 4.47)
Grades 5–6	Go Down, Moses (See Figure 3.25)
	Dry Bones (See Figure 4.54)
	Simple Gifts (See Figure 4.41)
	Matilda (Figure 4.70)
	Siyahamba (See Figure 4.55)
	Battle Hymn of the Republic (See Figure 4.45)

Figure 4.62

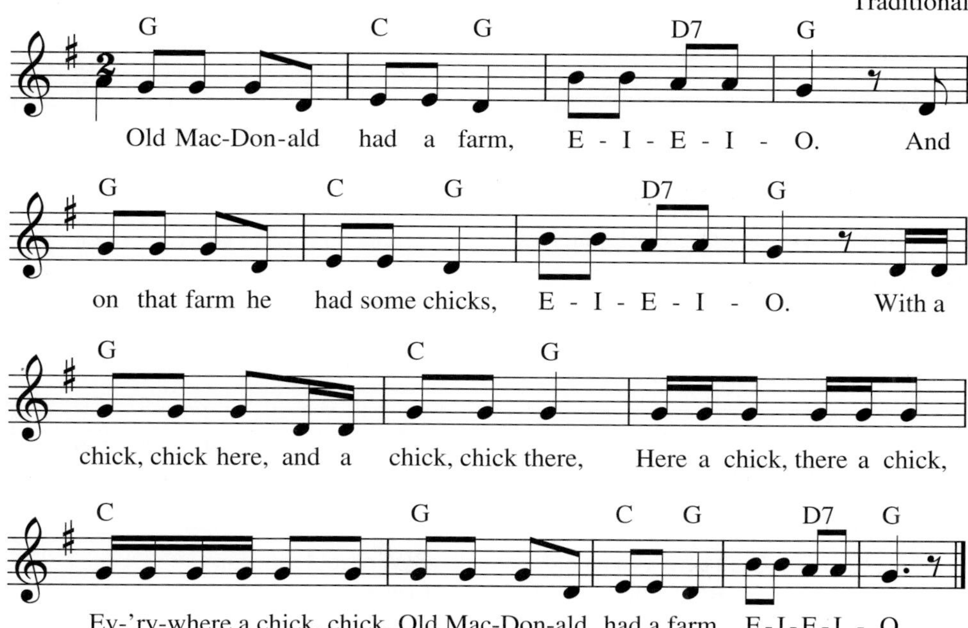
Old MacDonald
Traditional
G C G D7 G
Old Mac-Don-ald had a farm, E - I - E - I - O. And
G C G D7 G
on that farm he had some chicks, E - I - E - I - O. With a
G C G
chick, chick here, and a chick, chick there, Here a chick, there a chick,
C G C G D7 G
Ev-'ry-where a chick, chick. Old Mac-Don-ald had a farm, E-I-E-I - O.

2. . . . on that farm he had some ducks . . .
   With a quack, quack here . . .

3. . . . on that farm he had some pigs . . .
   With an oink, oink here . . .

Figure 4.63

The Farmer in the Dell

Singing Game

F
The farm-er in the dell, the farm-er in the dell,
F C7 F
Heigh - ho the der - ry - o, the farm - er in the dell.

2. The farmer takes a wife . . .
3. The wife takes a child . . .
4. The child takes a nurse . . .
5. The nurse takes a dog . . .
6. The dog takes a cat . . .
7. The cat takes a rat . . .
8. The rat takes the cheese . . .
9. The cheese stands alone . . .

Figure 4.64

Michael Finnegan

American Folk Song

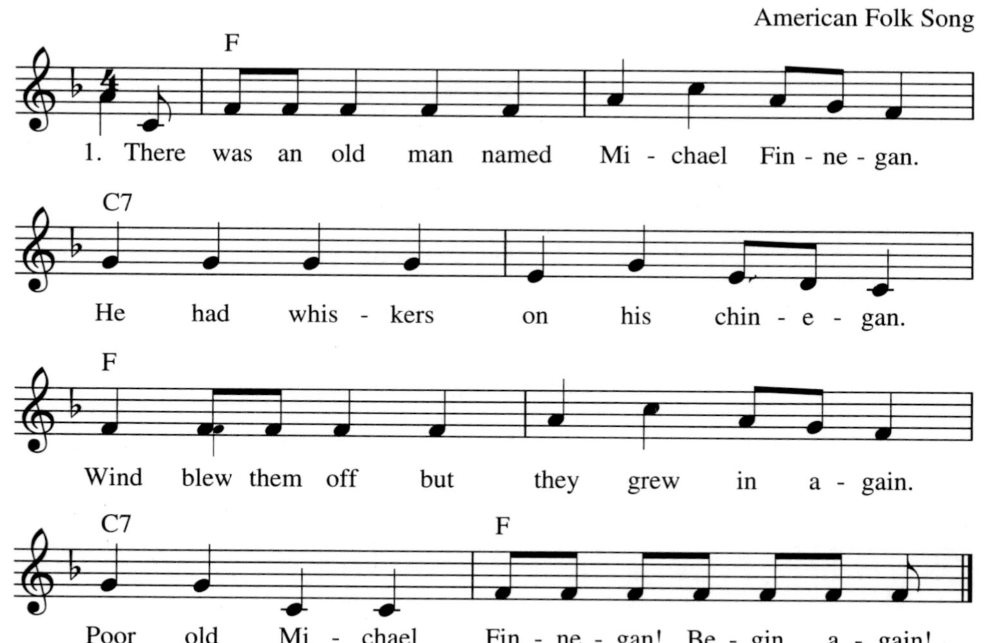
F
1. There was an old man named Mi - chael Fin - ne - gan.
C7
He had whis - kers on his chin - e - gan.
F
Wind blew them off but they grew in a - gain.
C7 F
Poor old Mi - chael Fin - ne - gan! Be - gin a - gain!

2. There was an old man named Michael Finnegan.
   Built a house of sticks and tin again.
   Wind came along and blew it in again.
   Poor old Michael Finnegan! Begin again!

3. There was an old man named Michael Finnegan.
   Went out fishing with a pin again.
   Caught a whale that jumped back in again.
   Poor old Michael Finnegan! Begin again!

Figure 4.65

One Little Elephant

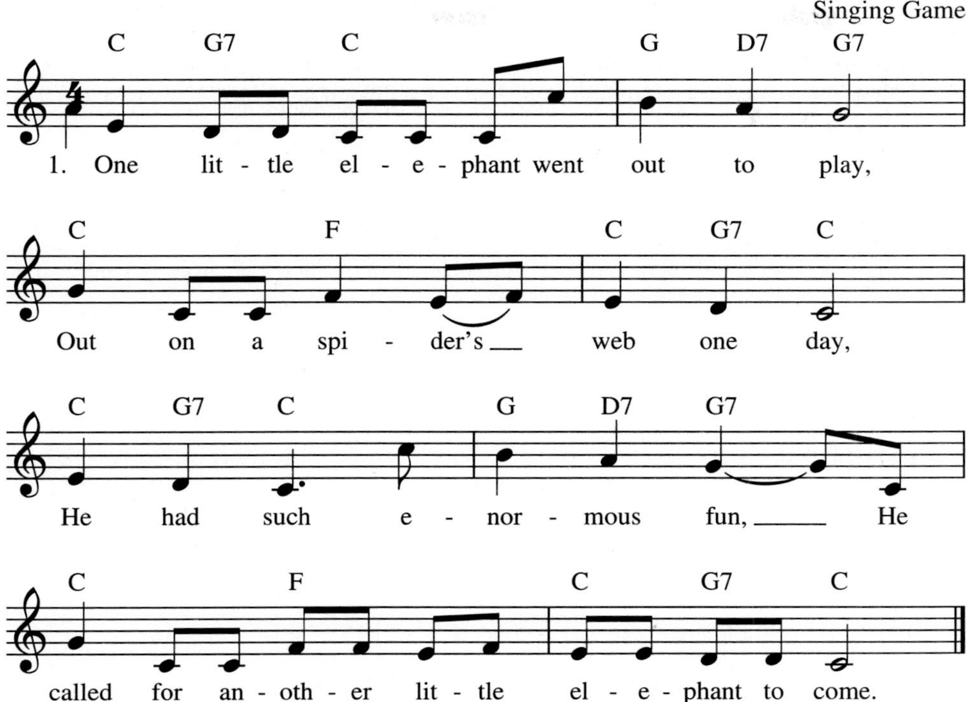

2. Two little elephants went out to play,
Out on a spider's web one day.
They had such enormous fun,
They called for another little elephant to come.

3. Three little elephants went out to play . . .

Figure 4.66

Three Pirates

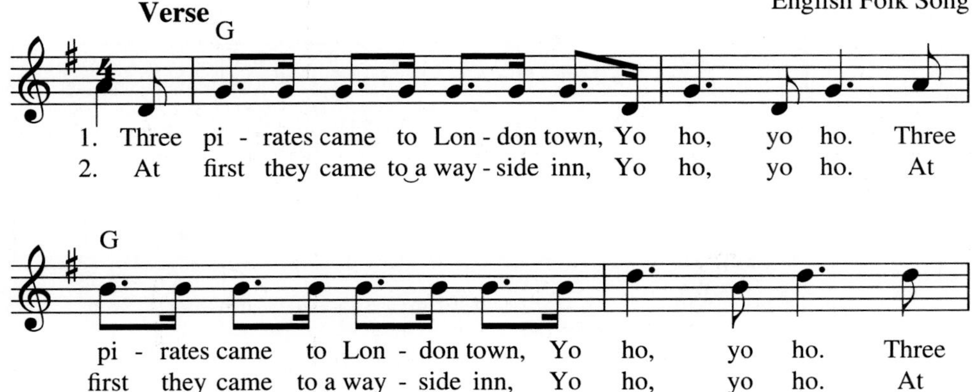

Figure 4.66 *continued*

C G D7 G D7
pi - rates came to Lon - don town To see the King put on his crown.
first they came to a way - side inn, And said, "Good land - lord, let us in."

Refrain

G
Yo ho, you lub-bers, Yo ho, you lub-bers, Yo ho, yo ho, yo ho!

3. "O landlord, have you lots of gold,
   Yo ho, yo ho.
   O landlord, have you lots of gold,
   Yo ho, yo ho.
   O landlord, have you lots of gold,
   Enough to fill the afterhold?" *Refrain*

Figure 4.67

America the Beautiful

Katharine Lee Bates — Samuel Ward

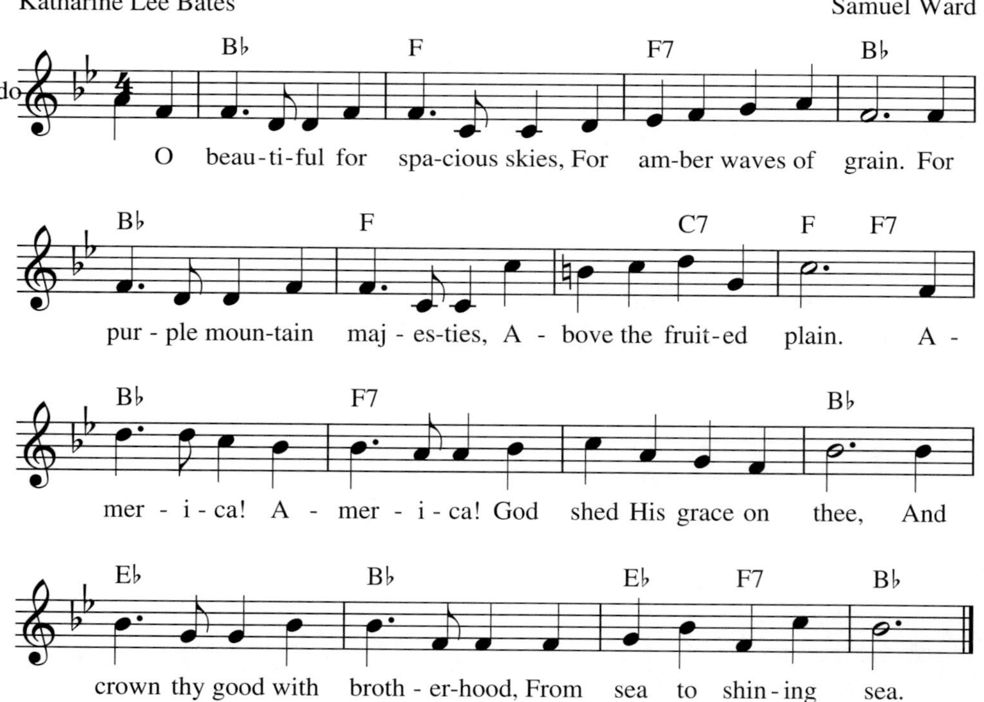
do
B♭ F F7 B♭
O beau-ti-ful for spa-cious skies, For am-ber waves of grain. For
B♭ F C7 F F7
pur - ple moun-tain maj - es-ties, A - bove the fruit-ed plain. A -
B♭ F7 B♭
mer - i - ca! A - mer - i - ca! God shed His grace on thee, And
E♭ B♭ E♭ F7 B♭
crown thy good with broth - er-hood, From sea to shin - ing sea.

Figure 4.68

Old Dan Tucker

Verse

American Folk Song

do

G

1. Old Dan Tuck - er's a fine old man.
2. Old Dan Tuck - er be - gan in ear- ly life, To

G D7 G

Washed his face in a fry - ing pan, Combed his head with a
play the ban - jo ___ and the fife. He'd play the boys and _

G D7

wag - on wheel, And died with a tooth - ache in his heel.
gals to sleep, And then in - to his bunk he'd creep.

Refrain

G C D7

Get out the way, Old Dan Tuck-er, You're too late to

G C

get your sup-per. Sup - per's o - ver and din - ner's cook-in', And

D7 G

Old Dan Tuck - er's just stand - in' look - in'.

Figure 4.69

Oh, Won't You Sit Down?

Figure 4.69 *continued*

G
C
D7
sit down? Lord, I can't sit down. 'Cause I
G7
C
D7
G
Fine
just got to Heav-en, gon-na look a - round.
Verse
1. Five thou-sand dol-lars, friend, I
Call
G
Response
G7
C
1. Who's that yon-der dressed in red? Must be the chil-dren that
2. Who's that yon-der dressed in blue? Must be the chil-dren that are
D7
G
Call
Mo-ses led. Who's that yon-der dressed in white?
com-in' through. Who's that yon-der dressed in black?
Response
G
Da Capo al Fine
D7
G
Must be the chil-dren of the Is-rael-ite.
Must be the hy-po-crites a-turn-in' back.

Figure 4.70

Matilda

Ma - til - da, Ma - til - da,

Figure 4.70 *continued*

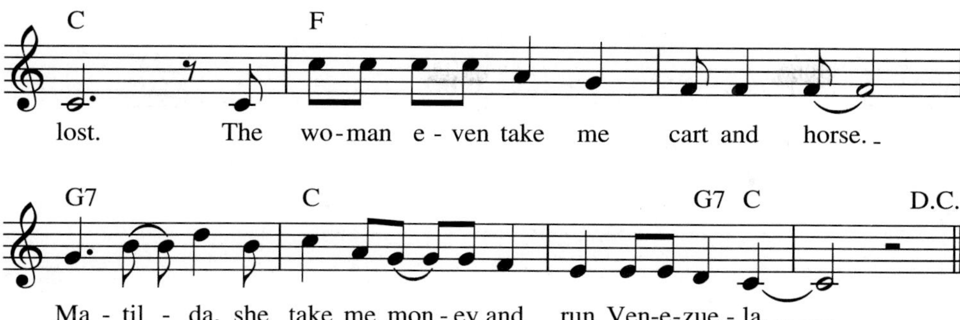

lost. The wo-man e - ven take me cart and horse.

2. My money was to buy me house and land,
   The woman she got a serious plan.
   Matilda, she take me money and run Venezuela.
   Refrain

3. Now the money was safe in me bed,
   Stuck in the pillow beneath my head,
   But Matilda, she find me money and run Venezuela.
   Refrain

4. Never will I love again.
   All me money gone in vain
   'Cause Matilda, she take me money and run Venezuela.
   Refrain

CHOOSING SONGS THAT YOUNGER CHILDREN WILL LOVE

After singing the songs in this chapter that the authors have identified as favorites of young children, you may wonder what there is about "One More River" and "Kye Kye Kule" that make them appeal to young singers. Even more importantly, how can you choose songs that will be hits with your class? You are going to practice analyzing the melody and words of songs in this section of the chapter. Here are two songs that could be used with young children. Look at each song carefully with a partner and make two lists. Title the first list "Words" and the second list "Tune." How can you describe the words and tune of each of these examples?

Figure 4.71

We Are Little Candles

Traditional

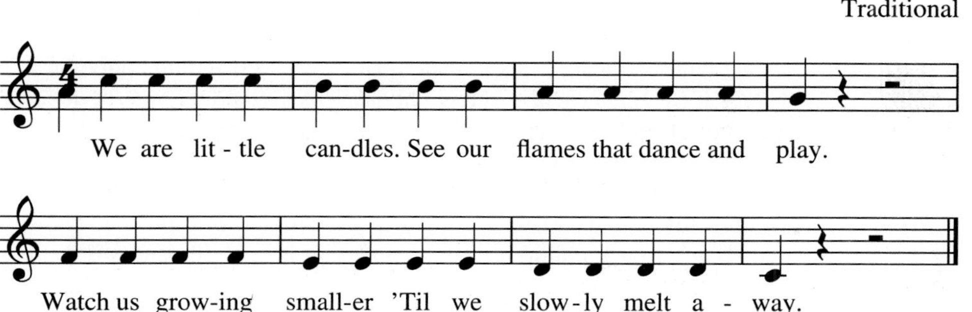

We are lit - tle can-dles. See our flames that dance and play.
Watch us grow-ing small-er 'Til we slow-ly melt a - way.

Figure 4.71 *continued*

Oh, My Aunt Came Back

Traditional

1. Oh, my aunt came back (oh, my aunt came back) from Hon - o -

lu (from Hon - o - lu), And she brought with her (and she brought with

her) A wood - en shoe (a wood - en shoe).

2. . . . from old Japan . . . a waving fan.
3. . . . from old Algiers . . . a pair of shears.
4. . . . from Guadalupe . . . a hoola hoop.
5. . . . from the New York Fair . . . a rocking chair.
6. . . . from the City Zoo . . . a monkey like you.

When you look carefully at "Oh, My Aunt Came Back," you will see that the words of the song are interesting and humorous and would appeal to children. The text of the song is very vivid in images and the continual addition of verses is a challenge for young singers. In contrast, the text of "We Are Little Candles" is banal and commonplace.

The melody of "We Are Little Candles" is only step-wise and the rhythm has no contrast at all. The melody of "Oh, My Aunt Came Back" has both skips and steps with contrasts of quarter notes and eighth notes. The repetition of each phrase contributes to making the song easy for children to learn. Based on this analysis, you would choose "Oh, My Aunt Came Back" and reject "We Are Little Candles" as a possible hit song for your class.

When you begin to select songs for your class you may be looking for a song that integrates with a topic in social studies, science, or another subject area. You may be pleased to find a song with text that seems to match. However, you should apply the following test to every song you choose for young children: study the text and the melody for appropriateness and appeal. You will be singing the song many times, and if you choose a song that has uninteresting words and melody, you will soon be bored—and so will the children. Singing with your class can be a pleasurable activity, but uninteresting songs will quickly dull the enjoyment for both you and your children. In addition, you want to insure that what you ask children to learn and sing is valuable and worth their time and energy.

As already noted earlier in this chapter, an excellent source of music for children is folk music. Folk music has evolved and been transmitted through the aural tradition. In order for a song to be remembered and shared with others, it had to have interesting text and melody. Whether you are looking for a counting song, a song about seasons, a holiday song, or a song about transportation, look for a folk song. Counting songs such as "This Old Man" or "Ten Little Angels" have endured and appeal to children not because they contain numbers but because they have text with strong images and the melody has an interesting tune and rhythm.

Some songs without repetition of text often contain images that can be demonstrated by gesture or pictures. "The Eency Weency Spider" (figure 4.7) is a favorite song of young children that includes no repetition of words; however, the hand gestures that accompany this song make it possible for children to remember the sequence clearly. "Barnyard Song" (figure 4.5) is also a favorite with children. The additive sounds of each animal are repeated at the end of each verse. Simple line drawings (see figure 4.87, the end of this chapter) make it possible for the entire class to remember the animal order.

Where will you go to try to find good singing literature for your class? Some excellent sources are the music series textbooks that have very clear and detailed indexes. There are currently two sets of music textbooks: one is published by MacMillan, the other by Silver Burdett/Ginn. Each series includes teacher textbooks for grades K–8 and student texts for grades 1–8. In addition, each grade level text has a CD set that includes all of the songs and listening selections. In addition to the currently published books, any of the older series texts also contain good material and clear indexes.

Check your public library for other sources, including books of folk songs for children such the Fireside Book of Folk Songs or the volumes compiled by Tom Glazer. Another good source for folk music is West Music. See Appendix F for additional resources.

You may be very tempted to buy tapes and CDs of music by popular performers of children's music and try to use these as teaching tools. While such music initially appears to be appealing due to catchy texts, the songs are often too long and are written in the adult vocal range at the adult level of difficulty. There are many tapes and CDs available that can be used with singing activities in your classroom. Many of these fine sources are listed in Appendix F. However, the authors of this text want to emphasize the importance of teaching children songs through the rote or whole song methods outlined in this chapter **BEFORE** you add any accompaniment to the children's singing. Accompaniments mask children's voices, making it very difficult for you to hear whether your students are really matching the pitches correctly. Accompaniments prevent children from hearing themselves and their classmates and actually reduce the accuracy of the class's singing. The rule of thumb for adding any accompaniment (including piano, guitar, or recorded music) is that unless the class can sing the song accurately on their own, they are not ready for any kind of accompaniment—even though the tape or CD is really appealing to both you and your students.

CHOOSING SONGS FOR OLDER CHILDREN

Music that older children love to sing is more complex than that used with younger pupils. The melody of the song should have a good mix of **skips** and **steps** and can include wider **intervals** as well. The rhythm should be fairly complex, using even and uneven rhythms and subdivisions of the beat. Children of this age also prefer songs that have a fairly quick and/or changing **tempo.** The texts of the songs should be interesting and tell an engaging or unusual story. The songs selected can be much longer and have multiple verses since the children are able to read the text.

Figure 4.72 presents two songs that could be used when teaching about types of work in different countries. As in the previous activity, look at each song carefully with a partner and make two lists, one titled "Text" and the other "Melody." How would you describe these characteristics in each of the following examples?

Figure 4.72

Sheep Shearing

Swedish Folk Song

F

1. Go get the sheep, we're clip - ping to - day,
2. Tell Moth - er dear we're card - ing to - day,

C7 F

Clip - ping their wool, yes, clip - ping their wool
Card - ing the wool, yes, card - ing the wool

F

So we can knit some stock - ings for you.
So we can knit a scarf for her, too.

C7 F

Then we shall dance till morn - ing.
Then we shall dance till morn - ing.

Refrain

C7 F C7 F

Surr, surr, surr, surr, surr, surr. Wheel spins a-round, now hear the sound:

C7 F C7 F

Surr, surr, surr, surr, surr, surr. Then we shall dance till morn-ing.

Click Go the Shears

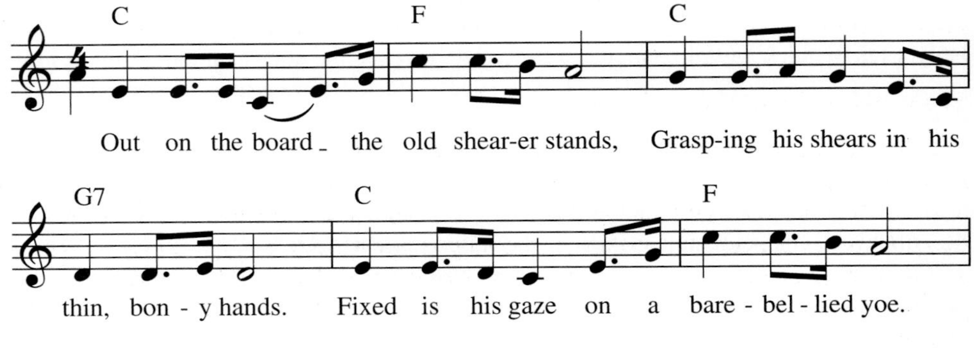

C F C

Out on the board_ the old shear-er stands, Grasp-ing his shears in his

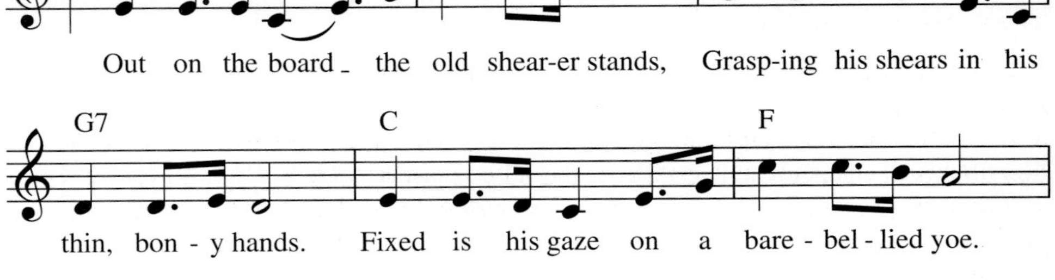

G7
C
F
thin, bon - y hands. Fixed is his gaze on a bare - bel - lied yoe.

Figure 4.72 *continued*

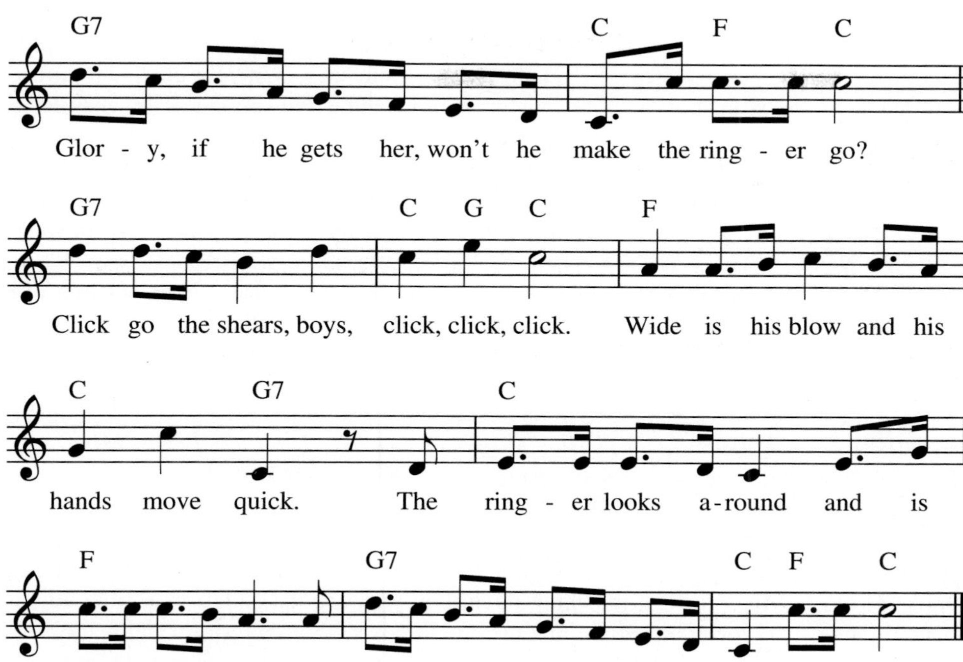
G7 C F C
Glor - y, if he gets her, won't he make the ring - er go?
G7 C G C F
Click go the shears, boys, click, click, click. Wide is his blow and his
C G7 C
hands move quick. The ring - er looks a-round and is
F G7 C F C
beat-en by a blow, And curs-es the old snog-ger with the bare-bel-lied yoe.

When you look carefully at "Sheep Shearing" and "Click Go the Shears," you will note that both songs have **refrains.** If you say the words in your head, however, you will compare the descriptive and alliterative text of the "click go the shears, boys, click, click, click" to the repetitive "surr, surr, surr." The Australian song text is very descriptive of the task and shearer while the Swedish song's text is less appealing to older children because the images are less clearly related to actual work.

The melody of "Sheep Shearing" contains many similar skips in the first two lines and repeated scale movement in the refrain. "Click Go the Shears" also has repetition in the verse section but the second phrase ends in a different manner than the first, providing more contrast and interest. In addition, the song has wider skips and a much more interesting dotted rhythm.

ACTIVITY Sing "Sheep Shearing" and "Click Go the Shears" with your instructor. Note the rhythmic interest and appeal of the dotted eighth and sixteenth notes in the Australian tune.

The same sources consulted for songs for younger children will also prove to be valuable resources for songs for older children. Series texts, no matter what the publication date, will include good examples of folk music and clear indexes to help you. Choosing good songs for children to sing is not a hit-or-miss proposition. It is a skill that you have learned in this chapter and will continue to develop throughout your teaching career. The time that you invest in choosing good songs for your class is time well spent.

SPECIAL NEEDS SINGERS

One of the greatest challenges for the classroom teacher who sings with the class is to help each child to use his or her singing voice effectively. Children with diagnosed learning difficulties often have trouble matching pitch and remembering the words to songs. Children who are otherwise academically "normal" may be "special needs" when it comes to singing. The good news is that any individual help you can provide will make a difference, although this difference is often incremental over time rather than immediate.

Music teachers label children with pitch-matching difficulties as "uncertain singers" rather than using other less-accurate terms such as "tone deaf." The problem of matching pitch with your singing voice is complex, calling on listening skills as well as vocal production skills. The best way for you to help the uncertain singers in your class is to infuse your teaching day with short activities that require listening and singing. Echo answering is one such activity. Instead of asking a math question in your speaking voice, sing the question using two comfortably low pitches. The answering child then sings her or his response on the same two pitches that you sang. You could use the same little echoing exercise to give transition directions such as "First row, line up." The students reply in song, "Yes, Mr. Davis!"

There is likely to be at least one child in your class who clearly does not improve over time and whose singing sounds much lower than that of the others. You can help this child improve through individual "singing tutoring" where no one else can hear you such as in the hallway or in an extra room. You can find the little time this takes in your school day if you look for it—perhaps five minutes during recess or at the very end of the lunch period.

The following exercise helps the child learn what it feels like to match pitch with someone else, something that uncertain singers need to learn. Have the child sing a pitch on the syllable "loo." Then you match this pitch by singing it back to the child, using the same syllable. Repeat the exercise, this time having the child sing a different pitch. Once he or she has felt the effect of matching pitch with you, ask the child to describe how it feels. In this way you can be certain that the child knows—both physiologically and cognitively—what it feels like when she or he is, or is not, matching pitch with someone else. This will begin to help the child monitor her or his own singing for pitch accuracy.

Another way to enhance the singing skills of special learners is to help them remember the melodic contour. This can be done by having them draw the shape of the melody in the air while singing it or look at a written graphic representation of the melodic contour. Special learners can also be aided in remembering the words of the song by posters that you can make with pictures or key words that represent the events of the song. Of course, while these aids will benefit everyone in your classroom, they are essential for children with special needs.

USING WHAT YOU HAVE LEARNED IN THIS CHAPTER

CASE STUDY

The last item on the agenda at the first teachers' meeting of the school year is the Patriot's Day celebration. Although this holiday occurs in April, it is a major event in your community, and all classroom teachers are expected to make it a priority in their planning from the beginning of the school year. Your principal, Laura Zawicki, is very supportive of musical and artistic activities and encourages all teachers to integrate the arts into their daily lesson plans wherever they can. In fact, she is quite a proficient piano player and often gives you copies of songs that you could use in the classroom. As she hands out a stack of music to all the teachers seated around the table, the principal says, "Here are the songs we need to teach to all our classes so they can sing them in the Patriot's Day concert." Scanning the list, you find the heading for Kindergarten and discover that you are to teach your class two patriotic songs, "Battle Hymn of the Republic" (figure 4.40, p. 114) and "The Star Spangled Banner" (figure 4.41, p. 115). You check your stack to make sure you have the music and notice that, sure enough, you have a copy of each of the songs you need. As the meeting winds down and you listen to the final comments from the principal, your eye scans the music, and you begin to worry.

Cooperative Questions to Discuss

1. Why are you worried?
2. What, if anything, would you say to the principal?
3. What suggestions would you make to solve the problem?

THE IDEAL CLASSROOM FROM THE CHILD'S PERSPECTIVE

American schools have always been the object of cyclical attempts at reform; the most recent began in the early 1980s. Current trends aimed at enhancing and improving schooling include site-based management, authentic assessment, and national standards. In spite of these trends, however, classroom activity does not look very different now than it did in the early 1980s. James H. Lytle, a superintendent of schools in inner-city Philadelphia, recently described his classroom observations in an article titled "The Inquiring Manager":[3] "A great deal of classroom activity was boring, repetitive, unengaging, and vapid. In many respects my observations were similar to those of John Goodlad [whose observations were reported in his 1984 book, *A Place Called School,* New York: McGraw-Hill].

In the rush to "improve" and "change" schooling in this country, it appears that we have misplaced an important tenet of education—that the learner be involved in constructing knowledge. Involvement, not passivity, is vital for learning to occur. Your task as classroom teacher is to create an essential learning atmosphere for your students through thoughtful and purposeful daily activities. Singing is one such activity that requires active immersion in learning and yields many additional nonmusical benefits.

Singing every day with your class will help establish a sense of community in your classroom that children will find unique in their school experience. Coming together to produce a group sound that depends on each member is a very different type of activity from what one usually finds in classrooms. The emphasis on skill and fact acquisition currently in vogue inevitably creates an atmosphere of individual competition rather than one of group cooperation. Yet, it is known that when they grow into adults, these children will need social and cooperative skills far more than they will need the facts memorized at different levels for state assessment tests. Singing is one way for children to understand that there are artistic activities where the product actually depends on everyone's participation.

Singing every day may be the most memorable aspect of a child's daily life in your classroom. There is a reason that children look forward to "special" teachers and "special" subjects such as art, music, and physical education. It is not because they get to go to a different room, but because in these subjects, children are actively involved in learning in different modes. A current writer in education, Howard Gardner, has hypothesized that there are seven different human intelligences possessed by all learners.[4] Musical intelligence is posited by Gardner as one of these unique ways to experience and learn about our world, and each child's musical intelligence should be nurtured through meaningful, engaging daily musical encounters.

The importance of helping young singers find their singing voice in early grades can not be stressed enough. Singing is one of those skills that adults find very difficult to master while children learn it easily, given the right instruction at the right time. Singing is as natural to young children as moving and breathing! The elementary classroom is a place where those children whose parents did not provide early singing experiences can be taught the important facets of vocal production so they may grow as singers and participants in a rich musical life. You provide an important part of a firm musical foundation for the children you teach when you guide them in singing every day.

NATIONAL STANDARDS FOR SINGING

The Federal Goals 2000 Legislation has provided an impetus for national professional organizations of various disciplines such as history, mathematics, and geography to develop discipline-based standards. The Music Educators National Conference cooperated with other arts organizations to develop K–12 standards in dance, music, theater, and visual arts. These standards are available in a publication titled *National Standards for Arts Education* (Reston, Va.: Music Educators National Conference, 1994). This publication is intended for everyone interested in the quality of arts education in America's schools.

The music standards are described in terms of what a child should be able to do by the end of Grade 4, Grade 8, and Grade 12. Following are the terminal outcomes for Grade 4 for singing:

Students:

1. Sing independently on pitch and in rhythm, with appropriate timbre, diction, and posture, and maintain a steady tempo.
2. Sing expressively with appropriate dynamics, phrasing, and interpretation.
3. Sing from memory a varied repertoire of songs representing ***genres*** and styles from diverse cultures.
4. Sing ostinatos, partner songs, and rounds.
5. Sing in groups, blending vocal timbres, matching dynamic levels, and responding to the cues of a conductor[5] (p. 13).

ACTIVITY Teach one of the songs from the "Greatest Hits" list for level 3–4 (p. 135) to a third- or fourth-grade child. When you think the child knows the song well, make an audio recording of the child's final performance of the song. Later, listen to the tape and evaluate it according to the national standards for singing outlined in the previous section. What singing skills are evident on the tape? Write a paragraph describing your findings.

PLAYING RECORDER

A NEW NOTE

The fourth note that you will learn to play on the recorder is C. The fingering for C is shown in figure 4.80.

Figure 4.73

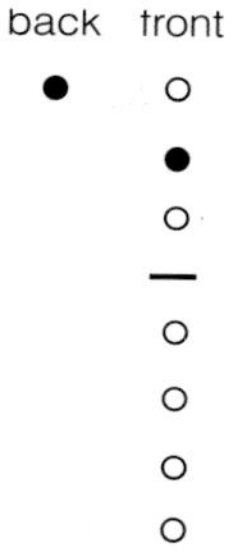

back front

In figure 4.74 you will find a number of notes that look unfamiliar. They are single eighth notes and are simply another way of writing this subdivision of the quarter note.

Figure 4.74

Now that you are familiar with four notes (G, A, B, C) on the recorder, you can explore the **intervals** or distances between the sounds. Figure 4.75 presents examples of these types of intervals—a second, a third, and a fourth. The interval of a second that you will play in figure 4.76 goes from B to A, from G to A, and from B to C. The interval of a third that you will play in figure 4.77 goes from G to B and from A to C. The interval of a fourth that you will play in figure 4.78 goes from G to C. You can determine the distance between two notes on the staff by counting the first note as one and counting the line(s) or space(s) to the next note. On the staves below you will play the three kinds of intervals —seconds, thirds, and fourths.

Figure 4.75

Figure 4.76

Figure 4.77

Figure 4.78

 **ACTIVITY** Practice each line in figures 4.76, 4.77, and 4.78 alone and then with your partner.

ANOTHER DOTTED NOTE

Figure 4.79 presents a line of stick notation for you to practice. Clap the notes at home and then in class with a partner or a small group.

Figure 4.79

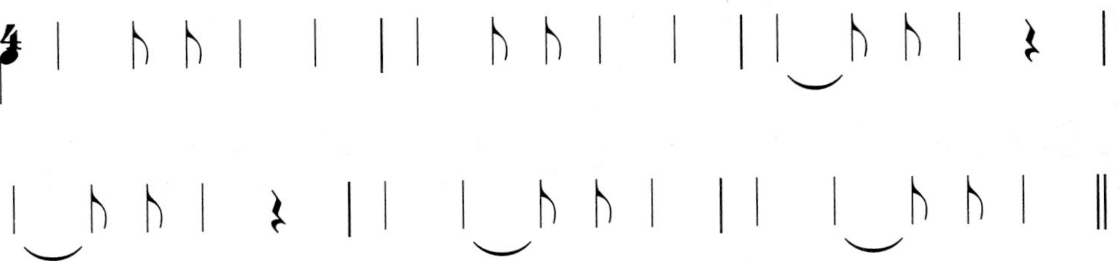

As you learned in the last chapter, there is a simpler way of writing this tied rhythm. Music notation usually uses dotted notes to indicate the tie that you just clapped.

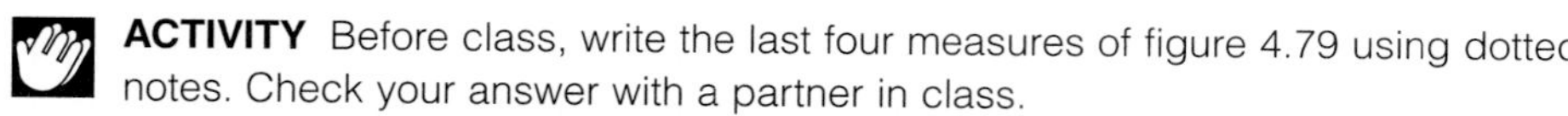

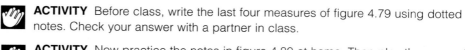

ACTIVITY Before class, write the last four measures of figure 4.79 using dotted notes. Check your answer with a partner in class.

ACTIVITY Now practice the notes in figure 4.80 at home. Then play the new note and the dotted note in class with your partner. After you practice, combine your performance with another pair of partners.

Figure 4.80

PLAYING ALL FOUR NOTES IN A MELODY

Figure 4.81 presents a simple melody that includes all four notes (G, A, B, C) that you have learned to play on the recorder. The example includes dotted notes. Practice playing the melody.

Figure 4.81

TWO DUETS WITH DOTTED NOTES

Practice each line of the duets in figure 4.82 at home so you will be able to play them with a partner. Then combine with another set of partners to play them. Share your performance with your classmates. Be sure that you follow the dynamic markings.

Figure 4.82

Figure 4.87 Drawings to Be Used with "Barnyard Song"

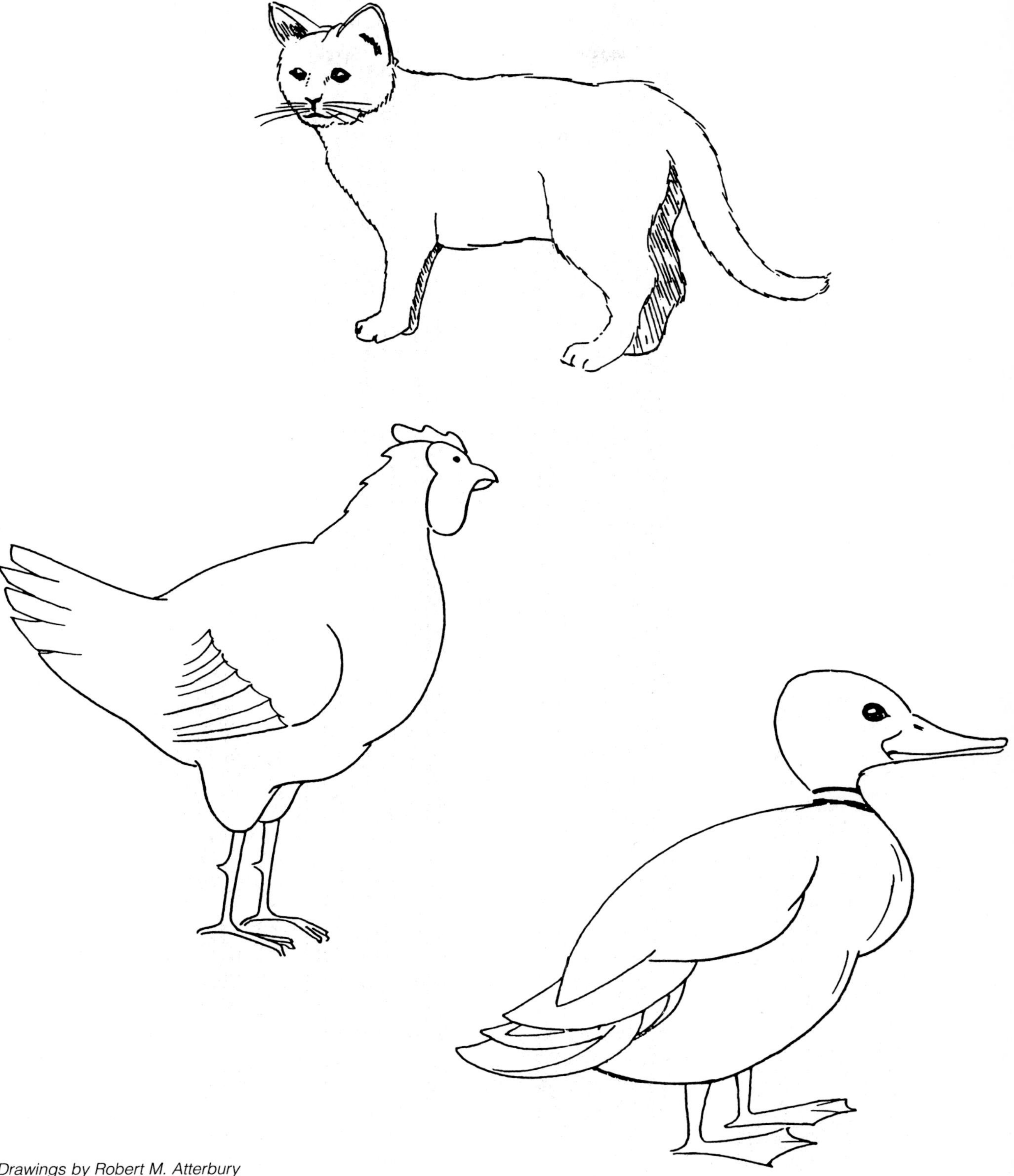

Drawings by Robert M. Atterbury

Music Fundamentals for Listening

What you will be able to do by the end of this chapter

- *Recognize repetition and contrast in songs and listening selections*
- *Identify the form of songs and pieces of music*
- *Follow listening maps*
- *Recognize the sounds of different voices and instruments (timbre)*
- *Play a new note on the recorder*
- *Play harmony with your classmates*

LISTENING ATTENTIVELY

The wonderful thing about listening to music is that human beings come readily equipped with the basic tools to enjoy sound. You don't have to take courses and read thick tomes to sing or to listen to music. Your experience can be so deep and meaningful that you may discover unique emotions that only occur when you are musically involved. Once you have had such an encounter you may realize what an uncommon event you have been involved in.

Even though most human beings are able to hear equally well, they may not really be careful or thoughtful listeners when it comes to music. Today our society needs a constant flow of sound. When most adults enter a quiet room they find some way to eliminate silence. They turn on the television or radio or put on a tape or compact disc to fill the room with sound. When we leave our homes or dormitories, most of our public spaces also have sound "piped in." Some of the music is selected to put shoppers or dental patients in the proper "mood." Many times, however, the music is not selected with any criteria—it is simply to fill silence so people will feel at ease in a particular setting. But all of this music, this constant flow of sound, can result in audiothrombosis. This is a condition where the primary symptom is a numbness to music.

Listening to music should be the opposite of audiothrombosis. When you hear a new song on the radio by your favorite singer or group, you change your usual passive music listening mode to one of active and careful involvement. You tune in very carefully to the sounds and decide whether or not you like what you are hearing. If you have a favorable first impression of the song, the next time you hear it you will listen even more actively and carefully so that you can remember some of the words and ideas that the song contains. This type of listening is very different from the daily musical environment where sound washes over you and leaves no residue behind. The ability to listen so carefully, to remember sounds, and to experience the resulting unique feelings is a basic facet of our humanity.

We often do not acknowledge that musical listening has always been a part of every society and culture. While we do not have any musical artifacts from ancient Greece, we do know that music was important from the writings of Aristotle and Plato and from the visual depictions of musicians on vases. In many other cultures, active listening always has been accompanied by movement, improvised or stylized. In other cultures, including our own, musical presentations are listened to by silent audiences.

The perspective presented in this chapter on the fundamentals of music listening reflects the traditional viewpoint of the western European music theorist. This view treats music as an object that can be isolated, lifted from its cultural context, and studied according to a prescribed set of invented theoretical constructs deemed to be "real." In such study, music must be written in order to be codified, categorized, analyzed, discussed, and understood. Such study includes descriptions of how pieces are put together or occur in time. This theoretical approach also requires a specialized vocabulary called musical terminology.

This particular system is pervasive in the western world as "the way" educated people know about music. Unfortunately, it does not capture the essence of the very music it works on. This essence is the spirit of the music, its richness and beauty, its ability to bring out in the performer or listener a wealth of emotions. In short, the exquisite humanness revealed and experienced in music has nothing to do with your success at knowing musical vocabulary. Such vocabulary does, however, provide a common language to use about music; for this reason, we have included some of it in this chapter.

As stated earlier, this theoretical approach does not deal with the cultural context of music. One facet of cultural context is the time and place in which the music was created or performed and another facet is the special meaning that the music has for a particular community, performer, or creator. This important information about the piece must come from another source. Music historians and ethnomusicologists are the specialists who study music in its cultural contexts as well as in its objective state. In this chapter we will share with you some of the cultural contexts of pieces we have selected for active listening experiences.

Music is valuable to all human beings because it is one of the basic ways that we know about ourselves and our world. Listening is the most accessible window into this type of knowing, but it is a difficult window to go through because careful and active listening is very, very difficult. Our minds can so easily be distracted by our thoughts and surroundings. But this special way of knowing has resulted in artistic expression that has existed and endured throughout human history. It is the hope of the authors that your own private reaction to and understanding of the musical examples in this text will be enhanced by the theoretical and cultural information we have included.

This chapter will introduce you to some important ideas about how we listen to music and in the process, you will become more aware of how exciting active musical listening can be. You will gain confidence in your ability to discriminate what you are hearing in music and you will become much more aware of the amount of music that exists in your daily life. You will listen to the music of many cultures and find that music has some very basic similarities, whether it is produced in America, Australia, or Asia. You will learn to use your innate music listening tools!

CHAPTER GOALS

The goal of this chapter is to enable you to learn how to listen to music in an active and participatory manner. Through class activities you will learn to discriminate, categorize, classify, and analyze different types of music. Some of the music will be songs that you will sing in class and some will be listening selections found on the compact disc that accompanies this text. Still other listening may involve your favorite performers or recording stars.

In all of this listening you will learn some very important concepts about music in general. The first is that all music contains two essential elements: repetition and contrast. The amount of each of these two characteristics determines how long and how intently you will listen to a song or a piece of music. A song that uses a similar melody for the verse and the refrain, such as "Battle Hymn of the Republic" (figure 4.46) is not as interesting to listen to as a song with a contrasting melodic idea in the refrain such as "Waltzing Matilda" (figure 3.30).

Music can also be described in terms of how it is constructed—its **form.** Songs with a verse and refrain such as "Waltzing Matilda" (figure 3.30) are in two-part, **binary,** or AB form while a song such as "One Bottle of Pop" (figure 4.65) with three different parts is in **ternary** or ABC form. You will learn how to determine form by listening to songs you already know, new songs, and music found on the accompanying CD.

Another important facet of listening is the ability to distinguish between the sounds you are hearing. Are there voices always singing or are there instruments alternating in the piece? If there are instruments, are they made of brass or wood or are the sounds being produced by electronic keyboards, synthesizers, or drum machines? The ability to discriminate in this manner makes it possible not only for your listening to be more refined and knowledgeable but for you to more fully experience all the sounds that actually exist in music.

Most of all, we want you to enjoy listening to music. We believe that the more active you are as a listener, the more you will realize that listening carefully to music is worth the extra effort and energy involved. We want you to understand the pleasure and thrill of knowing what you are hearing, how it is constructed, and how it works. Learning how to listen in this manner will affect you every day and will open up new sensations and feelings that you may not have been aware of before.

MUSIC HAS REPETITION AND CONTRAST

Music has sounds that our ears take in and that our brains make into patterns as we listen. These patterns of sounds may or may not reoccur. Even though most of us know almost nothing about music theory, we seem to listen for familiar patterns within a piece of music and are satisfied with the music when we can discern the patterns (or lack of patterns) within it.

Music is heard in terms of whether the part just heard is similar to or different from the part that preceded it. If it is the same, we call it repetition. If it is different, we say it is a contrasting section. A satisfying music listening experience includes the optimum amounts of repetition and contrast. Too much repetition is boring; too little repetition leads to confusion. Similarly, too much contrast is chaotic, and too little contrast can be boring. The following examples will help you recognize both repetition and contrast within pieces of music from Africa, Australia, and western Europe.

"Ghana Postal Workers," CD track #7

This example of repetition is from a field tape made by an ethnomusicologist. In it, you can hear the postal workers canceling stamps and whistling as they work. The first time that you listen, notice the two contrasting sounds in the example. The iconic map presented in figure 5.1 shows the outline of the melody. This melody occurs six times while the percussion accompaniment is continuous. See if you can follow the iconic map as you listen to this example a second time. The third time you listen, see if you can sing or whistle the melody and tap the steady beat.

Figure 5.1

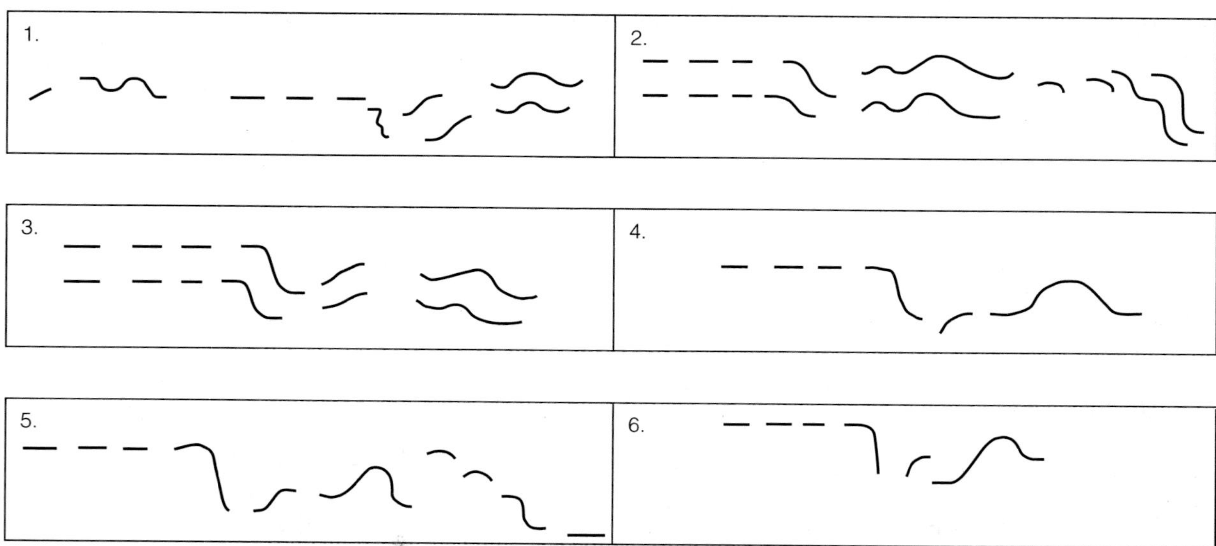

The next song is from the Australian vocal group Tiddas, made up of Aboriginal women of South Australia. It is a lullaby in which the mothers tell the children to go to sleep on the ground around the fire, while warning the goannas [large monitor lizards] to "Shoo!"

Look at the notation for "Inanay" (figure 5.2) and say the rhythm syllables for the song. Then clap the rhythm while you say the rhythm syllables a second time. Under the words in the figure write in the pitch or solfeggio syllables for the notation (start on "do" for the first note). Sing the solfeggio syllables without worrying about the rhythm. Now, see if you can sing both pitch and rhythm correctly.

Figure 5.2

Inanay

Traditional

In-a - nay ca-pu-a-na, In-a - nay ca-pu-a-na. Eh - eh - eh
u - la, u - la, u - la. U-la eh, yi-pi-eh, yi-pi - eh.

"Inanay," CD track #8

This live concert recording illustrates both repetition and contrast. There are two melodies or motives. A contrast occurs when the second melody appears. The first melody is the song you studied in figure 5.2; the second melody is a contrasting melodic idea. The following list shows the pattern of repetition and contrast in this example:

/\ melody one—one voice

/\ melody one—two voices

0 melody two

0 melody two

/\ melody one—three voices

0 melody two—two voices

"Pie Jesu," CD track #4

The following example, pronounced pee'-ay yay'-zoo, was first performed in 1985 and is taken from *Requiem,* a longer work for voices and orchestra by the contemporary English composer John Rutter. The requiem is sung in Latin because it is the traditional Catholic mass for the dead. The "Pie Jesu" is a prayer asking that God grant eternal rest to the departed.

Listen to the selection once to remind yourself of how it sounds. The second time you listen, follow the iconic map (figure 5.3), which shows how the melody is sung by a solo female voice and accompanied by the contrasting timbres of the male and female voices. When you listen a third time, see if you can hear the contrast between the soloist and the chorus. Circle the places on the map where this contrast occurs.

Figure 5.3 "Pie Jesu" (Rutter)

Instrumental Introduction

Pie Jesu domine Dona eis requiem

requiem ae ter nam Dona eis domine. Dona eis domine. Dona Dona Dona.

Pie Jesu Domine Dona eis requiem

Horn

Dona eis domine dona requiem aeter nam Dona Dona Dona

Pie Jesu Domine Dona eis requiem

Sempiternam Sempi Sempi Dona Dona Dona Dona Sempiternam

Pie Jesu Domine Dona eis requiem

Sempi ternam re qui em

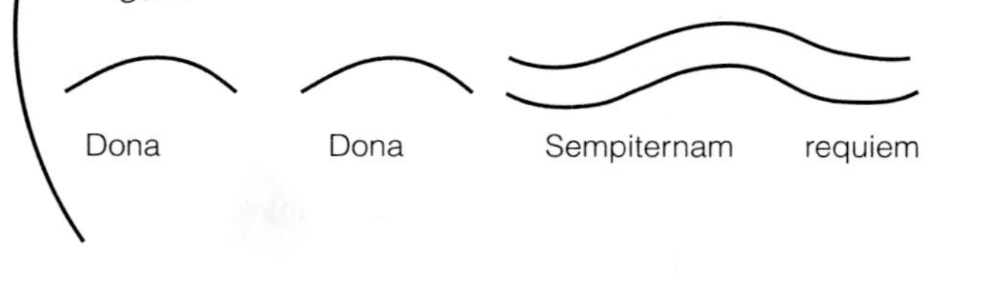

"Tanzen und Springen," CD track #9

This song was written in 1601 by German composer Hans Leo Hassler. It is a fine example of balance between repetition and contrast in both the melody and the text. The text contrasts meaningful words with nonsense syllables.

Look at the notation for "Tanzen und Springen" (figure 5.4) and say the rhythm syllables for the song. Next, clap the rhythm while you say the rhythm syllables a second time. Under the words in the figure write in the solfeggio syllables for the notation (start on "do" for the first note). Sing the solfeggio syllables without worrying about the rhythm. Now, see if you can sing both pitch and rhythm correctly.

The first melody (measures 1–8) is repeated at measure 9. The second melody (beginning at measure 17) is not repeated; instead, it is followed by a "fa la la" section that is sung twice. See if you can find any other examples of repetition and contrast as you sing this song. Circle any examples you find in red.

Kathleen Keenan-Takagi, Ph.D., prepared the following translation of the text of "Tanzen und Springen":

Dancing and leaping, singing and ringing,
Nor shall lutes and fiddles be silent
To make music exult
Remains my only wish

Figure 5.4

"Jesu, Joy of Man's Desiring," CD track #11

"Jesus, Lover of My Soul," CD track #11

The next two selections that you will listen to exemplify repetition and contrast in a different way. The first example, "Jesu, Joy of Man's Desiring," is from a cantata (a vocal form from the Baroque era [1600–1750] that contains a number of movements) by the German composer Johann Sebastian Bach (1685–1750). If this piece is not familiar to you, listen to it several times so that you will be able to recognize it in a new context.

The second example uses the accompaniment from "Jesu, Joy of Man's Desiring." Instead of the chorale written by Bach, the traditional gospel song "Jesus, Lover of My Soul" is sung. The effect here is quite different from the original Bach version. As you listen to this recording by the Richard Smallwood Singers, a contemporary gospel group, see if you can hear the accompaniment played by a piano and synthesized strings. Listen to both songs a second time: examine the diagram (figure 5.5) and note the areas of difference and commonality. As you listen again, add your own descriptors to the diagram for class discussion.

Figure 5.5 "Jesu, Joy of Man's Desiring" and "Jesus, Lover of My Soul"

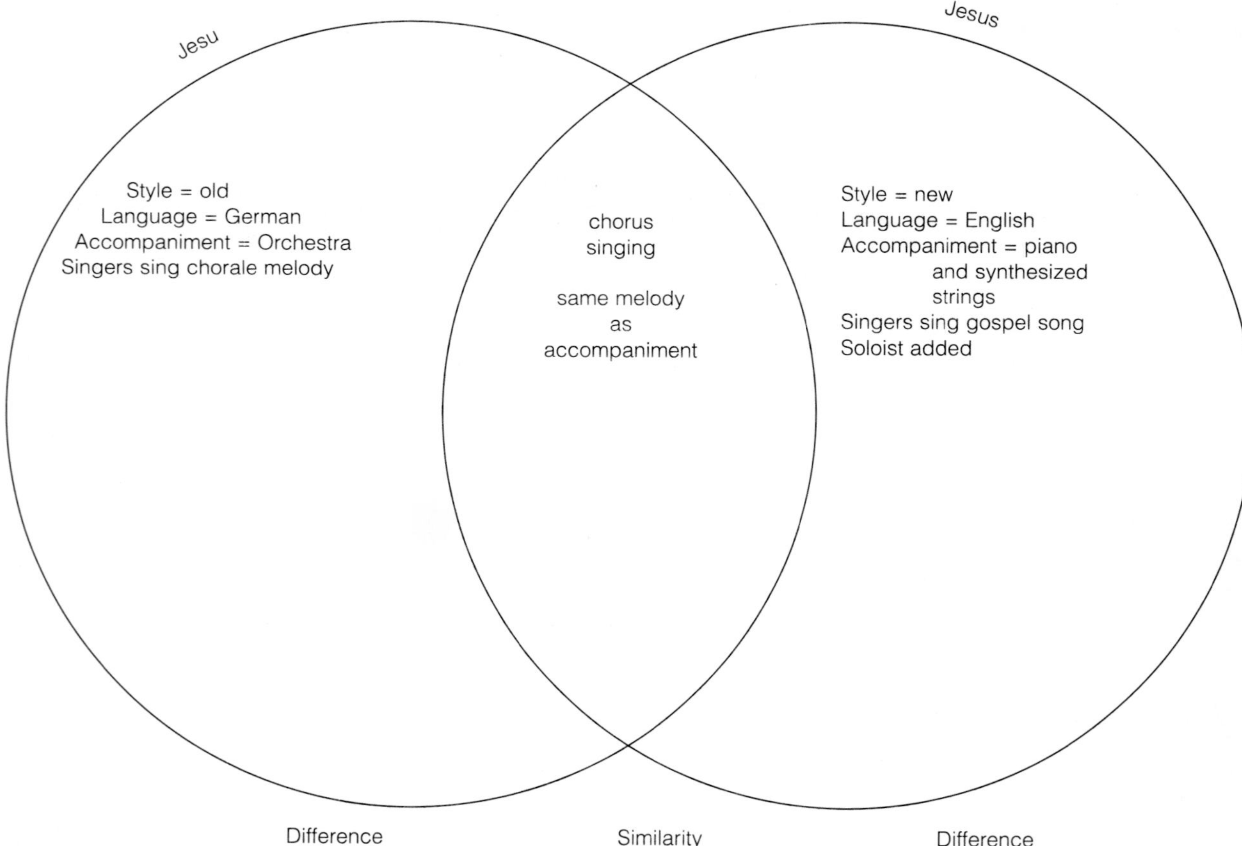

PREPARATION FOR CLASS: PHOTOCOPY THIS PAGE

As you listen to the following two examples, see if you can list the areas of similarity and contrast in the diagram below (figure 5.6). Include in your comparison all the musical information you notice while listening.

"Inanay," CD track #8

"Some People," CD track #5

Figure 5.6

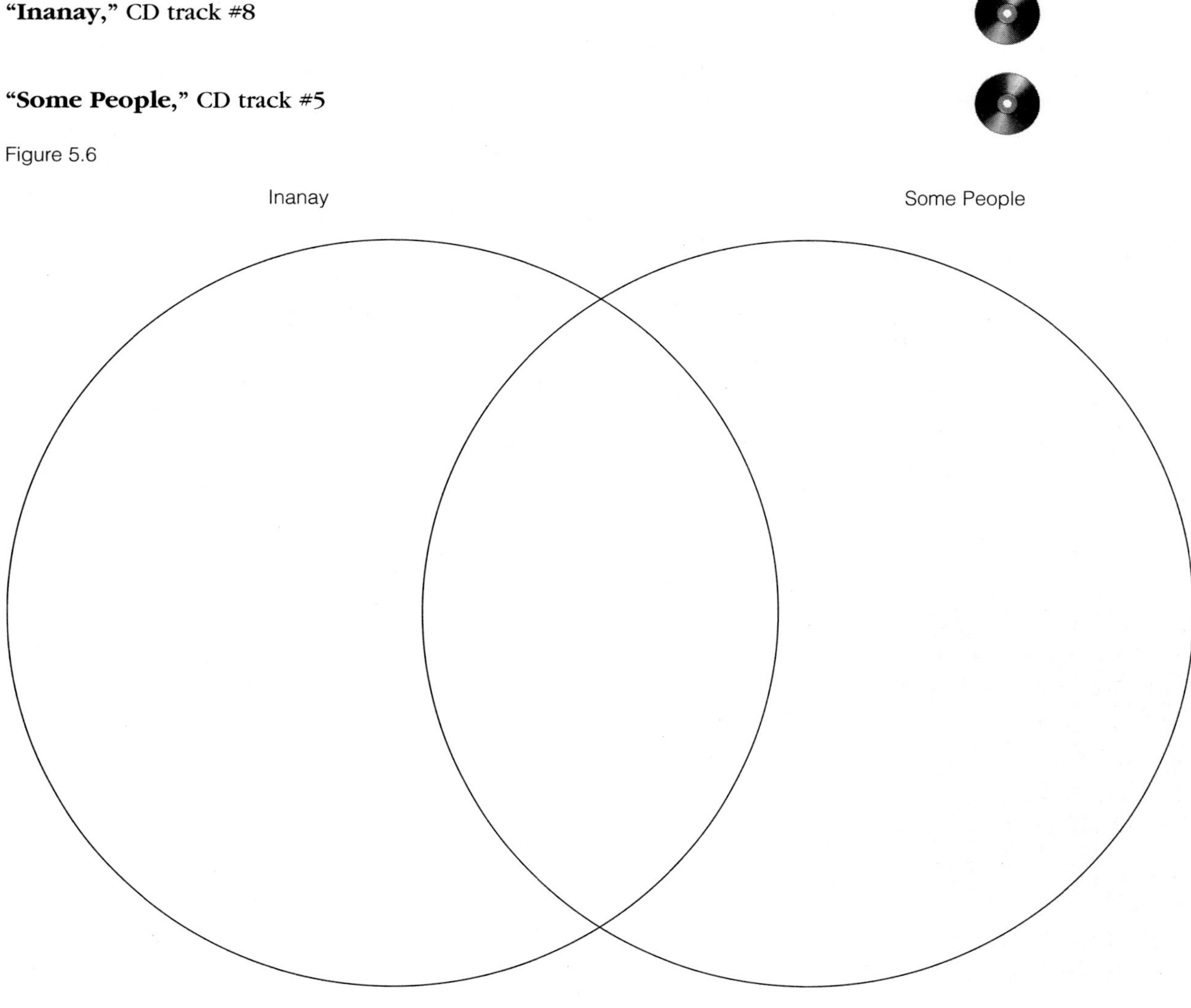

During subsequent listening in class, use a different color pen or marker to add newly discovered items to your list before you hand it in.

PREPARATION FOR CLASS: PHOTOCOPY THIS PAGE

From your personal tape or CD collection, select a favorite song and illustrate how the piece has repetition and contrast. Use any of the visual representations used in this chapter up to this point. Photocopy this page and bring it to class with the recording and a cassette or CD player. Be ready to share your illustration and recording with a partner.

MUSIC HAS FORM

Figure 5.7 presents the notation and text for the song titled " 'Til There Was You" that is found on the CD accompanying the text. As preparation for class, listen to the recording and follow the music in figure 5.7. As you listen a second time, try singing along with the recording.

Figure 5.7

'Til There Was You

Meredith Willson

If you look at the following iconic representation of " 'Til There Was You" (figure 5.8), you will see that the song has four sections, three of which are almost exactly the same (AABA). The composer, Meredith Willson, used contrast in the third line to make this song more interesting.

Figure 5.8 Graphic Representation of " 'Til There Was You"

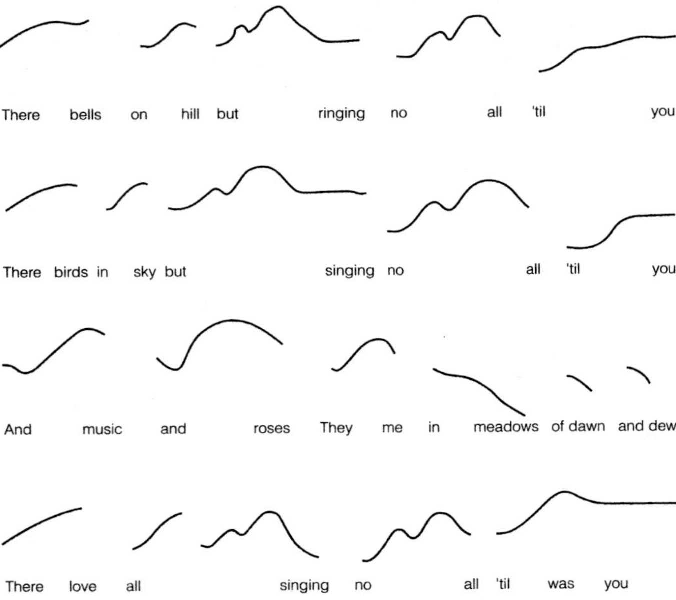

Another well-known song is "America." Look at the iconic representation in figure 5.9 and sing the song on "loo." This process will help you understand the simple changes that provide contrast and repetition within this short melody.

Figure 5.9 Graphic Representation of "America"

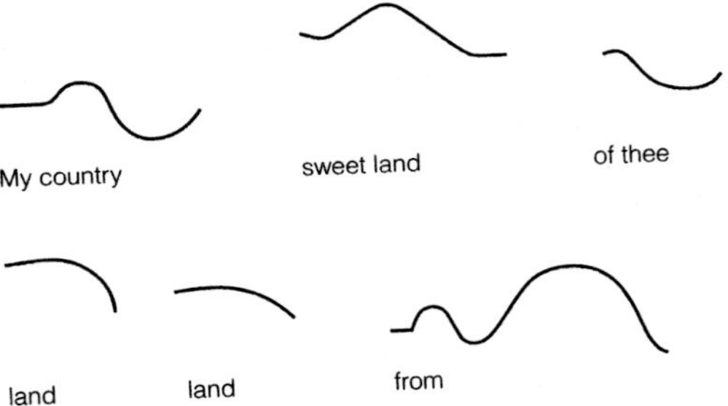

ACTIVITY In a group of four, choose one of the songs in chapter 4 and sing it together. As you sing, listen to the melody very carefully. Then, split up in pairs, and with your partner draw an iconic representation of the song. Compare your results with those of another pair of partners. How are they similar and/or different? What did each of your icons show about the form of the song?

"L'enfant et les sortilèges," CD track #12

Listen to Track 12, which is an excerpt from an opera by Maurice Ravel, titled *L'enfant et les sortilèges* (The Child and the Charms or Spells). At this point in the opera, Ravel's music describes a forest that is coming alive. The music is very impressionistic and sets the mood for the next scene in which the naughty child is transported into the beautiful forest. Eventually, the child expresses remorse for his misdeeds. As you listen the first time, decide if you hear any sections that repeat. During your second listening, follow the iconic representation in figure 5.10. As you listen a third time, listen for each of the contrasting sounds and enjoy the mood that the composer establishes in this very short example.

Figure 5.10 Graphic Representation of an Excerpt from Ravel's *L'enfant et les sortilèges*

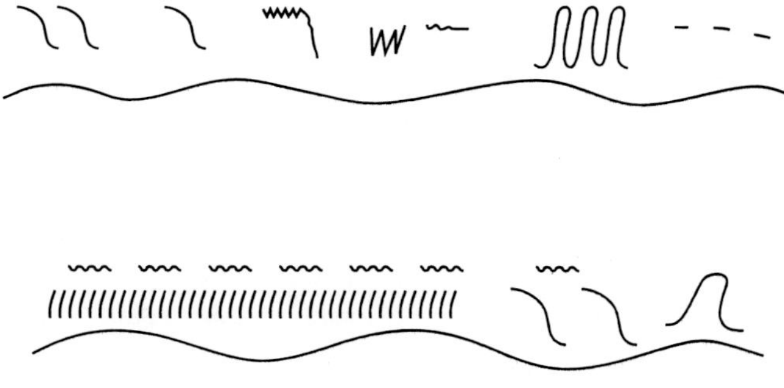

MUSIC WITH TWO PARTS

Many songs that you have already sung with your classmates have had two parts, which are commonly called a verse and a refrain.

ACTIVITY Look at pages 139–141 (chapter 4) as a homework assignment or in class with a partner. Decide which songs have two parts. List the songs that have a similar melody in the refrain and verse and then list those that have contrasting melodies.

Figure 5.11 presents the graphic representation and notation for the two-part song "Waltzing Matilda." Sing the song and follow the icons as you sing. What does the iconic representation show you about the refrain of this song?

Figure 5.11 Graphic Representation of "Waltzing Matilda"

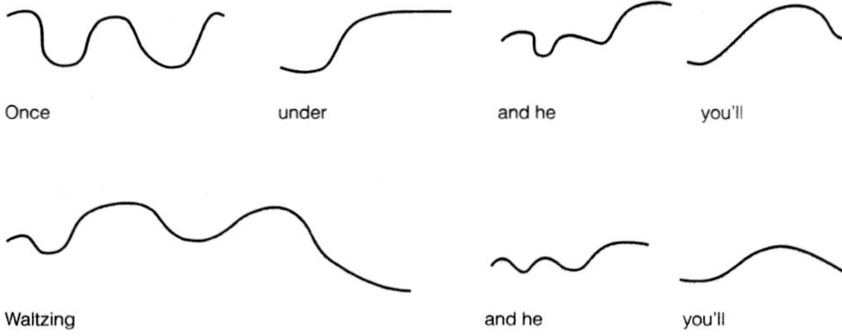

Figure 5.11 *continued*

Waltzing Matilda

Adapted from A. "Banjo" Paterson | Adapted by Marie Cowan

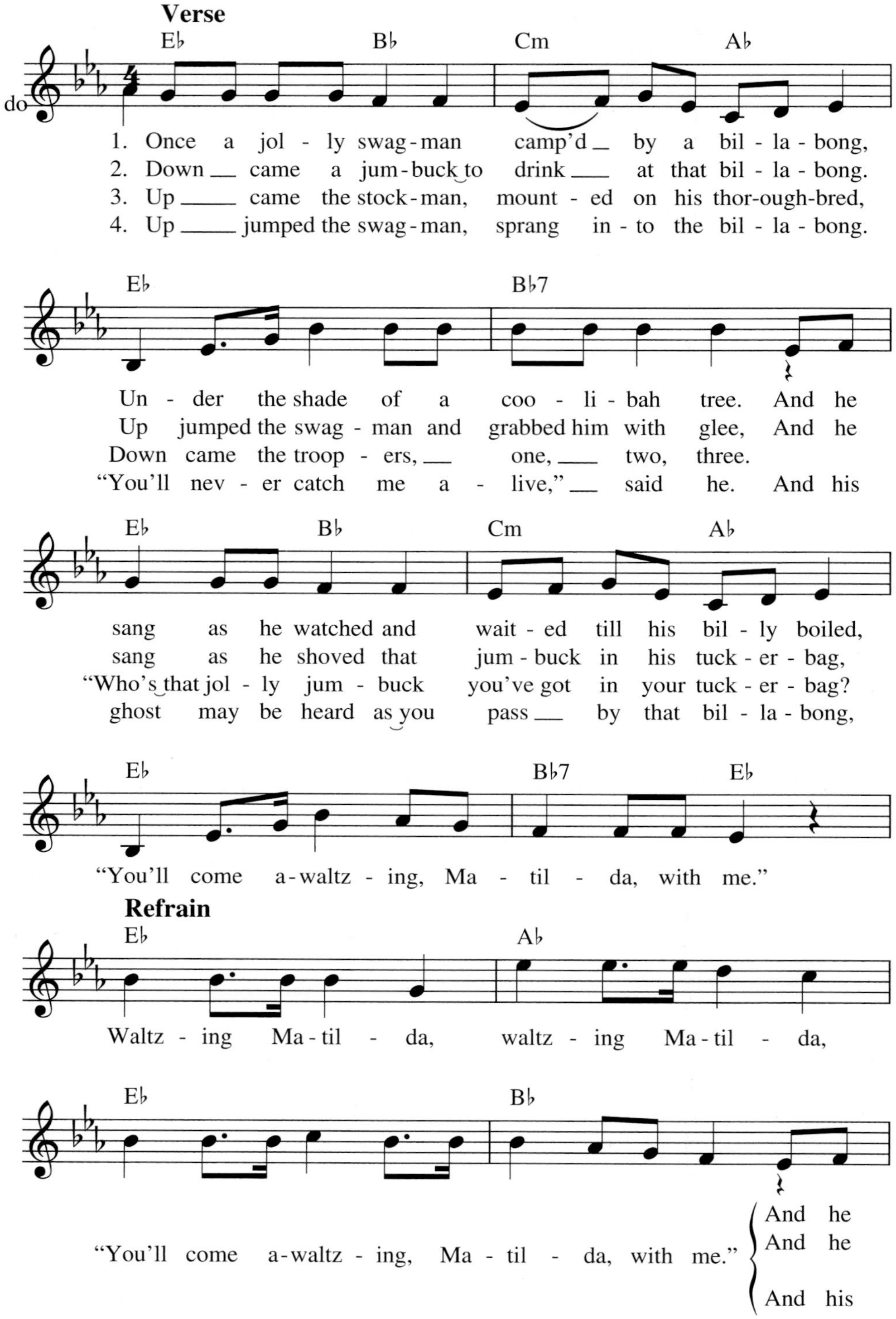

Verse

E♭ B♭ Cm A♭

do

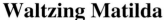

1. Once a jol - ly swag-man camp'd _ by a bil - la - bong,
2. Down _ came a jum-buck to drink _ at that bil - la - bong.
3. Up _ came the stock-man, mount - ed on his thor-ough-bred,
4. Up _ jumped the swag-man, sprang in - to the bil - la - bong.

E♭ B♭7

Un - der the shade of a coo - li - bah tree. And he
Up jumped the swag - man and grabbed him with glee, And he
Down came the troop - ers, _ one, _ two, three.
"You'll nev - er catch me a - live," _ said he. And his

E♭ B♭ Cm A♭

sang as he watched and wait - ed till his bil - ly boiled,
sang as he shoved that jum - buck in his tuck - er - bag,
"Who's that jol - ly jum - buck you've got in your tuck - er - bag?
ghost may be heard as you pass _ by that bil - la - bong,

E♭ B♭7 E♭

"You'll come a-waltz - ing, Ma - til - da, with me."

Refrain

E♭ A♭

Waltz - ing Ma-til - da, waltz - ing Ma-til - da,

E♭ B♭

"You'll come a-waltz - ing, Ma - til - da, with me." { And he / And he / And his

Figure 5.11 *continued*

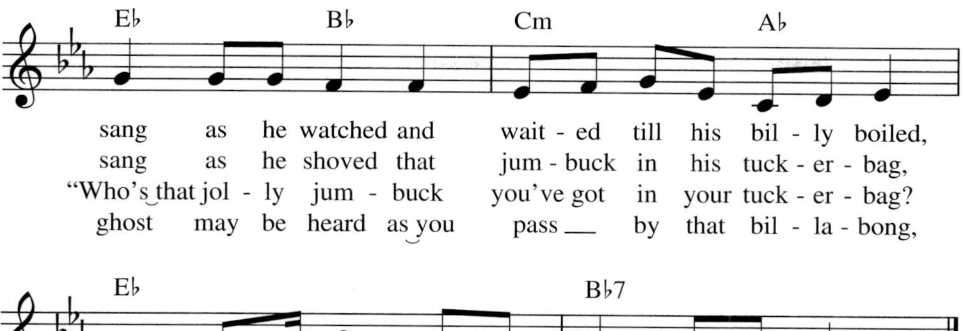
E♭ B♭ Cm A♭
sang as he watched and wait - ed till his bil - ly boiled,
sang as he shoved that jum - buck in his tuck - er - bag,
"Who's that jol - ly jum - buck you've got in your tuck - er - bag?
ghost may be heard as you pass by that bil - la - bong,

E♭ B♭7
"You'll come a - waltz - ing, Ma - til - da, with me."

Sonata for Recorder and Harpsichord, CD track #13

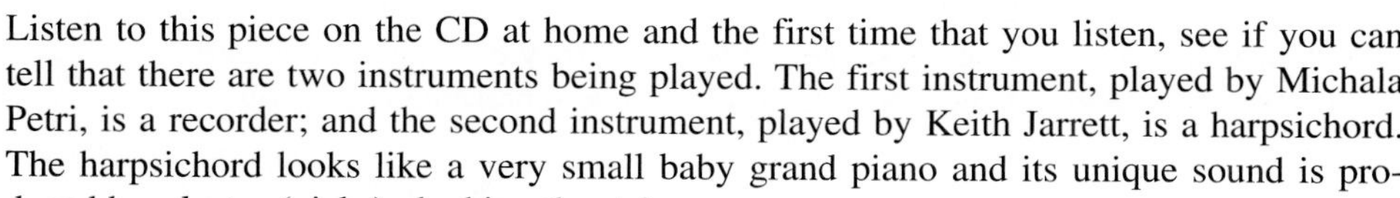

Listen to this piece on the CD at home and the first time that you listen, see if you can tell that there are two instruments being played. The first instrument, played by Michala Petri, is a recorder; and the second instrument, played by Keith Jarrett, is a harpsichord. The harpsichord looks like a very small baby grand piano and its unique sound is produced by *plectra* (picks) plucking the strings.

As you listen again, decide how the two sections contrast. As you listen a third time, look at the graphic in figure 5.12; then listen a fourth time while looking at the graphic in figure 5.13. Under each graphic write what you think is illustrated about the music. In the space provided in figure 5.14, draw your own graphic that illustrates the two contrasting parts of this music.

Figure 5.12

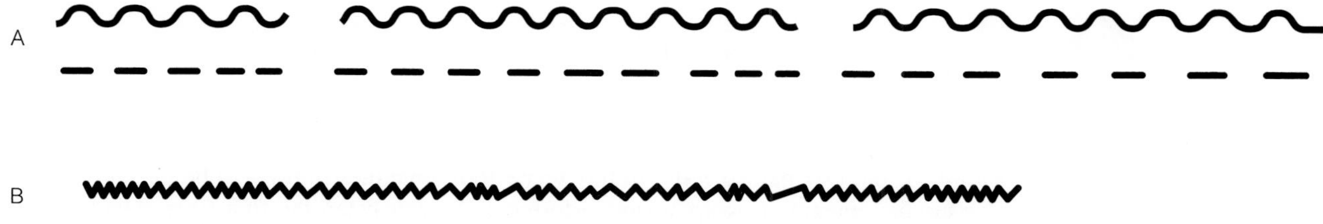
A
B

Figure 5.13

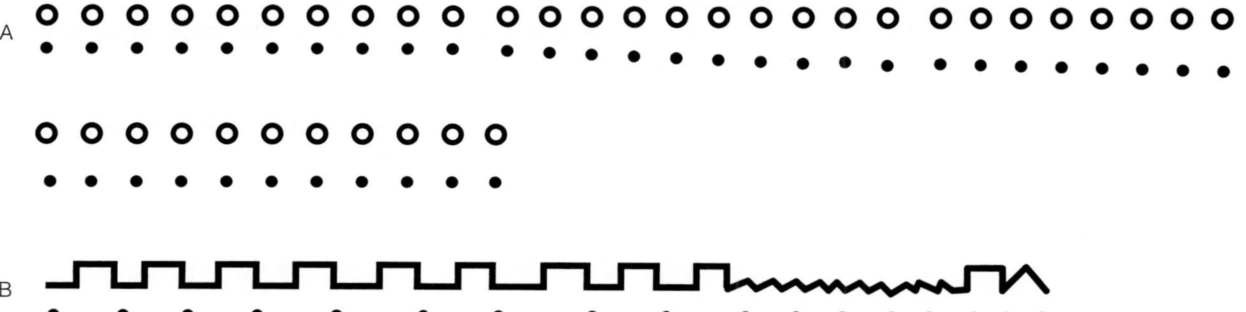
A
B

Figure 5.14

A

B

MUSIC WITH THREE PARTS

Two of the songs that you sang as a class are three-part songs: "Swing Low, Sweet Chariot" (figure 3.33, p. 65) and "One Bottle of Pop" (figure 4.60, p. 133). Sing each of these songs and see if you can describe the way that they each have three parts.

The parts of "Swing Low, Sweet Chariot" can be represented as follows:

△ ○ △

The parts of "One Bottle of Pop" can be represented as follows:

△ ○ □

If we describe the form of these two songs with letters of the alphabet, "Swing Low, Sweet Chariot" would be an ABA song and "One Bottle of Pop," an ABC song. Each of the songs is in ternary form, i.e., each has three parts.

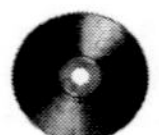

"Circus Music," CD track #14

"Circus Music" is from the soundtrack that Aaron Copland wrote for the film *The Red Pony.* The movie, based on a book by John Steinbeck, depicts a series of vignettes about a ten-year-old boy named Jody. In this scene Jody imagines himself to be the ringmaster of a circus, cracking a whip at the performers. As you listen the first time, decide what is the most obvious musical sound in the piece. Does the sound relate to the title of the music?

The rhythmic "ta-da" that reminds the listener of the end of an act at the circus separates each of the sections of the music. As you listen a second time, see if you begin to hear the repetition *within* the first section and the repetition *of* the first and third sections.

One way to represent the form of this piece would be with the same shapes as used above for "Swing Low, Sweet Chariot." But such simple shapes do not begin to show the musical complexity of this exciting piece of music. The following listening map (figure 5.15) shows more of the repetition and contrast within each section. As you listen to the recording a third time, see if you can follow the graphics for each melodic idea in the piece.

Figure 5.15 Graphic Representation of "Circus Music"

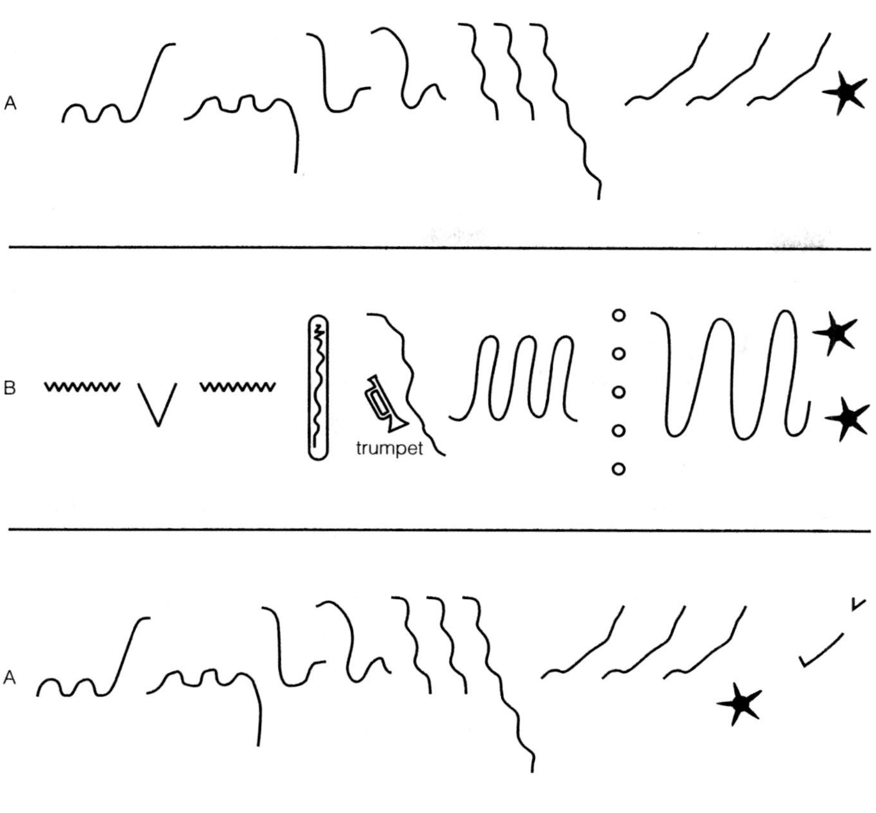

THEME AND VARIATIONS

Here are two versions of a song that has been used by American composer Morton Gould (1913–1996) in a theme and variations piece. The composer writes the theme (a folk melody) and then many repetitions, each of which varies slightly from the original song. The first version is an Irish folk song. You will notice that the meter signature in this song is quite different from what you have been using in your recorder playing. This meter, $\frac{6}{8}$, was introduced in chapter 2. When you first use this meter you will begin by counting six beats, one for each eighth note. As you become more proficient, you will begin to notice a strong feeling of duple or two beats that this meter implies.

 **ACTIVITY** Echo the rhythms in figure 5.16 after your teacher claps them.

Figure 5.16 Rhythm Echoes in $\frac{6}{8}$ Meter

After you have echo-clapped these rhythms with your instructor, carefully examine the notation for "Johnny, I Hardly Knew Ye" (figure 5.17). You will see a new notation symbol—a tie connecting the dotted quarter and quarter note. Look at the song and clap the rhythm notation with your classmates and instructor. Then listen to your teacher sing this Irish folk song and join in singing as soon as you are ready.

Figure 5.17

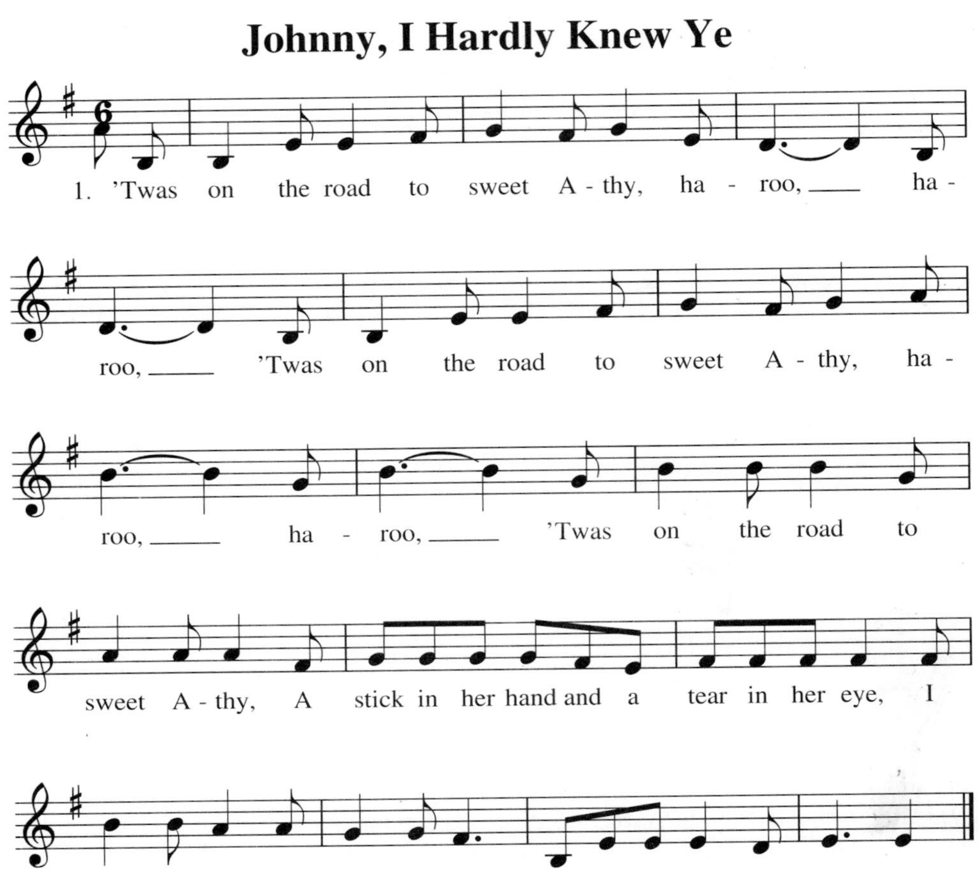
Johnny, I Hardly Knew Ye
1. 'Twas on the road to sweet A - thy, ha - roo, ha -
roo, 'Twas on the road to sweet A - thy, ha -
roo, ha - roo, 'Twas on the road to
sweet A - thy, A stick in her hand and a tear in her eye, I
heard a dole - ful dam - sel cry, "John-ny, I hard - ly knew ye."

2. Where is the leg on which ye run, haroo, haroo,
Where is the leg on which ye run, haroo, haroo,
Where is the leg on which ye run,
When first ye learned to carry a gun?
I think your dancing days are done;
Johnny, I hardly knew ye.

3. Where is the eye that looked so mild, haroo, haroo,
Where is the eye that looked so mild, haroo, haroo,
Where is the eye that looked so mild,
When my poor heart ye first beguiled?
Why did you leave your wife and child?
Johnny, I hardly knew ye.

4. They're rolling out the drums again, haroo, haroo,
They're rolling out the drums again, haroo, haroo,
They're rolling out the drums again,
But they'll never take our sons again.
No, they'll never take our sons again,
Johnny, I'm swearing to ye.

An American Civil War version of this song is titled "When Johnny Comes Marching Home." The text is much more celebratory and not as graphic as the original. Clap the rhythm of this song with your teacher and then sing the song with your classmates.

Figure 5.18

"American Salute," CD track #15

"American Salute" is a piece of music that takes this folk song melody and changes it many times in a form called **theme and variations.** As you listen the first time, you will hear music at the beginning and the end that does not resemble the folk song. These parts are called an **introduction** and a **coda.** Also listen for the ways that the composer provides variety while repeatedly using the same melody. When you listen the second time, count the number of times that the composer varies the theme. Finally, listen using the guide below.

"American Salute"

Introduction (does not use folk song)

Theme: "When Johnny Comes Marching Home" played by bassoon

Variation 1 . . . melody played by English horn

Variation 2 . . . melody played by strings

Variation 3 . . . melody played by flutes/oboes

Variation 4 . . . melody played by full orchestra

Variation 5 . . . melody played by full orchestra, then sections

Variation 6 . . . melody played much slower by brass and winds

Variation 7 . . . melody played by full orchestra

Coda: (special ending that does not use theme)

MUSIC HAS TIMBRE

Every musical sound you hear has a particular characteristic called **timbre** (pronounced tam'-bur or tawm'-bur). The timbre of a musical sound depends on the sound source producing it. If you clap your hands together, the sound you produce is a function of the speed with which you brought your hands together, the actual thickness of your hands, and the spot at which your hands touched. The timbre of your clapping sound can be modified slightly, depending on where you hit your hands together and whether you are wearing gloves or not. However, the characteristic timbre of a handclap remains, no matter how much you try to modify your performance. Because the sound originates with the air being pushed away from your hands, the type and shape of wave created in the air by the vibrating skin of your hands determine the characteristic of the sound.

The timbre of instruments also depends upon the sound source. The timbre of an oboe, for example, is a function of the vibrating double reed, along with the size, shape, and material of the instrument. The timbre of your singing voice depends on the shape and thickness of your vocal cords as well as on the way you use your instrument to produce sound. Both the oboe and your voice maintain their unique timbre no matter what pitch is played or sung.

Timbre is often referred to as **tone color.** While the term *tone color* actually confuses an aural metaphor with a visual metaphor, it might be helpful to your understanding of timbre to think of timbre as the sound equivalent of color.

Figure 5.19 presents the notation for the spiritual "Ev'ry Time I Feel the Spirit." As you sing through this well-known **spiritual,** think of ways that you could modify the timbre without any instruments if you were going to sing it with your class. Make a list of the ways your class could sing the spiritual so that there would be changes in timbre.

Figure 5.19

Ev'ry Time I Feel the Spirit
Spiritual
Refrain
Ev - 'ry time I feel the Spir - it mov - ing
in my heart I will pray, Yes, ev-'ry time I feel the
Fine
Spir - it mov - ing in my heart I will pray.
Up - on the moun - tain my Lord spoke; Out his
mouth came fire and smoke. All a - round me looks so
D.C. al Fine
shine, Ask my Lord if all was mine.

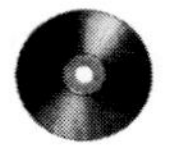

***Der Rosenkavalier*, act 2 (excerpt),** CD track #16

"The Iron Foundry," CD track #17

Each of these examples has the timbre of the symphony orchestra, yet they sound strikingly different. The example from the ballroom scene in Richard Strauss's opera *Der Rosenkavalier* has the full, rich string sound typical of a late-nineteenth-century orchestra. "The Iron Foundry" is a contrasting example of the way that the orchestral instruments can be combined and played so that their timbres evoke a factory rather than a ballroom. Listen to both compositions. As you recognize the instrumental timbres in each, list them under the headings below.

Der Rosenkavalier	**"The Iron Foundry"**

Each of the following examples features one or more musical timbres. As you listen the first time, focus only on the sound of the vocal and instrumental timbres. In subsequent listenings you can pay attention to other musical features such as repetition, contrast, and form.

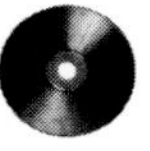

"Bes" (gyil, Ghanian xylophone), CD track #18

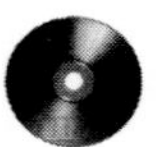

"Leang Dai" (Cambodian Tror Che), CD track #19

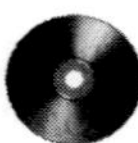

"Kima Duina" (Native American cedar flute), CD track #20

Trio (clavier, violin, and cello), CD track #21

"Slide, Frog, Slide" (Dixieland Jazz), CD track #22

MUSIC HAS TEXTURE

There are three different kinds of musical texture: **monophonic, polyphonic,** and **homophonic.** Monophonic texture is created when one instrument or voice plays alone without any accompaniment. The term is also used to describe the sound of many voices or instruments all singing or playing the same melody. An example of monophonic texture is Rimsky-Korsakov's "Flight of the Bumblebee." Listen to the selection as many times as needed to draw an iconic map of its melodic contour.

"Flight of the Bumblebee," CD track #23

Homophonic texture is created when a melody is accompanied by a less predominant harmony part. The melody can be sung or played on an instrument and the accompaniment can be vocal or instrumental. Listen again to "Pie Jesu" (track 4), which is illustrated in an iconic map on page 162 (figure 5.3). Listen only to the music that goes with the first quarter of the map. On a blank piece of paper, write down the names of the instruments you think are playing the accompaniment.

"Pie Jesu," CD track #4

Polyphonic texture is created when two or more independent melodies are played or sung simultaneously. Listen to Johann Sebastian Bach's "Two-Part Invention No. 13." You will hear one melody begin and then a second entrance of the same melody that produces the polyphonic texture. See if you can hear the two independent melodies through the entire excerpt.

Two-Part Invention No. 13, CD track #24

PLAYING RECORDER

A NEW NOTE

The fifth note you will learn to play on the recorder is D. The correct fingering for D is shown in figure 5.20.

Figure 5.20 Recorder Fingering for D

back front

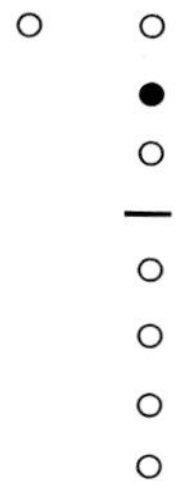

○ ○
●
○
—
○
○
○
○

The first staff of figure 5.21 presents eight bars of various notes that you can use to practice playing the D. The remaining three staves of figure 5.21 give you the opportunity to practice playing the D with the notes you learned in previous chapters.

Figure 5.21 Record Practice Notation

Now that you are familiar with five notes (G, A, B, C, D), you can explore another interval—the fifth. The distance from the lowest note you are able to play, G, to the highest note you are able to play, D, is a fifth. Intervals can be played one after the other as in the first measure of figure 5.22, or at the same time (by two players), as in the second measure of the figure.

Figure 5.22

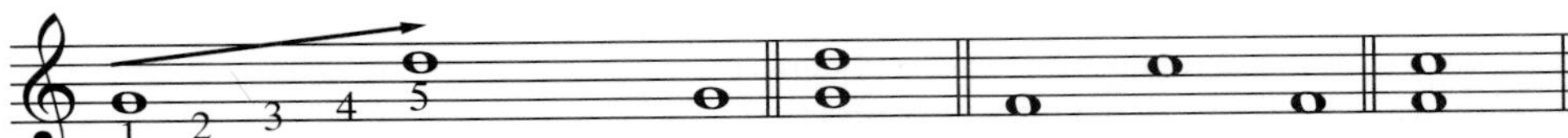

Figure 5.23 includes the symbol for a repeat :‖ and the symbols for first and second endings ⌐1.¬, ⌐2.¬. These symbols tell you to repeat part or all of a piece and end it differently the second time. The first time, you play through the first ending and then return to the beginning without missing a beat. When you get to the two endings, you then skip over the first ending and play only the second ending. The double bar at the end of the staff indicates "the end."

Figure 5.23 Four New Musical Symbols

Practice clapping the rhythm of figure 5.23 and then practice saying the names of the notes rhythmically using both endings. Then practice fingering the line without blowing.

MORE PRACTICE WITH FIVE NOTES

Figure 5.24 Practice for Playing Five Notes

PLAYING HARMONY

Practice playing each line in figure 5.25 before class so that you can play harmony with your classmates. If it will help you to practice correctly, write the names of the notes above or below the staff for each part. Before you play each line, practice clapping the rhythm and saying the rhythm syllables. Practice fingering the notes and saying the letter names in the correct rhythm.

Figure 5.25 Harmony Practice

TRIADS

The type of harmony you have played so far has used two notes that sound at the same time. Now that you can play five notes on the recorder, your class can begin playing triads. A triad is three notes that sound at the same time. The triad is identified by its bottom note. Figure 5.26 presents the notation for a G triad. After practicing each of the notes in figure 5.26 individually in class, you will be able to perform the melody and accompaniment in figure 5.27. (Note: You cannot play three notes simultaneously on a recorder!)

Figure 5.26 The G Triad

Figure 5.27 Melody with Triad Accompaniment

Practice each line of the following duets in figures 5.28 and 5.29 at home so that when you come to class you can play them with a partner. Then combine with another set of partners to play the duet. Share your performance with your classmates. Be sure that you follow the dynamic markings.

Figure 5.28 Duet for Recorder

Figure 5.29 Duet for Recorder

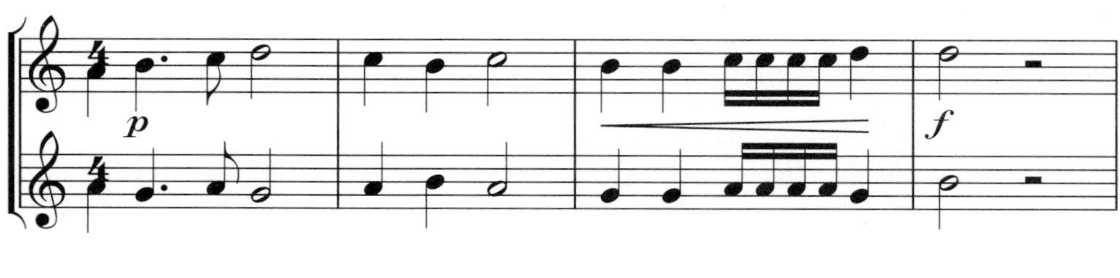

ACTIVITY After your performance, use the following blank staves to write an eight-measure song in $\frac{4}{4}$ meter using G, A, B, C, and D. Remember to include dynamic contrasts.

Figures 5.30 and 5.31 present the notation for two songs from "The Sweet Pipes Recorder Book" by Gerald Burakoff and William E. Hettrick. You must use your knowledge of rhythm and notation in order to play them correctly. After you have practiced them at home and in class, play them in a group of four.

Figure 5.30

Winter, ade

German

Figure 5.31

Quand j'étais mon père

French

MORE RECORDER PRACTICE USING FIVE-NOTE SONGS

Figure 5.32

Barnyard Song

Traditional

Figure 5.32 *continued*

Merrily We Roll Along

Traditional

Lightly Row

German Folk Song

Light-ly row, light - ly row; on the glass - y waves we go.
Soft - ly glide, smooth-ly ride on the qui - et tide.
Let the wind and wa - ters be min-gled with our har - mo - ny.
Sing and float, hum and float in our lit - tle boat.

FINISH THESE SONGS

Figure 5.33 presents the beginning notation for two different songs. Write in the necessary notation on the staves to complete each of the songs. Be sure to note the different meter signatures. Once you complete the notation, practice playing the songs.

Figure 5.33

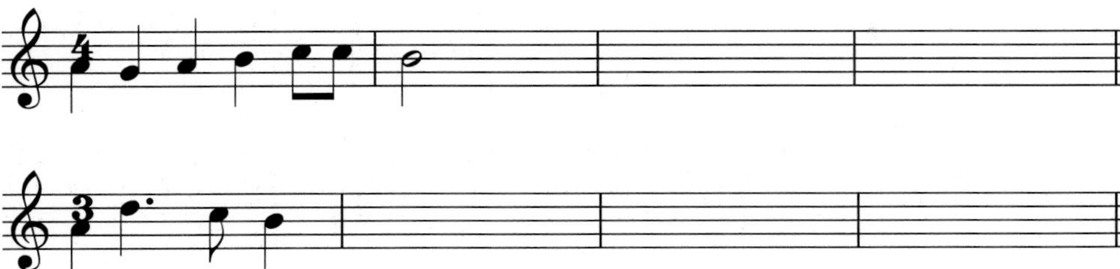

FOR YOUR OWN COMPOSITIONS

Figure 5.34 presents three blank staves, each of which begins with a different meter signature. On each of the staves compose a brief song for the recorder. Practice playing your new songs and share them with your classmates.

Figure 5.34

FURTHER PRACTICE

The first two exercises for this section require you to photocopy the next three pages from the text before you begin.

PREPARATION FOR CLASS: PHOTOCOPY THIS PAGE

1. From your personal tape or CD collection, select a favorite song and illustrate how the piece has repetition and contrast. Use any of the visual representations presented at the beginning of this chapter. Bring this page to class with the recording and a cassette or CD player. Be ready to share your illustration and recording with a partner.

PREPARATION FOR CLASS: PHOTOCOPY THIS PAGE

2. Compare and contrast the musical features of two selections of your choice from the accompanying CD.

   Piece #1 ____

   Piece #2 ____

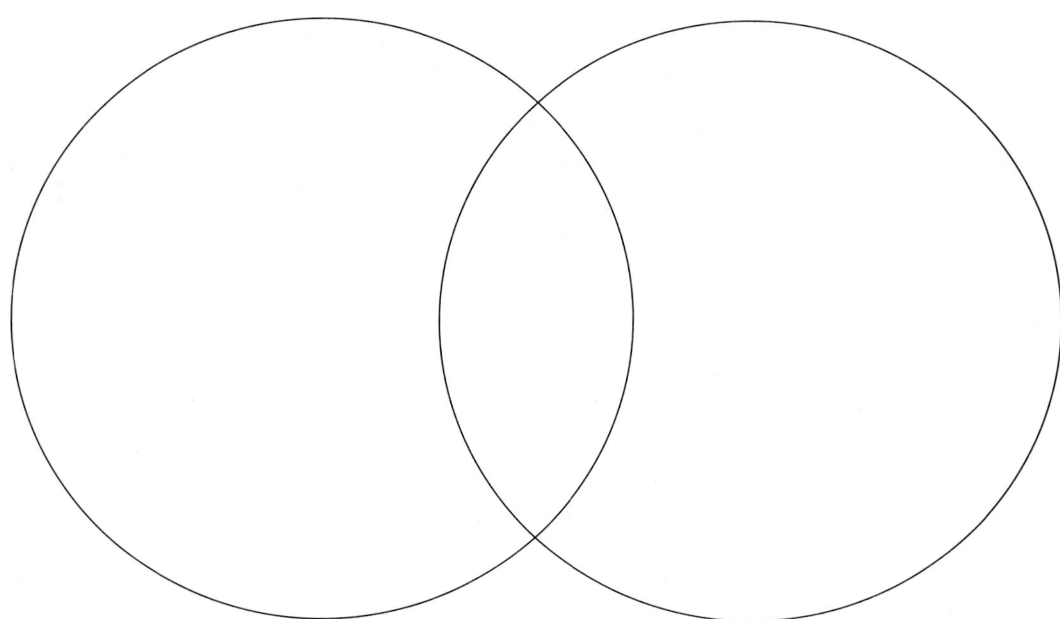

3. On figure 5.35, write the letter name of each note above the staff and the rhythm syllable for each note below the staff.

Figure 5.35

Figure 5.35 *continued*

Music Listening with Children

6

What you will be able to do by the end of this chapter

- *Make listening part of the classroom routine*
- *Choose appropriate music to integrate with your curriculum*
- *Write lesson plans that incorporate listening*
- *Use music listening to develop higher level thinking*
- *Understand a different type of musical meter*
- *Play a new note on the recorder*

THE LISTENING CLASSROOM

Music listening is the one musical activity that can provide all students with lifelong pleasure, both as future audience members and as purchasers of recordings. Too many adults feel so uncomfortable with music listening that they never attend a single live concert or listen to music regularly. The important window of opportunity to develop skills in intelligent music listening is wide open during the formative elementary school years, and the classroom teacher, who spends thirty hours per week with these children, is perfectly positioned to open children's ears to the richness of the music in the world.

Your primary task as an elementary classroom teacher is to help your students negotiate their way in the world of learning, using whatever means necessary to help them increase their learning skills: listening, reading, thinking, and writing. Focused music listening not only opens the world of music to your students but gives them essential practice in focusing their attention, following aural phenomena carefully, and reflecting on what they have heard. Short-term memory is exercised through focused music listening and can be a powerful tool for remembering information in other contexts. Reflective thinking, the process through which children make sense of their experiences, is expanded as children discuss what they have heard, compare it to previous listening examples, and formulate evaluative statements about musical examples. In addition to nurturing these essential listening and thinking skills, however, regular music listening enhances other, equally important aspects of children's development.

Our world is inundated with sound no matter where we turn. Therefore, young children come to elementary school with a wide range of music listening experiences already in place. We have become a culture where music is our 24-hour companion: our homes, day care centers, shopping malls, grocery stores, and restaurants are filled with musical sounds. Unfortunately, this constant exposure to music serves to anesthetize rather than enhance children's listening skills, and the challenge is to teach children how to focus their attention on musical sounds so that they can fully experience the power of music. Without careful and consistent listening experiences throughout the elementary years, children do not learn how to focus their attention on anything more than the powerful steady beat or catchy lyrics of the most accessible popular tune. And they grow into adults whose music listening pleasure is extremely limited.

One of the greatest challenges facing the teacher is how to deal with the affective component of music. We acknowledge that all musics have the power to move us in ways that we cannot express in language, and that much of what we hope will happen to children musically will be something that we can't expect them to be able to verbalize directly. The best way to handle the ineffable personal musical response is to keep your lesson focused on the features of the music that seem to grab the children's attention and help them understand how and why the music has this powerful affect on human beings. Essential to this process is a classroom atmosphere in which all answers are given a receptive hearing and children are encouraged to offer divergent points of view. Due to the widespread use of music as a background in cartoons, films, and commercials, certain styles, instruments, and genres have become stereotyped icons for a particular mood, feeling, or occasion. While you are not charged with correcting the major musical misapprehensions of American culture, you should take care to teach your students that a particular piece of music is neither happy nor sad, but is simply capable of eliciting feelings. You must emphasize that each person will experience different feelings and have different reactions to a piece of music, but that each is an equally valid, correct response.

Since young children are uninhibited music listeners and gladly listen to and enjoy music from all musical styles and genres, you will find it very rewarding to regularly include music listening in your classroom. Music from every source available to you, including your own tape or CD collection, will bring the richness of our musical heritage to your students' appreciative ears and can add a new dimension to learning in other curricular areas. No matter what the context in which you present music listening examples, your enthusiasm for a wide variety of musical genres and styles will be emulated by your students. In short, you are largely responsible for the music listening development of your students, and you can meet this challenge through regular active listening activities.

CHAPTER GOALS

In this chapter you will learn how to use the listening skills developed in chapter 5 in your role as a classroom teacher of either primary- or intermediate-school students. You will learn to incorporate active listening to music in your daily classroom planning and curriculum, and you will learn how to direct and involve your students' listening in ways

Whatever type of mapping exercise you use to get children involved in a musical excerpt, you need to remember that the mapping is just a means to an end, not the end itself. The desired end in this case is a deeper understanding of the piece of music under consideration and a better grasp of how it does what it does. If the mapping exercise is not followed with a synthesizing activity that focuses on the musical context, the child will have a vague sense of having accomplished something rather like a workbook exercise.

FINAL SYNTHESIS IN LISTENING

After repeated listenings, you should find a way for the children to synthesize and express all they have heard. Creating an individual or group listening map may be one approach. You might have the students work in pairs to create their own movement compositions that show their understanding of the music. Their own maps may even serve as a beginning catalyst for such movement. Some children might explore other facets of the piece such as its cultural setting or the composer's background and find ways to relate this information to topics studied in the classroom through writing, drawing, painting, acting, or combinations of any of these.

At other times, you may want to have the children learn to enjoy listening just for listening's sake. Directions such as "What else can you hear in the music as we listen?" or "Now that we know a lot about the instruments in this music we're going to listen one last time and see how the instrument sounds fit with all the other parts" will provide youngsters with an opportunity to truly interact with and experience the music. Such synthesis activities allow the musical import of the piece to resurface and take the child's full attention. Teaching that puts the child into the experiential and responsive mode is satisfying for both teacher and student and is the desired outcome of music listening.

THE IMPORTANCE OF VARIETY

The selections you choose for your class listening should portray accurately the wide variety of music found in the world. Young children take great delight in all kinds of music, and it is up to you to ensure that they hear every possible type of music in your class. All children will not like all kinds of music, nor should you expect them to. Remember that all children do not like long division or multiplication, either. The point is that the elementary curriculum is designed to expose children to a broad range of experiences and disciplines. You never need to ask "Did you like this music?" any more than the math teacher needs to ask "Did you like this problem?"

LISTENING TO MUSIC WITH OLDER CHILDREN

When you begin your teaching career, you may discover that the children you are teaching have not had *any* listening experiences. The carefully built foundation that should have been established in primary grades may not exist. You can deal with this problem most effectively by introducing music listening with very short selections (as described earlier for primary grades) and gradually expanding the length of the listening pieces.

Intermediate-age children are members of the "three-minute" listeners' club because the commercial music selections they hear outside of school never exceed this length. Commercial producers know they must not inundate young listeners with long and complex pieces, so they rely on short, repetitive selections, which produce immediate recall as well as short-term musical gratification. Teachers need to incorporate this powerful marketing strategy as well. Even though intermediate-school children are older and have more sophisticated cognitive abilities, their listening attention span still needs to be accommodated with fairly short selections.

One effective way to provide children with the tools and skills needed for eventual sustained listening is to begin with a short excerpt of a piece and gradually add successive sections. For example, after listening to Copland's "Circus Music" on your CD, you may wish to find a CD of the entire *Suite from "The Red Pony"* and have your class listen to other segments, such as "Morning On the Ranch," "Walk to the Bunkhouse," or "Grandfather's Story." Each segment might be a separate listening, and eventually your class would know enough of the music to listen to the entire piece. Since the piece was written for a film, you might have your students explore the entire genre of film music.

The attraction of commercial or popular music becomes even stronger for children in intermediate grades than when they were younger, and the possibility that students will perceive a distinction between "school" music and "real" music is also strengthened. For this reason, it is imperative that your choice of listening selections be as eclectic as possible. Your selection of music must demonstrate to impressionable listeners that quality music has no boundaries.

The social effects of peer and media approval are a much stronger influence in the intermediate grades than during the primary years. It is interesting, however, to note the finding by Finnas[2] in 1989 that seventh-grade music preferences for classical and folk music were much higher when expressed privately as opposed to public expression with their peers. It is important to remember that the loudly expressed groan or negative comment will influence other students, particularly if this negative affect is expressed by a popular student or one who is a class leader. Preplanning is the key to preventing such possibilities. Knowing exactly what you are going to say to intrigue or challenge intermediate students, in addition to not allowing such interference, will enable you to overcome this possible obstacle.

Selecting a repertoire of challenging listening selections for intermediate grades requires consideration of other factors. As in earlier grades, it is important to select music that has characteristics children will be able to hear easily. This will enable you to prepare clear, directed listening questions that will focus each listening experience. But because of older students' cognitive growth, listening becomes much more exciting for you and your class because you are able to direct them to listen to not just one but several musical aspects in a single piece.

It is important to balance accessibility with complexity. Musical selections in which all of the content can easily be perceived should be a very small part of children's musical diet. You don't want to announce a listening selection and have children groan at the thought of listening to the piece "again." (Remember the "top 40 syndrome"—there's nothing worse than listening to a pop tune everyone knows backward and forward). Most of the music you select should be of moderate complexity and provide some challenge. It is also good to choose a few pieces that will represent more substantial listening challenges. These selections will provide students with the opportunity for continued refinement of their listening skills.

MATERIALS AND SOURCES

Listening lessons with intermediate-age children can be made more imaginative and exciting through the use of a wide variety of materials. Because they can listen for longer periods of time and can focus on increasingly complex and subtle musical ideas, you need to be continually on the lookout for ways to expand your musical offerings for these students. One cognitively appropriate way is to compare recordings of different groups and different artists. Yet another way to show more subtle musical contrasts is to compare an audio recording and a videotape of the same performer in the same work. Because there are so many excellent classical music videotapes (see Appendix F) available today, it is important to use their powerful visual influence to engage children in musical learning. While it may seem that adding the visual element does take the student's attention away from the music, the focus of your lesson will determine where the attention is paid. It is up to you to plan your questions carefully so that the comparisons made are essentially musical ones.

There are many ways to expand listening opportunities for students through recorded musical encounters but you must never forget that no matter how fine your CD player or tape deck is, recorded music is only a reproduction. Real instruments and singers sound very different from the reproductions, and students need opportunities to experience the richer, fuller sounds of live performances. One important source of listening experiences is the community in which you live and teach. No matter where you are, there will always be many talented musical adults about whom you will know little or nothing and who could enrich your classroom.

The best way initially to tap into this resource is to ask your students if they have musical parents or friends and then follow up on their suggestions. Some schools may already have a parent resource guide that will help you find performers to come to your class. In communities with a large variety of ethnic groups, you may uncover parent performers who can bring a taste of world music to your classroom. In addition, be alert to concert announcements in local papers or on bulletin boards in malls and grocery stores. You may be able to discover performing groups that do not include parents of your students but that are willing to share their talents with your students. Live performance is a powerful means of expanding the musical world for your students and is well worth your extra effort and planning.

Another way to provide enrichment opportunities for your students is to investigate what is available through your local or state arts commissions. Many states, counties, and even individual communities have arts councils that are partially funded by the National Endowment for the Arts. These organizations provide matching funds for a variety of artistic endeavors, one of which can be bringing professional musicians into school settings. The matching funds are either supplied by the school district or, in some places, the parent-teacher association (PTA). Often states or regions even have a catalog available that lists and describes approved artists and musical ensembles.

All symphony orchestras, opera companies, and concert associations now recognize the necessity of educating the audiences of the future. Indeed, these organizations are deeply concerned that their audiences are aging and that younger listeners are not attracted to their offerings. Each organization approaches this task quite differently and with varying degrees of effectiveness. Some groups provide concerts for young listeners for a "bring-your-class-to-the-symphony" experience; others provide pop offerings or other attempts at lighter entertainment. Still others provide small groups of musicians who will perform a concert in your school. Many groups have education directors or committees who prepare and distribute helpful written materials and tapes for teachers to use in preparing students for concerts.

Taking students to a performance outside of school is a complicated but rewarding experience. After obtaining approval from your principal, you may have to collect money for tickets, make reservations, arrange for a school bus, and ensure that adequate numbers of parent chaperons will also attend. And, of course, your students must be prepared as well. Daunting as all this preparation may seem, the efforts are worthwhile when you remember that so many adults never enter a concert hall because they perceive it as a foreign place and one where they are unsure of correct behavior. When you take your students to a concert hall to listen to live music, you are giving them a gift of social ease and access that they may be able to use all their lives.

DIRECTED MUSIC LISTENING

An active listener is one who is involved as the music moves through time. Every encounter that intermediate students have with listening to music must be preceded by clear directions that focus student attention in such a way as to require active participation. Teachers can use simple verbal directions as well as elaborate visual prompts to focus children's listening. Students who are directed to put their thumbs up when they hear a new section or instrument or a change in melodic direction cannot help but be active listeners. Moving a hand or arm in a arc to indicate sections or counting the number of repetitions of a musical element also requires attentive listening. Active listening can also be fostered with the use of teacher-made listening maps and call charts, as well as student-made maps. Teacher-made listening maps for intermediate students should be quite different from those used in primary grades, since more musical content needs to be made accessible to listeners. A listening map for intermediate grades of Copland's "Circus Music" should show the form and the contrasts of melody in the B section as well as melodic direction in the B section (see figure 6.2).

Figure 6.2 "Circus Music" Listening Maps

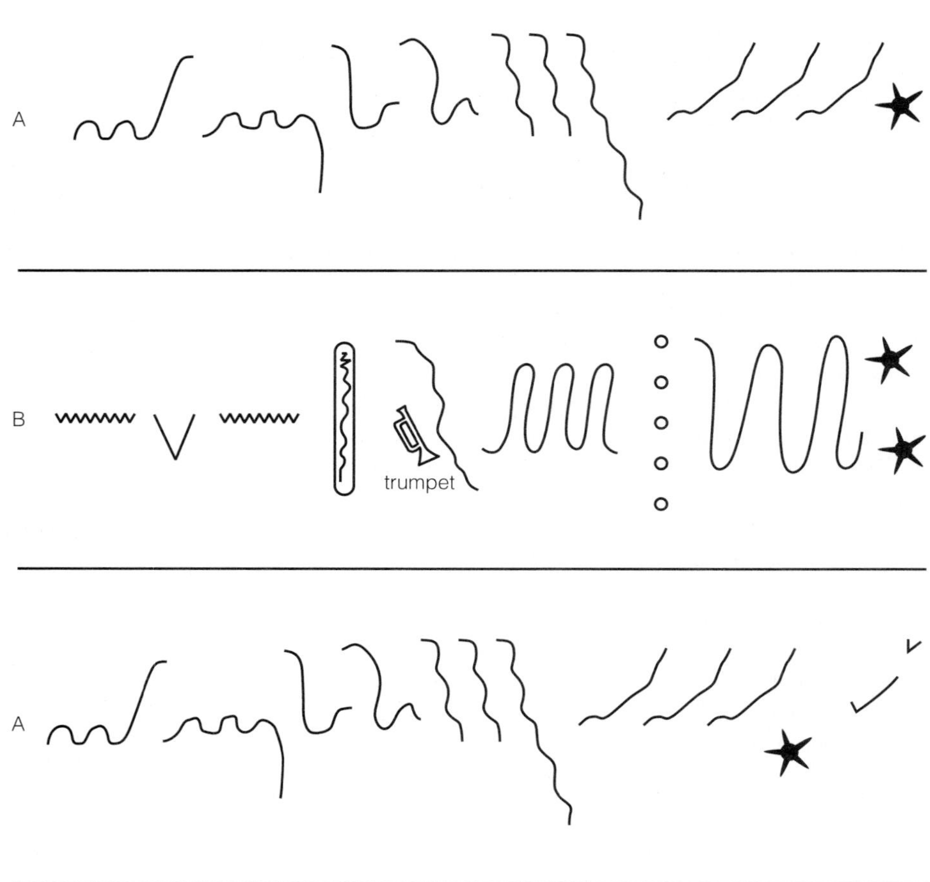

Call charts contain information about the music, usually in a verbal format, and require the teacher to interrupt the music by calling out a number. The listener then reads what is happening in that particular section of the music. The chart that directed your listening to "American Salute" in chapter 5 (p. 176) could easily become a call chart for fifth or sixth graders as you call the number out before the beginning of each variation in the piece.

SPECIAL LEARNERS AND MUSIC LISTENING

The trend toward including every handicapped child into typical classrooms means that your planning may need to include ways of accommodating a vast range of learning and motor abilities within your class. For this reason, your use of listening responses that rely completely on the understanding and/or writing of language may need to be supplemented or completely replaced for some students. Responses that require students to write answers should be used very sparingly when children listen to music because writing is a very difficult task. The act of writing requires the student to remember the motor patterns involved in forming each letter, the correct spelling and syntax, and the musical vocabulary and meaning. Effective individual evaluation for intermediate learners should be constructed in a way that supplies the learner with a choice of words or symbols to circle or check. In this way, you will be able to evaluate musical listening rather than writing or spelling ability.

The present emphasis in many areas is on the complete inclusion or assimilation in general classrooms of children with handicaps ranging from mild to severe. This type of inclusion often presents classroom teachers with issues of social acceptance as well as educational adaptation. The text of the song "I'm a Little Cookie," track 26, provides a clear metaphor for individual differences and can be used as a catalyst for class discussion of social issues in inclusive classrooms.

NURTURING THINKING SKILLS THROUGH MUSIC LISTENING

The place of thinking in the elementary school curriculum is firmly established, thanks to the wide-scale reforms that have swept through the educational world during the last 10 years. One of the last places one would expect to find a focus on thinking, however, is in musical classroom activities, where the focus is traditionally on physical involvement: performing songs, playing instruments, listening and moving to music, and creating with sounds. We expect to see what children are able to do and what they have produced in the domain of music.

Yet each musical activity can provide exciting and exhilarating opportunities to take children beyond mere doing to a more sophisticated level of understanding and appreciation. How can a classroom teacher enhance children's level of musical expertise and appreciation, given the time constraints of the typical elementary curriculum? An essential link in this process is teacher questioning that allows students the opportunity to think within the domain of music, use their musical knowledge and understanding, and find their own meanings in what they performed, heard, or created. Each classroom teacher can pose questions that lead children to three different kinds of thinking in music: convergent, divergent, and critical thinking.

CONVERGENT THINKING

When teaching specific subjects within the curriculum, teachers often cause students to engage in convergent thinking by prompting them to give the single correct answer to a question. Such questions tap only the lowest level of cognition, which includes remembering or recalling specific terms, symbols, facts, or classifications. An example of convergent thinking during a math lesson might be coming up with correct answers to addition problems.

In a music listening activity, students might be asked to label the timbre of three different examples. Whether the convergent response is verbal or gestural, it is important that you accept children's terminology and reasoning as a valid way of explaining their answers to your question. Students often use metaphors to explain their musical responses and understanding. If you encourage such responses you will often get a clearer understanding of how they've processed the musical experience than if you require them to use "musicianly" language exclusively.

DIVERGENT THINKING

When you ask a question that does not have a right or wrong answer, you are asking children to engage in divergent thinking. Questions that lead to divergent responses include: "If you were the composer, what could you do to make it sound more like a circus?" "How might you change the timbre so that it would sound like a march?" You can list all the verbal responses to divergent questions on the chalkboard and show the class that although each response is different, each one is valid. Although divergent thinking is prized as the source of inventions and marvels of modern science, divergence is not valued highly by our society. It seems that teachers, who have been trained to expect a single right answer, often don't know what to do with responses that differ from the norm. Encouraging divergent responses to music is one of the easiest ways to help children engage the feelings that we know are a necessary and important part of reacting to music. This type of discussion highlights and validates this important and often neglected aspect of children's cognitive development.

CRITICAL THINKING

Critical thinking is a term that has a variety of definitions and applications in education. In some schools, students are taught critical-thinking skills and are shown how to apply them in each area of the curriculum. Critical thinking in math, for example, requires the student to reason as a mathematician would, using the terminology and concepts of mathematics to solve problems. Thinking poetically requires students to think as a poet would, using the terminology and concepts of poetry to construct or discuss a poem. Critical-thinking skills are practiced in the context of solving a problem in a particular content area, and the skills involved are related to logic: presenting well-reasoned arguments supported by ample evidence and based on valid assumptions.

Critical-thinking experiences in the domain of music enable children to make decisions and judgments about music in the same way the musician and music critic do. Children engaged in critical thinking in musical activities use their knowledge and skills, musical imagination, and individual internal response to the music in arriving at decisions. Although the level of the elementary child's musical sophistication will not approach that of the adult musician or music critic, elementary children can still engage in musical thinking as young connoisseurs, given the right questions.

Questions that focus on skill issues can easily lead children to draw on their musical knowledge to make musical decisions: "How can we improve the sound of the song we just sang?" "How can we make this accompaniment fit the story better?" "How can we make sure the audience can understand our words?" Questions that focus on the musical expressiveness of the performance can lead to a rich discussion: "How did this way of singing change the way the song made you feel?" "What can we do to make this chant sound more interesting?" "Which of the two ways we just tried to play this sounded better? Why?"

It is important that classroom teachers give children the opportunity to engage in convergent, divergent, and critical thinking as part of each musical activity, whether it is listening, playing, singing, moving, or creating. Through the inclusion of carefully crafted and differentiated questions in all parts of the musical encounter, children hasten along the path to becoming musical thinkers. One benefit for you as the classroom teacher is that the focus is no longer on just presenting the musical content correctly, but on how well you are able to lead the children to think in the musical domain. The biggest bonus of all is that you are suddenly coach to a roomful of young thinkers who, through the depth and innocence of their thinking, can further your own understanding of the music.

PLANNING INTEGRATED LESSONS WITH APPROPRIATE MUSIC

One effective way to regularly include music listening in your classroom is through integrated listening lessons that enhance another portion of the elementary curriculum. Three types of integrated listening lessons are included in this chapter. The first is based on a nonmusical theme or topic (manufacturing); the second requires the application of a nonmusical concept in a musical context (punctuation); and the third requires application of concepts shared by visual art and music (repetition, pattern, symmetry). The following script shows how a fourth-grade teacher teaching a thematic lesson on manufacturing incorporates a music listening example. This piece illustrates how one composer took the concept of turning raw materials into a finished product and translated the process into sound.

INTERMEDIATE TEACHING SCRIPT: THEMATIC LESSON ON MANUFACTURING

We've been working on our manufacturing unit for a few days now, and I've got something new for you to think about today. Before we go to today's activity, though, I'd like to review our class rules for music listening: ears open, mouths closed. I'd like you to listen to a piece of music called "The Iron Foundry." While you listen the first time, see if you can hear anything in this piece that reminds you of what you've learned about the manufacturing process. Be ready to tell me what you've discovered after the first listening. Play recording, monitoring students' responses.

Who can tell me what you remember about the manufacturing process as the result of listening to this piece? Take a few responses.

This time, let's listen with our eyes closed and see if you can find a sound or rhythm pattern that repeats. If you find a repeating sound or rhythm pattern, use your hand or arm to show the way the sound or pattern moves. Play example again, monitoring "eyes closed," and note those unable to find a repeating pattern or sound.

I noticed that most of you found the percussive pattern of the rhythm that time. This time I'd like you to listen for and show something that is a pitch or melodic pattern; you can even sing along with it every time you hear it. But make sure you keep your eyes closed. Play example again, monitoring the class to see if anyone is unable to find a melodic figure in the example.

I saw a lot of variety that time. Many of you noticed a lot of the little melodic figures in this mass of sound. Great listening! Now, can anyone tell me something about how the composer used dynamics to make this piece sound like an iron foundry? Take a few answers.

Can anyone tell me something about the character of this piece? Take a few answers.

How would you describe it to someone who has never heard music before? Think for a few minutes, then take out a sheet of paper and write at least one sentence that describes this music. Be prepared to read your sentence to the class in about three minutes. Solicit readers, then write on board key words from each description.

There are almost as many different descriptions of the piece as there are listeners in this class! Isn't it amazing how we each respond to music in our own way, hearing different things and interpreting them as different moods or feelings? Thanks for your hard work today!

The following lesson plan format summarizes the steps used in the integrated listening teaching script.

INTEGRATED LISTENING LESSON PLAN: GRADE 3

Theme: Manufacturing

I. Learning Outcome or Objective:
Entry ability: Students understand the concept of the manufacturing process: taking raw materials and developing them into a finished product. Students' listening skills include ability to find repetition, recognize and label dynamic levels within a piece, show a steady beat, and discern melodic materials.
Exit ability: Students will be able to synthesize what they know about repetition, dynamics, and musical character or mood to formulate a description of a piece of music that illustrates the theme of manufacturing.

II. Lesson Evaluation Procedures:

Teacher will note those students who are unable to synchronize their movements with rhythmic or melodic themes or who have difficulty applying musical vocabulary.

III. Materials: "The Iron Foundry," track 17; CD player

IV. Teaching Procedures:

A. Setting the Stage: Remind class about manufacturing unit and review listening rules.

B. Developing the Lesson:
Step 1: Introduce listening with focus question. Play recorded selection: take comments after first listening.
Transition: "This time, let's listen with our eyes closed and see if you can find a sound or rhythm pattern that repeats."
Step 2: Listen a second time and use hand or arm to show the way the sound or pattern moves.
Transition: "This time I'd like you to listen for and show something that is a pitch or melodic pattern."
Step 3: Students listen to piece again.
Transition: "Can anyone tell me something about how the composer used dynamics to make this piece sound like an iron foundry?"

Step 4: Solicit answers and discuss.
Transition: "Can anyone tell me something about the character of this piece? How would you describe it to someone who has never heard it before?"
Step 5: Students think for a few minutes, then each student takes out a sheet of paper and writes at least one sentence that describes this music. Each student reads his or her sentence to the class. Teacher writes key words on board from each description.

C. **Concluding the Lesson:** Discuss the wide variety of answers, and reflect on the wide variety of ways each of us responds to musical materials.

Another type of lesson that integrates music listening into the elementary curriculum focuses on particular skills concepts that translate across the curriculum. In the following primary script, the punctuation concept of "the period" is illustrated through a music listening example. Notice how this script makes explicit how the concept of punctuation in language parallels that of punctuation in music.

PRIMARY TEACHING SCRIPT: ILLUSTRATING PUNCTUATION THROUGH MUSIC

Today during language arts time we're going to use what we've learned about punctuation to figure out how one composer used punctuation in a piece of music. Our first question: How many sections does this piece have? Before we listen, remember the rules for listening: mouths closed, ears wide open. Now let's listen to this piece with our eyes closed and see if you can tell me how many sections are in this piece. Be ready to tell me what you've found after the first listening. Play recording of "Circus Music," track 14, monitoring eyes closed; then take responses to the focus question.

This time, I'd like each of you to listen with your eyes closed again and pay special attention to what happens in the music at the end of each of the three sections. See if you can decide what kind of punctuation mark the composer would use if she or he had to write it in English rather than in music; then use your finger to write the punctuation mark on top of your desk at the very moment it happens in the music. Play recording again, monitoring "eyes closed" and watching students as they write their punctuation marks on the desk tops.

How many of you wrote a comma? A period? A question mark? An exclamation point? Tally up the total votes for each, then ask for reasons for these decisions.

This time as you listen, I'd like you to think about the title you'd give this piece if you were the composer. As soon as you've got it, write it across the top of a piece of paper and be ready to share your title with the person on your right. Monitor listening and writing, noticing those who are not writing. Offer help and encouragement by circulating among students and looking at what they've written.

Now, under your title, along the left side of your paper, I'd like you to write the numbers 1, 2, and 3. These stand for the three sections of this piece. Next to each number, write one sentence about what you think happens in the music of each section. Think about this for a moment; then we'll listen to the piece again so you can check to see if you've remembered all the details of each section correctly. Listen to selection again.

I'd like you to exchange lists with the person on your right; people on the right end of the row walk over to the end person on the left end and give your paper to them. Take a few minutes to discuss how your interpretations of the piece differ. Monitor interactions, moving toward those students who look like they need assistance.

Who would like to share their title and three descriptions with the whole group? Take several responses, highlighting the differences between individual interpretations.

You've done some fine work today, class, both in listening and in thinking about punctuation. It's been interesting to see how punctuation works in both music and language. Great job!

The following lesson plan format summarizes the steps used in the integrated listening teaching script on punctuation.

INTEGRATED PRIMARY LISTENING LESSON PLAN: PUNCTUATION

I. Learning Outcome or Objective:
Entry ability: Students understand the concept of punctuation, titles, and events in sequence. Students' music listening skills include ability to find ends of sections.
Exit ability: Students will be able to draw parallels between the use of punctuation in music and its use in language.

II. Lesson Evaluation or Assessment Procedures:
Teacher will note those students who are unable to create a title for the piece of music, have difficulty formulating concept of musical punctuation, show expertise in thinking across genres of language and music.

III. Materials and Board/Space Preparation: "Circus Music," track 14, paper and pencils, CD player.

IV. Teaching Procedures:

A. Setting the Stage: Remind class about listening rules and introduce listening.

B. Developing the Lesson:
Step 1: Play recorded selection; take comments after first listening.
Transition: "See if you can decide what kind of punctuation mark the composer would use if she or he had to write it in English rather than in music."
Step 2: Listen a second time and students use fingers to write the punctuation marks on top of desks. Discuss how many wrote comma, period, question mark, and exclamation point.
Transition: "Listen a third time. Think about the title you'd give this piece if you were the composer."
Step 3: Students write the title across the top of a piece of paper and share their titles.
Transition: "Under your title, along the left side of your paper, I'd like you to write the numbers 1, 2, and 3. These stand for the three sections of this piece. Next to each number, write one sentence about what you think happens in the music of each section."
Step 4: Listen to the piece again, exchange papers.
Transition: "Who would like to share their title and three descriptions with the group?"
Step 5: Teacher highlights the differences between the interpretations of each speaker.

C. Concluding the Lesson: Thank them for good work and have them discuss the focus of the lesson.

GESTURAL LISTENING MAPS: WINDOWS TO CHILDREN'S MUSICAL UNDERSTANDING

Some teachers have children draw to music as a way of bringing music into the classroom. This visual translation is very different from the musical gesture maps shown earlier in this chapter. Although children find drawing to music enjoyable and it gives them a pleasant break from the regular routine, this activity teaches children that all music is a sound track to which one can put a story. This type of drawing usually focuses on scenes that the children think of in response to the music, often creating a cartoon for the musical sound track. Although some music was created to illustrate a plot line, most was not. In fact, music is music, period. It contains musical information that moves us because it is a human art form that seems to move the way our feelings do. Great care must be taken so that children's musical activities lead them toward an understanding of the art of music, rather than its utilitarian uses as background ambient noise or sound tracks.

So far in this text you have learned to follow and construct iconic listening maps that are graphic representations of particular aspects of musical selections, such as melodic contour or repetition and contrast. The following teaching script introduces gestural listening maps. Gestural maps go beyond representation of single musical concepts to a more global representation of the music because they develop from the individual listener's kinesthetic response to the music listening selection.

Gestural maps are described by Richards in *Aesthetic Foundations for Thinking.* Richards suggests three steps in the process of gestural mapping. First, the listener focuses on the music listening selection and simply listens to the music. During the second listening, the listener is instructed to move to the music in a way that shows how the music moves, using either the whole body or a single part, such as an arm or hand or the head. The movement should capture the way the music moves. The next step involves translating the whole-body or single-part movement into a single point, such as the index or pointer finger, top of the head, or even the nose. The final step has the listener recording the trace of this single-point movement through the point of a pen or pencil on a blank sheet of paper, resulting in a visible representation that can readily be shared with others.

Each listener's gestural map will represent a given musical selection differently, and children can learn valuable lessons about the variety of ways people respond to music when they exchange gestural maps and try to follow each other's gestural icons. Even primary-school-age children are capable of making their own graphic representations of music, and your elementary class will have a much richer music listening experience when they are allowed to create their own gestural maps.

INTERMEDIATE CONCEPTUAL INTEGRATION LISTENING SCRIPT WITH GESTURAL MAP

Figure 6.3 Sydney Opera House

We've been working with the ideas of pattern, repetition, and symmetry in our art lessons, and today I'd like us to think about how these ideas might work in music. Just to review these ideas, take a look at the photograph of this famous building (figure 6.3) and if you can spot any pattern, repetition, or symmetry, take 30 seconds to explain this to a partner. Allow 30 seconds' discussion between partners, then ask for reports from pairs.

By the way, can anyone tell us the name of this building? Take volunteer response.

Now let's listen to a piece of music and see if we can hear any pattern, repetition, or symmetry. But before we begin, who can tell me the rules for music listening? Take a volunteer to explain: mouths closed, ears wide open.

For our first listening, let's close our eyes and just focus on the sounds. Play first minute and 13 seconds only of Haydn, Symphony no. 94, second movement (Andante), track 27.

You seemed to like the surprise that the composer put into that part of the symphony! I'd like to play it again, and this time I'm going to follow a listening map of the selection (figure 6.4).

As my finger traces the path of the map, I'd like each of you to trace it in the air with me. Are you ready? Here we go. Trace the map while keeping an eye on the students' responses. Begin at the S in the upper left corner, tracing with your pointer along the graphic, from top to bottom. The "surprise" in the music is represented by the circle. The two long phrases that occur after the "surprise" should also be traced from top to bottom, finishing at the "F" at the end of the selection.

Figure 6.4 Figural map of Haydn's Symphony no. 94, Second Movement (Andante)

How many of you felt that the map moved the way the music did? Take a few responses for discussion. Emphasize that all responses are correct.

Can someone look at this map and tell me if there are any patterns or repetition in it? Take a few responses and ask for explanations of why they think so.

Is there any symmetry? Take a few responses.

Let's make our own drawings now as we listen. Show the repetition, pattern, and symmetry of the music. Please let your imagination go wild here, and make your drawing as visually interesting as you want; use lots of color, too. We have about 30 minutes to work on these, so let's get started! When we are finished we will share our different ways of expressing these ideas.

The following lesson plan format summarizes the steps used in the gestural mapping listening lesson.

INTERMEDIATE CONCEPTUAL INTEGRATION LISTENING LESSON PLAN

Concept: Repetition/Pattern/Symmetry

I. **Learning Outcome or Objective:** Students will be able to demonstrate understanding of repetition, pattern, and symmetry in music.
   Entry ability: Students understand the concepts of repetition, pattern, and symmetry. Students' music listening skills include the ability to listen and move with music.
   Exit ability: Students will be able to produce drawings that illustrate the repetition, pattern, and symmetry of the music.

II. Lesson Evaluation Procedures: Teacher will note those students who are unable to apply concepts of repetition, pattern, and symmetry in visual representation.

III. Materials: Haydn, Symphony No. 94, track 27, paper and drawing pencils, colors, CD player.

IV. Teaching Procedures:

A. Setting the Stage: Review concepts of repetition, pattern, and symmetry by looking at photo of Sydney Opera House.

B. Developing the Lesson:
Step 1: Discuss with partner pattern, repetition, and symmetry in photograph and report to class.
Transition: "Who can tell me the rules for music listening?"
Step 2: Volunteer explains rules.
Transition: "For your first listening, let's close our eyes and just focus on the sounds."
Step 3: Listen to the music.
Transition: "As my finger traces the path of the map, I'd like each of you to trace it in the air with me."
Step 4: Students listen and trace map in air along with teacher. Discuss whether map moved the way the music moved and whether there was pattern, repetition, or symmetry.
Transition: "Let's make our own drawings now that show the repetition, pattern, and symmetry of the music."
Step 5: Students create own drawings.

C. Concluding the Lesson: Class discusses and shares their gestural maps.

Figure 6.9 *continued*

Figure 6.10 A New Triad

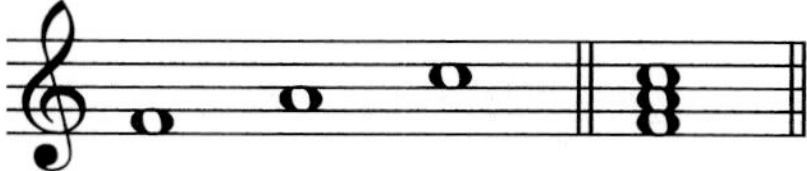

Figure 6.11 Playing More Harmony

PLAYING SONGS

Figure 6.12 Here Comes a Bluebird

Here Comes a Bluebird

Figure 6.13 Button, You Must Wander

Button, You Must Wander
North American Singing Game
But - ton, you must wan - der, wan - der, wan - der,
But - ton, you must wan - der ev - 'ry - where.
Bright eyes will find you, sharp eyes will find you.
But - ton, you must wan - der ev - 'ry - where.

Figure 6.14 Who's That Tapping at the Window

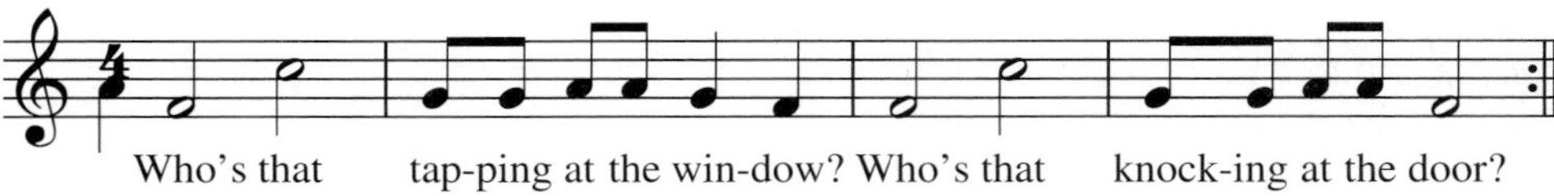
Who's That Tapping at the Window?
North American Singing Game
Who's that tap-ping at the win-dow? Who's that knock-ing at the door?

At the beginning of this song you will see a new symbol, an upside-down half-circle with a dot. This is called a **fermata,** and it means to hold the sound for an indefinite amount of time. It is up to you how long you hold each note. When you play with others, however, someone (probably the course instructor) will decide!

Figure 6.15 Long-Legged Sailor

Long-Legged Sailor
North American Singing Game
Did you ev - er, ev - er, ev - er, in your long - leg - ged
No, I nev - er, nev - er, nev - er, in my long - leg - ged
life, Meet a long - leg-ged sail - or with a long - leg-ged wife?
life, Met a long - leg-ged sail - or with a long - leg-ged wife.

Figure 6.16 Rocky Mountain

Rocky Mountain

Appalachian Folk Song

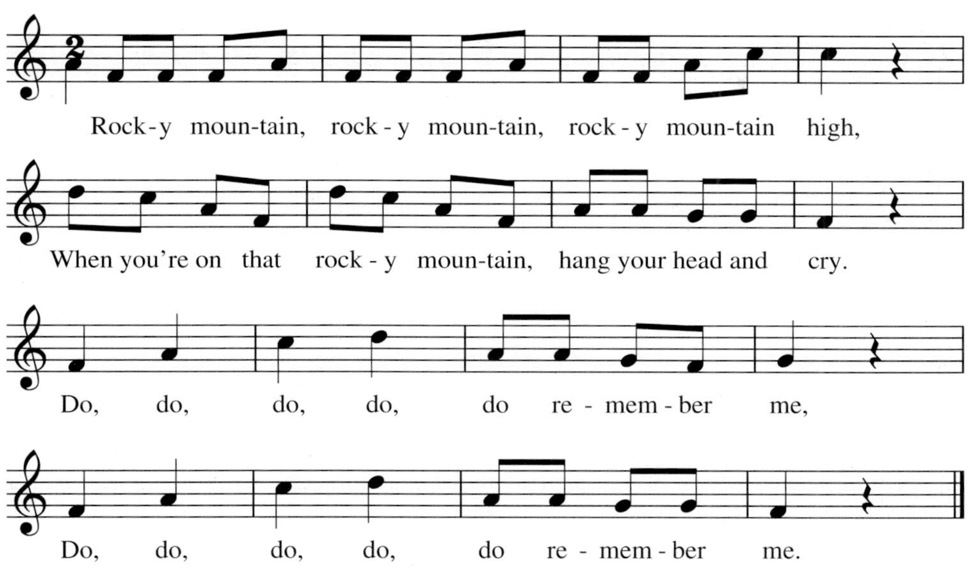

Rock-y moun-tain, rock - y moun-tain, rock - y moun-tain high,
When you're on that rock - y moun-tain, hang your head and cry.
Do, do, do, do, do re - mem - ber me,
Do, do, do, do, do re - mem - ber me.

Figure 6.17 Great Big House

Great Big House

Louisiana Play Party Song

Great big house in New Or - leans For - ty sto - ries high, __

Ev - 'ry room that I been in Filled with pump-kin pie.

Figure 6.18 Oats, Peas, Beans, and Barley Grow

Oats, Peas, Beans, and Barley Grow

English Folk Song

Figure 6.19 Little Tom Tinker

Little Tom Tinker
Traditional
1.
2.
Lit-tle Tom Tin-ker got burned by a clin-ker, and he be-gan to cry,
3.
4.
"Ma, ___ Ma, ___ what a good boy am I."

FURTHER PRACTICE

1. Using your elementary curriculum expertise from another class, develop a lesson plan from another area of the curriculum that would incorporate both singing and listening. Use the following format to organize your plan.

LESSON PLAN

Grade Level:

Type of Integrated Listening Lesson:

Concept:

I. **Learning Outcome or Objective:**

   Entry ability: Students can

   Exit ability: Students will be able to

II. **Lesson Evaluation or Assessment Procedures:**

III. **Materials and Board/Space Preparation:**

IV. **Teaching Procedures:**

   A. Setting the Stage:

   B. Developing the Lesson:

   Step 1:

   Transition:

   Step 2:

   Transition:

   Step 3:

   Transition:

   Step 4:

   C. Concluding the Lesson:

2. Here are four more children's maps of Copland's music. Figure out which musical elements are depicted and write on the map which symbols illustrate these elements.

Figure 6.20 Four Representations of "Circus Music"

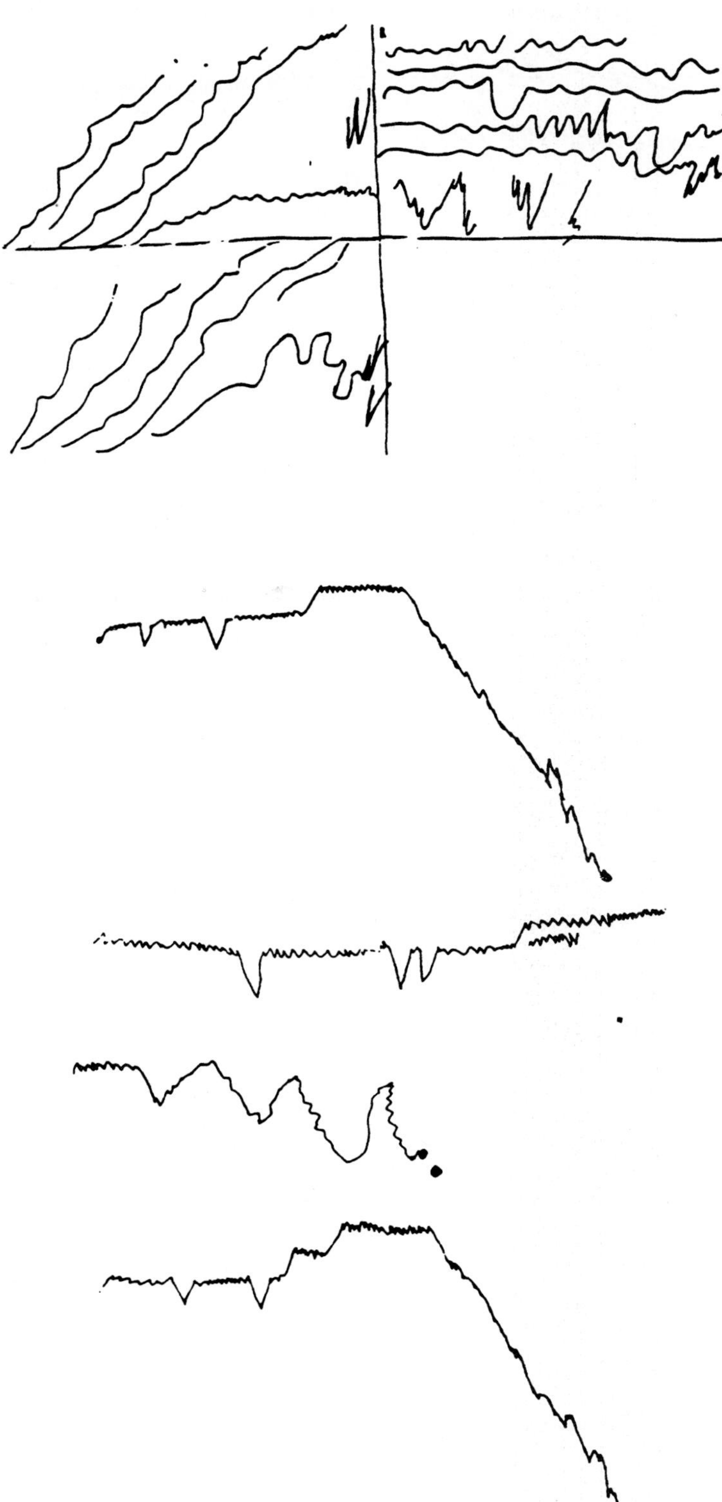

Figure 6.20 *continued*

End

A.

B.

A.

NOTES

[1]Mary Helen Richards (1980). *Aesthetic Foundations for Thinking.* Part 3: The ETM Process. Portola Valley, CA: Richards Institute.

Music Fundamentals for Playing Instruments

THE JOYS OF PLAYING

Since the dawn of time, musical instruments have been part of human culture the world over. From simple percussive sound makers fashioned out of logs to electric guitars and keyboards, human beings have always found a way to create musical sounds that delight and satisfy them. Even in our electrically powered techno-culture, where people are often surrounded by musical sounds most of their day, many adults enjoy music through playing instruments. The current sales figures of electronic keyboards and guitars stand as testimony to this fact, as do the plethora of garage rock bands. Well-known writers such as Stephen King, Amy Tan, and Dave Barry have played in an authors' rock band. For the less famous, summer community bands and year-round community bands and orchestras attest to the value of instrumental playing and participation.

Playing musical instruments is a vital and important way to become engaged in musical experiences. Indeed, the verb used to describe the action used with instruments, "play," implies not only the action of producing sounds but the idea that we think of play as fun and pleasure, not work. As you know, there is a wide range of instruments which require different levels of proficiency and practice. One becomes a piano soloist, for example, by beginning lessons at a very young age and practicing many hours every day throughout childhood, adolescence, and adulthood. Becoming a reasonably proficient recorder player is possible in the course of a semester, again with adequate practice. Other instruments, such as Autoharps, Chromaharps (TM), resonator bells, and Orff-type xylophones and metallophones are played with a minimum of instruction and produce fine sounds that can be combined to create either melodies or harmony. It is indeed possible for you to play instruments in this class and produce valid musical sounds that will be rewarding and satisfying.

When you are beginning to learn how to play recorder, the instrument may not seem to produce a viable and satisfying sound. But once you begin to experiment with dynamic contrasts, play harmony with your peers, add other instruments to accompany your music making, and perhaps have your instructor play the piano or a different-sized recorder while the entire class is playing, you will quickly realize that the recorder is indeed rewarding to learn and lots of fun to play.

The more you practice any instrument, the easier it will be to derive the feelings of accomplishment and satisfaction that await you both as a soloist and as a member of an instrumental ensemble. You will quickly learn what all players know: that time becomes immaterial when you are producing satisfying musical sounds. Your mental focus is on the sound—on how to make a better individual tone as well as produce a variety of delightful sounds. This type of focus is quite different, of course, from memorizing facts or analyzing and applying information, and you will find that practice time and class time pass more quickly than you ever thought possible.

What you will be able to do by the end of this chapter

- *Identify classroom instruments*
- *Perform rhythm patterns accurately on unpitched percussion instruments*
- *Read and play accurately melodic patterns on resonator bells*
- *Write and play major scales*
- *Read and play triads to accompany songs*
- *Lead ensembles of your peers through simple conducting gestures*
- *Play a new note on the recorder*

CHAPTER GOALS

The most crucial determinant of whether you will include music in your daily classroom life is your comfort level with the musical activities you encounter in this class. The activities in this chapter are designed to raise both your comfort level and your musical confidence as you gain further instrumental experience.

The musical skills and knowledge you've developed in previous chapters will be further expanded in this chapter. Your recorder playing will include a new note (E) and incorporate more sophisticated rhythm reading. Your music reading skills will grow as you begin to read rhythm patterns and experiment with the classroom percussion instruments commonly found in elementary schools.

You'll gain performing experience on a wide array of classroom instruments, which will give you the confidence and expertise required to lead your class in the kinds of creative musical activities that enhance the school day. While you won't be expected to achieve symphony-performer status, you do need to look and feel like an expert performer before you can successfully model playing skills for your students, and you will easily achieve this goal by the end of this chapter.

RHYTHM REVIEW PRACTICE

Here are four rhythm patterns (figure 7.1) using the different types of rhythmic notation you learned in your recorder practice in previous chapters. When you practice the patterns at home, first be sure you establish the feeling of a steady pulse by tapping your foot for at least two measures. Then clap each rhythm. After you have practiced each line, write a rhythmic variation underneath it. To write a variation, use some of the original rhythm and change other parts. For example, you could keep measures 1 and 2 and change the next two measures, or you could keep measures 1 and 4 the same and change the measures in between. Practice clapping your new rhythms.

Then decide on a new sound source to use other than clapping. You might use different mouth sounds or sounds you can make on your body, such as tapping your cheek with your mouth open, snapping your fingers, or patting your knees. After you practice with this sound, look around your room or house for a new sound source you can bring to class. Try to find a sound source that will make two different sounds. You might use a comb, which you can snap the teeth of and hit on a desk, or you might use a can of hair spray that you can hit and tap. Look around carefully and experiment, as there are many sound sources that are never thought of as instruments that make wonderful new sounds.

After you select your best sound source, practice the original rhythms and your variation. Try playing one measure with one sound and the next measure with the second sound. Bring your new sound source to class to share with your classmates and instructor.

Figure 7.1 Rhythm Review

Figure 7.13 *continued*

work hand in hand. As they la - bor all day __ long, __
__ They __ lift their voi - ces in song.

TWO MORE CHORDS

The next two chords to learn are the D major and A7 chords. Practice moving from D to A7 by playing each chord four times and then switching. When you can do this smoothly, practice your guitar playing with the following songs.

Figure 7.14 Alouette

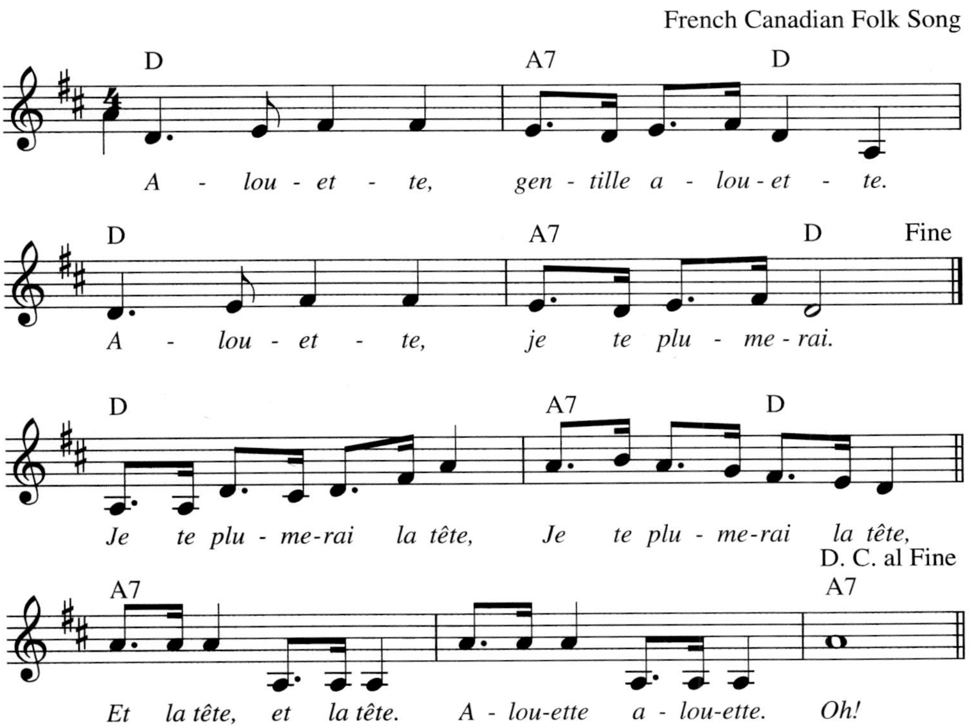

French Canadian Folk Song

A - lou - et - te, gen - tille a - lou - et - te.

A - lou - et - te, je te plu - me - rai.

Je te plu - me-rai la tête, Je te plu - me-rai la tête,

Et la tête, et la tête. A - lou-ette a - lou-ette. Oh!

Figure 7.15 Dry Bones

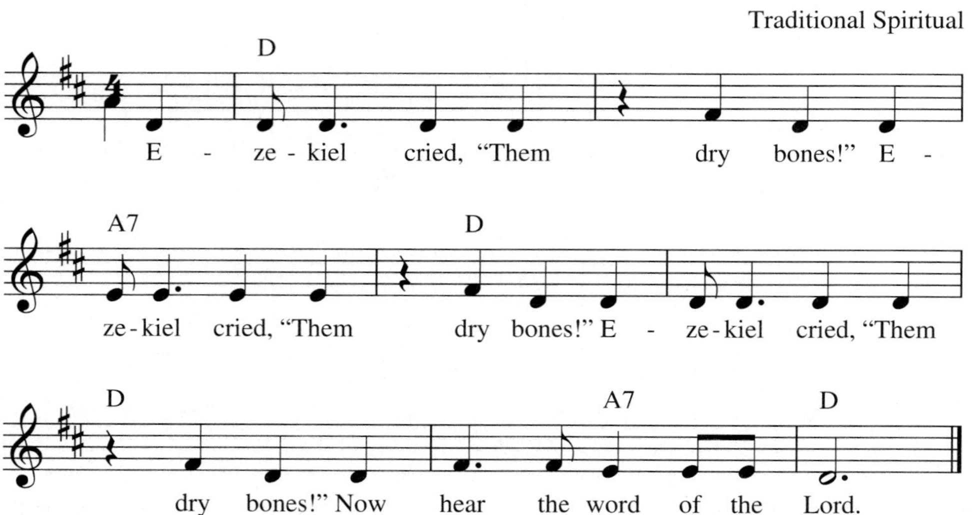

A FOURTH CHORD

To play songs that use three chords in the key of D, you need to learn the chord built on the fourth scale degree, the G chord. Practice playing each chord four times, as shown below:

////	////	////	////	////	////	////	////	////	////	////	////
D	D	G	G	A7	A7	D	D	G	A7	D	D

Then practice the following song, which uses three chords in the key of D.

Figure 7.16 You Are My Sunshine

In Appendix E you will find fingering diagrams for the chords. To master these chords will take practice every day, but when you can play chords in a few keys you will be able to accompany most of your classes' singing, and you will have a tool that enables you to provide wonderful classroom music experiences for your students.

PIANO AND ELECTRIC KEYBOARDS

The piano or electric keyboard is more difficult to master than the recorder, but it is a wonderful classroom tool if you had piano lessons as a youngster or if your instructor spends the needed time on helping you develop this skill in this course. The keyboard set-up at first looks bewildering to a novice, but with careful attention to the order of the black and white keys, you can see that there is indeed a very clear pattern. Looking at and playing any set of keys surrounding the sets of two and three black keys will produce sounds that are repeated at higher (to the right) or lower (to the left) *octaves.* The picture below shows this pattern.

Figure 7.17 Piano Keyboard

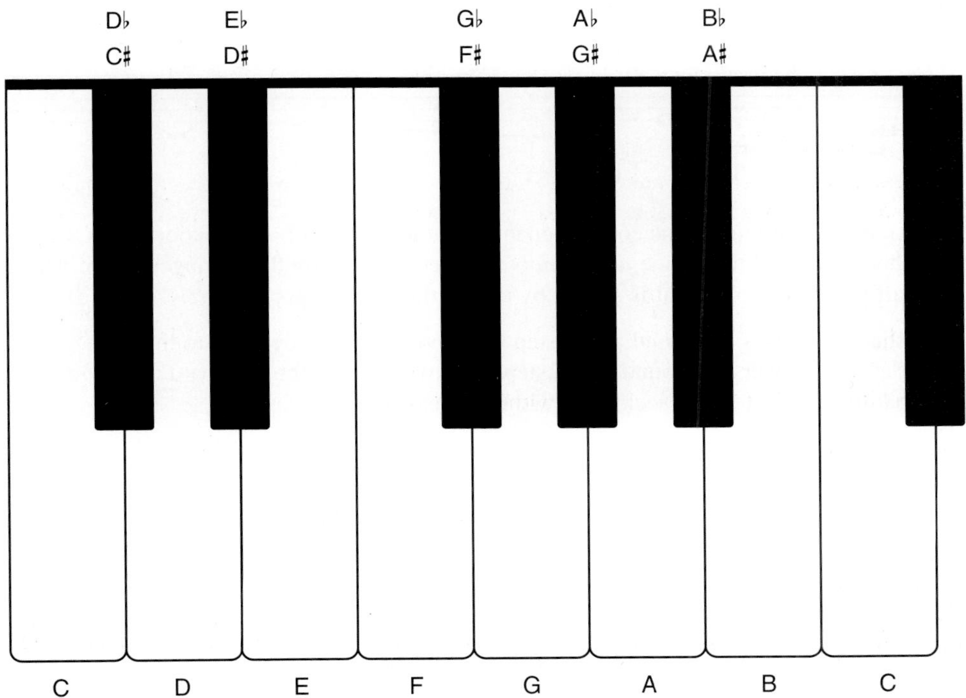

WHOLE AND HALF STEPS

You have played intervals on your recorder in previous chapters. The first important idea to learn about the piano keys is that between every key, the sound produced is called a half step. In each octave, some of these half steps are from a white key to a black key, and two others are between two white keys. On the picture of the keyboard above, find the two places where there are two successive white keys. If you have access to a keyboard, play these naturally occurring half steps as well as the half steps that occur between every white and black key. You will find that the naturally occurring half steps are between E and F and between B and C.

Whole steps are made up of two half steps. Therefore, the interval from C to D is a whole step because of the black key between them. Look at the piano keyboard in figure 7.17, and complete the following exercise by underlining the correct answers as in the first line.

Half- and Whole-Step Exercise

The interval C–D is a <u>half</u>	whole	step.
The interval D–E is a half	whole	step.
The interval E–F is a half	whole	step.
The interval F–G is a half	whole	step.
The interval G–A is a half	whole	step.
The interval A–B is a half	whole	step.
The interval B–C is a half	whole	step.

The arrangement of these whole and half steps is an important idea because the set of pitches from C to C is our model for the major scale. It uses one note for each letter name, and the last note has the same letter name as the first. You sang this scale in chapter 3 with syllables and know it has a very distinctive sound. The sound is due to the following arrangement: whole step, whole step, whole step, half step, whole step, whole step, whole step, half step. In other words, a major scale has a half step between the third and fourth pitches and between the seventh and eighth pitches, and whole steps between all the other pitches.

Figure 7.18 C to C Notation with Half and Whole Steps

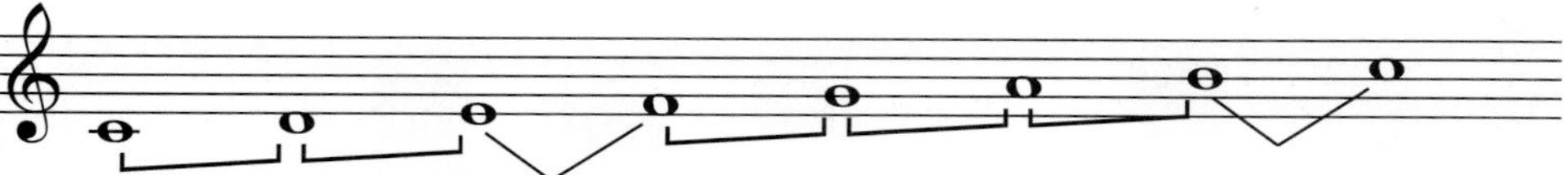

An understanding of this concept enables you to figure out other major scales, but all the others will need to include *accidentals* in order to maintain this arrangement of whole and half steps. An accidental is shown by one of the following symbols:

♯ (sharp): raises the sound a half step by moving up the keyboard to the right
♭ (flat): lowers the sound a half step by moving down the keyboard to the left
♮ (natural): negates any accidental within a measure

In the next example, let's look at the pattern of whole and half steps in the row of notes from G to G.

Figure 7.19 G to G Notation with Whole and Half Steps

This is not a G-major scale yet. In order to make it sound like a G-major scale, we need to superimpose the pattern of whole and half steps from the C-major scale. Look at the C-major scale in figure 7.18 and the G-major scale in figure 7.19. You will see that for the latter, the distance between the F and the G needs to be changed to make a half step. In order to make a half step between F and G, we must raise the F a half step to the right, making the note an F-sharp.

Now put a row of notes from F to F on the staff in figure 7.20.

Figure 7.20 Practice with F Major

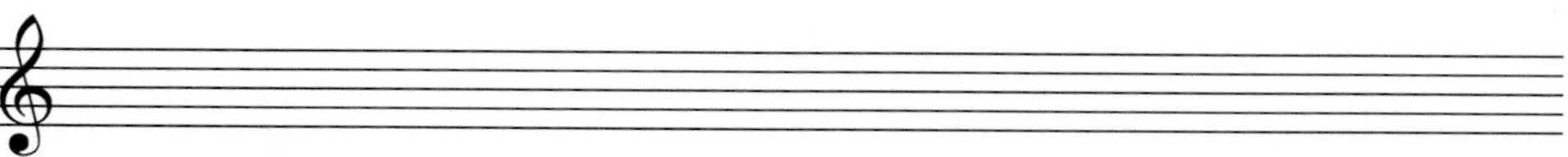

Determine where to write in the correct half- and whole-step symbols for this set of notes. Now compare this pattern of half and whole steps with the pattern for a major scale (see figure 7.18). Circle the note or notes that need to be changed to make the half- and whole-step pattern of the major scale. (You should have circled the B.) The distance from B to C needs to be a whole step for this row of notes to sound like a major scale. Put a flat on the B, to the left of the notehead, in order to make a half step between A and B.

Each note on the keyboard can be the beginning of a major scale and will sound correct if you keep your arrangement of whole and half steps the same, as shown and discussed above. On this practice page, use the keyboard picture at the bottom of the page and figure out more major scales.

Figure 7.21 Practice Page

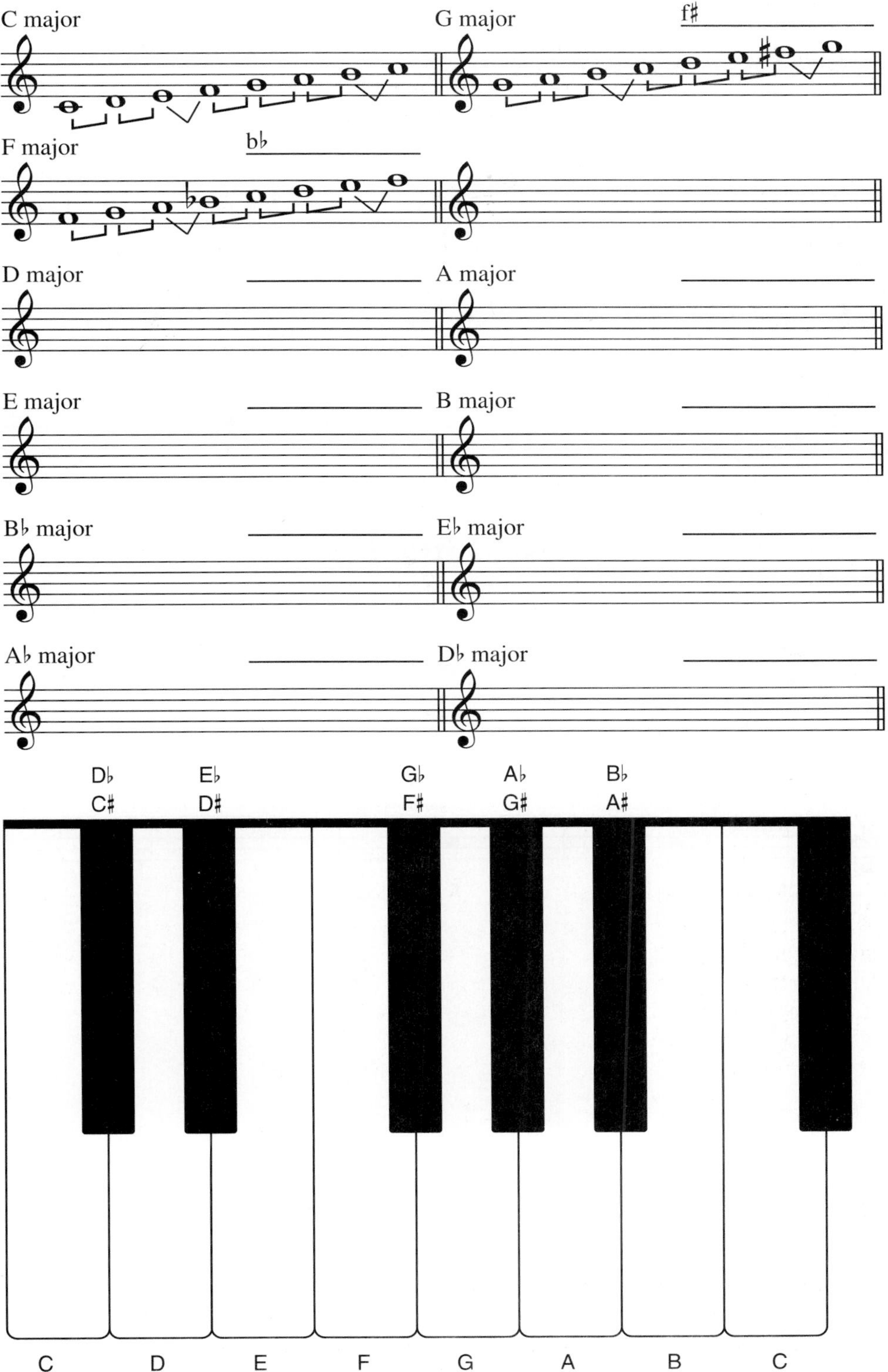

KEY SIGNATURES

Each of the scales that you have written and heard has a similar sound in that you can sing the syllables with them, but each begins on a different pitch on the piano. These different major scales are the source of the collections of accidentals that you find at the beginning of printed music. Such a set of accidentals tells us the name of the scale or of *do* and is called the *key signature.* For example, here is a song you may already know, written in two different keys. The one B-flat at the beginning of the first version tells you that the key of the song is F (the major scale that uses only a B-flat). The one F-sharp at the beginning of the second version tells you that the key of the song is G (the major scale that uses only an F-sharp).

Figure 7.22 Hush, Little Baby in F and G

Hush, Little Baby

Traditional

sol mi mi mi fa mi re re re

sol sol re re re re mi re do do

Hush, Little Baby

Below you will find the major-key signatures for each of the scales that you just wrote on p. 231.

Figure 7.23 Major Key Signatures

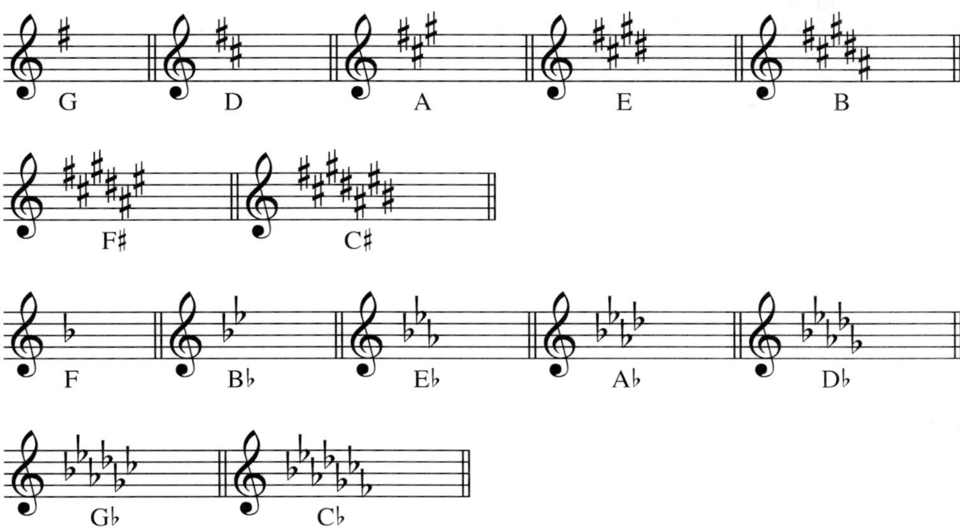

As you sing songs in different keys, you will find that some keys are very comfortable ones for you to sing in. Some keys may use pitches that strain your voice. For this reason, it is good to know that you can sing the song in a more comfortable key. If you look carefully at figure 7.22, you will see that the pattern of the notes and syllables is identical, even though the starting note is different in each version. The starting note is low *sol,* or the fifth note of the scale. When you sing this song in these two different keys in class, note if one is more comfortable for your own voice.

You can write this song in another key very easily. This process is called *transposing.* On the first staff in figure 7.24, you will find the major scale and syllables for A major. On the second staff you will find the beginning of "Hush, Little Baby" written in A major. Finish writing the song in this new key by using the same syllables as those used in the song in figure 7.22.

Figure 7.24 "Hush, Little Baby" transposition

Hush, Little Baby

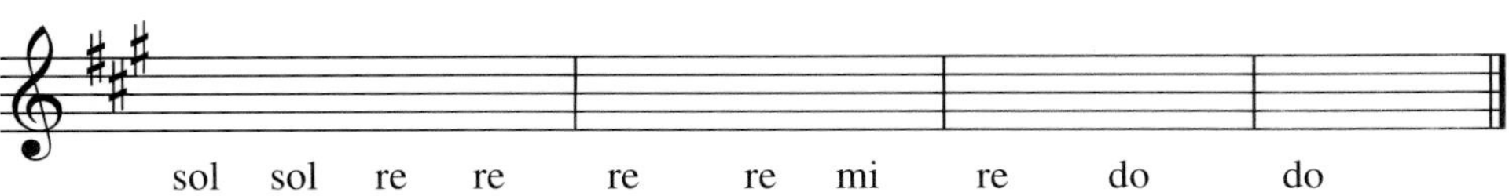

TRIADS AND CHORDS

One of the most enjoyable ways to enhance singing is to add a simple accompaniment based on the harmonic structure of the piece. The added notes, called **triads** (three notes sounded at the same time), can be played along with the melody on a piano or other keyboard instrument, or as a **tremolo** on resonator bells (holding the mallet in your right hand and the bell in your left, hit the bell quickly and repetitively several times to sustain the tone for the required duration). The point is that it is fun to sing along with an accompaniment, and many printed songbooks include triad symbols that are easy to read and translate into musical tones.

In your recorder practice you have played triads with your classmates, but because your recorder can only produce one sound at time, you cannot produce triads or chords to play harmony alone. Triads are sets of three notes, and chords are sets of four or more notes that are sounded at the same time. The harmonic accompaniments of most of the songs you will use with children generally use only three triads or chords. These are based on the first, fourth, and fifth scale degrees and have the name of the letter of the bottom pitch.

In the following example (figure 7.25), the song "Hush, Little Baby" appears with letter symbols above some of the notes.

Figure 7.25 "Hush, Little Baby" with Letter Symbols

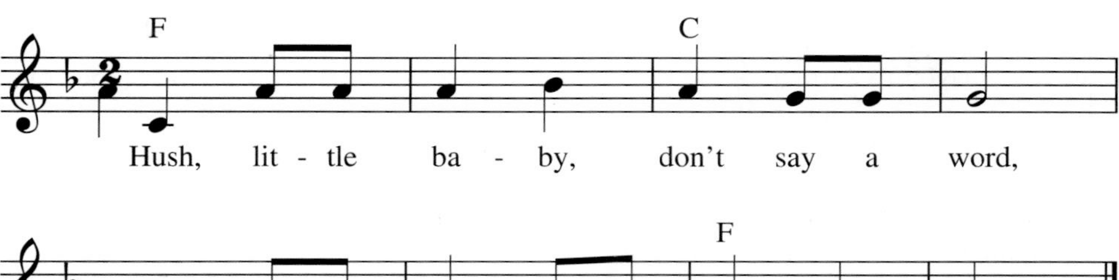
Hush, Little Baby
F
C
Hush, lit - tle ba - by, don't say a word,
F
Ma - ma's gon - na buy you a mock - ing - bird.

2. If that mockingbird don't sing,
   Mama's gonna buy you a diamond ring.

3. If that diamond ring turns brass,
   Mama's gonna buy you a looking glass.

4. If that looking glass gets broke,
   Mama's gonna buy you a billy goat.

5. If that billy goat don't pull,
   Mama's gonna buy you a cart and bull.

6. If that cart and bull turn over,
   Mama's gonna buy you a dog named Rover.

7. If that dog named Rover don't bark,
   Mama's gonna buy you a pony cart.

8. If that pony cart falls down,
   You'll be the saddest little boy/girl in town.

To translate these symbols into playable notes, simply follow these rules. First, the letter name of the triad stands for the bottom note of the three-note stack. The first triad symbol in this song is F, so we'll build the stack or triad on F and use the notes F, A, and C.

When these are sounded at the same time, the result is the F triad, and it sounds pleasant with the words "Hush, little baby." You'll notice that the next triad is C, and it is meant to sound on the words "don't say a word" and "Mama's gonna buy you a" in the second line of the song. This is followed by another F triad on the word "mockingbird." The other verses of the song follow the same pattern.

Building triads is quite easy if you use your picture of the keyboard and your knowledge of scales and key signatures.

1. Find the letter name of the triad and write it on the staff. This becomes the bottom note of the triad.
2. To build the triad: if you are on a note that is written in a space, write the next note on the next space up the staff. If you are on a note that is written on a line, write the note on the next line up the staff. From where you are now, go up one more line (if you started on a line) or space (if you started on a space) and write a third note.
3. You now have three notes written, and they should sound at the same time either on the piano or on resonator bells. Each of the written notes of the F triad should be sitting in a space.

Figure 7.26 F and C Triads

The greatest challenge in performing the accompanying triads is not in figuring out what notes to play but in changing from triad to triad as the song moves along. The easiest way to become fluent at performing the accompaniments is to practice the triads first, then try to play them along with the song while singing it very slowly at a steady tempo. You'll soon find that, with a bit of practice, you can begin to read ahead in the musical line and get ready for the triads before you need to perform them.

ACTIVITY In groups of three or four, figure out the note names of the triads in "Alouette" (figure 7.14) and "You Are My Sunshine" (figure 7.16). Write in the letter names of these triads next to the chord symbols above the staff, then try to play the accompaniment while some members of your group sing the song.

FACETS OF ENSEMBLE PLAYING

An important aspect of ensemble playing, and ensemble leading, is establishing a steady beat for yourself and your fellow performers and then keeping that tempo throughout your performance. From the work you did in earlier chapters, you've gained skill in setting and maintaining a steady beat in your musical performances, and in this section you will gain further experience at setting and keeping a steady beat for others.

The most common problem encountered by novice musicians is speeding up. You can avoid this problem by putting the steady beat into some part of your body and then focusing on keeping it very regular and accurate. Some students feel most comfortable using an index finger as a vertical pendulum, tapping it up and down in the air to keep the steady beat.

Your index finger is easier to control than your whole foot, which is another favorite appendage for keeping the beat. Tapping your foot requires many more muscles than simply tapping your finger and also inhibits your ability to stand upright. This simple up-and-down motion of the finger has been called the *tactus* and can actually show the beat as accurately as a second hand on an analog clock.

Once you understand the concept of the tactus, it is easy to put the steady beat into a more conventional conducting pattern of two or three, or duple or triple. All music is either in duple meter (a beat pattern of two or a multiple of two) or triple meter (a beat pattern of three). To show duple meter, simply use your index finger as you did for the tactus or steady beat and follow the pattern illustrated in figure 7.27.

Figure 7.27 Duple-Meter Conducting Pattern

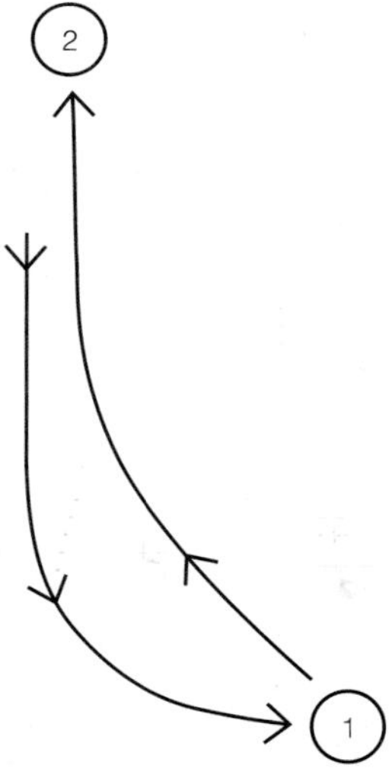

To show triple meter, use your finger again to follow the pattern illustrated in figure 7.28.

Figure 7.28 Triple-Meter Conducting Pattern

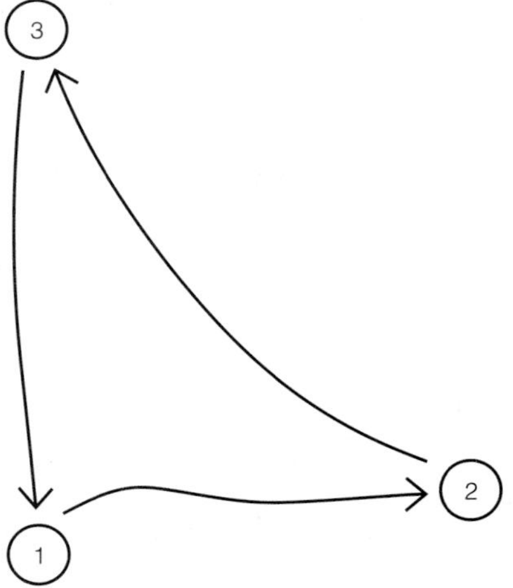

ACTIVITY As directed by your instructor, determine the meter of each of the following CD selections and then practice conducting the duple or triple pattern.

Tanzen und Springen, CD track 9
Coal Quay Market, CD track 3
Try to Remember, CD track 6
American Salute, CD track 15

Now that you can tell from looking at the meter signature how many beats there are in each bar or measure, conduct your classmates. As you already know, the top number in the meter signature defines the number of beats in a measure. Once you've determined the meter, you know whether you should use the duple or triple conducting pattern. Then you just count one whole bar or measure aloud ("one-two" or "one-two-three") and begin the conducting pattern on the first beat of the measure or bar.

For example, look at "Try to Remember" (figure 7.29).

Figure 7.29 Try to Remember

Try to Remember

The meter signature is $\frac{3}{4}$, so the pattern you'll use is triple (down, right, up). To begin the song, you'll need to know the starting pitch (B) and the tempo. Play a B, hum it to yourself, and then decide the speed of the beat that you'd like to use for this song. Now sing the pitch, B, while counting a whole bar or measure ("one-two-three"), so that you know exactly what the pitch and steady beat will be. Try it again, this time counting "one-two-three" while singing it on the pitch B, and begin singing the song and conducting yourself up to "mellow."

You are now ready to try this whole procedure in front of a mirror so you can see how it looks to someone who needs to watch you, such as your classmates whom you will conduct. When you try it in front of a mirror, you may notice how important it is to make eye contact with your fellow performers before the song starts, during the preparatory beats (the measure in which you are counting out loud), since you will want to signal to them exactly when each beat of the song occurs and when the initial note will sound. It is very important that you look directly at your performers during the preparatory beats so they will all be exactly together with you and begin singing together precisely at the same time, on the correct pitch.

ACTIVITY Conduct small groups of peers (three or four people) as if they were going to perform "Try to Remember," following the procedure outlined above. Repeat the procedure until you are successful at establishing both the pitch and the tempo. Then discuss this experience in pairs.

The procedure for conducting instruments is exactly the same, except that you need not sing the starting pitch. Simply determine the pattern you need to use, duple or triple, and count aloud one full measure or bar at the speed you intend to follow.

If you look back to Chapter 5 for the recorder example in figure 5.13, "Quand j'etais mon père," you'll find one further complication: an incomplete first measure or bar. To start this piece, you'll need to first establish that you should use the triple pattern, and then count out one complete bar of three. Then conduct beats 1 and 2 to silence and bring in the performers on beat 3.

Conductors use their gestures as well as their eyes to indicate to the performers when they should begin, and in measures where the performers begin on beats other than 1 or 2 it is particularly important that the performers know that they should not begin on the first beat. You can reinforce this fact by using your left hand to indicate the third beat, raising both hands for beat 3, and then just using your right hand for the rest of the song.

The other challenge, in addition to bringing all the performers in at the same time, is getting them all to stop at the same time. This is called the **cut-off**, and it can be indicated in a variety of ways, including bringing your index finger and thumb together in a pinching motion, making your hands into a fist shape, or pretending to pull two ends of an imaginary piece of elastic horizontally in front of you. Since most music ends with longer-held notes, it is important that you maintain eye contact with the performers and indicate very clearly exactly when you want them to stop the sound. With practice, these simple conducting skills become easier and quite fun to do, especially when the result is enjoyable music making.

CONDUCTING A ROUND

Now that you've mastered the conducting basics of keeping the beat, maintaining either the duple or triple beat pattern, and bringing in and cutting off the performers, you're ready to master the art of conducting a round. You already have all the skills required for this task, but you'll need to use them in a more complicated way. Instead of just bringing in the whole group at once, you will be bringing in several groups in succession.

Study the music for "Rise Up O Flame" (figure 7.30). You'll notice first that this piece is in triple meter and begins on the first beat of the measure. The first and last notes are both C. The numbers 1, 2, 3, and 4 appear above the staff at the first, second, third, and fourth measures. These numbers tell you that this is a four-part round and also indicate the point at which you as the conductor should bring in the various voices. Voice 1 begins the song, and when voice 1 gets to the word "flame," voice 2 should sing "Rise." When voice 1 gets to "by," voice 3 should sing "Rise," and when voice 1 gets to "glow-," voice 4 should sing "Rise."

It is the task of the conductor to make sure each successive voice begins the round at the right time. This means that the conductor must know where each group of performers is so that he can look at them and give them the signal to begin when it is their turn. Conducting a round is a bit like doing several tasks at once, such as walking across the street while chewing gum and working out a math problem on a calculator. But keeping the steady beat and looking at the correct group just before it is their turn to start singing are the most important aspects of the task, and they are easily manageable with a little practice.

ACTIVITY To begin this task, learn the round "Rise Up O Flame," found in figure 7.30. Your instructor may teach it to you by rote or using another method. Once you have learned it, work in groups of five, with one person as conductor and the other four as singers. The conductor should bring in each singer in turn and cut each one off after he or she has sung the round twice. Allow each member of the group to serve as conductor, and rotate the order in which the individual singers come in (i.e., don't have the same person start the round each time). Pay particular attention to the different ways each conductor uses his or her facial expressions and hands to indicate entrances and cut-offs. Discuss this experience and be ready to report your findings first to the larger group, then to the entire class.

Figure 7.30 Rise Up O Flame

ADDITIONAL PLAYING EXPERIENCE

The following musical activity is provided to give you further playing experience. Your instructor will direct you in the activity in class, playing a single note from each triad on tone bars. You can prepare for class by looking the activity over to familiarize yourself with the musical requirements of this task. (Note: The entire listening example takes four minutes, thirty seconds, and requires you to play the accompaniment figure 26 times. You may choose to use just a portion of the entire listening example for this activity.)

Figure 7.31 Pachelbel Canon Triads

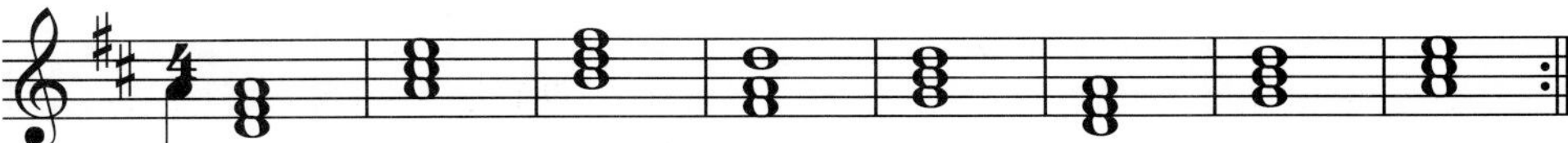

ACTIVITY

1. Four-Part Rhythm Scores

The following four-part rhythm scores are meant to be played by four people at the same time. Each person will read only one line of four bars or measures. Notice the different meters, rests, and note values in each score. At home, practice clapping the patterns needed to perform each part in each score. Then be prepared to perform any of the parts in any of the scores in small groups in class. Decide which percussion instruments you might want to use for each score. Practice conducting each of the scores, paying attention to your beat pattern (duple or triple) and the cut-off.

Figure 7.32 Rhythm Scores

2. Rhythm Improvisation

The following two-bar rhythm patterns include many that you learned in previous chapters. Clap through the complete set of rhythms without observing the repeat sign. Then try them all again observing the repeat sign. Now you are ready to play them in class. (a) In groups of five (with one person serving as conductor), assign different families of instruments to the various two-bar patterns (woods, metals, and membranophones). (b) Decide the order in which the patterns will be played. (c) Have the conductor start the group. (d) After the first time through, discuss the degree of success you had during this performance and decide how you'd make the next attempt sound better. (e) Perform the patterns a second time and evaluate your second performance. (f) The third time through, have one person from your group make up a different rhythm pattern and play this pattern on another instrument as accompaniment for the group. This improvised (newly made up on the spot) pattern can then be changed and modified by another person in the group, and he or she can play the new instrument while the group continues to play the notated rhythms.

Figure 7.33 Rhythm Improvisations

3. Recorder Textures

In previous chapters you learned various musical textures, including monophonic, polyphonic, and homophonic. "Monophonic" means one voice only, while "polyphonic" refers to many different independent voices moving in independent melodies. "Homophonic" means a single melody with accompaniment. The following three-part recorder round, "Sweetly Sings the Donkey" (figure 7.34), can be played in each of the three textures.

Figure 7.34 Sweetly Sings the Donkey

(a) Read through the melody, fingering your recorder while resting it on your chin without blowing into it. (b) Read through it again, saying the note names while fingering the notes, still resting your recorder on your chin and not blowing. (c) Now try blowing the notes as you read through the melody, observing a steady tempo. You are now ready for the next activity. (d) In groups of four, perform "Sweetly Sings the Donkey" three different ways. Three people will be recorder players, and one will be the conductor. (1) First, have all three recorder players play the round monophonically, with the fourth person serving as conductor. Observe the breath marks and hold the half notes for a full two beats. (2) Decide who will play parts one, two, and three of the round. Have the conductor bring in each of the three parts as the group performs the entire round twice through. (3) Have two people play the first recorder part while the rest of the group adds the chordal accompaniment in figure 7.34 to create a homophonic texture. See if you can do it without a conductor. Discuss the experience with your peers.

A NEW RECORDER NOTE: F♯

Figure 7.35 Recorder Fingering for F♯

● ●
●
●
—
○
●
●
○

You will note that beginning with the fourth example in figure 7.36, the F-sharp is placed in the key signature. Remember that you must now play an F-sharp every time you read an F in these lines.

FURTHER PIANO PRACTICE

SONGS WITH TWO CHORDS

Figure 7.42 Go, Tell It on the Mountain

Figure 7.43 Hot Cross Buns

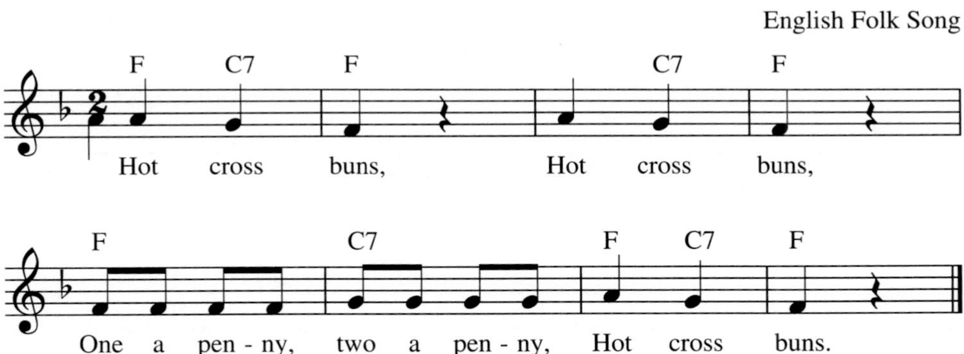

Figure 7.44 The More We Get Together

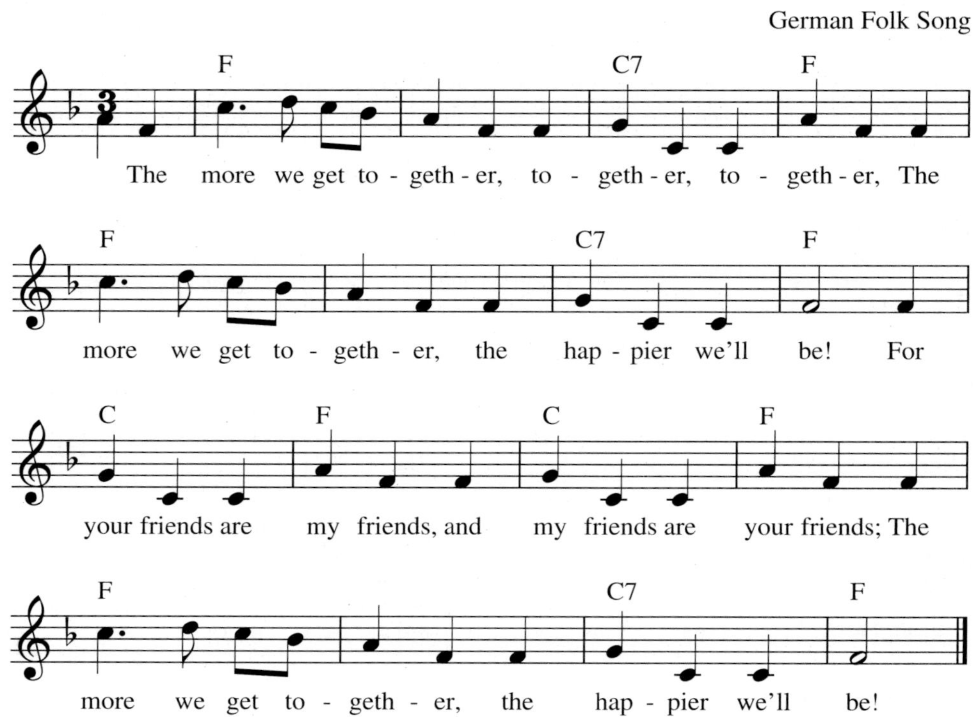

Figure 7.45 Buenos Días, Amigo

Figure 7.46 Old Blue

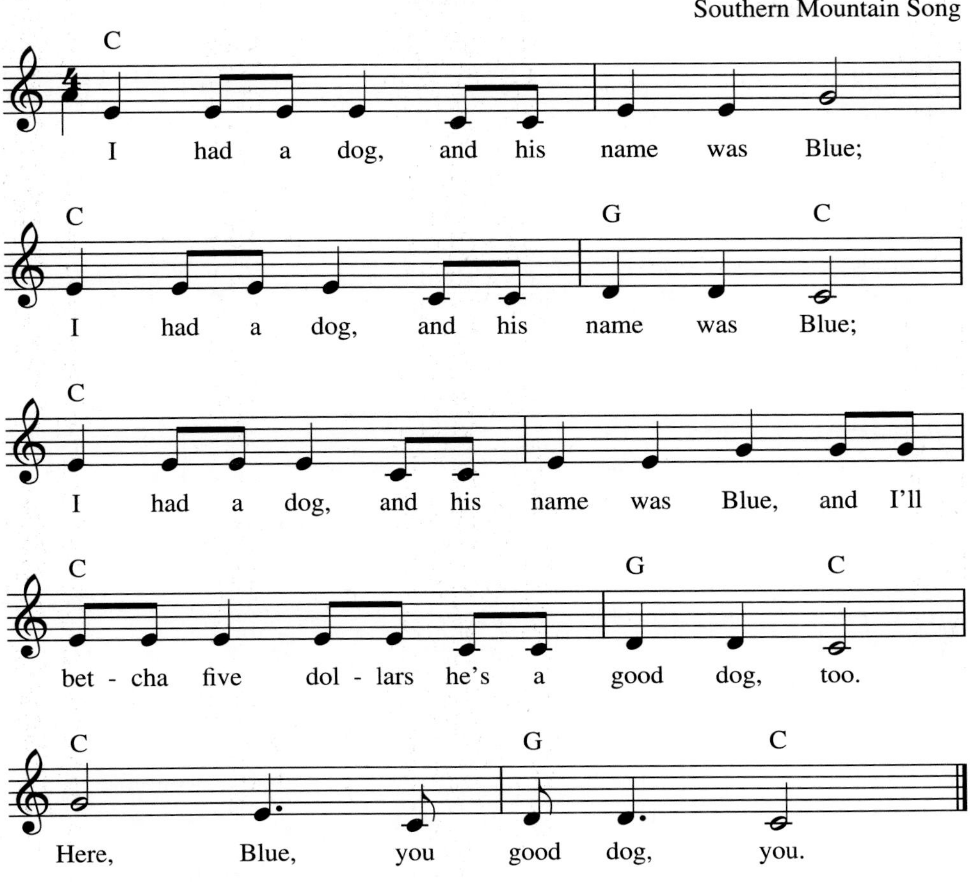
Old Blue
Southern Mountain Song
C
I had a dog, and his name was Blue;
C G C
I had a dog, and his name was Blue;
C
I had a dog, and his name was Blue, and I'll
C G C
bet - cha five dol - lars he's a good dog, too.
C G C
Here, Blue, you good dog, you.

Figure 7.47 Vamos a la mar

Vamos a la mar
Guatemalan Folk Song
C G7
Va - mos a la mar, tum, tum, a co - mer pes -
C C G7
ca - do, tum, tum. Bo - ca co - lo - ra - da, tum,
C
tum, fri - ti - to y a - sa - do, tum, tum.

Figure 7.48 Shoo, Fly

SONGS WITH THREE CHORDS

Figure 7.49 You Are My Sunshine

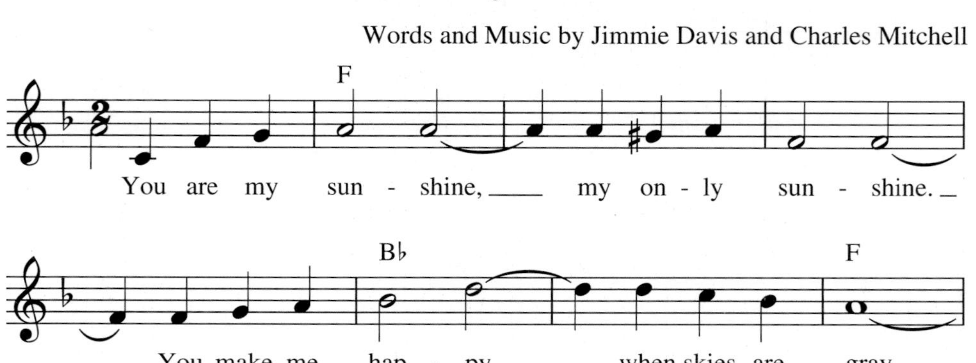

Figure 7.49 *continued*

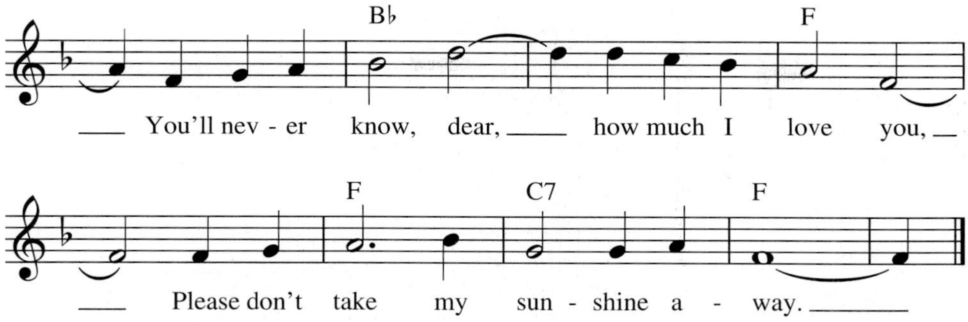

Figure 7.50 Mister Frog

Figure 7.51 Little Chickens

Figure 7.52 This Old Man

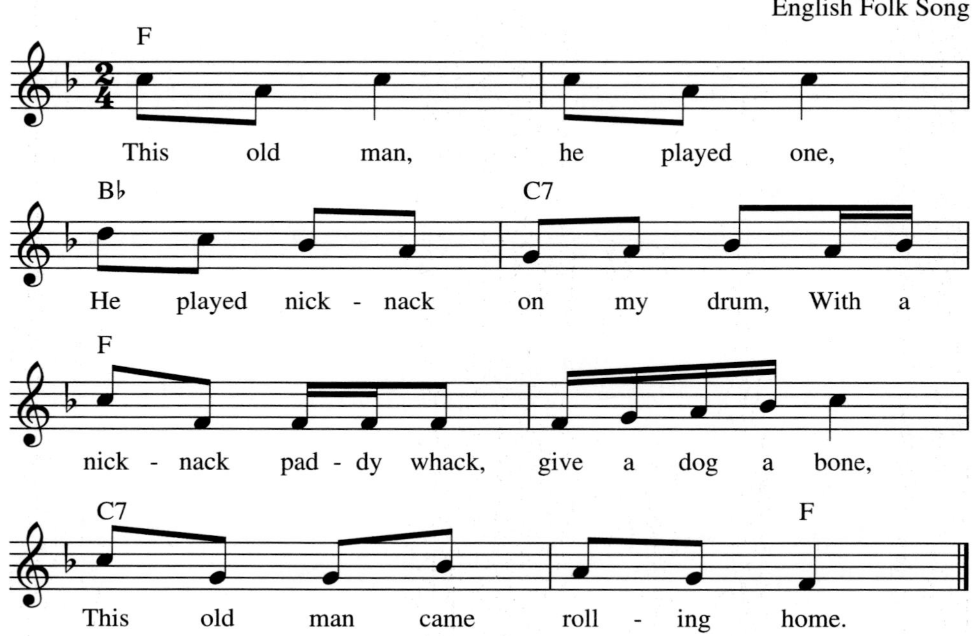

Figure 7.53 If You're Happy

Figure 7.54 All Night, All Day

All Night, All Day

G C
All night, all ___ day, An - gels watch-ing o - ver

D7 G
me, my Lord. _ All night, all ___ day,

D7 G
An - gels watch - ing o - ver me.

Figure 7.55 She'll Be Comin' 'Round the Mountain

She'll Be Comin' 'Round the Mountain

FURTHER PRACTICE

1. Look at "Sweetly Sings the Donkey" (figure 7.34). In groups of seven, assign the following parts: three people to play the melody as a round, one conductor, and three people to play the chordal accompaniment on resonator bells. Use the following questions to focus your discussion as you rehearse and improve your performance:
   a. How well did it work?
   b. Does one part need to be practiced alone?
   c. How can the conductor help you more in your performance?
   d. Can you do anything with dynamics or tempo to make your performance sound more musical?

   Practice the piece again after reassigning all the parts.
2. As preparation for class, write a four-measure rhythm pattern in the space below. This pattern will be used in combination with two others to make a three-part rhythm score.

   All three group members should first rehearse each line of rhythm. Then create a three-part texture by having everyone clap their own rhythm simultaneously. After your group can clap the rhythms together, play your score using three different timbres of classroom instruments (woods, metals, and membranophones, for example).
3. Select a recorded piece of music that appeals to you and bring it to class to use for conducting practice.
4. On the melody staves below (figure 7.56), write one primary song from chapter 4 with the chord symbols. Then, on the triad staff, write the notation for the triads in whole notes.

   Name of Song______________________________ Page no. ______

Figure 7.56 Melody and Triads

5. On the following staves (figure 7.57), complete the labeled major scales, using the needed accidentals. Label the whole and half steps using the bracket symbols found in this chapter.

Figure 7.57 Major Scales Practice

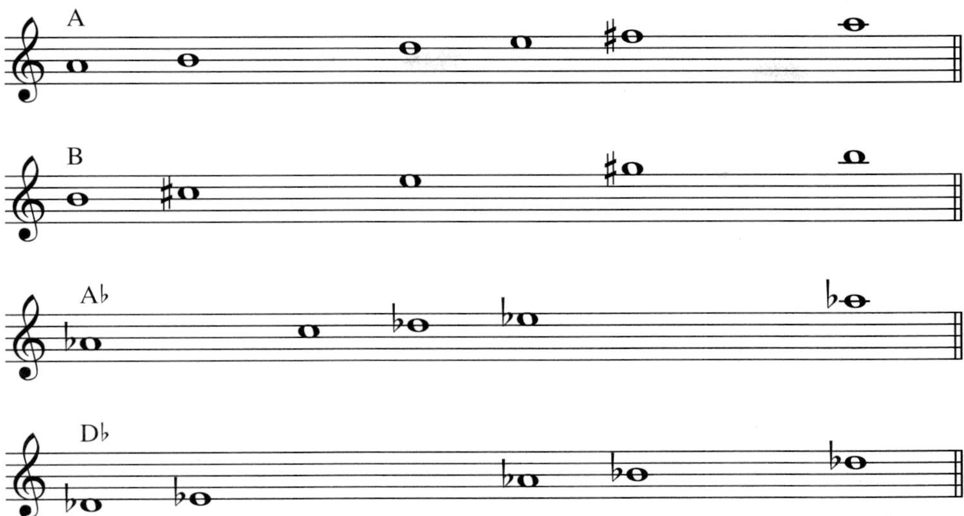

6. Transpose "Sweetly Sings the Donkey" (figure 7.58) to the key of D major. Use the correct key signature and write in the letter names of the triads you would use in this key.

Figure 7.58 Sweetly Sings the Donkey

Playing Instruments with Children

What you will be able to do by the end of this chapter

- *Make playing activities part of lesson planning*
- *Devise ways to enable children to listen more intently*
- *Categorize and classify sounds*
- *Explore alternate ways of producing sounds*
- *Develop a lesson plan that includes playing instruments*
- *Accompany original writing with instrument sounds*
- *Play a new note on the recorder*
- *Play more children's songs on the recorder*

INSTRUMENTAL ENJOYMENT

Playing musical instruments is another way for children to express themselves in your classroom in a very satisfying activity. Young children love to experiment and explore the sound-producing possibilities in their home and play environments. Older children are fascinated by the possibilities of actual instruments, and even a single drum can be a magnet for children of all ages. Exploring a variety of available sounds and incorporating them in imaginative play, whole-language experiences, and other curriculum areas is a vital way to enhance learning for both younger and older learners.

As mentioned in chapter 7, we speak of "playing" an instrument, and children think of play as fun and pleasure, not work. The addition of instruments to any activity keeps children interested and provides more opportunities for repetition. Often this type of repetition will provide children who have different learning styles with the needed amount of time to assimilate that which is being taught. Playing instruments is also a way to enhance your classroom community, because the social skills involved include group effort and cooperation as well as group decision making.

Musical instruments can be used singly or in endless combinations. Young children can explore the timbre contrasts possible in a single instrument or the contrasts between two or more instruments while deciding which sound will best complement a song they have learned in class or a text they have written in whole-language experiences. Older learners can enrich original stories, poems, or songs by including instrumental sounds they have carefully considered and selected. All children learn best when they are actively involved in the process, and the addition of classroom instruments to a well-planned, well-executed lesson never fails to entice children further into the experience. Sound explorations not only extend listening ability, critical thinking, and particular subject matter, but they also enhance children's affective knowing.

Children need to explore, assimilate, and enjoy the variety of sounds possible from each individual instrument you have in your classroom. They may experiment with a xylophone by using mallets with rubber, plastic, or felt heads, or by using beaters that they invent from other materials. They may discover the differences in sound when a drum is tapped with the fingers on its edge or struck in the middle with the palm of the hand or with any of the xylophone mallets. Such exciting contrasts can be important additions to the quality of sound produced by a group of children singing or speaking, and a wide variety of sounds can extend and refine children's musical and classroom experience.

Playing instruments is another way to relate the many curriculum areas that children experience in their elementary classrooms. The inclusion of musical instruments with the songs of particular cultures enhances classroom learning as children actually experience the sounds of the culture. A wide variety of objects as well as actual instruments can reinforce science units about sound in enticing ways. Including instrument playing is a natural way to extend and enrich the curriculum and will provide interest and motivation in your classroom.

Another result of playing instruments in the elementary classroom is competence in making musical sounds as a soloist and as part of an ensemble. And as in any ensemble, it is possible to vary the difficulty of the parts so that each class member participates successfully. Children who are gifted and children who are developmentally delayed derive equal pleasure from playing instruments, and this musical activity can easily be adapted to accommodate the wide range of abilities found in every class. Every child, therefore, can participate in procedural, kinesthetic, and affective musical knowing when engaged as an instrumental performer.

Instrumental accompaniments are popular additions to musical public performances and are a simple way to augment children's singing. Parents and administrators respond well to performances by children and the instrumental playing need not be complicated to elicit this response. The current educational restructuring, which is focused on the value of "outcome-based" and "performance-based" education, supports the sharing of classroom learning and endeavors and is a delightful way for you to present what children have accomplished and learned about many different curriculum areas.

CHAPTER GOALS

In this chapter you will practice using your playing skills as well as your singing and listening skills in the role of classroom teacher of younger and older children. You will learn how to incorporate playing experiences into the daily curriculum and be a confident model for your students. You will also learn many ways to enhance your students' listening and playing development.

An important aspect of playing instruments with children is knowing when the inclusion of additional sounds will best enhance classroom endeavors. This chapter will help you understand this important concept. You will also learn how to lead children in exploring sounds from found objects as well as standard instruments and how to write lesson plans that include this process.

Like previous chapters, this one is designed to enable you to become confident in your ability to lead children in playing experiences. We want you to understand that playing instruments is such an exciting experience for children that it must not be omitted from your classroom, leaving it to be experienced only occasionally, in the music room. Producing and experiencing sounds other than speech and song are important parts of children's daily classroom lives.

CASE STUDY

Mrs. Saba stands up in front of her first-grade class and says, "Everyone please take out the pair of big white socks that you brought from home today. We're going to put them on over our shoes right now and go outside on a 'sock walk.' When we come back from our walk, we'll take a look at our socks to see what we can learn about where we've been." She directs the class to form a double line, and they follow her out of the classroom, down the hall, and out the front door of the school. After half an hour of walking, the class returns to the room and Mrs. Saba goes around to each child's desk to help them take off their big socks and place them carefully on their desktops. She then begins: "Let's see what we've brought back with us from our walk. What can you see on your socks?" The children study their not-so-white socks, and several hands go up. "I've got a lot of little tiny seeds stuck in my socks," offers Sara. "Me, too," interjects Rashid, "but I've also got some sticky stuff that looks like tar!" The class laughs, and Mrs. Saba continues, "Let's all look very carefully at our own socks and then write out a list of what each of us finds. You may take out your pencils and notebooks and begin writing as soon as you can identify something on your socks."

After a flurry of activity during which pencils and notebooks are produced, the class settles into the task of writing their invented spellings for what they've found. A few minutes later, Mrs. Saba says, "Now we're each going to read from our lists one thing that we found, and I'll put the words up on the board for all of us to see and read." Starting with the first child in the first row, Mrs. Saba calls on each child to name one item from his or her list. She writes each child's response on the board, resulting in a sizable list by the time the last of the 28 children has responded. Mrs. Saba then says, "We seem to have brought back everything from dust to spiders on our socks, first grade! This is a pretty big list, and I'm wondering if there's a way we can rearrange these words into groups, somehow, so that things that are similar can go together." After a few seconds Brita raises her hand and says, "We could put all the 'w's together, like 'water' and 'web'!" "Yes, that's one way to do it," replies Mrs. Saba. "Let's see how that would work. Are there any more 'w' words besides 'water' and 'web'?" Damian pipes up, "No, but there are lots of 'd' words: 'dirt,' 'dust,' 'dog doo'!" "You're right, Damian!" laughs Mrs. Saba. "Let's use the alphabet chart to help us group all the words by their starting sound, starting with 'a.' " The class progresses quickly through the list, grouping all the words by their starting sound, and Mrs. Saba concludes the activity by saying, "That was good thinking, class. Let's save this list, though, and we'll have another look at it this afternoon when we do another grouping activity."

After lunch Mrs. Saba brings out several boxes of rhythm instruments and places them around the room. She says, "Remember our sock activity this morning, class? We're going to do another grouping lesson with these instruments now, and I'm wondering how we might group these instruments." She takes a large drum from one of the boxes and holds it up. "How would you group this one?" she asks. Damian bursts in without putting his hand up, "It's a 'd' word, of course, just like me!" The class laughs along with Mrs. Saba, who says, "Yes, it is, Damian, but you forgot to put your hand up. And there are other ways to group all of these instruments besides by the starting sound of their names. We can group them by the way we make sounds on them such as hitting, plucking, or shaking, or by the material from which they are made, such as wood, metal, or shell. Let's look at these two instruments and see how we could group them." She holds up the drum and a triangle. Gregory is waving his hand, and she calls on him. "The two instruments have different shapes. One is round and one is a triangle." "That's right," says Mrs. Saba. "How else could we group these instruments?" The children look at her, puzzled. "Well," she says, "how do these instruments make a sound?" "Oh," says Gregory, "you hit them, of course." "Yes," says Mrs. Saba, pulling out a maraca. "Does this instrument belong in this group also?" Loren has his hand up, and Mrs. Saba says, "Well, Loren, what do you think?" Loren responds, "That's one of those shaker things, I think, so it would not go in this group." Mrs. Saba says, "Right. We now have two groups, instruments that we hit and instruments that we shake. Now I'd like each of you to work with a partner and draw all the instruments in the box nearest your desk. Then color with the same color those instrument pictures that belong in the same group. Let's get busy with a partner right now." The pairs scurry to the boxes nearest their desks and begin the task.

Cooperative Questions to Discuss

1. Write the rest of this case, showing how Mrs. Saba could synthesize their discoveries and conclude the lesson.
2. Is there anything about this case that bothers you? How would you modify the lesson to fix it?
3. Design and describe the follow-up lesson that you'd do with the initial sock walk list to help children grasp the concept of grouping as learned in the instruments lesson (i.e., that there are multiple ways to group things).

THE IMPORTANCE OF LISTENING

One important aspect of all learning in the elementary grades is the need for focused listening and attention in the learning environment. Children need to be taught to listen to and respect their own thoughts and ideas as well as those of their classmates, their teachers, and their siblings and parents. The ability to focus one's attention on an aural phenomenon, hear its message, and react to it is a foundational skill basic to all learning.

Making music a regular part of your classroom day gives students a different kind of listening experience from the verbally based learning they encounter most of the day. The musical timbres you offer them in the classroom are the raw materials from which they derive listening pleasure and experience a different type of decision-making process. By asking children to use their musical memory in the grouping activity, for example, Mrs. Saba was able to bring the aural dimension to the rather abstract thinking required of the task in a way that children find immediate and appealing.

USING INSTRUMENTS WITH YOUNGER CHILDREN

CATEGORIZING AND CLASSIFYING SOUNDS: MATERIAL

Young children need repeated opportunities to explore the variety of sounds that can be produced by different materials. Classroom explorations should begin with the sound made by a single material, such as two pieces of wood hit together. The wood may be actual instruments, such as wood sticks or claves, or it may be two pieces of scrap lumber from a woodshop or home workshop. Then these first sounds should be contrasted with a very different one, such as that made by two pieces of metal. Again, actual instruments, such as a triangle or finger cymbals, can be used, as well as two long bolts, metal tools, or pieces of scrap metal. The focus needs to be on contrasting sounds and why they are different, rather than the actual names of instruments.

After this type of introduction, you may wish to use two other contrasting sounds from two other materials, such as plastic or cardboard. Then the sounds produced thus far can be discussed by the children, and the effect of materials upon sound can be discovered.

Such initial experiences may be used as an introduction to classifying and categorizing sounds. One way to begin is to collect a large number of sound sources in a cardboard box and assign partners or small groups to discover the "sounds" in the box. Or you may just leave it in your classroom and wait for the children to investigate the objects and the purposes for which they can be used. Your box can include actual instruments, but such a collection does not depend upon having a lot of extra money for classroom instruments. It is fairly easy to produce a box of interesting and contrasting sound sources from home workshops, kitchens, storage closets, and drawers.

PRODUCTION

After young students have learned to differentiate sounds according to the actual material that the source is made of, a second important way to vary sounds should be introduced. How a particular instrument or object is played affects the sound. A pair of rhythm sticks, one of which is notched, can provide the introduction by contrasting the sound made when the sticks are struck with that produced when they are rubbed back and forth. If you don't have a set of such sticks, any object that can produce two different sounds when hit and rubbed will illustrate the same idea.

Following this introduction, a demonstration for your class of how single objects or instruments can produce varied sounds through scratching, hitting, or shaking should be adequate to return eager learners to the "sound box" for continued investigations. Again, you will want to structure the investigations so that once initial discoveries are made, the children move to careful listening and determining which sounds are similar and which are dissimilar.

Of course, you do not have to be the sole provider of sound sources. Your students and parent volunteers can be asked to contribute to the box from their homes, just as you request them to bring materials for other curriculum projects. You should not overlook your community, either, in your quest for unusual sound sources. Merchants often have interesting and unusual packing materials that they are glad to recycle for an educational cause.

THE PLACE OF IMAGINATION

While it is important for young children to learn that particular sounds depend upon the material of the instrument or object and the manner in which the sound is produced, it is also meaningful for young learners to become involved in using the sounds in imaginative and unusual ways. Whether it be a poem about falling leaves that could be reread with accompanying sounds, a Halloween story or song that would be improved by ghostly, cat, or monster sounds, or a whole-language story written by the class about the first snowfall with added soft background sounds, the curriculum offers many opportunities that can be expanded to include sounds for mood or atmosphere.

It is as vital to allow young children to use their sound imagination as it is to explore their potential for visual or linguistic creativity. Sound does not always have to be accompaniment, but sometimes sounds can provoke imagination. The class "sound box" can be a place to begin whole-language experiences. Your class, either together or as individuals, can select one, two, or three unusual sounds and use them as a topic or as part of a story. Children can be made more aware of their sound environment and bring sounds to share just as naturally as they share new objects or experiences.

Often, because of children's television experiences, particular sounds will provoke identical responses or naming from them. Such sounds as loud claps for thunder, repeated rhythmic drumming for American Indian ceremonies, or pentatonic instruments for Asian backgrounds may be part of their sound stereotypes. Sound clichés certainly exist and can be useful at times in your curriculum. And there are indeed particular musical sounds representative of individual cultures that children should experience when they learn about the cultures. Finding the balance between accepting these clichés and expanding the ability of your students to think in divergent and critical ways is an essential part of good teaching. Accepting a child's response that the sound of a yogurt container containing rice is "rain" could lead to an activity wherein one or more children are sent to the "sound box" to classify the sounds according to weather. This exploration could then be extended to an art or language project. The important aspect of using diverse sounds in your classroom is that you provide another way for children to enlarge their ways of thinking and listening.

PRIMARY TEACHING SCRIPT: CATEGORIZING SOUNDS

Today we are going to be working with partners. Who can remember what our class rules are for choosing a partner? Take responses; if the class has not devised rules, take the time to do so.

What are our rules for working with a partner? Take responses; if the class does not have rules, devise a set that stresses taking turns, listening to each other, respect, etc.

Would you choose your partner and hold hands up in the air right now, please? As you look around the room this morning, you will see that I have put out some containers for us to explore today. You are going to do this activity with a partner. If your class contains an uneven number of children, designate which set of three will be today's trio.

I have here a set of film containers, and each one makes a sound when I shake it. Listen carefully and see if you can tell which ones sound the same and which are different. Put rice in one container and two small bolts in two other containers. Shake the containers in order and put them in front of the children. Take responses and redo as many times as needed to get the children to focus on the sound, not the container. It may be necessary to have the children listen with their eyes closed in order to really focus on sound.

Here is another set of different sounds. It looks like yogurt and ice cream containers but they sound different also. I want you to listen to all four carefully and then decide how we will group them by sound. Place sand in one ice cream and one yogurt container and stones in the other two containers. Again demonstrate, take responses, and redo until the entire class understands the concept of similar sounds.

Now partners are going to explore the boxes and containers I have put around the room. You and your partner are to listen carefully to the sounds and decide which ones belong together and which are different. When you have made your decision, come back to the gathering area with your containers. Be ready to share your decision with the class. To avoid mass chaos, you assign partners to different areas of the room. Have three, four, or five sets of sound containers placed together on tables, shelves, etc., with enough space between them so the children can experiment and listen. Use film, yogurt, ice cream, margarine, or other plastic containers, as well as small cardboard boxes, oatmeal containers, or any container you have two of. The contents can be sand, gravel, small stones, metal bolts, washers, nails, sugar, oatmeal, beans, rice, etc. Be sure that at least two sound the same, whether or not they look the same.

Now it is time for us to share what we have decided. Everyone please come back to the gathering area. Which partners would like to be first to share their decision? As you listen to these sounds, first decide if you think the partners found the two sounds that were alike. Have two children demonstrate their sounds and explain their decision.

I want you to close your eyes and be very quiet and try to remember the sounds that your objects made. Are there any others in the class that are similar? Raise your hands if you think the sounds you have were like the ones we just heard. Have partners volunteer to demonstrate and explain. Then compare the two sets of sounds and see if you have three or four containers that sound the same. Continue in this manner until all the children have shared their findings.

Now that we have heard all the sounds we have today, we need to decide why some of these boxes and tubs have the same sounds. Shake several that are filled with the same material, such as sand, sugar, or rice.

What do you think is the reason? Take responses and let the class discuss this topic. Open as many containers as needed to illustrate the finding.

We did a nice job of working with a partner today and discovering something new about sounds. When we write our class story this afternoon, we'll use some of these sounds as well.

LESSON PLAN: PRIMARY TEACHING SCRIPT: CATEGORIZING SOUNDS

I. Learning Outcome or Objective:
Entry ability: Students are able to distinguish varied shapes and work with a partner.
Exit ability: Students will be able to hear contrasts in sounds and categorize sounds.

II. Lesson Evaluation Procedures: Teacher will note which students have difficulty categorizing sounds.

III. Teaching Procedures:

A. Setting the Stage: Introduce activity with reference to classroom set-up. As you look around the room this morning you will see that I have put out some containers for us to explore.

B. Developing the Lesson:
Step 1: Demonstrate one set of three identical-looking containers with one different sound. Take responses and guide discussion.
Transition statement: Here is another set of different sounds.
Step 2: Demonstrate second set of four containers. Two are ice cream and two are yogurt containers. One of each kind contains sand and the other two contain small stones. Take responses and guide discussion.
Transition statement: Now partners are going to explore the boxes and containers I have put around the room.
Step 3: Students work with partners in listening and categorizing.
Transition statement: Now it is time for us to share what we have decided.
Step 4: Students share their sounds and categorizing decisions. Other partners decide if they have similar sounds. Teacher guides students to discover why sounds are similar or not.

C. Concluding the Lesson: Praise students for working and tell them when you will use the sounds again that day.

EXPLORING ALTERNATE WAYS OF PRODUCING SOUNDS

The typical classroom instrument holdings of the elementary school often include pitched and unpitched percussion (including hand drums, maracas, guiros, triangles, wood blocks, and finger cymbals), as well as Autoharps, recorders, larger cymbals, and tambourines. The instruments may be hidden away in each classroom, or there may only be one cache in the music room. Wherever they are to be found, these simple instruments are a great source of classroom enhancement, as they can provide instant timbral interest for any of your activities.

However, these simple instruments are also a great source of discovery for students when they are asked to use them in nontraditional ways. Students can be asked to see how many different ways they can find to produce a sound on a single instrument. They can also have a great time making unusual sounds on "found objects," such as kitchen equipment, discarded metal pipes and sheets, junk wood scraps, and wire. The local recycling depot or scrap metal collection point can be a great source for inexpensive and interesting sound-producing objects.

While the timbral appeal of well-constructed musical instruments is undeniable, children love to explore all kinds of sound sources, particularly those that let them make big sounds, such as metal tubes, sheets, and bars. As a classroom teacher, you'll want to collect a variety of these found sound sources, as they often inspire the student's aural imagination in ways that expensive instruments cannot. The following script illustrates an exploratory lesson for young children using found sound sources.

PRIMARY TEACHING SCRIPT: SOUND EXPLORATION

Look what's inside this box! Teacher pulls out metal pipe, piano wire with bottle tops attached, glass jars of various sizes, a conch shell, a large brass platter, and several other dissimilar objects.

These things all look very different from each other, don't they? But we can figure out how they are similar and different. I'll show you an object, and I want you to think of a way I could make it produce a sound. Raise your hand when you have an idea. Take several suggestions.

There are lots of ways to produce sounds on these different objects, and I'd like you to explore them today. I'll give everyone a chance to experiment with each object and see how many different sounds you can produce. Just for review, though, what are the ways we make sounds with objects? List responses on the board until you have a nice variety—rubbing, shaking, hitting, scraping, blowing, etc.

I'd like you to work with your group and try out each object, making as many different kinds of sounds with it as you can. Pass it around the group and listen carefully to each other as you experiment. Then, when you receive it for your turn, use it in a different way from the previous people. After each person has had a turn, talk about which sounds you liked the best. When everyone in your desk group has had a turn with one object, we'll exchange objects so that everyone will have a turn at every object. When we're all finished, we'll talk about it as a class. Let's begin! Distribute all the objects, giving one to each table group. After a few minutes, assist the groups in redistributing the objects, continuing until everyone has had a turn at every object.

I'm going to collect all the objects right now. Arrange all the objects on a long table in front of the chalkboard.

Let's look at all the objects in front of us and and see if we can put these objects into groups. Do any of them belong together? Take responses from the class.

Now let's try to group them another way. I'm going to put some words on the board. Watch. Write "hitting" on the far left, "blowing" next to it, "shaking" right of center, and "scraping" on the far right. Ask for volunteers to read each word, then ask the class to rearrange the objects by placing them under the word that produces the best sound. Lead a class discussion of their decisions and summarize that grouping has occurred by the way musical sounds are produced in each object.

Thank you for your good thinking and good listening today, class. You worked well with each other, and you really used the objects in interesting ways to produce a lot of different sounds.

LESSON PLAN: PRIMARY LESSON: SOUND EXPLORATION

I. Learning Outcome or Objective:
Entry ability: Students understand similarity and difference and are able to place things in categories or groups.
Exit ability: Students will be able to categorize objects according to the ways in which one produces sound on the object.

II. Lesson Evaluation Procedures: Teacher will note which children are able to offer suggestions and place objects in the correct categories.

III. Teaching Procedures:

A. Setting the Stage: Introduce box of objects.
Look what's inside this box!

B. Developing the Lesson:

Step 1: Display each object and ask the class to think of ways to produce a sound using the object. Lead class discussion, focusing on alternate ways to produce a sound. Review blowing, scraping, tapping, and shaking.

Transition statement: Let's experiment with these objects.

Step 2: Work in desk groups trying out each object to make many different sounds, each child having a turn. Redistribute objects when all have completed their experiments so that each child has worked with each object.

Transition statement: I'm going to collect all the objects right now.

Step 3: Put all objects on long table in front of the chalkboard.

Transition statement: Look at these objects and see if we can put them into groups.

Step 4: Lead discussion, take suggestions.

Transition statement: Now let's try to group them another way. I'm going to put some words on the board. Watch!

Step 5: Children rearrange objects into new categories under correct headings, discussing their choices as a large group.

C. Concluding the Lesson: Summarize the categories and groupings used and learned today. Praise for good thinking (if appropriate).

LANGUAGE ARTS AND INSTRUMENTS

Opportunities to incorporate instrument playing and sounds in language arts abound throughout the primary grades. The earliest pre-reading experiences can be enhanced through the addition of sounds as experience charts about a walk, a visit to a fire engine, or a visiting musician are constructed. The sounds can be an integral part of the story construction or can be thought of as accompaniment and decided by the children after the story is finished on the chart. When children progress to writing their own stories or writing in a daily diary, they can continue to incorporate sounds as a way to emphasize particular words in their texts, as well as important ideas, climaxes, or endings. Individuals or pairs of children can compose and illustrate stories with sound effects from the class box and tape them for their classmates or parents.

When teaching word recognition, instruments or sound sources can also be incorporated as effective reinforcers. Particular words in a story about a spring walk, such as peepers, jack-in-the-pulpits, and robins, may each have their own distinctive accompanying sound selected by the class. When individual word cards are used to match these words on the story chart, the sound should be included. Word cards may be used to teach colors as well as the alphabet, coordinated with the many picture books used in primary classrooms, and reinforced by sounds. After the first reading of *Brown Bear, Brown Bear, What Do You See?* (Bill Martin, Jr., illustrated by Eric Carle; New York: Rinehart and Winston, 1983), the "sound" of each color can be decided by the class and added, or each child can make up a different color story with sounds.

Folktales from different countries also lend themselves to instrumental accompaniment. Repeated patterns of text can be accompanied by sounds or an invented melody, and the text pattern can be written on strips for reading recognition and matching practice. In *The Pancake Boy* (Lorinda Bryan Cauley; New York: G. P. Putnam's Sons, 1988), a Norwegian version of the familiar gingerbread boy story, the phrases "Good day pancake" and "The same to you" are repeated each time a new animal is encountered. *How the Ostrich Got Its Long Neck* (Verna Aardema, illustrated by Marcia Brown; New York: Scholastic, 1995) is a retelling of a folktale from the Akumba tribe in Kenya. The picture book includes a repeated pattern—"Don't do it"—that lends itself to a phrase strip for reading recognition, and the sounds of each animal are written in nonsense language—"Kwark" (fish eagle), "ku-PU-tu" (kudu), "tih, tih" (crocodile tears)—inviting the addition of instrumental or sound accompaniment.

Common folktales of our own country also lend themselves to enhancement through sound. The appeal of these tales to children is in the repetition of word patterns and visual images, each of which can be reinforced by sound. Children can choose appealing sounds or compose melodies to stand for such characters as the three billy goats gruff, the three bears, or the three little pigs. Rebecca Emberley's *Three Cool Kids* (Boston: Little, Brown, 1995) is a retelling of the three billy goats gruff story in an urban setting: the goats trip over a sewer grate, under which lives a gruesome rat. The picture book provides opportunities for instrumental reinforcement ("squincha, squincha, squinch went his sneakers") and could also serve as a model for teachers in urban settings to have their children write and retell other familiar folktales from outside the city setting.

Many of the poems used in primary classrooms also lend themselves to instrumental or sound accompaniment that reinforces repeated patterns or illustrates descriptive words or phrases. The poems found in *Joyful Noise: Poems for Two Voices* (Paul Fleischman, illustrated by Eric Beddows; New York: Harper & Row, 1988) titled "Grasshoppers," "House Crickets," "Whirligig Beetles," and "Honeybees," as well as many others, include delightfully musical language with phrase and word repetition. As with folktales, poems used in classrooms also provide a motivation for children to write their own original poems. Again, including the potential for sound reinforcement is a wonderful way to motivate young learners.

PRIMARY TEACHING SCRIPT: ENHANCING A STORY WITH INSTRUMENTS

Today's story is about some insects that were friends and a lot of different animals as well. Let's find out what one friend did for another. Read the picture book *Grasshopper to the Rescue: A Georgian Story* (translated from the Russian by Bonnie Carey, illustrated by Lady McCrady; New York: William Morrow, 1979). After reading the story, lead the discussion of friendship and sort out the sequence of the animal actions using pictures and word cards for the ant, grasshopper, pig, raven, hen, barn, mouse, cat, and cow.

Before we reread the story and match our words to the story, who would like to go to the music room and borrow a xylophone from Mr. Cole so the grasshopper can have his own music each time he goes to another animal? Choose one child and someone to accompany him or her.

Tell Mr. Cole why we want to borrow an instrument so he will let you choose a mallet that will make a grasshopper sound. While we're waiting for the instrument to play a grasshopper song, let's move our sound box over here and decide on a sound for each of the other animals in the story. Use word cards and pictures for each animal in order and have children choose the sound they think fits best. Then arrange individuals for each animal or object in a row or line in front of the class, with the word cards of their animals pinned to their chests. This arrangement will allow them to do the backward sequence at the end of the story when the grasshopper brings grass to the cow who gives him milk, which he takes to the cat who stops chasing the mouse, and so on.

Now that we have a xylophone for our grasshopper song, how do you think our song should sound? Lead a discussion of how a grasshopper moves and how the song could reflect jumping, bounding, and fast sounds.

I am going to draw one name from our "turn envelope" and that person will compose our grasshopper melody today. Draw one name and let the child have time to experiment with the instrument and have the class listen closely for grasshopper sounds. Lead discussion and focus children's listening on the types of sounds and the animal.

I think we are all ready to reread this picture book together with animal sounds for each animal and a song for the grasshopper. Read story, cueing individual animal sounds as needed.

Children, that was a wonderful performance (praise as appropriate) **and one we can share at a morning meeting. I will talk to the teacher-leader for this week and see which day will be our turn to share a story.**

PRIMARY TEACHING SCRIPT: ENHANCING A STORY WITH INSTRUMENTS

I. Learning Outcome or Objective:
Entry ability: Students are able to follow picture-book story and are learning sight words via word cards.
Exit ability: Students will be able to identify words of animals in story and illustrate an additive sequence through instrument/sound accompaniment.

II. Lesson Evaluation Procedures: Teacher will note which children are able to identify animal words and track the sequence of the story.

III. Teaching Procedures:

A. Setting the Stage: Introduce book with reference to major theme. **Let's find out what one friend did for another.**

B. Developing the Lesson:
Step 1: Read story and lead discussion of friendship. Use prepared word cards and pictures to establish the sequence of animals mentioned in story.
Transition statement: While we're waiting for the instrument to play a grasshopper song, let's move our sound box over here and decide on a sound for each of the other animals in the story.
Step 2: Use word cards and pictures and lead decision making about which sound to use for each animal. Arrange children in order of animals and practice the sounds.
Transition question: Now that we have a xylophone, how do you think our song should sound?
Step 3: Lead discussion of how a grasshopper moves and how a song could be composed to reflect that movement. Choose one child to compose the melody.
Transition statement: I think we are all ready to reread this picture book together with animal sounds for each animal and a song for the grasshopper.
Step 4: Read story, cue children to play sounds and song if needed.

C. Concluding the Lesson: Praise if appropriate and tell children how they can share what they have learned.

USING INSTRUMENTS WITH OLDER CHILDREN

IMPROVISING WITH THE CLASS

Improvisation is free play with musical materials: adding new notes to a melody as you sing it, playing a contrasting rhythmic pattern over an existing accompaniment, or just filling in the rests with body-percussion sounds. The element of play that is the basis of improvisation makes it especially appealing to us as humans: we love to play. And improvising with your intermediate class can serve as both a listening and a lightening-up activity, a change of pace during the regular school day. There's an element of surprise, risk taking, and pure joy involved in musical improvisation, and this "fun quotient" enlivens children's attention and refocuses them in ways that other activities cannot.

The German composer Carl Orff (1895–1982) was an important proponent of musical improvisation for children and had a great influence on music education practices worldwide. Orff's approach to teaching music involves a specified sequence of musical activities that are designed to lead children into an understanding of musical concepts and skills based on a prescribed teaching sequence. Orff believed in beginning with rhythmic speech, then moving to imitative singing and to instrumental accompaniment taught through imitation, and finally adding movement. Orff called his approach to music "elemental" and wrote, "What does it mean? . . . Never music alone, but music connected with movement, dance, speech—not to be listened to, meaningful only in active participation. Elemental music . . . contents itself with simple sequential structures, ostinatos, and miniature rondos . . . It can be learned and enjoyed by anyone. It is fitting for children."[1]

Improvisation is an integral element of this approach, as it allows the child musician to make musical decisions within a carefully prepared set of parameters that provides a framework for the musical exploration. Orff conceived the idea of the instrumentarium known today as "Orff instruments": barred percussion based on Javanese gamelan instruments that were both easy to play and beautiful to listen to. For further information regarding this interesting approach to music teaching, as well as summer certification courses and workshops for classroom teachers, contact the American Orff-Schulwerk Association (American Orff-Schulwerk Association, P.O. Box 391089, Cleveland, OH 44139-8089; phone: (216) 543-5366).

The improvisation suggested in the following script includes many of the components of the Orff approach: beginning with rhythmic speech, moving to song, and improvising in the call-and-response format.

INTERMEDIATE TEACHING SCRIPT: CALL-AND-RESPONSE IMPROVISATION

Today we're going to review a song you've already learned and do something new with it called improvisation. Improvisation is just playing around with the music and making up something new as you do it. Remember when we had the poet come to our class and she had us play around with lots of different words and phrases? See if you can remember this song. Teacher sings "Funga Alafia" (figure 8.1), pointing to self, and then indicates class should join in by pointing to them at the end of the four-bar phrase.

Figure 8.1 Funga Alafia

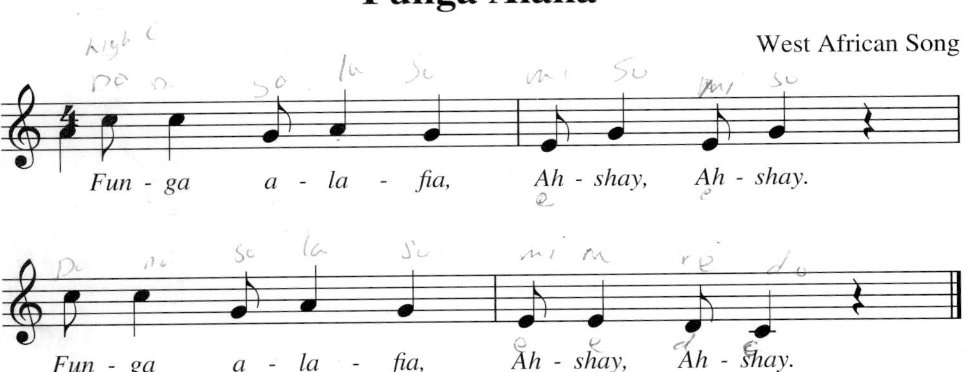

Funga Alafia
West African Song
Fun - ga a - la - fia, Ah - shay, Ah - shay.
Fun - ga a - la - fia, Ah - shay, Ah - shay.

Let's review the words of this one, since the Yoruba language is a bit tricky. Says "fung a a la fya a she a she," etc., pointing to self, and then points to class to indicate that they are to say it. **Does anyone remember what these words mean? *Alafia* means good health or peace, and *ahshay* is close to *oh-shay*, which means "thank you" in Yoruba. Let's sing it again now that we've got a better handle on the words.** Leads class as above. **That was great! Now let's take a look at the pattern I've drawn on the board.** Shows class box-circle-box. **In music, this means that something starts, something happens that is different, and then the first part happens again. Today I'd like to have us try to sing our song as the box** (points to it) **and then make up something new for the circle** (points to it). **For the circle, we'll make up a new rhythm pattern four beats long.** Demonstrates the length of four beats. **This will be the call. Then someone else will make up another pattern, also four beats long, to answer or repond to it; this will be the response.** Demonstrates with a volunteer child: Teacher claps a four-beat pattern, child responds with another. **I was the call, s/he was the response. Let's have someone take my place as the caller: who would like to do this?** Choose one child; have her or him do two sets of call-and-response for a total of four bars. **Great work! We now have an improvisation section for our circle; let's put it together with the square** (points to board) **for a three-part composition.** Class sings song, call-and-response clappers do their part, and class sings song a second time. **How could we put these patterns into unpitched percussion instruments to get the most contrast between them?** Take suggestions and try playing just the middle section. Discuss which are effective and which are not. **Now let's try performing the piece with two sets of people doing the circle** (percussion call-and-response) **and the rest of the class singing.**

Box = "Funga Alafia" (four bars, repeated once)
Circle = call-and-response rhythms played on percussion by alternating pairs of people for eight bars
Box = same as first time
Try it; discuss what happened. Try again with different improvisers; discuss.

That was a great set of improvisations, class! You used lots of different rhythm patterns and lots of interesting timbres, and it had lots of energy. You worked really well as a class, and your singing was terrific! (if appropriate). **We'll do some more improvisation soon.**

INTERMEDIATE LESSON PLAN: CALL-AND-RESPONSE IMPROVISATION

I. Learning Outcome or Objective:
Entry ability: Students are able to sing "Funga Alafia" (*Share the Music,* book 4, page 55) and are able to recognize ABA sections in a musical example.
Exit ability: Students will be able to transform four-bar song into four one-bar call, one-bar response patterns and use unpitched percussion to improvise call and responses for B section.

II. Lesson Evaluation: Teacher will note which children are able to (1) keep the correct number of beats in each of the sections of the call-and-response and (2) play the improvisation patterns only during the B section.

III. Teaching procedures:

A. Setting the Stage: Teacher relates idea to poetry experience, reviews song learned previously, and introduces idea of improvisation. **Today we're going to review a song you've already learned and do something new with it, called improvisation.**

B. Developing the Lesson:
Step 1: Review the song by first singing it, then saying the words, and reviewing the translation. Then sing it again.
Transition statement: Now let's take a look at the pattern I've drawn on the board.
Step 2: Show how box is song and circle is new material, followed by repeat of song. Teacher makes up a four-beat clapping pattern as the call and asks a chld for an answering four-beat rhythm as the response. Teacher then asks for someone to take her place as caller and do the two sets of call-and-response. The four-bar call-and-response improvisation is the circle, and the whole class performs the square-circle-square pattern.
Transition statement: Great work! We now have an improvisation section for our circle: and let's put it together with the square (points to board) for a three-part composition.
Step 3: Perform song with clapping call-and-response for the circle.
Transition question: How could we put these patterns into unpitched percussion instruments to get the most contrast between them?
Step 4: Have volunteers try various instruments and patterns. Discuss which are effective, which are not, and why.
Transition statement: Now let's perform the piece with two sets of people doing the circle (percussion call-and-response) and everyone else singing the song.
box = "Funga Alafia" (four bars, repeated once)
circle = call-and-response rhythms played on percussion by alternating pairs of people for eight bars
box = same as first time
Step 5: Try it, discuss what happened, then try it again with different performers and discuss result.

C. Concluding the Lesson: Reiterate definition of improvisation as making up something new and trying it. Praise, if appropriate, for fine work.

ADDING SOUNDS TO POEMS AND STORIES

Intermediate children are capable of more sophisticated use of instrumental enhancements to poems and stories. While as primary children they may have added single sounds to specific words or phrases, older children are able to add subtler variations of sounds to enhance the meaning of words or phrases. They can also create their own rhythmic ostinato accompaniments to create new forms from poems of either their own or others' creating. The following script shows how an intermediate class can create an instrumental accompaniment for a haiku poem.

INTERMEDIATE TEACHING SCRIPT: ENHANCING HAIKU WITH INSTRUMENTS

Today we're going to create some beautiful music, class! You may not believe me, but sometimes the simplest music is the most beautiful, just as the simplest poetry can be the most full of images and ideas. There's a type of poetry called *haiku* that does not rhyme, is usually three lines long, and has a pattern of five, seven, and five syllables, for a total of only seventeen syllables. It is an ancient style of poetry that comes from Japan, and it has been described as looking at a beautiful, brief moment in slow motion. Here is a haiku poem that was written by the poet Jōso who lived from 1662–1704. It does not follow the traditional pattern exactly, but is still considered haiku:

"I've just come up
From a place on the bottom" is the look
On the little duck's face.

Jōso, 1662–1704

I'll read it to you and you listen. Teacher reads it. **Now who would like to read it for us this time, using your voice to make it sound interesting?** Take a few volunteers. **Notice how it sounds different with each reader's different vocal timbre and inflection. Now we need to figure out what instrument sounds we might add to this poem to make it more interesting to listen to. Can anyone think of some sounds that this poem suggests?** Take some responses and list them on the board. **Let's try them.** Try a few and evaluate.

Now let's think of a sound that might come before the poem starts that would help us get into the poem more quickly—that would set our ears up for what the poem has in store. Can anyone think of a sound? Solicit answers: something moving in an upward motion, low to high, perhaps a splashy sound. Try it and see what the response is.

Let's try to add the sound before the poem starts and then do it again at the end of the poem, for symmetry. Try it and see what the response is. Then try another kind of instrument, substituting a more subtle version of it in the next try. Next, try adding a sound for every syllable, replicating the rhythm pattern of the words exactly. See what the response is; discuss.

How does playing the rhythm pattern of the words change the way the poem sounds to you? Now go back and read the poem again without any accompaniment; discuss how it has a different meaning this time.

I'd like you to work in pairs to create your own versions of the poem now. Try to vary your inflection, timbre, and accent as you read the poem. You can also vary the accompaniment. Listen to all pairs, record them, and discuss in large group. List on the board all the characteristics of a pleasing, well-accompanied poem.

Did you notice how important the accompaniment is to the meaning of the poem? Sometimes just a hint of sound can be more effective than many sounds. Thanks for working well and for listening carefully to each other's performances.

INTERMEDIATE LESSON PLAN: ENHANCING HAIKU WITH INSTRUMENTS

I. Learning Outcome or Objective:
Entry ability: Students are able to read and comprehend a haiku poem and to manipulate classroom instruments in a variety of ways with varying degrees of subtlety.
Exit ability: Students will be able to identify, discuss, and compare ineffective and effective ways of enhancing the meaning of the haiku poem.

II. Lesson Evaluation Procedures: Teacher will note which children participated in exploration, discussion, and evaluation of the accompaniments.

III. Teaching Procedures:

A. Setting the Stage: Introduce ideas of haiku and musical subtlety. **Today we're going to create some beautiful music, class.**

B. Developing the Lesson:
Step 1: Show poem to class on overhead projector and read it aloud, then ask for volunteers to read it with different vocal inflections and intensities. Discuss.
Transition question: Who can think of some sounds that this poem suggests that we could try to add?
Step 2: Assign task of adding accompaniment to enhance the meaning of the words. Take suggestions, then try them.
Transition question: Who can think of a sound that could come before the poem starts that would prepare us for the images of the poem?
Step 3: Experiment with several different sounds that could be used as an intro to the poem. Then try repeating the sound after the poem, to achieve symmetry. Discuss. Then try it with a more subtle instrumental sound and compare the effect.
Transition question: How would adding a sound for every syllable of the poem change the way the poem sounds—its effect?
Step 4: Try using unpitched percussion on every syllable; discuss.
Transition question: What would happen now if you listened to the poem without any accompaniment? How would it be different?
Step 5: Have volunteers read the poem with no accompaniment; discuss.
Transition statement: I'd like you to work in pairs to create your own versions of the poem.
Step 6: Students work in pairs to create their own performance, with vocal inflection, accent, dynamic changes, and accompaniment. Record these performances and listen to them again, then discuss.

C. Concluding the Lesson: Create a list of the class's findings about the characteristics of a pleasing accompaniment for the haiku genre. Thank them for working well and listening to each other.

USING INSTRUMENTS IN AN INTERMEDIATE SCIENCE LESSON

There are many ways to integrate instruments and instrument playing when teaching about sound in intermediate science lessons. The beginning experiences with vibrations can be illustrated with a tuning fork or a large triangle when it is struck, put into water, and touched to stop the sound. Particularly useful is the inside of a piano, where children can see the hammers hit the strings and watch the vibrations of strings of different lengths and thicknesses. Other instruments that you have in the classroom can be similarly explored in order for children to compare, predict, and make interpretations about how sound is produced.

When you are ready to teach about differences in sounds, you can begin with simple classroom demonstrations with wooden chalk or cigar boxes or a board "guitar" made with a 20-inch board and some nails at each end (or at different points on the board). When you stretch different thicknesses of rubber bands or guitar strings along the length of the board, you provide simple contrasts of sounds and materials that will stimulate student interpretation and classification. After the relationship between the speed of vibration and the pitch level has been discovered, your students will want to explore other string instruments and each instrument played by a class member to discover how pitch vibrations vary.

Teaching each of the other sound concepts can be similarly enhanced by the use of either simple instruments or the actual ones being learned by individuals in your class. The idea that sound travels can initially be demonstrated by hitting pipes on different floors of your school; but if your building is on one level, using instruments in the classroom and experimenting with different materials (such as a wooden table, a necktie, or water) as sound conductors will enable students to predict and infer that sound travels through air, solids, and liquids. The loudest instrument played by a class member will serve as the best demonstration of the speed of sound if you can move your science lesson outside and have the student a good distance from your class.

Content Standard: Performing on Instruments, Alone and with Others, a Varied Repertoire of Music

Students:

1. Perform on pitch, in rhythm, with appropriate dynamics and timbre, and maintain a steady tempo
2. Perform easy rhythmic, melodic, and chordal patterns accurately and independently on rhythmic, melodic, and harmonic classroom instruments
3. Perform expressively a varied repertoire of music representing diverse genres and styles
4. Echo short rhythms and melodic patterns
5. Perform in groups, blending instrumental timbres, matching dynamic levels, and responding to the cues of a conductor
6. Perform independent instrumental parts while others sing or play contrasting parts

A NEW RECORDER NOTE: E

Fingering Chart

● ●
●
●
—
●
●
○
○

Figure 8.2 Practice Playing the New Note, E

Figure 8.3 Two Songs Using the New Note

Southwell

English (16th century)

Folk Tune

Welsh

New rhythm patterns using sixteenth notes and eighth notes

There are a variety of rhythm patterns than can be created with these two types of durations. If you look carefully at figure 8.4, you will see that two sixteenth notes can be combined with an eighth in several ways.

Figure 8.4 Rhythm Syllables with Eighth and Sixteenth Notes

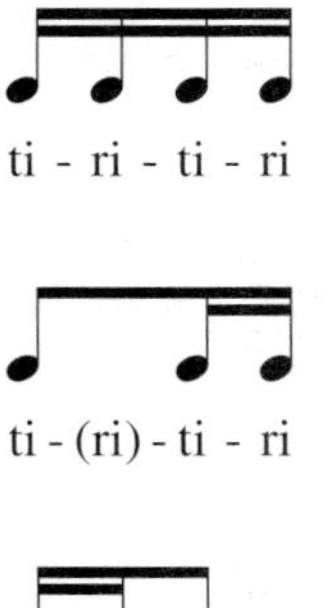

ti - ri - ti - (ri)

Figure 8.4 *continued*

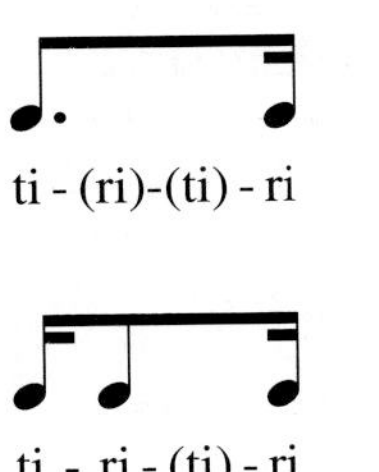

Practice saying these rhythms at home and also in class with your instructor.

Figure 8.5 Rhythm Practice

Now practice playing these rhythms on the recorder.

Figure 8.6 Recorder Practice

Figure 8.6 *continued*

Figure 8.7 Children's Songs Using the New Note and New Rhythms

Ridin' in the Buggy

Western Play Song

Rid - in' in the bug - gy, Miss Mar - y Jane, Miss
Mar - y Jane, Miss Mar - y Jane, Rid - in' in the bug - gy, Miss
Mar - y Jane, I'm a long way from home.

Figure 8.7 *continued*

Hop, Old Squirrel

Traditional

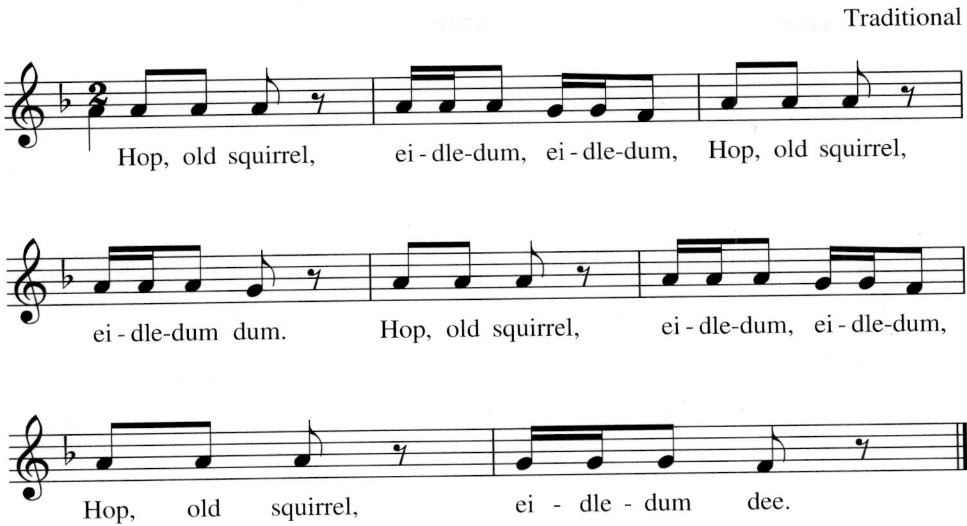

ei - dle-dum dum. Hop, old squirrel, ei - dle-dum, ei - dle-dum,

Burn, Little Candles

Hebrew Folk Song

Burn, lit-tle can-dles, burn, burn, burn, Burn-ing bright and clear.

Burn, lit-tle can-dles, burn, burn, burn, Ha - nuk - kah is here.

Jingle Bells

Words and Music by James Pierpont

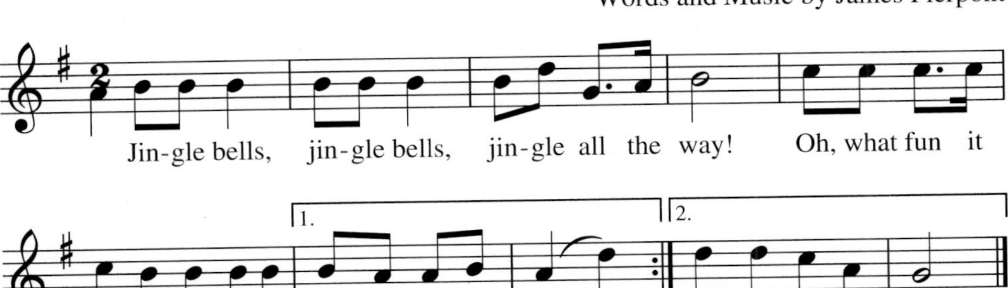

Jin-gle bells, jin-gle bells, jin-gle all the way! Oh, what fun it
1.
2.
is to ride in a one-horse o - pen sleigh! one-horse o - pen sleigh!

Figure 8.7 *continued*

Shoo, Fly
American Folk Song
Shoo, fly, don't both - er me, Shoo, fly, don't both - er me,
Shoo, fly, don't both - er me, For I be-long to some-bod - y.
Annabelle
Camp Song
An-na-belle, where are you go-ing? Up-stairs to take a
bath. Your legs are like two tooth-picks,
Your neck like a gi - raffe! An-na-belle, pull out the
stop-per, An-na-belle, look down the drain.
Oh my good-ness, oh my soul, There goes An-na-belle down that hole!
An - na - belle? An - na - belle? Glug.

FURTHER PRACTICE

1. Look at the songs in chapter 4. Choose one that you would like to teach, copy it onto the following staves, and underneath it write an ostinato accompaniment using two unpitched percussion instruments. Come to class prepared to teach it to your peers and describe how you would use it to enhance another area of the curriculum.

2. Write your own haiku poem in the space below. It should be based on a theme of your choice. It should have 17 syllables and appear in three lines of 5, 7, and 5 syllables each. It should not rhyme. Build an accompaniment for it that enhances the meaning of the poem. Notate your accompaniment under the poem below. Be prepared to teach your poem and accompaniment to the class.

3. Using either your own children's literature collection, your local library, or the children's section of your favorite bookstore, find a picture book appropriate for young children and design an accompaniment that illustrates some of the words. Make cards for each of the words you chose to illustrate with sound. Come to class prepared to share it with your peers.
4. Interview a fifth or sixth grader using the questions below. Then write a one to two page reflection paper on what you learned from this interview experience. Be prepared to share your findings with your peers in class.

Interview Questions

1. When do you listen to music?
2. What kinds of music do you listen to?
3. Do the other kids in your class like music?
4. Do you have a music teacher?
5. What's the best part of what happens in your music class?

6. What's the worst part of what happens in your music class?
7. Do you do music with your classroom teacher?
8. What do you do musically with your classroom teacher?
9. Do you think your classroom teacher is a good musician? Why?
10. Do you study an instrument?
11. What instrument do you study?
12. What's the best part of playing your instrument?
13. What do you want to be when you grow up?

5. Write a lesson plan for a music-playing activity at a grade level of your choice. Show how you will use music to enhance a lesson in any content area in the curriculum.

Grade Level:

Content Area:

Materials Needed:

Concept:

I. Learning Outcome or Objective:

Entry Ability:

Exit Ability:

II. Lesson Evaluation Procedures:

III. Materials and Board/Space Preparation:

IV. Teaching Procedures:

A. Setting the Stage:

B. Developing the Lesson:

Step 1:

Transition statement:

Step 2:

Transition statement:

Step 3:

Transition statement:

Step 4:

Transition statement:

C. Concluding the Lesson:

NOTES

[1]Carl Orff (1963). "The *Schulwerk:* Its Origins and Aims." *Music Educators Journal* 50, no. 8: 70.

Fundamentals of Movement

9

What you will be able to do by the end of this chapter

- *Demonstrate the Laban qualities of movement*
- *Illustrate the difference between structured and creative movement*
- *Create individual and group movement compositions*
- *Move to syncopated rhythms*
- *Develop movements that demonstrate understanding of the elements of pitch*
- *Participate in structured folk dances*
- *Play a new note on the recorder*

MOVING OURSELVES TO MUSIC

Movement, like music, has been a basic way for human beings to express their feelings since the beginning of recorded time. Depictions on Egyptian tombs and Greek vases reveal that it was an important part of these early civilizations. Many other cultures have perpetuated their particular dances and movements even though they are not shown on preserved objects or documents. Some philosophers, such as Susanne Langer, have proposed that movement and music became intertwined as soon as human beings began expressing themselves.

This partnership of music and movement is a logical one because each of these art forms moves through time. We are unable to stand and ponder a dance or a piece of music in the way we do a painting or a piece of sculpture. Certainly music and movement have existed together from the earliest civilizations and cultures until the present.

Many cultures have evolved very distinct movement forms that are recognized as representing a particular group of peoples. We instantly distinguish the uniqueness of American Indian dances, Spanish flamenco, and Hawaiian hula dancing, among many others. Whether the dance be in a circle or a straight line, performed by one person or many, the movement and the accompanying music have special meaning for a particular culture. We know, of course, that the term "American Indian dance" includes the dances of many different tribes. Within each tribe, there are very different dances for specific ceremonial occasions and very clear expectations as to gender roles in the execution of these dances. The stylized and improvised movements of each culture have a similar complexity and uniqueness that contributes to the richness of this important part of human expression.

When we think of the ways that most adults move in our culture, we call up some pretty staid images: walking, sometimes running, and occasionally dancing. These are quite different from the exuberance and joy that we express through movement as children. Unfortunately, as we mature, we also become extremely self-conscious about moving our bodies. Most adults are quite restricted in their movements, just as they are in their music making, believing that movement as expression is a specialized field open only to those who train to be professionals. However, most adults sometimes respond to music with movement. Often the movements are very structured, as in aerobics classes or line dancing, and at other times the movements are as subtle as tapping a toe or finger.

Indeed, most music provokes some type of a movement impulse. Consider the difficulty that you have controlling your own foot or finger while looking at MTV. This natural human impulse is a valid one, as it is propelling you toward further engagement and involvement with what you are hearing. The performers and producers of these videos understand the appeal of movement. That is why they do not feature a singer or group simply standing still holding microphones and reproducing their recorded songs. These videos are produced to appeal to viewers with a combination of music and movement.

This chapter will introduce you to some important ideas about movement. In the process, you will become more aware of how exciting moving to music can be. You will gain confidence in your own ability to move to music and will become much more aware of the amount of movement that exists in daily life. We also hope you will derive feelings of satisfaction and enjoyment from the many different types of movement activities we have compiled for this chapter.

CHAPTER GOALS

The goals of this chapter are to enable you to understand the fundamentals of movement and develop more comfort in actually moving to music. Through class and homework activities you will experience both structured and creative movement using the music on the CD that accompanies this textbook. In these activities you will use the listening skills of discrimination and analysis that you acquired in chapter 6 and develop movements that illustrate different musical qualities. You will revisit many of the ideas about musical elements learned in earlier chapters and expand your understanding of rhythm in music as well.

In all of this moving, you will experience the meaning that music has for listeners in a very different way. You know that all music contains repetition and contrast and that it can be described in terms of how it is constructed (its form) and how it is produced (its timbre). After becoming acquainted with the different qualities of movement, such as force and space, for instance, you will experience ways to use these qualities and illustrate the musical ideas that you can recognize and identify. These experiences will enable you to more fully experience all of the sounds that exist in music.

Most of all, we want you to enjoy moving to music. We believe that the more active you are, the more you will realize that moving to music is worth the extra effort and energy involved. We want you to understand the pleasure and thrill of responding to music and illustrating in a very different way how music is constructed and how it "works." Learning how to move in this manner will affect your everyday life and open up new sensations and feelings that you may not have been aware of before.

TYPES OF MOVEMENT

FUNDAMENTAL MOVEMENTS

This type of movement includes all of the basic locomotor ways that human beings move, including walking, jumping, and skipping, as well as nonlocomotor movements such as stretching, clapping, or bending. The inclusion of these basic motor skills in singing or listening to music implies, of course, that all participants will be doing the same motor activity at the same time.

The locomotor movements are usually based on the feeling of a steady pulse. The easiest fundamental movement is walking, followed in difficulty by running, jumping, skipping, galloping, and hopping. There are many ways to develop the feeling of pulse necessary for these movements. For example, you can begin by echoing simple patting movements on the body while giving a verbal cue ("head, head, shoulders, shoulders, knees, knees," and so on) and then put that feeling in your feet and walk in place. Simple verbal cues can then be replaced by speech patterns and rhymes with a strong sense of pulse, and locomotor movements can be coordinated with the pulse.

ACTIVITY Try this at home and then in class with your peers: Say the following rhyme, putting the pulse on the underlined parts or on whole words.

Icky spiffy
Double do
Is this movement
Good for you?

Then say the rhyme and clap the pulse while speaking. Next, say it and pat the pulse on different parts of your body. Start from the top or bottom and move the pulse up and down while you speak. After this step, add one or more of the fundamental movements described in the above paragraph. (You may want to practice this initially when your roommate is not in the room. When you are comfortable with the movement, share it.)

Another way to experience locomotor movements is to move while singing a familiar song. Once you have established the feeling of a pulse while singing, you can decide whether to use the same movement throughout the entire song or to change your movement at the beginning of a new section. For example, while singing "When the Saints Go Marching In" (chapter 4, page 128), practice the marching movement in the first verse and then change your movement for each successive verse (get your roommate to move with you this time).

ACTIVITY Look at the songs you learned in chapters 3 and 4, choose one you really like, and decide how you could move in two different locomotor ways while singing it. Be ready to share your decisions with your classmates and have them move and sing with you.

Fundamental locomotor movements can be devised to accompany rhythm patterns as well. Patterns in simple meter (where the pulse is divided into two equal parts), such as 2/4, 3/4, and 4/4, can be walked, marched, jumped, and hopped, while rhythms in compound meter (where the pulse is divided into three equal parts), such as 6/8 or 9/8, can be skipped or galloped.

ACTIVITY Before your next class meeting, write out two rhythm patterns, each four measures long. One should be in 4/4 meter and the other in 6/8 meter. Look at your recorder pages from previous chapters if you need help with possible rhythm combinations. Be sure that the rhythm you bring to class is one that you can clap correctly for your classmates. In class you will combine your rhythm patterns with those of a partner, practice them on rhythm instruments, and decide which fundamental movements to use in your composition.

Nonlocomotor movements provide yet another way to add different gestures to music. What are the possible ways that you can move your body while standing still? Swaying, bending, stretching or clapping your hands are just a few. Each becomes even more interesting when contrasted at different body levels. The space surrounding the body at low, medium, and high levels can be explored with each of these nonlocomotor movements. In addition, you can add the idea of directional changes and different pathways to these movements. The directions can include forward, backward, up, down, and diagonal. The pathways can be straight or curved as well as large or small. Exploring all of these movements enables you to add to your basic repertoire of movement possibilities.

ACTIVITY Before your next class meeting, arrange a movement sequence that lasts for 16 pulses. In this time (which you count internally), use at least two body levels and two pathways. Use both locomotor and nonlocomotor movements. Be ready to share your sequence with a partner; that partner must be able to identify the levels and pathways you use.

CREATIVE MOVEMENT

This category of movement implies that you express your understanding of what you hear through movements that you invent. When college students initially are asked to originate movements to songs or music, they often appear confused or indecisive. This reaction is completely normal. However, once you understand the movement qualities described below, you will be able to combine them with fundamental movements to create interesting and expressive ways to respond to music.

According to Laban, the four movement qualities are weight, space, time, and flow. If you are alone as you read this paragraph, try moving your body in each of the following opposite ways, focusing solely on how your body feels during the movement. Weight can be light or heavy. Move your arms in such a way that they express each of these two words. Space can be described as narrow or wide. Stand up and make your body as wide as you can, then as narrow as possible. Time opposites are slow and fast. Just use your fingertips and move them these opposite ways in time. Flow can be sustained or it can stop. Move your arm in a smooth, flowing manner and then suddenly stop it.

The quality of weight is expressed through light and heavy or strong and weak movements. Imagine the movement of a butterfly and then think of an animal or object that you think moves in the opposite manner, such as an elephant or a bulldozer. Using these images assists in inventing contrasting movements that feel heavy or strong. An important aspect of all creative movement is accepting all possibilities: there is no "right" way to move lightly or heavily. You can explore these two qualities with your fingertips, arms, legs, or feet, as well as with your entire body. Weight movements are particularly useful in expressing the contrasts of dynamics and texture heard in music.

The quality of space can be experienced through the contrasts of up/down, narrow/wide, or in/out. The space surrounding your body can be explored with nonlocomotor movements in different levels using pathways that are straight, serpentine, spiraling, or even geometric. You can also move in space using more abstract vocabulary, such as "growing," "spreading," "exploding," and so on. These movements need to be first explored without sound, then added to simple sounds, and finally used to demonstrate changes in music such as register or dynamics.

Time movements include the opposites fast and slow as well as gradual, sudden, short, and long. Time can be expressed through both locomotor and nonlocomotor movements; in addition, you can add levels and pathways to these explorations. Time movements can accompany the pulse or particular rhythms in poems, sayings, songs, or music.

Flow is the expressive movement quality that can be sustained or sudden; it can even stop. You can express this movement quality by moving in a floating or gliding manner and then contrasting with flicking or slashing movements. This movement quality is a particularly apt way of expressing musical duration as well as different articulations.

Reading about these movement qualities is only the beginning of becoming comfortable with movement. In the rest of this chapter you will find many experiences that provide opportunities for you to combine the effort elements, locomotor and nonlocomotor movements, and space levels and pathways. We begin with simple activities that need no sound and then ask you to combine your movements with chants or poems, instruments, songs, and music from the CD.

ACTIVITY Select two movement qualities (weight, space, time, and flow), two locomotor movements, and one pathway. Create a movement composition that illustrates AB form. After you have practiced with a partner or a group, add two nonpitched instruments to your composition.

Select two movement qualities, two nonlocomotor movements, two space levels, and two pathways. Create a movement composition that lasts for 16 pulses. After you practice it together several times, try it as a round, with half of the group beginning together and the second half starting from the beginning when the first half reaches beat 4.

Choose your own combination of movement qualities, fundamental movements, space levels, and pathways. Create a movement composition that has an introduction, a middle, and an end.

Choose your own combination of movement qualities, fundamental movements, levels, and pathways. Create a movement composition that is accompanied by unpitched instruments and lasts for thirty seconds. This composition should begin with a theme and then have two variations of the theme.

MOVING TO MUSIC COMFORTABLY

The following movement activities are designed to get you moving, incorporating the concepts of fundamental, locomotor, nonlocomotor, and creative movement in interesting ways. The first activity will introduce you to structured movement to accompany one of the listening selections from the CD, "Coal Quay Market." The second movement activity will give you the opportunity to experiment with creative movement to accompany the percussion piece "El Dorado." Both of these activities are meant to get you into the music, so get ready to have a little fun!

STRUCTURED MOVEMENT

Coal Quay Market, track #3

This piece has two parts: the verse, which tells the story of a bad shopping trip, and the refrain, which is in nonsense syllables. The structured movement that you will use to accompany this piece is a combination of hand jive and foot jive.

To begin, stand up and place your book on a table or chair in front of you so you can see the directions. There are eight beats of drumming in the beginning before the verse starts. Don't do anything during these eights beats but listen and get ready for the hand jive. The hand jive takes 16 beats, and you perform it twice during each verse as follows: Pat thighs twice, clap twice, pound fists together twice with left fist on top, pound fists together twice with right fist on top, snap fingers of both hands twice on the left at shoulder height, snap fingers of both hands twice on the right at shoulder height, pat shoulders twice, pat head twice.

The foot jive takes 16 beats as well, but you only perform it once during each refrain as follows: Standing with your weight on your right foot, touch your left heel to the floor in front of you, then shift to point your left big toe to the floor on the next beat (heel-toe). Do this sequence twice (heel-toe-heel-toe) for the first four beats of the refrain. Then step left with your left foot, slide your right foot across to the left foot, step left with your left foot, and slide your right foot across again (step left–slide left–step left–slide left). Repeat the whole sequence with your weight on your left foot and leading with your right foot: right heel–right toe–right heel–right toe, step right with your right foot, slide your left foot across to your right foot, step right with your right foot, slide your left foot across to your right foot. In the diagram of the foot jive (figure 9.1), the X marks the moving foot, and each square represents one beat of the refrain. When you have practiced both the hand and foot jives, try putting them together while the music is playing. Your instructor will give you further directions about whether you will perform this with your peers in class.

Figure 9.1 Foot Jive Diagram for "Coal Quay Market"

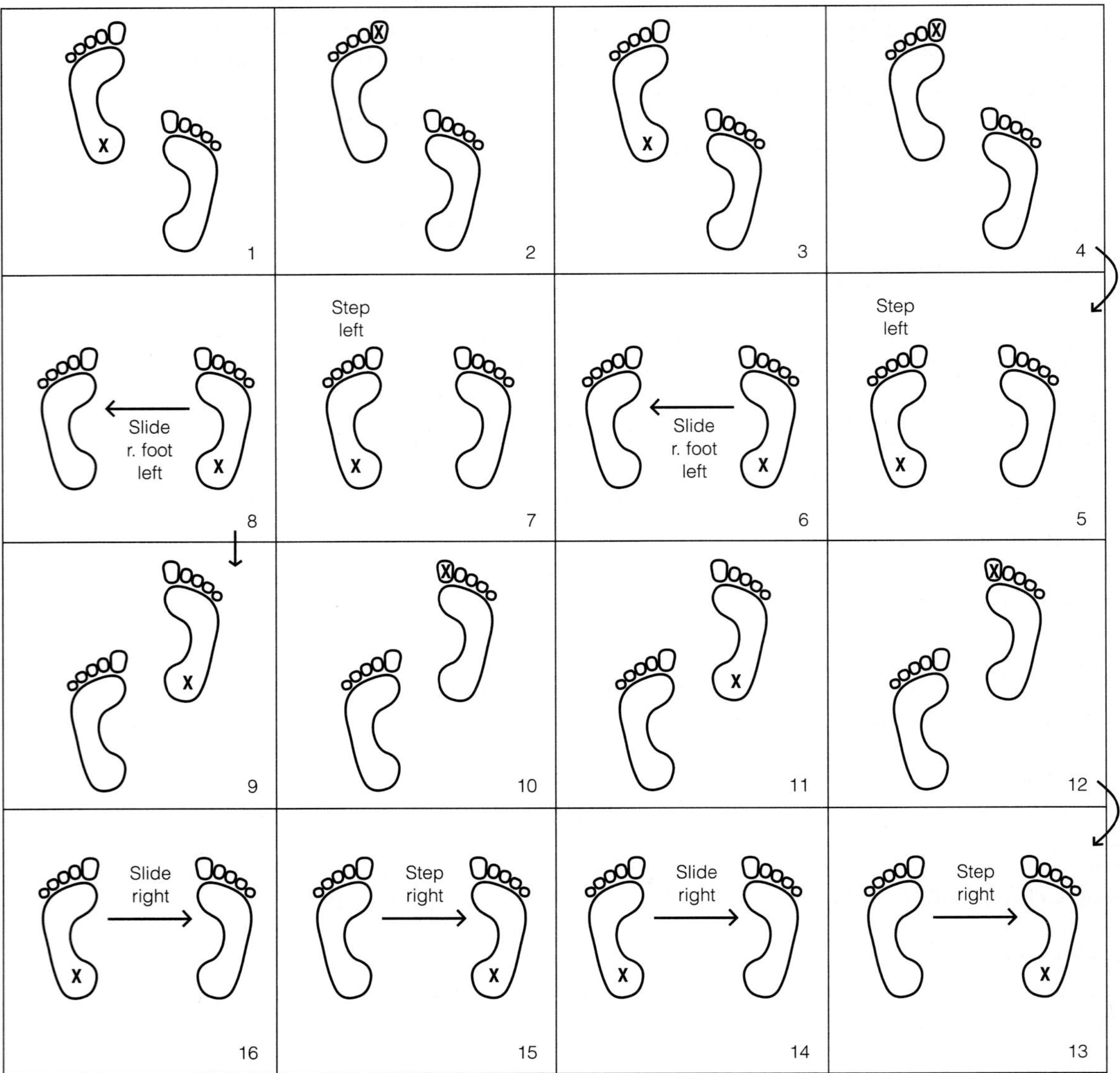

CREATIVE MOVEMENT: "EL DORADO"

El Dorado, track #29

This activity uses only the first 50 seconds of the selection, the A section. Using your own watch or clock, listen to the music and pause or stop the CD player when the piece has played for 50 seconds. This part of the selection will serve as the basis for the creative-movement activity.

How would you describe this music in terms of the movement qualities explained in this chapter: (weight, space, time, and flow)? Was it heavy or light? Narrow or wide? Slow or fast? Sustained or stopped? Up or down? Did it grow or contract? You can use these metaphorical descriptions, as well as your own personal descriptions, as stimuli for your own movement accompaniment for this selection.

Now sit on the floor or on a chair and listen to the selection again with your eyes closed, this time letting your upper body (head, shoulders, arms, hands, and fingers) show the movement qualities you discovered during the first listening. Make sure that your movements mirror the way the music moves as you listen to it and that the character of your movements matches your description of the piece.

Each of these movement activities gave you a different kind of experience that related your musical understanding to the simple joy of moving your body through space. Perhaps you noticed something different in the music as you moved to it while listening. Or perhaps you just got lost in the activity and enjoyed the kinesthetic action. No matter what your response, movement experiences with music can be an enjoyable means to getting to know music in a more intimate way. They may also help you free your musical self and let you respond to music more fully.

REVIEW OF FUNDAMENTALS THROUGH MOVEMENT

RHYTHM REVIEW

Listen to each of the musical selections listed in the boxes below. For each example, create a movement or series of movements that illustrates the musical feature listed in the box. You may use pictures, graphic notation, or verbal descriptions to help you remember your movement. Come to class prepared to share your movement examples with a classmate or the whole group. Your instructor may ask you to hand in this assignment.

Galway Hornpipe, track #1

Musical concept: Beat

Tanzen und Springen, track #9

Musical concept: Rhythm pattern in the first two measures

Try to Remember, track #6

Musical concept: Meter

Slide, Frog, track #22

Musical concept: Meter

SINGING REVIEW

"Funga Alafia"

Here are the pitches that are used in a Liberian song. Sing them using syllables and hand signals.

Figure 9.2 Pitches in "Funga Alafia"

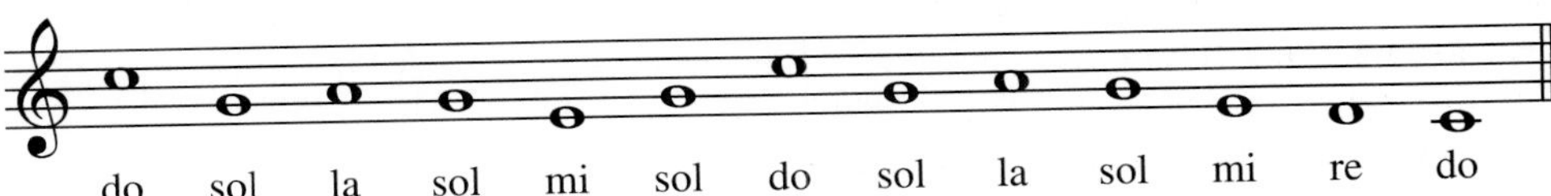

Next say the rhythm of the first three notes of each measure. Then say the rhythm syllables as you clap the rhythm pattern four times.

Figure 9.3 Rhythm of First Three Notes

Then say the rhythm syllables of the entire song and then clap and say the rhythm of the entire song.

Figure 9.4 Rhythm of Entire Song

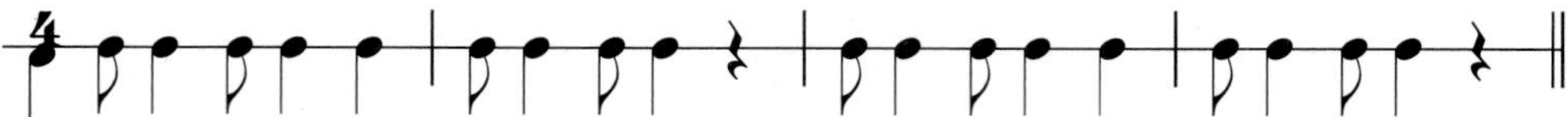

Now it is time to combine the pitch and rhythm you have figured out.

Figure 9.5 "Funga Alafia"

As you sing the song a second time, tap a slow pulse with your fingertips each time you see an X below a word. The next step in this process is to move into a large circle and, while singing the song, take a step to the right each time there is an X. Now it is time to add your hands to this movement activity. While your instructor sings the song, step to the right and then raise your hands and softly clap the hands of the person on either side of you.

Next, sing the song and step and clap as you sing. Now you are singing a syncopated rhythm and moving to a steady beat.

Figure 9.6 "Funga Alafia"

PHOTOCOPY THIS PAGE: PITCH REVIEW

Listen to "Pie Jesu," track #4, and sing the melody along with the recording. Refer to the map of this selection on page 162 to help you remember the melodic contour. Create a movement composition that shows the melodic contour of this selection. Using either graphic notation, verbal description, or pictures, notate your composition in the space below.

FOLK DANCES FROM AROUND THE WORLD

Folk dance is a type of structured movement that not only gets you physically involved with music, but also gives you a window on the culture in which the music and dance originated. In the following two dances, you will have the opportunity to experience kinesthetically, through structured dance movements, a bit of what it feels like to participate in the Israeli and Japanese cultures, to "move the way those folks do." Sampling these cultures through folk dance is similar to tasting Israeli food or watching a Japanese film. However, the cuisine, film, and dance of a people all have their own unique ways of informing us about the cultures in which they originated and, consequently, lead us to different insights about the peoples involved. The authors of this text propose that the insights you will gain from this brief cultural encounter through folk dance are just as important to your development as a teacher as is your physical grasp of the steps and the sequence of the movements.

ISRAELI FOLK DANCE: THE HORA

The *hora* is a circle dance that has come to be identified with Israel. It is usually danced in a closed circle, with each dancer's arms around the waists or over the shoulders of those on either side of him or her in the circle. You will learn by doing it with your hands first, before putting it into your feet.

Hold your hands up in front of you at a 90-degree angle to your arms. Your palms should face out, away from you. Your hands will dance the pattern: right step, left behind, right step, hop, left step, right step, left step (in place), left right. Try this pattern a few times, saying the directions while you dance it with your hands. When you feel confident about the pattern, try doing it with your feet instead of your hands, saying the directions while your feet move. When you are ready, try the pattern while listening to "Hava Nagila," track #30. Perhaps your instructor will have you perform this dance in class with your peers so that you can feel what it is like to dance in a joyous circle formation.

JAPANESE BON DANCE: TOKYO DANTAKU

Tokyo Dontaku [don-tah-koo (no accent)] is a Bon dance, done at the annual Buddhist-Shinto celebration of the Feast of the Dead. Named for the city of Hakata-Dontaku on the southern island of Kyushu, it was introduced in North America in the early 1960s by Madelynne Greene, a respected folk dance teacher. She learned it in Honolulu in 1960 from the Japanese Hawaiian community. The version of the dance presented here is for arms and hands only, with the performers seated on the floor in a straight line. Even the most novice dancer may experience Japanese movements and music by learning just the hand gestures.

Hand Movements

Part 1:

Clap hands in front of chest (beats 1 and 2), sweep hands down and out to sides with palms down (beat 3), sweep hands up in front of chest (& of beat 3), clap hands in front of chest (beat 4).

Part 2: Paddle, paddle, shade your eyes

Move both palms backward on left side as though paddling a boat (beat 1); repeat on right side (beat 2). Shade eyes with left palm at left ear and right arm extended in front, palm forward (beat 3), reverse hands (& of beat 3), reverse again (beat 4 &).

Part 3: Make a tree and make a tree

Facing a bit right, touch fingertips with palms down about thigh level and arms rounded, then swoop arms up to touch fingertips above head with palms facing ceiling (beats 1 & 2 &). Repeat, facing a bit left (beats 3 & 4 &).

Part 4: Brush your sleeve and brush your sleeve

With right arm bent and palm facing cheek, left hand brushes kimono sleeve below right elbow three times (beats 1 & 2 &); repeat the three brushes with right hand below left elbow three times (beats 3 & 4 &).

It has been a very good season for pumpkins.
Two birds are flying in the sky.
A man catches a woman's attention, thinking she is a real beauty.
But when she turns around, oh my, she isn't.

(Song translation by Fumiko Watanabe. Dance notes, translation, and directions © 1997 Sanna Longden. Used by permission.)

A NEW RECORDER NOTE: D

Figure 9.7 Recorder Note D

● ●
●
●
—
●
●
●
○

Practice playing the new note and reviewing rhythms you know.

Figure 9.8 Practice with D

The first song below is a well-known Shaker folk song. After you have practiced the canon at home, you will be able to play it with a partner or your class as a canon, an imitative melodic device. In order to play this song as a canon, after one section of your class begins to play, another section begins at the beginning. Your instructor will explain when each part starts. In this piece, you can have two, three, or even four parts. The sign at the beginning of the canon is a different meter signature called cut time. It means that the common time of 4/4 is divided by two; therefore, with this symbol, the time signature is 2/2. There are two beats in each measure, and the half note receives one beat.

Figure 9.9 "Simple Gifts" and Canon

Simple Gifts

Canon

Thomas Tallis

Songs Using the New Note

Figure 9.10 Songs Using the New Note D

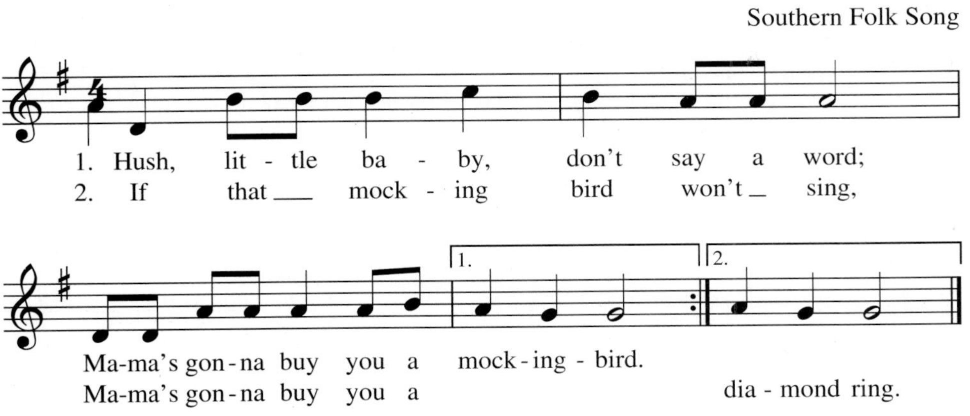
Hush, Little Baby
Southern Folk Song
1. Hush, lit - tle ba - by, don't say a word;
2. If that mock - ing bird won't sing,
1.
2.
Ma-ma's gon-na buy you a mock-ing - bird.
Ma-ma's gon-na buy you a dia - mond ring.

Old MacDonald
Traditional
Fine
1. Old Mac-Don-ald had a farm, E - I - E - I - O.
And on this farm he had some chicks, E - I - E - I -
O. With a chick, chick here and a chick, chick there,
D.C. al Fine
here a chick, there a chick, ev - 'ry - where a chick, chick.

2. . . . ducks . . . quack, quack here, . . .

3. . . . pigs . . . oink, oink here, . . .

4. . . . cows . . . moo, moo here, . . .

Figure 9.10 *continued*

Jolly Old Saint Nicholas

Traditional
Jol - ly Old Saint Nich - o - las, Lean your ear this way.
Don't you tell a sin - gle soul What I'm going to say.
Christ-mas Eve is com - ing soon; Now, you dear old man,
Whis-per what you'll bring to me; Tell me if you can.

La Muñeca

Spanish Folk Song
1. Ten - go u-na mu - ñe - ca ves - ti - da de a - zul;
2. Dos y dos son cua - tro y cua - tro y dos son seis.

Za - pa - ti - tos blan - cos, ca - mi - sol de tul.
Seis y dos son o - cho y o - cho die - ci - seis.

Figure 9.10 *continued*

All Night, All Day

Little Tom Tinker

Down in the Valley

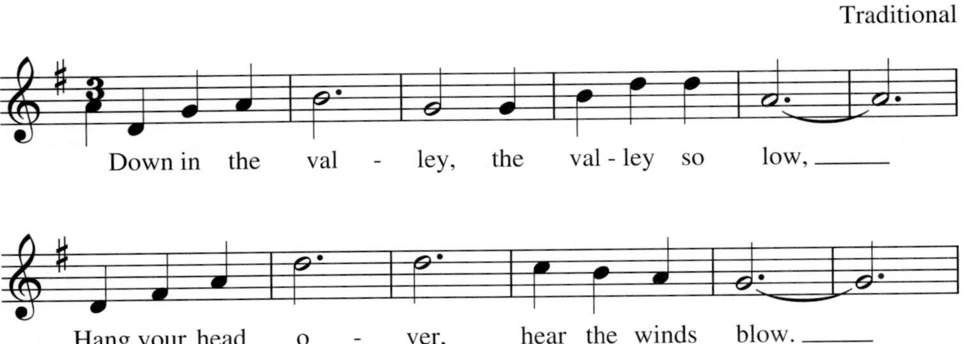

Figure 9.10 *continued*

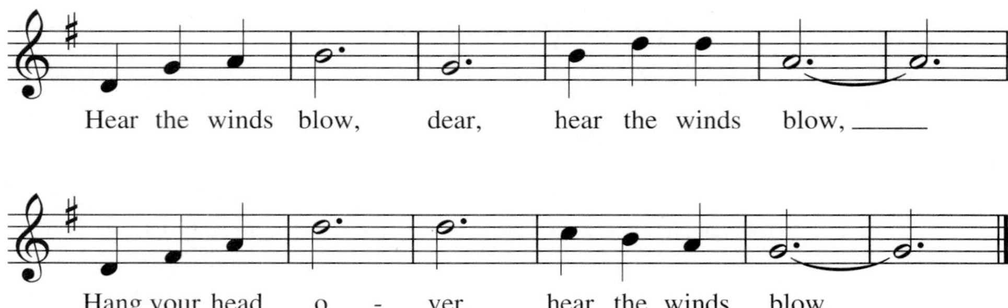
Hear the winds blow, dear, hear the winds blow, ___
Hang your head o - ver, hear the winds blow. ___

Kum Ba Yah

Traditional

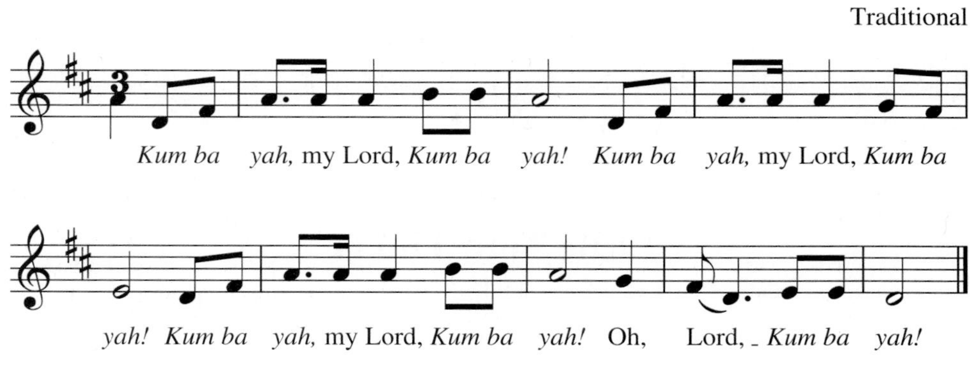
Kum ba yah, my Lord, *Kum ba yah!* *Kum ba yah,* my Lord, *Kum ba*
yah! *Kum ba yah,* my Lord, *Kum ba yah!* Oh, Lord, _ *Kum ba yah!*

When the Train Comes Along

American Folk Song

When the train comes a - long, _ When the train comes a - long, _ I'll
Fine
meet you at the sta - tion when the train comes a - long.
It may be ear - ly, it may be late, But I'll
D.C. al Fine
meet you at the sta - tion when the train comes a - long.

Figure 9.10 *continued*

Tom Dooley

American Folk Song

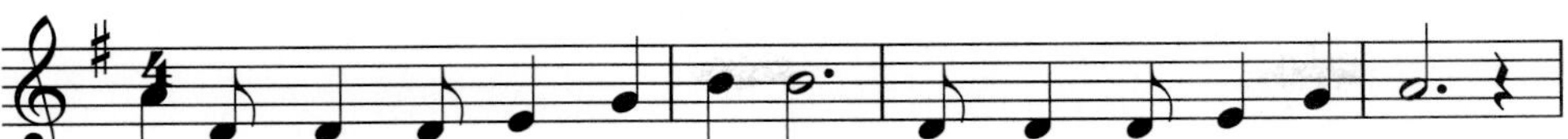

Hang down your head, Tom Doo-ley, Hang down your head and cry.

Hang down your head, Tom Doo-ley; Poor boy, you're bound _ to die.

Good King Wenceslas

English

When the snow lay 'round a - bout, Deep and crisp and e - ven.

Bright-ly shone the moon that night, Though the frost was cru - el,

When a poor man came in sight, Gath-'ring win-ter fu - el.

FURTHER PRACTICE

Listen to "Water Drum I" from the Baka Forest People, track #32. Using either structured or creative movement, create your own movement composition to illustrate this musical selection. Use a notation system of your choice to record notes for your composition that will help you remember it. Be prepared to teach your composition to either a partner or the whole class.

Figure 10.1 *continued*

Tra la la la la la la, Tra la la la la la la;

All who born in Jan - u - ar - y, skip a - round.

Figure 10.2 If You're Happy

If You're Happy

Traditional Folk Song

If you're hap-py and you know it, clap your hands. If you're

hap - py and you know it, clap your hands. If you're

hap-py and you know it, Then your face will sure-ly show it. If you're

hap - py and you know it, clap your hands.

Do remember, however, that singing and moving at the same time is relatively difficult for children. It is really important that they know the song you are using very well. If they do not, you should have them listen and do the movements while you perform the song for them.

Three fundamental movements are particularly difficult for many handicapped children. When you have youngsters skip or gallop to the music, you should be prepared to suggest a simpler alternative, such as walking or running, for children who are not at the same motor level as their age mates. Similarly, many developmentally delayed youngsters have a very difficult time hopping on one foot, and the easier jumping movement should be included in your directions as a "way to move to this song."

STRUCTURED MOVEMENT

As you will recall from chapter 9, structured movements are simply organized patterns of movement. They may range from simple to intricate patterns of any of the fundamental movements, from walking the beat in a circle to intricate folk dances for older children. Hand jive and foot jive, such as you learned in the previous chapter, are forms of structured movements that help children demonstrate their understanding of the form of songs or listening selections. When students create their own hand and foot jives to accompany songs or listening selections, they synthesize many learning concepts in addition to the musical: number, structure, pattern, symmetry, and repetition. The social learning environment fostered by group movement-composition activities aids students further in shaping and refining their conceptual understandings through interaction with their peers.

Structured folk dances are an excellent means of exploring and experiencing the nature of different cultures, and elementary students love to learn them. There may be adults in your community who are willing to share their knowledge of traditional dance with you and your students. Invite these individuals to meet with you before they come to your class so that you can help them tailor their teaching to your students' ability level. If this initial experience with the adult dance expert proves exciting, you may want to explore the possibility of involving this adult in an entire day or week of folk dance so that the whole school may benefit. Of course, organizing a special event for the whole school would require a lot of consultation with your principal and teaching colleagues. But the result of your extra effort can be very worthwhile.

The four songs included in the following structured-movement activities were chosen to broaden your repertoire, as they are from a variety of countries around the world. Each song presents its own challenge, such as testing your ability to pronounce a foreign language or sing an unfamiliar rhythm pattern. After you've worked through each song, look at the structured-movement suggestions included after it. Try the movements yourself, saying the directions as you move. When you are confident about the pattern, go back and try to say the words of the song while you do the movements. When you are secure in this, try doing the movements while you sing the song. Your instructor may want you to perform these songs in class with your peers.

Figure 10.3 Hummingbird

Figure 10.3 *continued*

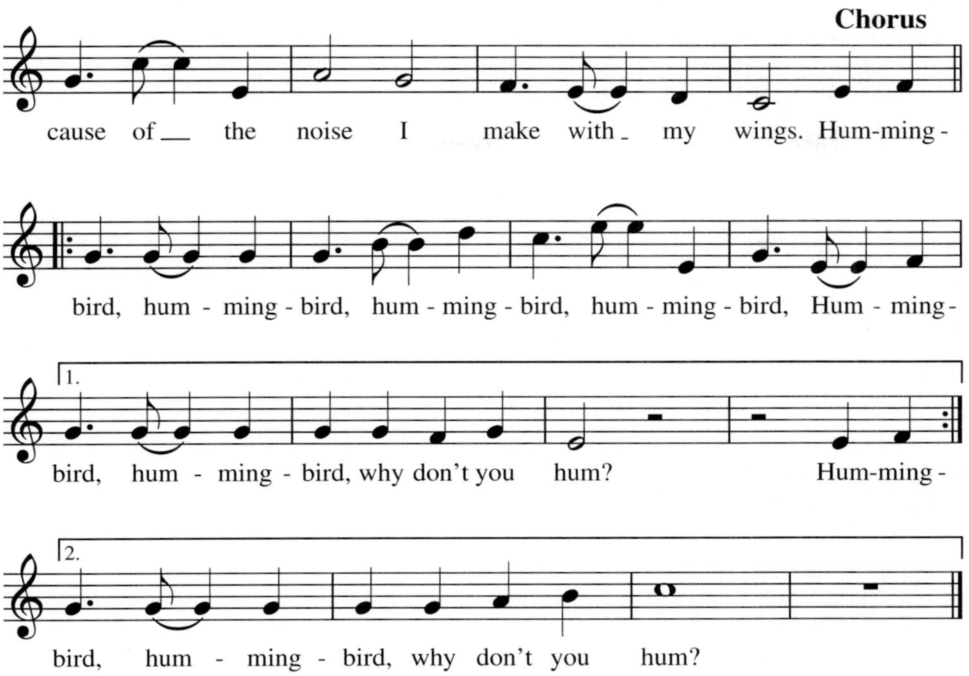

Figure 10.4 Hummingbird Hand Jive for Verse

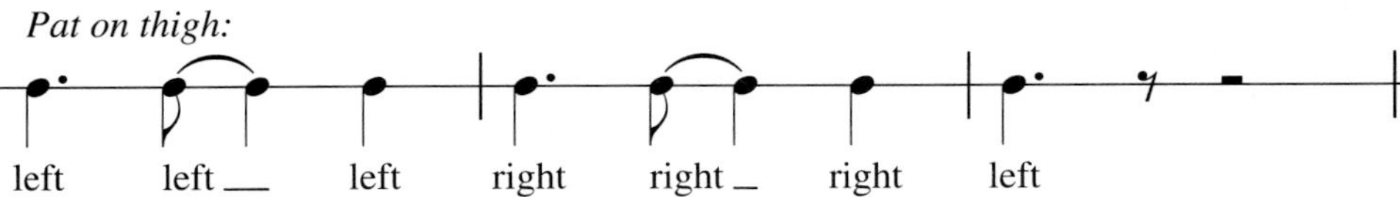

Figure 10.5 "Sambalele": Story and Music

"Sambalele"

There was an old woman who lived in a hut in a clearing in the great Amazon forest. She was an old woman, but she was also very strong and very capable. She built the house herself and planted a garden around it. A garden with all kinds of fruit and vegetables. Some you know, like pumpkins, beans and peas, and some you may never have seen, like cassavas, mangoes and papayas. Every morning, after looking after the garden, she used to go to the river to fish.

Now, somewhere far away in the forest, there lived Sambalele. Sambalele was a little monkey, and he lived with his tribe in a very dense and overgrown patch of forest. Sambalele wasn't a very nice monkey. He was very mischievous, always playing little jokes (which were not very amusing) on the other monkeys, like for example setting their tails on fire. One day, Sambalele, bored and having done every kind of mischief he could think of, decided that he was going to leave his tribe and go in search of adventure. So, to the general relief and happiness of the whole tribe, off he went.

Well, he jumped from tree to tree for a whole day, then he slept in a very big tree. Next morning, refreshed, he continued traveling, far and far away. And at the end of the third day he found the clearing. He looked at the house with great interest and then he realized that there was a garden full of the most amazing and beautiful fruit and vegetables that he had ever seen in his life. His eyes opened as wide as saucers in his head.

At that time of the day, as usual, the woman was down at the river fishing, washing clothes, and swimming. And since Sambalele found that there was no one around, he dived headfirst into the middle of the garden, and began eating everything he could lay his four hands on (because you know monkeys have four hands, they don't have feet like ours). He plucked everything he could, even fruit that was still green, and he ate so much that after a while he crawled very slowly on his belly back into the brush, where he lay sick for a few hours.

The sun went down and the old woman came back from the river with two very big fish that she had caught, and a pile of neat and clean clothes in a basket on her head. She came into the clearing and immediately noticed the destruction. Everything was torn apart, fruit thrown all over the place, vegetables strewn, young seedlings scattered and trampled on. She was so surprised and shocked that she let the basket fall from her head, and the fish fell to the ground. She was in such distress, she almost cried. But she was a very strong woman, so instead of crying she looked very carefully all around, and thought, "This mischief could only have been done by a monkey. I have no monkeys around here, but there must be a monkey somewhere that has come into my garden and created this destruction."

So there and then she decided that she was going to get that monkey. She picked up some logs and went into her hut, closing the door after her. All night you could hear her working away and the lights and the fire kept on burning and burning while she hammered and worked and put things together. When the sun came up the old woman, very tired but happy, came out into the garden with a doll which looked just like a little five-year-old girl. This was what she'd spent the night making. She took a pot of tar, and painted the doll all over so she was sticky from head to toe. Then she took this lovely little girl with a nice grin on her face and stood her in the middle of the garden. Very pleased with herself, the woman took up her clothes and her fishing rod and went back to the river.

At twelve o'clock, Sambalele woke up and started scratching his face. He'd had a very uncomfortable night, because he'd eaten so much. Nevertheless, all he could think of was going back to the garden and eating some more. So he crawled back to the garden, jumped into the middle, and was stuffing his mouth with corn and mangoes when he suddenly realized that someone was looking at him. O-oh. Maybe he had been caught. So he turned and looked and there was this very nice looking little girl, grinning from ear to ear. Sambalele thought, "Well, I can eat some more later, maybe I should go and ask if this girl will play with me."

After all, he was very lonely being away from all the monkeys he knew, having no one to talk to and no one to brag to. So he went to the little girl and said, "Good morning, little girl, I am Sambalele. I am a very important monkey in my tribe. I am very clever, very intelligent, very rich, and I jump from the tallest of the trees."

And he went on boasting like this, and finally asked the little girl (who was, of course, silent), "What's your name?"

The girl just grinned.

"Well," said Sambalele, "maybe you'd like to play with me. We could run around the garden, then we could go and try to find something interesting to eat, and perhaps we could sing some songs together."

The little girl stayed silent.

So Sambalele said, "Hey, haven't you got any manners? I'm talking to you. Won't you answer me?"

But the little girl just grinned.

"Listen, when I talk to you you should answer me, because I am Sambalele, a very clever and important monkey. Answer me! I'm getting very annoyed with you."

He stamped his feet with impatience.

Now of course all the girl did was grin her lovely wide smile behind the tar. So Sambalele smacked her very hard in the face, and to his surprise his hand stuck.

"Let go of me!" he said. "Let go of me, or I'll smack you again!"

But the girl just grinned, so he smacked her on the other side of her face, and to his surprise his other hand stuck.

"Let go," he said, "or I'll kick you."

So he kicked her, and his foot stuck fast. More furious than ever, he kicked her with his other foot, and that foot stuck too.

"You stupid little girl, let me go or I'll hit you with my head!"

So he hit her with his head, and that got stuck. Finally, he switched his tail at her, and now . . . he was completely stuck!

At sundown the old woman came back and as she came into the garden she heard the howling and screaming of Sambalele. Now, this time she had a bamboo stick with her and she was smiling.

"Well," she said to Sambalele, "so *you* are the pest who has been destroying my garden and eating the green fruit and breaking my plants. You are the nasty thing who destroys what you cannot eat and breaks what you cannot take away. Right, now I've got something for you."

And she gave him such a whack on his bottom that Sambalele broke free from the tar girl with a yell and a scream. But his tail was stuck so fast that it wouldn't come away. He pulled so hard, it broke off, and he ran into the forest, leaving it behind. He didn't stop running until he got to his tribe of monkeys, to whom he told his tale—very much changed.

"Ah," he said, "I'm so glad to be back. I've been in a terrible place, a place in the forest where there lives a sorceress and her daughter. The daughter doesn't speak, and the sorceress is thirty feet tall!"

But all the monkeys laughed and sang, and made mockery of his story. He was a monkey without a tail! The other monkeys made up a song about him which said:

Sambalele is sick, he has a sore head.
Sambalele deserves a handful of smacks!

Sambalele

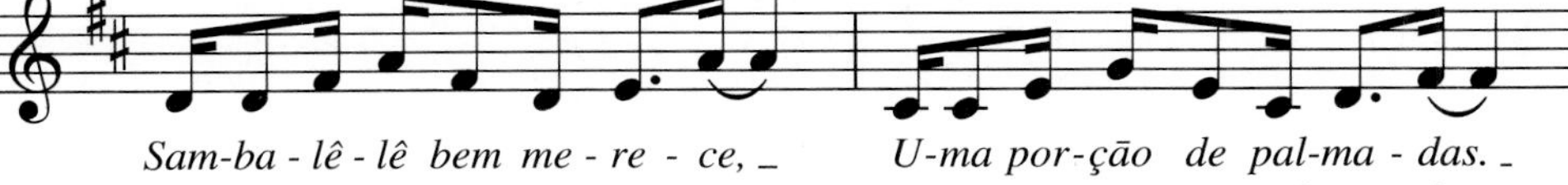

Figure 10.6 "Sambalele": Hand Jive for Verse

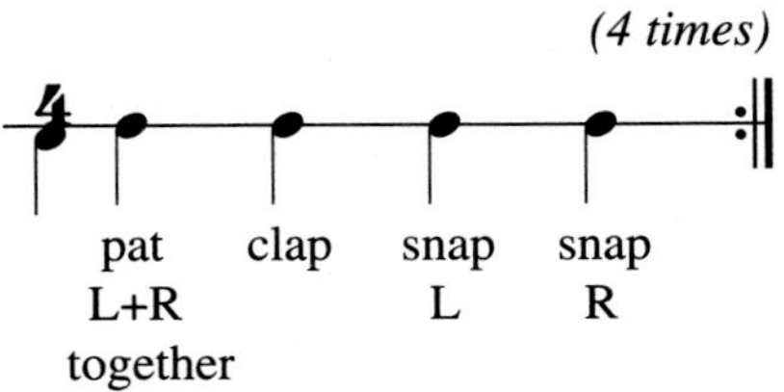

Figure 10.7 "Sambalele": Foot Jive for Chorus

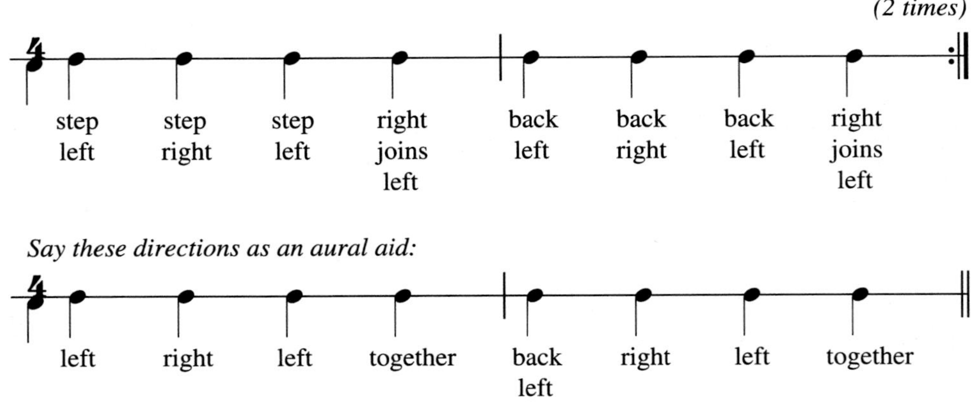

Figure 10.8 "Serra, Serra Serrador"

Serra, Serra, Serrador
Saw, Saw, Lumberjack

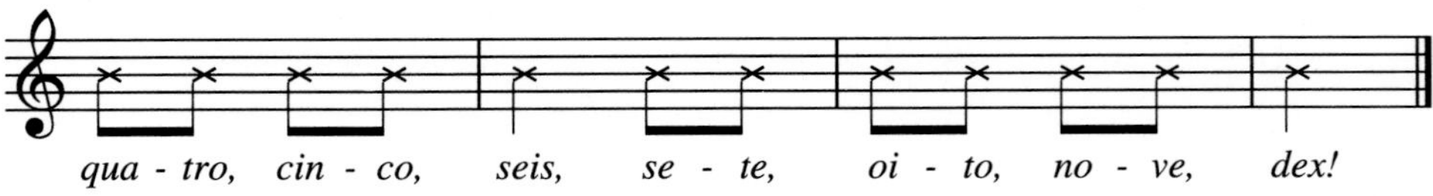

Translation:
Saw, saw, lumberjack.
How many pieces of wood do you saw, sir?
One, two, three, four, five, six, seven, eight, nine, ten.

Movement Directions

During the singing, walk in a circle formation clockwise around the circle, stepping the beat, and stop on last note of song ("serou?"). Then turn to face the center of the circle and, with arms extended in front of you as if holding the handle of a big saw, count (in speaking voices). With each count, pull and push the saw (pull-push-pull-push) as you count to 10 ("dez!").

Figure 10.9 "Inanay" Song and Hand Jive

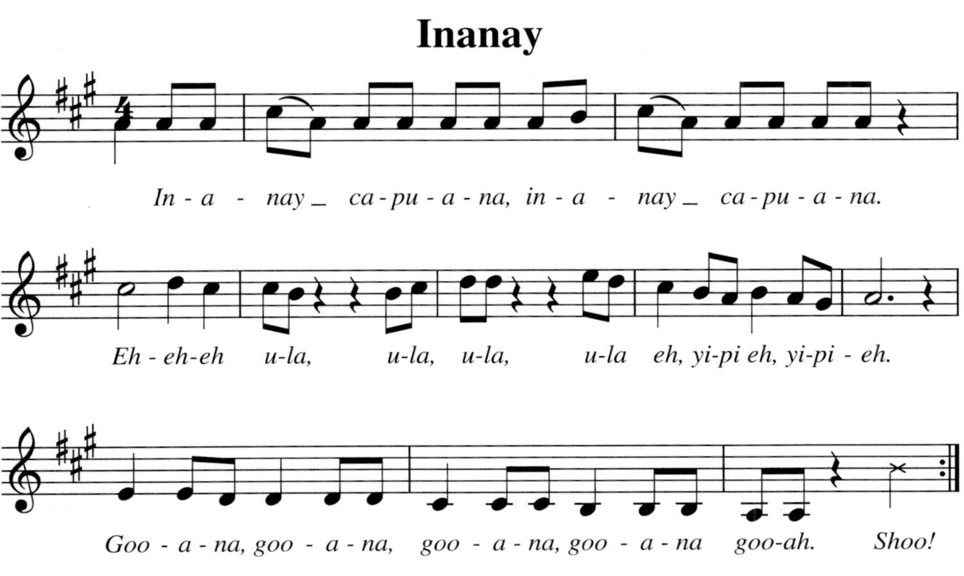

Hand jive for lines 1 and 2: *(4 times)*

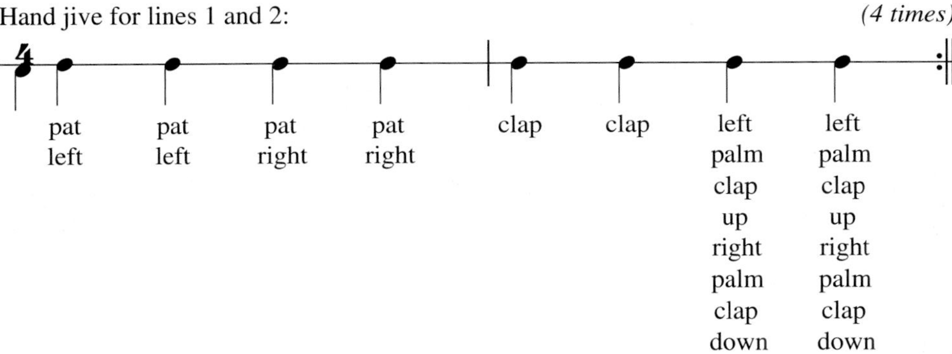

Hand jive for line 3: *(2 times)*

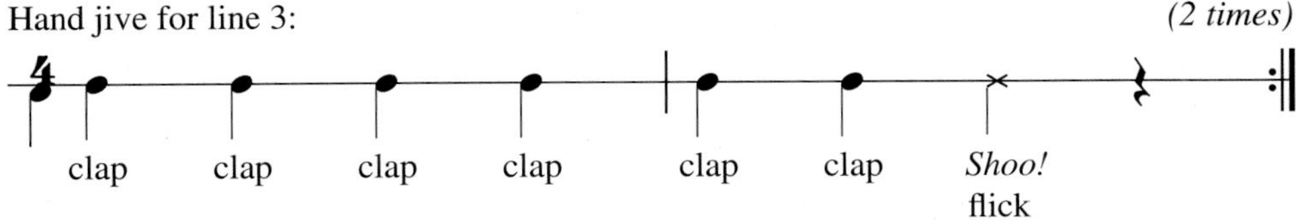

Movement Directions

For the first part ("Inanay" to "yipi-eh a"): Seated on the floor in a circle with legs crossed ("school style"), the hand jive is: Pat left thigh twice, pat right thigh twice, clap twice in center, extend arms to sides with left palm up and right palm down, and pat neighbor's hands twice (four times).

For the second part ("Gooana"): Clap hands six times, then on "Shoo!" raise both arms in front and extend all fingers in a flicking motion (two times).

Figure 10.10 "Kaeru no Uta": Song and Hand Jive

Kaeru no Uta (Frog's Song)

Translation:
The song of the frog
I can hear:
Gwa gwa gwa gwa
Gero gero gero gero gwa gwa gwa

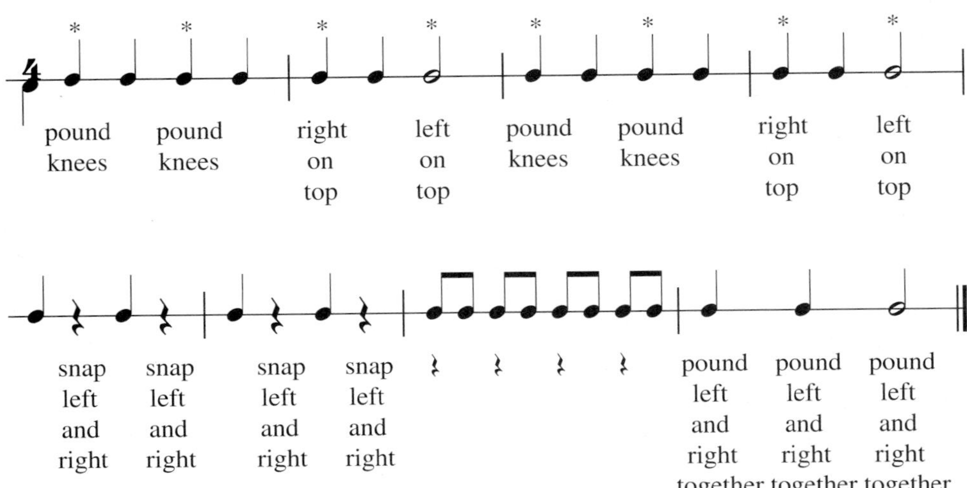

Movement Directions

Seated on the floor in a tight circle, with legs crossed ("school style") for first line (up to "ku-ru-yo"): Pound fists on knees twice, then pound right fist on top of left fist, reverse to pound left fist on top of right fist. (two times).

For the second line ("Gwa!"): Snap on each rest (four times), rest on "gero," pound both fists on both knees for the remaining "gwa"s.

CREATIVE MOVEMENT

Children can invent movements to express their understanding of what they hear in a musical selection, whether it is a song they're singing or a listening example. When children are asked to originate movements to music, they are often confused or indecisive. You may be disappointed when you ask your class to create their own movements, only to see some class members imitating a child who is using a fundamental movement, while others stand still and appear uninvolved. This reaction is due to a lack of prior movement opportunities and indicates that you need to provide your students with a basic movement repertoire.

Creative movement should be organized around a planned sequence of instruction with the four movement qualities of weight, space, time, and flow. When you have introduced students to each of these qualities, they can gradually begin to combine them and devise original movements that express what they feel and hear. Each movement quality can be introduced effectively with examples of opposites (light/heavy, narrow/wide, slow/fast, and sustained/stopped). If you introduce these qualities initially without sound, you can then accompany them with unpitched percussion instruments, and finally with music.

The quality of weight is expressed through light/heavy or strong/weak movements. Elementary-school children can easily imagine an object or an animal that moves lightly and imitate that movement. You can then explore the opposite quality in a similar way. An important aspect of this initial activity is establishing the acceptance of all possibilities —there is no "right" way to move lightly or heavily. After your students have explored many possibilities using their fingertips, arms, legs, feet, and entire bodies, you can add light and heavy sounds on a single instrument. You can then use two contrasting instrumental sounds, such as a tub drum and finger cymbals, and have the class indicate which they hear through movement.

The quality of space can be experienced through the contrasts of up/down, narrow/wide, or in/out. Younger children initially respond best to imitating the movement of an animal or object, but intermediate-school children should consider ways to use space while learning movement vocabulary. In addition, they can be challenged to incorporate ways of moving in space using more abstract vocabulary, such as growing, spreading, exploding, and so on. This sequence—movement exploration without sound, adding simple sounds, and then using the movements to demonstrate musical changes in dynamics or tempo—can be used in both primary and intermediate classes, depending upon the children's background in movement.

The movement qualities of time and flow are very helpful in reinforcing musical learning. You can easily introduce time (slow/fast) when discussing the pace at which a piece moves. Ask primary-school children to imitate the falling of autumn leaves at different tempi and then use either the same movements or new ones when you play a maraca or triangle, as if they are responding to changes in the wind. You can then ask children to create movements to represent changes in tempi when you improvise on a hand drum or a xylophone. Intermediate-school children can demonstrate contrasts in tempo in an activity in which they choose three words from a list (for example, drip, slither, bounce, float, glide, and scamper), decide on an order, practice in groups, and then share their movement compositions with their classmates. Their compositions can accompany either teacher-selected sounds or sounds they choose themselves.

Flow (sustained/stopped) is an expressive movement quality that relates to musical duration as well as to different articulations. Primary-school children can easily imitate moving through honey or glue; then, as they listen to a flowing piece from the CD, such as "Pie Jesu" (track #4), they can think about how they will move. With adequate preparation, children can create their own movements. Older children will find sustained flow more difficult, especially if they have not had numerous movement experiences in their primary years. One way to help them overcome self-consciousness is to give them three-foot pieces of crepe paper to move in a flowing fashion and then have them translate that movement into their bodies.

One important aspect of developing children's movement competence is to monitor your classes carefully and decide when you think children are ready to move beyond the preparatory experiences to create their own original movements. If you spend regular amounts of time in activities that incorporate movement into your school day, your students will be empowered to move in creative ways to whatever sounds they hear. Becoming creative in movement requires experiences in a comfortable repertoire of motions and gestures, and you can provide some of this on a regular basis in your classroom.

INTEGRATING MOVEMENT AND MUSIC IN THE CURRICULUM

TEACHING SCRIPT: LANGUAGE ARTS LESSON

Figure 10.11 "Quilla Bung": Story and Song

"Quilla Bung"

One day, a man and his wife had nothing to eat for dinner. So the man went out with his gun to see if he could shoot something. As he was going along he heard a song:

Laleelu come quilla, come quilla,
Bung, bung, bung quilla bung.

Quilla Bung

La - lee-lu come quil-la, come, quil-la, Bung, bung, bung quil-la bung.

He looked up, and what did he see? A whole flock of geese flying overhead, and they were all singing. The man licked his lips, lifted his gun, aimed, fired, and BANG! he shot one. But as it fell down from the sky, it sang:

Laleelu come quilla, come quilla,
Bung, bung, bung quilla bung.

He took it home and gave it to his wife to cook. She laid it down, and began to pluck it. But every feather she plucked flew out of her hand and floated out the window. And all the while, the goose kept singing:

Laleelu come quilla, come quilla,
Bung, bung, bung quilla bung.

Well, she finished at last, and she put the goose in the stove to cook it. But all the time it was cooking, she could hear in muffled tones from inside the stove:

Laleelu come quilla, come quilla,
Bung, bung, bung quilla bung.

Anyway, they sat down to dinner, the husband and wife, and she put the goose on the table between them. And the man picked up the carving knife to carve it, but all the while it sang:

Laleelu come quilla, come quilla,
Bung, bung, bung quilla bung.

And as he held up the carving fork ready to stick into the goose, there came a tremendous noise. In through the window flew the whole flock of geese, and they were all singing as loud as could be:

Laleelu come quilla, come quilla,
Bung, bung, bung quilla bung.

Then each one took out a feather, and stuck it into the goose, and then all together they lifted that goose right out of the dish. And up it flew and followed them, and round they went and out the window.

And the man and his wife sat there with empty plates and open mouths, and stared. But all they got for dinner that night was a song!

Laleelu come quilla, come quilla,
Bung, bung, bung quilla bung.
Laleelu come quilla, come quilla,
Bung, bung, bung quilla bung.
Laleelu come quilla, come quilla,
Bung, bung, bung quilla bung.
Laleelu come quilla . . .
(Repeat, gradually fading.)

Today we're going to work on a traditional North American story called "Quilla Bung." (See figure 10.11.) Before we begin work on it, though, I'd like to teach you a little song that we'll need to know for this story to make sense. I'll sing it, and you listen. Teacher sings song once, then repeats it. **This time, I'll sing it again, and when you are ready, join me.** Teacher sings it again. **That was a little tricky, wasn't it? Let's go over the words now, to make sure everyone has them.** Teacher reads words from overhead projector while pointing to them so class will read along. **Let's try the song again, now that we've got the words down.** Teacher leads class in song. **That was a lot clearer and easier to understand that time.**

Now I'd like you to take a look at the story on your desk. Let's all read it together as different people read it aloud. Whenever we get to the song words, let's all sing the song instead of reading it. Who would like to volunteer to read the first section, up to the song? Teacher surveys the group and chooses one child with hand raised, and the reading begins. When the volunteer finishes the section, the teacher continues. **I'll play the starting pitch on the tone bar and we'll sing the melody now.** Teacher plays the D and class sings. Teacher then assigns volunteer readers for the rest of the story, and the lesson continues as readers alternate with the whole class singing the little melody to the end of the story. **That was great for a first time through. Now I'd like us to add some movement to this story so that we can show each time something unusual happens with the goose or geese. I've made a list of four unusual things that involve the goose or geese. Let's read through my list and see what it says.** Teacher asks for volunteers to read the listed items, and they read them as follows: (1) falling from the sky, (2) feathers flying up, (3) geese coming in the window, and (4) geese lifting up the cooked goose and all flying away together.

Let's experiment with some movements before we figure out what to do. What are some ways that we can show flight? Yes, I see everyone has the idea: you're all flapping your arms like birds. But what about other movements that also show flight? Teacher takes a few suggestions, ranging from delicate hand movements to fixed-wing bombers, each demonstrated by students. **If we look back at my list, we've got four different activities that we'll need to portray in movement. I'd like us to work in four groups for the next few minutes, each group working on just one of the items. I'm going to assign each of you to a group with the letter name A, B, C, or D. I'll count you off now, so pay attention to your assigned letter.** Teacher goes down the rows, assigning a letter to each student. **The A group is in this corner, the B group in that corner, the C group is in the front of the room, and the D group can meet in the hallway, just outside our door. You've got about five minutes to get your suggestions out and get them ready to try out with the whole group. Be ready to show your group's favorite movements to the whole class when we come back in five minutes.** Students move to groups as assigned and teacher circulates among them, watching and listening. After five minutes teacher continues: **Time's up, class.** When students have returned to their seats, teacher continues: **Let's have group A show us their movements.** Groups remain at their seats but demonstrate their movements as an ensemble in turn. When all groups have shown their movements, teacher continues: **Now we have to make a decision about which of the movements from each group we'd like to use with our story. We'll do this by popular vote, which means that I'll ask each of you to vote for the four choices you feel best show the action of the geese.** Teacher leads class through voting process. When decision is reached for all four categories, teacher continues: **Now let's try out the movements we've chosen when they happen in the story. I'll need another group of volunteers to do the reading.** Teacher makes assignments for new volunteers, then continues: **I think we're ready to begin. The only thing I've forgotten to do is assign the title. Who is supposed to read the first section?** A girl raises her hand and says, "I am." **Would you read the title, too?** She nods, and teacher thanks her.

Here we go! When the story is finished, teacher continues: **That was a good first try, class. Everyone worked very hard to listen carefully, sing the little melody accurately each time, and remember the movements for each section. Now, if we were going to do it again, how could we make it a little better?** Teacher takes suggestions, then works through all the components (reading, singing, and movements) to incorporate all the suggestions. **You've all worked really well on this story today, class. When we come back to it tomorrow, we'll use your suggestions and see how we like our new, improved version. If we're happy with it, we'll invite Mrs. Salaman's first-grade class to come in so we can perform it for them. Now it's time for recess!**

LESSON PLAN ACTIVITY

Use this form to help you derive the lesson plan for the "Quilla Bung" script you've just read.

Grade Level:

I. Concept:

II. Learning Outcome or Objective:
Entry ability:

Exit ability:

III. Lesson Evaluation Procedures:

IV. Materials and Board/Space Preparation:

V. Teaching Procedures:

A. Setting the Stage:

B. Developing the Lesson:

Step 1:

Transition statement:

Step 2:

Transition statement:

Step 3:

Transition statement:

Step 4:

Transition statement:

C. Concluding the Lesson:

INTERMEDIATE TEACHING SCRIPT: INTEGRATING MOVEMENT AND MUSIC IN SIXTH-GRADE SOCIAL STUDIES

We've been studying two countries this spring, and we are getting closer to the time when we'll share what we've learned with your parents in our annual exhibitions. We have learned many things about both India and Japan. What are some of the ways in which these countries are similar? Take class contributions and list them on the board under the name of each country. **Now let's change our thinking and try to remember what we've learned about how these countries are different.** Take class contributions and list them on the board. If you do not get a contribution of contrasts in music, art, and folklore, bring up specific examples of such contrasts they have studied, such as haiku they have read and written.

Later this week we are going to organize the lists we have just put on the board and decide how to let your parents know what you know. Some of the information is best shared in picture form, and we may want to make a big class mural. Today, we are going to learn something new from only one of these countries. Here is some music for you to listen to. Can you decide which country it comes from? Play "Tokyo Dontaku," track #31. Take responses from class.

The music is indeed from Japan, and there is a great set of movements that I want to teach you today that go with the music. I want you to listen to the music again and watch my arms as I move them. Play CD track #31 again and model movements as follows:

Part 1:

Clap hands in front of chest (beats 1 and 2), sweep hands down and out to sides with palms down (beat 3), sweep hands up in front of chest (& of beat 3), clap hands in front of chest (beat 4).

Part 2: Paddle, paddle, shade your eyes

Move both palms backward on left side as though paddling a boat (beat 1); repeat on right side (beat 2). Shade eyes with left palm at left ear and right arm extended in front, palm forward (beat 3), reverse hands (& of beat 3), reverse again (beat 4 &).

Part 3: Make a tree and make a tree

Facing a bit right, touch fingertips with palms down about thigh level and arms rounded, then swoop arms up to touch fingertips above head with palms facing ceiling (beats 1 & 2 &). Repeat, facing a bit left (beats 3 & 4 &).

Part 4: Brush your sleeve and brush your sleeve

With right arm bent and palm facing cheek, left hand brushes kimono sleeve below right elbow three times (beats 1 & 2 &); repeat the three brushes with right hand below left elbow three times (beats 3 & 4 &).

I want us to try practicing the movements without the music first. I will do a movement and then you be my echo. We'll go through the entire set of motions this way. Model movements four beats at a time and have class echo movement.

Now I want you to watch one more time while I do the movements with the music, and then we'll try it together. Play music and model movements for class. **It's time for everyone to try moving to this great piece of Japanese music. I want you to stand, and let's try it all together.** Play music and continue to model movements. Repeat practicing movements alone if necessary and repeat moving with music, if necessary. **You did a great job today, class. With a little more practice each day, we'll be able to share this music and movement with everyone soon.**

PHOTOCOPY THIS PAGE

Fill in the details for this lesson plan, based on the previous teaching script.

LESSON PLAN FOR INTERMEDIATE INTEGRATED MOVEMENT LESSON PLAN

I. Learning Outcome or Objective:
Entry Ability:

Exit Ability:

II. Lesson Evaluation Procedures:

III. Materials and Board/Space Preparation:

IV. Teaching Procedures:

A. Setting the Stage:

B. Developing the Lesson:

Step 1:

Transition statement:

Step 2:

Transition statement:

Step 3:

Transition statement:

Step 4:

Transition statement:

Step 5:

C. Concluding the Lesson:

INTERMEDIATE TEACHING SCRIPT: INTEGRATING MOVEMENT AND MUSIC INTO FIFTH-GRADE SCIENCE

Today is the day that your picture assignment is due. I hope that each group has many pictures of different types of weather. These pictures are going to be a way for us to further explore the topics of evaporation and condensation that we have been studying this month. Have group members take out pictures and put them on tables. **You already have a lot of scientific data collected about these two topics. Which group would like to share their observations from this week on evaporation?** Take responses and put on board. **When we look at these observations, we can try to make some predictions. What do you think will happen next with the quart of water on the windowsill?** Take responses. **Today's task involves creating a model of what happens with one or both of these processes. Here is your group assignment.** Move to the board and pull up the screen which has been covering the following directions.

1. Look at all the pictures your group has.
2. Decide which can be used to illustrate either evaporation or condensation or both.
3. Arrange your pictures into a logical sequence.
4. Decide movements that will demonstrate your sequence AND your classmates' understanding of the topic.
5. Practice your movements together very carefully.
6. Choose which section of "The Seasons" you will play with your movements.
7. Practice your movements with the music. You may use any picture as a prop or create another picture if you need it.

Please read these directions carefully. If there are any that are not clear, you know that it is best to ask before you begin. Take questions and provide clarifications, if needed.

When your group is finished and ready to demonstrate your science concept, you must remember that your classmates will be trying to decide which concept you are illustrating and also the sequence you are following. I have borrowed the camcorder from the library so we can videotape this assignment. You will have exactly half an hour to work together on this task. Let's get to work.

Rhythm pattern should be 4 measure long you should be able to clap your rhythm

Find a poem & lesson plan

PHOTOCOPY THIS PAGE

Fill in the missing details based on the previous lesson script.

INTERMEDIATE LESSON PLAN: INTEGRATING MOVEMENT AND MUSIC INTO FIFTH-GRADE SCIENCE

Theme: Weather: Condensation and Evaporation

I. Learning Outcome or Objective:

Entry Ability:

Exit Ability:

II. Lesson Evaluation Procedures:

III. Materials and Board/Space Preparation:

IV. Teaching Procedures:

A. Setting the Stage:

B. Developing the Lesson:

Step 1:

Transition statement:

Step 2:

Transition statement:

Step 3:

Transition statement:

Step 4:

Transition statement:

C. Concluding the Lesson:

PRIMARY TEACHING SCRIPT: ART LESSON ON PATTERN

The following script is for a second-grade art lesson on pattern. The stimulus for the lesson is a photograph of the Sydney Opera House (figure 10.12).

Figure 10.12 Sydney Opera House

Remember this morning's social studies lesson about Australia? Well, we're going to use one of the photographs from that lesson to give us ideas for an art activity now. Take a look at this photograph, class. Teacher uncovers slide of figure 10.12 on overhead projector. **Who can remember the name of this famous building?** Teacher calls on child, who correctly identifies it as the Sydney Opera House. **This building is unique because it sits right out on the water and was designed to look like sails on a ship. Some people say it also looks like seashells. Remember what a pattern is? A pattern is something that happens more than once—in fact, many times—so that it becomes the way of organizing something. I'd like each of you to look very closely at this photograph now and think about whether you can see any patterns.** Teacher waits for a minute, then continues. **Did anyone see a pattern in the way the building is put together?** Several hands shoot up, and teacher calls on one child, who states that the shape of the triangles in the roof makes a pattern. Another child says that the light color of the roof makes a pattern, too. A third child explains that the dark shapes in the middle of the photo make another pattern. **These are all great answers, class, and I can see that many of you are still studying this photo carefully for more pattern clues. What I'd like each of you to do now is draw your own pattern, using both color and line. It doesn't have to look anything like our photo, so use your imagination and see what you discover. You may work quietly on your own for the next 10 minutes, and then we'll check our work.** Teacher moves around the room, monitoring students as they settle down to work. After 10 minutes, teacher continues. **I'd like each of you to show your work to a partner at your table now and see if your partner can find the pattern in your work.** Each student turns to a partner, and they discuss how pattern appears in their works. **Let's look once again at our opera-house photo. Can you imagine how we could move to show the pattern in this photo? Perhaps we could just trace in the air the way the outline of the roof looks to our eyes. Let's try that. We'll start on the left and trace the outline to the right.** Teacher uses a pen point on the overhead projector to trace the contour of the roof while the students trace along in the air with their fingers. **Is there another way we could move our fingers that would produce another kind of pattern in this photo?** Several hands go up, and one child is called on. "We could draw all the triangles as we find them with our eyes," she says. **Let's try it.** Teacher traces over all the triangles in the photo and continues. **Let's stand up now, and this time let's trace the outline of the triangles with our noses. Ready, go!** The class tries this and begins to break into giggles. **It's kind of funny to draw**

with your nose, isn't it? Let's try one more idea. I'd like you to use your upper body this time—your head, shoulders, arms, hands, and fingers—and move in the pattern that your eye follows as you look at the photograph. Let's try it. Teacher monitors class as they all create their own movements while looking at the photograph. **What I've noticed in doing this activity with you is that what we call movement in art is really the movement of our eyes as we take in the details of the artwork. Nothing in this photograph, or in our own pattern works, actually moves, does it? So the point of our work today was to discover what movement is in an artwork, one that has a pattern. Thanks for your good work today, class.**

PHOTOCOPY THIS PAGE

Use this form to help you derive the lesson plan for the art and movement script you've just read.

Grade Level:

I. Concept:

II. Learning Outcome or Objective:

Entry ability:

Exit ability:

III. Lesson Evaluation Procedures:

IV. Materials and Board/Space Preparation:

V. Teaching Procedures:

A. Setting the Stage:

B. Developing the Lesson:

Step 1:

Transition statement:

Step 2:

Transition statement:

Step 3:

Transition statement:

Step 4:

Transition statement:

C. Concluding the Lesson:

SPECIAL LEARNERS AND MOVEMENT

Movement activities can be extra challenging for special learners for a wide variety of reasons. Movement activities are typically led by verbal directions alone, and special learners benefit from a combination of verbal and visual reinforcement. You can easily represent your directions on the chalkboard through key words ("turn," "step") or pictures and drawings (right arrow and footprint for "step right"). Many children appear to be "left-right impaired"—unable to remember which is which. Visual cues will help in this case, too.

Visually impaired children need you to "show them" the movements by talking them through the directions while moving them physically, first by letting them hold on to you while you do the movement. You can also pair the child with a sighted child to act as a movement guide, once you've given the extra help described here.

Some children with attention difficulties find the freedom of movement activities to be too chaotic for them, and they benefit from having more structure. You can provide this by staying in close proximity to the particular child, asking her or him to be your partner, and using her or him to help you to demonstrate the movement sequence.

MOVEMENT IN THE CLASSROOM: THE CHILD'S PERSPECTIVE

For the elementary-age child, movement is life, and the teacher who makes movement activities part of the regular classroom routine allows children this very necessary means of learning. Some people are naturally kinesthetic learners, which means that they cannot learn to do a thing unless they actually do the thing (physically). No matter what their learning style, however, both primary- and intermediate-age children need the physical activity that movement lessons can provide. When you take the time to include a wide range of movement activities in your daily routine, children become more body competent; the result is that they move more freely, exhibiting a wider movement vocabulary. Also important is the enjoyment factor: movement activities bring smiles to the faces of your students and make the little bit of extra planning required to fit them into other subject lessons well worth your trouble.

NATIONAL STANDARDS FOR MOVEMENT

The following achievement standards for elementary-school students are included here to underscore the importance of the movement concepts presented in this and the previous chapter.

1. Students accurately demonstrate nonlocomotor movements such as bending, twisting, stretching, and swinging.
2. Students accurately demonstrate eight basic locomotor movements such as walking, running, hopping, jumping, leaping, galloping, sliding, and skipping.
3. Students create shapes at low, middle, and high levels.
4. Students demonstrate accuracy in moving to a musical beat and responding to changes in tempo.
5. Students use improvisation to discover and invent movement and to solve movement problems.
6. Students explore, discover, and realize multiple solutions to a given movement problem, choose their favorite solution, and discuss the reasons for that choice.
7. Students perform folk dances from various cultures with competence and confidence.

A NEW RECORDER NOTE: LOW C

Figure 10.13 Fingering for Low C

Figure 10.14 Practice the New Note

Figure 10.15 A Duet with the New Note

Figure 10.16 Practice Songs

My Bonnie Lad

Scottish

Tanz

Melchior Franck (ca. 1579–1639)

Een kint gheboren in Bethlehem

Dutch (16th century)

Figure 10.17 Children's Songs You Can Play

My Head and My Shoulders

Zulu Singing Game

My head and my shoul - ders, My chest and my mid - dle, My
knees and then my toes, Oh, my knees and then my toes, oh.

When the Saints Go Marching In

African American Spiritual

Oh, when the saints ___ go march-ing in, ___ Oh, when the

saints go march-ing in; ___ Oh, Lord, I want to be in that

num - ber ___ When the saints go march - ing in. ___

Old Dan Tucker

American Folk Song

Old Dan Tuck-er was a might-y man; He washed his face in the

fry - ing pan, Combed his hair with a wag-on wheel, Had a tooth-ache

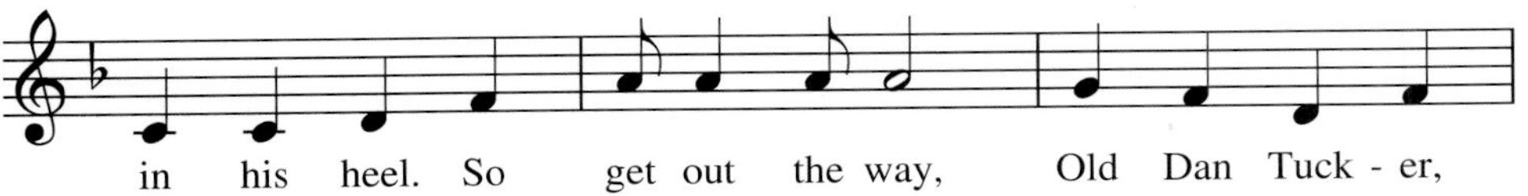
in his heel. So get out the way, Old Dan Tuck - er,

Figure 10.17 *continued*

Get out the way, Old Dan Tuck - er. Get out the way,

Old Dan Tuck - er, You're too late to get your sup-per.

Down at the Station

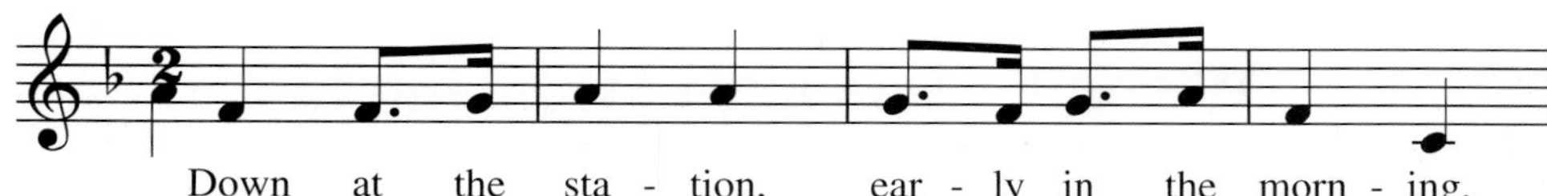
Down at the sta - tion, ear - ly in the morn - ing,

See the lit - tle puf - fer-bil - lies all in a row.

See the en - gine driv - er pull the lit - tle han - dle.

Chug! Chug! Woo! Woo! Off we go!

Camptown Races

Stephen C. Foster

Camp-town la - dies sing this song,
Went down there with my hat caved in,
Doo - dah, doo - dah,

Camp-town race - track five miles long,
Came back home with a pocket full of tin,
Oh, doo - dah day.

Figure 10.17 *continued*

Goin' to run all night, Goin' to run all day;
Bet my mon-ey on the bob-tailed nag; Some-bod-y bet on the bay.

Mister Frog Went Courtin'

American Folk Song

Mis-ter Frog went court-in', and he did ride, mm - hmm.
Mis-ter Frog went court-in', and he did ride,
Sword and pis - tol by his side, mm - hmm.

Little Red Caboose

Traditional Children's Song

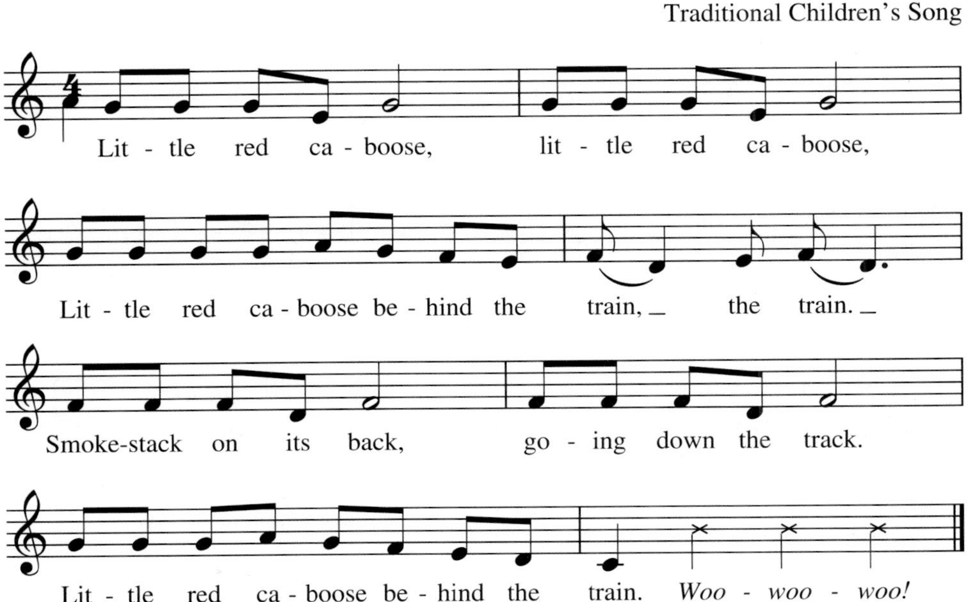

Lit - tle red ca - boose, lit - tle red ca - boose,
Lit - tle red ca - boose be - hind the train, the train.
Smoke-stack on its back, go - ing down the track.
Lit - tle red ca - boose be - hind the train. Woo - woo - woo!

Figure 10.17 *continued*

Cotton-Eye Joe

Alabama Folk Song

Where did you come from? Where did you go?
Where did you come from, Cot - ton - Eye ___ Joe?

Tideo

American Singing Game

Skip one win-dow, ti - de - o, Skip two win-dows, ti - de - o,
Skip three win-dows, ti - de - o, Jin-gle at the win-dow, ti - de - o;
Ti - de - o, ti - de - o, Jin-gle at the win-dow, ti - de - o.

London's Burning

Fire! Fire! Fire! Fire! Pour on wa - ter, pour on wa - ter.

FURTHER PRACTICE

1. Using the following form, prepare a lesson plan which includes music and movement for a grade and curriculum area of your choice.

I. Learning Outcome or Objective:

Entry Ability:

Exit Ability:

II. Lesson Evaluation Procedures:

III. Materials and Board/Space Preparation:

IV. Teaching Procedures:

A. Setting the Stage:

B. Developing the Lesson:

Step 1:

Transition statement:

Step 2:

Transition statement:

Step 3:

Transition statement:

Step 4:

Transition statement:

C. Concluding the Lesson:

---

2. From a school or public library, select two children's books about holidays that could be integrated with movement and music. Write a short paragraph for each that describes why you think this book is appropriate. In your second paragraph, describe how you would use it in a classroom. Then use the above form and write a lesson plan for your favorite grade level.

PHOTOCOPY THIS PAGE

3. Develop a lesson plan for creative movement using one of the selections from the CD accompanying this textbook. Fill out the lesson plan format and fill in each section in as much detail as possible. Be prepared to hand this in to your instructor.

Grade Level:

I. Concept:

II. Learning Outcome or Objective:

Entry ability:

Exit ability:

III. Lesson Evaluation Procedures:

IV. Materials and Board/Space Preparation:

V. Teaching Procedures:

A. Setting the Stage:

B. Developing the Lesson:

Step 1:

Transition statement:

Step 2:

Transition statement:

Step 3:

Transition statement:

Step 4:

Transition statement:

C. Concluding the Lesson:

---

4. Using a lesson plan that you've developed for one of your other teaching subjects, add a section that incorporates movement into the lesson. Come to class prepared to teach the movement section of your lesson to a partner.

Music Fundamentals for Creating Music

What you will be able to do by the end of this chapter

- *Read triplet and dotted eighth–sixteenth note patterns*
- *Create and perform rhythmic ostinati*
- *Read and perform major and minor modes*
- *Recognize I, IV, and V chords*
- *Create a rap piece*
- *Create a blues song*
- *Play a new note on the recorder*

PLAYING WITH SOUND

The process of musical creation has remained cloaked in mystery over the centuries, and even in our technological age the average person knows next to nothing about the compositional process. Composers themselves are usually not interested in revealing how they work—how the musical product comes into being. So we are left with the impression that music somehow comes to them fully formed, packaged perfectly for the listener's ears. The truth is that there are as many compositional processes as there are composers, and what they actually do is not much different from what other creative artists do: they "mess around" with sound, working on a musical idea until it satisfies them.

In this chapter you will have an opportunity to take on the role of the composer and use your musical knowledge and imagination to create unique musical products. In messing around with sound, you will synthesize various types of musical learnings and use your musical knowledge in new ways. It is the hope of the authors of this text that you'll even experience some of the joy of creating that is at the heart of the composer's role.

CHAPTER GOALS

In this chapter you will review the music fundamentals from earlier chapters, with particular emphasis on pitch, rhythm, and harmony. You will have the opportunity to improvise music, using your singing voice and your recorder to play with musical ideas as a means to discovering new ones. In the role of composer, you'll learn to write songs in two popular musical genres: rap and blues. You'll also learn a new note on the recorder.

REVIEW AND EXTENSION OF MUSIC FUNDAMENTALS

RHYTHM

Triplet

The **triplet** was introduced briefly in chapter 2. It is a way of subdividing the beat in simple meter such as 2/*, 3/*, or 4/*. This even subdivision of three is fairly rare in children's music, but it certainly provides another way to vary rhythm and make it more interesting for the performer and the listener. Figure 11.1 is a rhythm score using triplets. Practice each line at home after you write in the rhythm syllables where indicated.

 **ACTIVITY** In class, perform the rhythm score using rhythm instruments assigned by your instructor. Be sure to follow the dynamic markings indicated.

Figure 11.1 Triplet Rhythm Score

Below is a Korean folk song that uses a triplet. The title of the song is the name of a famous hill outside of Seoul, South Korea. Look at the song carefully and say the rhythm pattern at home, tapping the beat softly to ensure that you say the triplet evenly on one beat. If you have been learning recorder in this class, you can practice this song on your instrument. If you have not, your instructor will teach you the song in class.

Figure 11.2 Arirang

An **ostinato** is a repeated rhythmic, melodic, or harmonic pattern in music. Ostinati can often be used to accompany songs. Here are two possible ostinati to use with "Arirang." Write the rhythm syllables under each one and then practice tapping or clapping each so you will be ready to play one of them on rhythm instruments.

ACTIVITY Have members of the class play each ostinato, listening carefully to determine which one sounds best with "Arirang." Take a vote to decide which ostinato to use for the accompaniment, and sing the song with it. Then work in small groups and make up your own ostinato for "Arirang." Practice it with the song and share it with your classmates.

Figure 11.3 Ostinato Figures

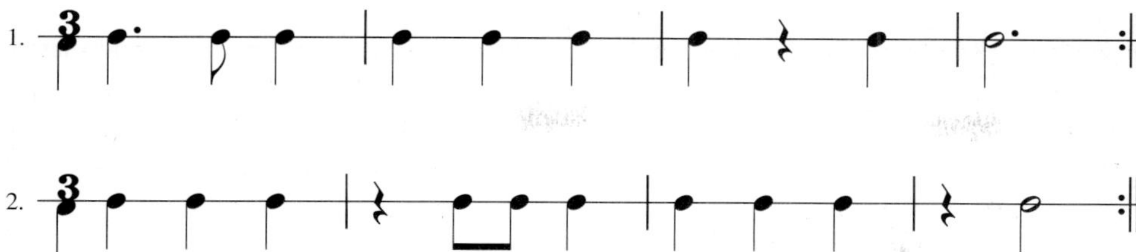
1.
2.

More Rhythm Review

The combination of a dotted eighth note and a sixteenth is frequently used to provide an uneven and interesting rhythm (see chapter 2). Below is a song that contains this pattern and its reverse (a sixteenth followed by a dotted eighth).

Figure 11.4 The Boatman

The Boatman

African American Folk Song

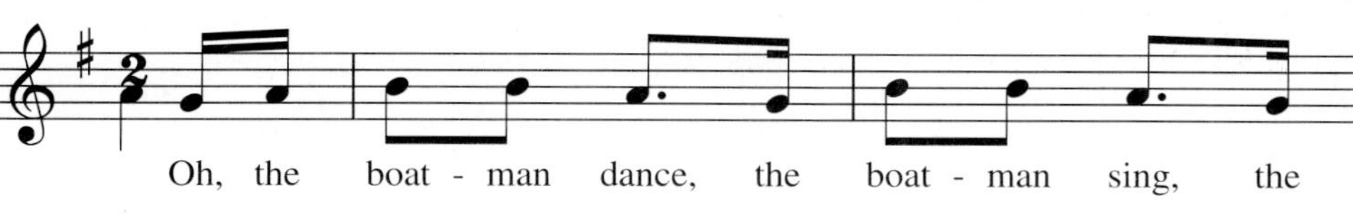
Oh, the boat - man dance, the boat - man sing, the

boat - man up to ev - 'ry - thing. When the boat - man

come on shore, he spend his mon-ey, and he work for more.

As you read this section before class, look at the song and write the rhythm syllables over the top of each line of the song. Circle the measures that have *even* rhythms (no dots). Practice the rhythm syllables for these measures first. Then tap four sixteenth sounds for each beat and say the rhythm syllables. In this way, you will help yourself be accurate with each of the dotted rhythms.

If you have been learning recorder in this class, practice the song on your recorder also. If you have not, your teacher will sing the song for you in class. You might want to try to figure out the sound, since the song only uses three syllables: do, re, and mi. The first three notes are those three syllables in order (do, re, mi).

Here is a rhythm ostinato to play on rhythm instruments with the song. Prepare at home by establishing a steady beat and saying, clapping, or tapping the rhythm syllables for the pattern twice.

Figure 11.5 Ostinato for "The Boatman"

PITCH

Two New Scales

You learned in chapter 7 about the major scale. This scale has a distinctive sound that is the result of its arrangement of whole and half steps. A variation of the major scale is the **minor scale,** which has a different pattern of whole and half steps (figure 11.6).

Figure 11.6 Minor Scale

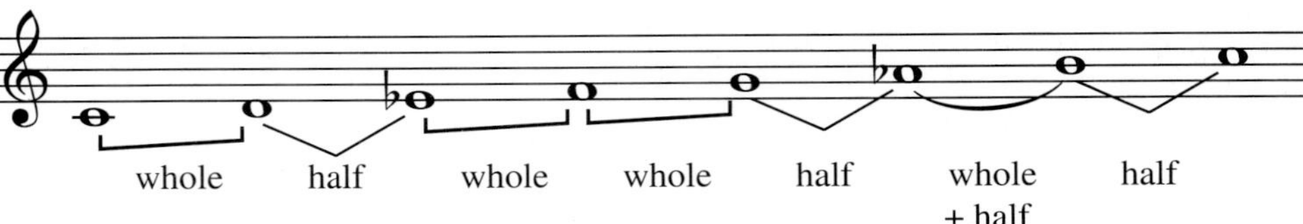

The minor scale sounds quite different from the major scale; it is often described as darker or gloomy. See if you can spot the differences in whole- and half-step configuration in these two scales, both starting and ending on C (figure 11.7).

Figure 11.7 C Major and C Minor Scales

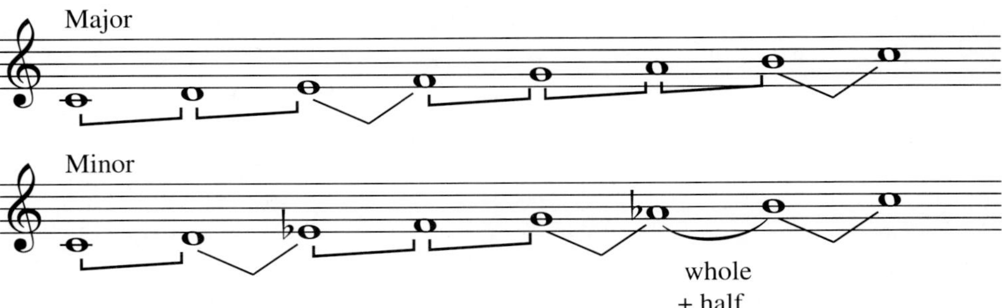

Another scale that is the basis for much folk music is the **pentatonic scale** (see figure 11.8). You can tell from its name how many notes it has (*penta* means "five"). A very easy way to play a pentatonic scale is to begin on C-sharp and play the five black keys.

Figure 11.8 Black-Note Pentatonic Scale

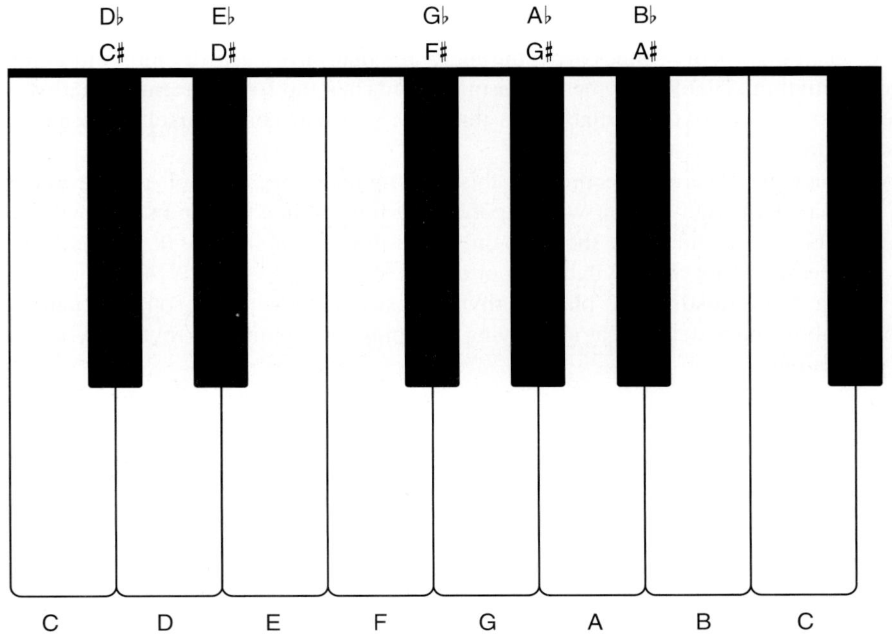

Write your words out on a sheet of scratch paper, and when you are satisfied with them, copy them onto the blues outline that appears in figure 11.22. Note that you will need to add your own chord symbols for the second and third verses.

Figure 11.22 Blues Writing Exercise

Verse 1

A	___ ___ ___ ___	___ ___ ___ ___	___ ___ ___ ___	___ ___ ___ ___
	I	V	I	
A	___ ___ ___ ___	___ ___ ___ ___	___ ___ ___ ___	___ ___ ___ ___
	iv	V	I	
B	___ ___ ______	___ ___ ___ ___	___ ___ ___ ___	___ ___ ___ ___ ‖
	V	iv V^7	I	

Verse 2

Verse 3

Now that you have all the words and chord symbols in place, you need to create the melody for your song. As you may have noted from listening to Bessie Smith, blues songs are typically sung in the lower vocal register rather than in head voice. This contributes to the characteristic "low" sound that enhances the blues feeling. As the composer of this song, you may choose any key you want for your song, but first take a look at figure 11.23. Here the chords for the key of G have been written out so that you know which pitches to include in the accompaniment.

Figure 11.23 Chords to Play

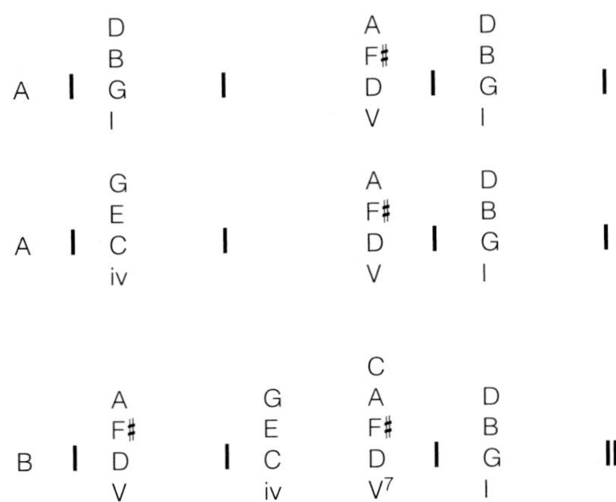

Practice playing these triads and chords. Try to change quickly from chord to chord, especially between the third and fourth bars in each line.

Now that you've got the sound of the chords in your head, you can create the melody for your song. To do this, speak the words in the correct rhythm a few times. When you are comfortable doing this, try chanting the first line on the note G. Now try chanting it again starting on G, this time moving to other pitches in the first line and ending on G on the last word of the line. You've now created the first two lines of melody, since the melody you made up for the first line is repeated exactly in line two. You're now ready to create the melody for the third line. Use a different starting pitch for line three and follow the same procedure that you used for the first two lines. Then try to sing all three lines. It may be helpful to notate your melody in whatever way is most comfortable for you: letter names, pitches on the treble staff, or just squiggles (as in chapter 5, figure 5.8, p. 168).

You are now ready to sing all three verses. Practice a few times, then record yourself as you sing. When you listen to your tape, be generous to yourself! Note all the musical things you did, such as singing with good breath support, making the line flow smoothly, and using dynamic changes to bring out the meaning of your lyrics. Note also the places where you could make your voice sound stronger or pronounce the words more clearly. Musicians are seldom completely happy with any performance, even those who tour the world as concert artists. So ease up on yourself, and sing it again.

Try to let the spirit of the blues guide your voice to add some blue notes this time by lowering the third note of the key (the B becomes B-flat) as well as the sixth note of the key (E becomes E-flat). It is amazing how, simply by lowering these two pitches, you can change the very character of your song. Blues singers often slide between the lowered and unlowered versions of these notes, so try to do this, too. In other words, play with your melody and see if, by adding blue notes and slides between notes, you can make it sound as if it were written for Bessie Smith. If you record each of these different attempts at "playing with" your song, you will be able to hear the effects of your modifications and decide which ones you like best.

Your instructor may have you perform your blues song in class, with the class providing the accompaniment. On your recorder, practice playing one note from each of the triads or chords in figure 11.21 so that you can accompany your classmates. If you have keyboard skills, you may want to try to play the entire chord or triad. Your instructor may choose to have the class play the accompaniment on resonator bells, as you did for the Pachelbel Canon in chapter 9.

You will notice that in the recording of "Reckless Blues," the organ accompaniment does not play all the triads or chords as blocks of sound but rather sounds one note of the chord on each beat, moving from the lowest to highest note in the chord. This is called an **arpeggio**, and it produces a lighter, more active sound to the accompaniment than would a block chord or triad. If you are using your recorder, you can only sound one note at a time. If you are using a keyboard, try to play your accompaniment both ways: first by sounding all three or four notes of the chord at the same time, and second as an arpeggiated chord. Which one sounds best to you? Be prepared to explain your choice in class.

A NEW RECORDER NOTE: HIGH E

Figure 11.24 Recorder Fingering for High E

◒ ●
●
●
—
●
●
○
○

Figure 11.25 Practice the New Note

Figure 11.26 A Duet with the New Note

Figure 11.26 *continued*

Figure 11.27 Three Songs from Sweet Pipes

Figure 11.27 *continued*

Parson's Farewell

English

Figure 11.28 Children's Songs You Can Play

Twinkle, Twinkle

Traditional

Jingle Bells

Words and Music by J. Pierpont

Figure 11.28 *continued*

Mister Frog Went A-Courtin'

American Folk Song

FURTHER PRACTICE

1. For each of the following songs write the roman numerals which could replace the letter chord symbols given.

   "Mi Chacra" (p. 96) ____________________

   "Dry Bones" (p. 121) ____________________

   "Click Go the Shears" (p. 144) ____________________

2. Choose a character from a folktale or fairy tale. Using the rap format given in figure 11.19, write a rap that illustrates your chosen character's point of view. Be as creative as you like, since you are putting words into the character's mouth that have never been written before. Practice speaking your character's words with the rap track on the CD. Be ready to perform your rap for your peers. (Bring a prop that will help you get into character!)
3. Using the rap piece you created in figure 11.19, create a percussion ostinato that enhances the two parts already written (the lyrics and the percussion rap track). Notate your ostinato so that someone else could play it. Come to class prepared to teach it to your classmates.

Creating Music with Children

12

What you will be able to do by the end of this chapter

- *Make creating music part of your classroom*
- *Choose appropriate ways to integrate composition with your curriculum*
- *Write lesson plans that include creation and composition opportunities*
- *Use composition to develop synthesis in other curriculum areas*
- *Play duets with your classmates on the recorder*

CHILDREN AS SOUND MAKERS

Just as the goal of reading instruction is to enable children to enjoy independent reading for their entire lifetimes, the goal of music experiences is to empower all students to realize that they are also musical beings who can express themselves in musical sounds. When you include creating and composing activities in your classroom, you provide yet another way for children to become musical.

The elementary classroom is an ideal place for every child to experience all of the facets of music. One of the important aspects of this educational encounter is learning to use the materials of music as a composer does. Understanding music in the role of the composer develops the child's musical thinking beyond the level of performer or re-creator to that of musical decision maker.

"Messing around with music" as a composer does is the perfect way to let each child synthesize the musical understandings he or she has gained through singing, listening, playing instruments, and moving. Because music is a nonverbal art, composition allows students to experiment with elements of music that they have experienced in teacher-led activities and to begin to use them independently. When elementary students are actually free to create their own music, you give them proof that all music making need not be initiated and led by an adult.

Because all children are naturally creative, their inclination is to play with whatever materials are available to them. Making sounds and recombining them is both stimulating and fun for children, particularly in our age of prepackaged entertainment and video-induced passive enjoyment. Making sound sources accessible for the simple enjoyment of manipulating them enhances children's understanding of how sounds behave when combined in random or haphazard ways. These activities provide the foundation for later use of the same sounds in well-thought-through ways.

Musical thinking involves a very different kind of cognition or knowing. So many of our musical decisions cannot be verbalized because we intuitively *feel* that certain sounds should be manipulated in different ways. For us to verbalize this feeling is often impossible. The opportunity to experience similar thinking must also be available to all children.

Young children "make" art of some kind almost every day from a very early age in day care, preschool, and elementary-school art classes. While most of these artistic explorations are not "museum quality," every house with young children has displayed on the refrigerator door original works of art that youngsters have proudly carried home. Most of us believe that composers are "special" people, but children can learn composition skills very easily. Parents do not compare their child's drawing with that of Michelangelo, and they will not compare their child's musical compositions with those of Bach. Each child's artistic expression is a unique and valued part of their education. An important part of your job is to ensure that every child creates music, just as they write their own books, paint, and make clay bowls and vases.

CHAPTER GOALS

In this chapter you will build on the creative experiences you gained from the previous chapter, as well as your singing and listening skills in the role of classroom teacher of younger and older children. You will learn how to incorporate creative experiences into the daily curriculum and be a confident model for your students. You will also learn many ways to enhance your students' compositional development.

An important aspect of incorporating composition is knowing when to use it in your classroom. This chapter will help you understand this important concept. You will also learn how to lead children in composing different types of music such as rap, instrumental scores, and blues songs and how to write lesson plans that include creating and composition.

Like previous chapters, this one is designed to enable you to become confident in your ability to lead children in these experiences. We want you to understand that creating original music is an exciting experience for children that can enhance their learning and understanding in many ways. It must not be omitted from your classroom and only experienced occasionally in a music room. Producing and experiencing this important human reaction is an important part of children's overall education.

CASE STUDY

Mr. Lao stands in front of his fifth-grade class and says, "To complete our unit on 'The City' we're going to do something different today for social studies. We're going to write a blues song based on what we now know about cities. I know you've all listened to and sung blues songs in music class. But today we're going to write our blues song that tells what we really saw when we went on our field trip to the city. Let's call it 'City Blues.' " Mr. Lao writes this title in capital letters on the chalkboard and continues, "I want you to work in groups of four. Your blues song needs to be 12 verses long, using the classic blues format. And your song must be in the key of G. You have twenty minutes to complete this task. You may begin." While the class dissolves into chaos, several students approach Mr. Lao with questions. "I've already told you the directions," says Mr. Lao to the small group assembled in front of him. "You obviously were not listening." The students look at each other silently, then turn around and return to their seats. Mr. Lao notices that the noise level is too high, and even his most focused students are not on task. "I was sure this would be a great lesson. I wonder what happened?" he thinks to himself.

Cooperative Questions to Discuss

1. With a partner, rewrite the directions that Mr. Lao gave to get this activity started. Include all the details that this fifth-grade class would need to make this lesson a success.
2. Think about the last time you were in a classroom (either as a student or as a teacher) that was out of control. As you reflect on this experience, try to remember what you felt and how the situation was resolved (if at all). Explain this to a partner.
3. Propose a list of materials that Mr. Lao should have had ready for the class before starting this lesson. Compare your list with that of a partner.
4. Describe what Mr. Lao should say next to get this lesson back on track.

INTEGRATING COMPOSITION IN THE CURRICULUM

PRIMARY TEACHING SCRIPT: INTEGRATED SCIENCE LESSON

Mrs. Saba stands up in front of her first-grade class and gives the opening direction. **Everyone please go out to the coat hooks and put on your raincoats and boots. We're going for a rain walk today.** After everyone has their rain gear on, she has them come back to their seats for final instructions.

We're going to be careful lookers and try to figure out what the rain does after it falls from the clouds. When we come back from our walk we'll talk about where we think the water is going. She then directs the class to line up in two lines, and they follow her out of the classroom, down the hall, and out the front door of the school. When they get to the front drive, she directs their attention to the water. **Can anyone figure out what the rain is doing here?** Several children notice the little streams, and others point out the presence of the water drain. Others also tell Mrs. Saba that some of the water is sitting in puddles. She then leads the class over to the schoolyard and the sandbox.

Now where is the rain? The children study the ground and the sandbox and are able to tell her that the water is going in the ground. **Who would like to dig down in the sandbox and see how deep in the sand the water has gone?** Jamie volunteers, and the class gathers around the box to see how far he digs before he finds dry sand. They then walk over to the paved playground surface. Here several tiny streams are carrying the rain into the grass. **Now where is the rain going?** Again the children call out their answers. Mrs. Saba then has the class line up again, and they go back into the school and leave their rain gear outside the classroom. When everyone is sitting in their seats, Mrs. Saba says, **I want you to show what we learned about the rain in a different way today. As I call your row, I want each person to get a piece of drawing paper and a box of crayons from the shelf.** After everyone has their materials, she says,**Your first way to show our rain discoveries is by drawing something you saw.** A few minutes later, she says, **Let's make a word list of what we drew about the rain. We'll put it on the board, and after lunch we'll use our list a different way.** She begins calling on individuals, and soon the list includes their observations of puddles, tiny streams, drains, and water soaking into the ground.

After lunch and recess, the class settles down to listen to Mrs. Saba read them a story about a rainy day. **Now we're going to decide how we can make a sound story that helps to tell all we saw outside this morning. After we make our rain composition, we'll invite Mrs. Major's class to come and listen.** Mrs. Saba brings out several boxes of rhythm instruments and places them around the room. **First, we need a group to produce the rain sounds that we heard while we were outside. Who would like to be in that group?** She assigns them to a corner of the room and asks them to sit quietly while she continues. She has two or three volunteers for each idea move to an instrument box and then tells them their task. **You're to experiment with the sounds in your box and choose which will best illustrate what the rain is doing. We'll work on this for a few minutes, and then we'll write a class story and add the rain and water sounds.**

PHOTOCOPY THIS PAGE

PRIMARY LESSON PLAN: INTEGRATED SCIENCE LESSON

Use the previous script to fill in the lesson plan form.

I. Learning Outcome or Objective:

Entry Ability:

Exit Ability:

II. Lesson Evaluation Procedures:

III. Materials:

IV. Teaching Procedures:

A. Setting the Stage:

B. Developing the Lesson:

Step 1:

Transition statement/question:

Step 2:

Transition statement/question:

Step 3:

Transition statement/question:

Step 4:

Transition statement/question:

Step 5:

C. Concluding the Lesson:

PRIMARY TEACHING SCRIPT: CREATING A STORY WITH ACCOMPANIMENT

Step One: Story

Use the following prompts to have the class compose a story. Be sure to use only one prompt at a time. Put each prompt on a separate overhead transparency, which you show only after the class has filled in the blank. Read the prompt, then write in the response, then read the next prompt. Decide ahead of time how to choose children for responses. You may want to go down rows or alternate blue eyes and brown eyes or birthday months. Whatever you do, explain your procedure to the class before you begin constructing the story.

1. Once upon a time there was a ______________________.
2. (He/She/It) lived in a great, big ______________________.
3. (He/She/It) had lots of ______________________, and liked to ______________________.
4. One day, as the ________________ was playing in the ______________, (he/she/it) saw a ________________ in the ________________.
5. "Oh, dear!" thought the ______________. "That ______________ is so ______________, I'm sure it will ______________!!!"
6. The ______________ ran as fast as (he/she/it) could to the ______________.
7. But it was too ______________. (His/Her/Its) heart was pounding as (he/she/it) ______________.
8. Suddenly the sky looked ________________ and (he/she/it) heard birds ______________.
9. Then a friendly old ______________ came out of the ______________ and said "______________."
10. Now the ______________ felt much better. (He/She/It) ran back to ________ and said, "I'll never ________________ again!"
11. So (he/she/it) walked along home and ______________________.

THE END

Step Two: Adding Appropriate Sounds

When complete, read the entire story through and let the children follow along by reading the overhead transparency. **Now let's add some sounds that help to make the story more interesting. There are many ways to do this. We could add a different sound for each line, or we could only add a few sounds. We could add certain sounds to particular words, or we could only add sounds in between words. Let's begin by trying out some different sounds with the first line. We'll have to read it once more and suggest a few sounds to try. Ready?** Using your predetermined method for choosing children to respond, take suggestions for each line or section and let the class add sounds that they feel enhance the meaning of the story. Try several suggestions per line or section and allow the group to discuss which sounds enhanced the meaning of the story for them. If you guide the discussion carefully, the focus will remain on the quality of the sound enhancement, rather than on whether they like a particular student's suggestion.

Step Three: Recording and Evaluating the Performance

When they have added sounds to the entire story, have the class try performing the entire set of sounds as children read the different lines. Record the performance and play it back for them immediately. Then lead a discussion based on the following questions:

1. Which parts were particularly interesting to you? Why?
2. Which parts would you like to change? Suggest alternatives.

3. What did you notice as you listened to each of the different children's voices while they read? Is there anything you'd like to suggest that would make the reading more effective?
4. How did the sounds that we used change the story for you? Did the sounds make the story feel different to you? Describe.
5. If we were to start over again and do this completely differently, what would you do this time?

Take suggestions and work with them, as time permits. Conclude by saying (if appropriate), **That was fine work, children! You worked well together and you listened carefully to your own composition.**

PHOTOCOPY THIS PAGE

PRIMARY LESSON PLAN: CREATING A STORY WITH ACCOMPANIMENT

Use Primary Teaching Script (p. 353) to fill in the lesson plan.

I. Learning Outcome or Objective:

Entry Ability:

Exit Ability:

II. Lesson Evaluation Procedures:

III. Materials:

IV. Teaching Procedures:

A. Setting the Stage:

B. Developing the Lesson:

Step 1:

Transition statement/question:

Step 2:

Transition statement/question:

Step 3:

Transition statement/question:

Step 4:

Transition statement/question:

Step 5:

C. Concluding the Lesson:

INTERMEDIATE TEACHING SCRIPT: RAPPING IN LANGUAGE ARTS

It is 2 P.M. on the day that she has to hand out report cards at 3 P.M. Mrs. Panetti faces her fifth-grade class and says, **I'd like each of you to put everything away except for one pencil. When you have done that, sit up tall and look at me. When I see all eyes, we'll begin.** She waits patiently while her students find their pencils. When the last student is ready, she continues. **I know that some of you are looking forward to getting your report cards at 3 o'clock, while others of you are not looking forward to it at all. We've all worked hard today, and our next activity is going to be just for fun.** Mrs. Panetti points to herself and chants, in 4/4 time, **We're gonna write a report card rap (rest)!** When she gets to the end of the chant, she points to her class, and they chant, "We're gonna write a report card rap (rest)!" Mrs. Panetti continues. **Our rap is going to tell the world about how it feels to get your report card. To write our rap we'll need everyone's help. I've got an outline of the form that we'll use to create our rap. When you get the sheet, please look at it carefully.** She hands stacks of the outlines to the first person in each row, and they take one and pass the rest to the person behind them. After a minute, during which everyone scans the rap outline (found in chapter 11, figure 11.18), Mrs. Panetti continues. **This is the outline for the rap track that is going to be the accompaniment for our rap. It will make it sound like a rap you'd hear on the radio. See if you can follow the outline while we listen to the rap track accompaniment.** Mrs. Panetti plays the rap track through once while the class follows the outline. **How many beats do we need to write for each line?** Mrs. Panetti calls on John, whose hand was up. He says, "Eight." Mrs. Panetti agrees, and continues. **The form of our rap song is going to be ABABAB. Each A section is 16 beats long, and each B section is 8 beats long. All we have to add are the words that tell what it is like to get your report card. I'd like each of you to work on this individually for the next five minutes, writing your own lines that use only eight beats.** The class works quietly for five minutes, and Mrs. Panetti continues. **Now I want each of you to contribute to the piece. I'll take your suggestions for the first line.** Mrs. Panetti calls on students, they offer their suggestions, and she decides whether their first line should be used or not. If a suggested line is not used, she tells the student, "I'll come back to you." In this way, each student contributes to the process.

When all the lines are filled, she says, **Now let's see how this sounds. We're going to speak the words with the rap track, and while we're speaking we also need to listen and see if we need to rework anything.** The class reads the words from the board and speaks them along with the rap track. Mrs. Panetti takes suggestions for changes, and they repeat the process. When the class seems settled on the final product, Mrs. Panetti says, **We're now ready to record our performance of "Report Card Rap."** After making the recording, Mrs. Panetti continues. **We now have to make some musical decisions. As you listen to our performance, figure out if there are things that we need to change to make our performance better.** After the class listens, Mrs. Panetti takes suggestions, they try them, and she re-records the performance. After listening to the recording of their improved performance, a big cheer goes up from the class. Mrs. Panetti says, **I think we're ready to share this with the whole school! I've arranged with Dr. Duff to have us perform our rap in the office and put it over the PA system. I've copied it from the board and can make copies so we'll each have our own copy to read from. Here we go!** The children file out of the room, excitedly whispering to each other.

PHOTOCOPY THIS PAGE

INTERMEDIATE LESSON PLAN: RAPPING IN LANGUAGE ARTS

Use Intermediate Teaching Script (p. 356) to fill in this lesson plan.

I. Learning Outcome or Objective:

Entry Ability:

Exit Ability:

II. Lesson Evaluation Procedures:

III. Materials:

IV. Teaching Procedures:

A. Setting the Stage:

B. Developing the Lesson:

Step 1:

Transition statement/question:

Step 2:

Transition statement/question:

Step 3:

Transition statement/question:

Step 4:

Transition statement/question:

Step 5:

C. Concluding the Lesson:

SPECIAL LEARNERS AND COMPOSING

Special learners can succeed in small-group composition activities if you construct the groups carefully. You will want to create the most comfortable mix of social abilities and learning needs. Special learners benefit from having smaller tasks to complete, so breaking the composition task into small increments ("In two minutes you need to have agreed on one sound for the A section") is preferable to "You have fifteen minutes to complete this task." Developmentally delayed children may react to group composition tasks in an immature way, such as acting silly or banging randomly on the instruments, which their classmates find inappropriate. It helps to stay physically close to such a child, perhaps working as a member of the child's assigned group to model appropriate behavior. All learners benefit from having a clear visual representation of the assignment, in addition to the verbal directions. A list on the board outlining the steps required can be referred to easily by all groups.

THE LOGISTICS OF COMPOSING WITH YOUR CLASS

WORKING IN SMALL GROUPS

As is evident from the opening sections of this chapter, your role in the group composition process is one of mentor, coach, and source of suggestion, rather than critic and fount of all wisdom. In the spirit of the creative process you are more of a bystander than in other class activities. Because of this subtle shift in role, your experience when you teach a music or writing composition lesson may be different from what you're used to feeling when you teach reading to a small group or sing a song with the whole class.

It may be frightening to allow students to move into groups, pick up noisemakers, and start making all sorts of sounds over which you have no control. You may feel that you have lost your ability to manage your classroom. You may also feel confused by all the scattered activity and not know where to focus your attention, or even whom to answer when several students in different groups raise their hands and invite you to come to help their groups.

These feelings are to be expected when engaging in a more student-focused activity. Be assured that in spite of the seeming confusion, musical learning is happening. Getting control of your feelings of discomfort and inadequacy is easier when you realize that all your students really need from you in this activity is an enthusiastic ear and some helpful suggestions. Children love to create their own music, and you are the lucky one who has the privilege of watching, listening to, and enjoying their creative efforts.

Effective classroom management techniques will enable your class to pursue many successful composition activities while enhancing their learning in other subjects. These techniques include an ability to give precise directions, to provide children with a sense of security, and to impart a sense of purpose. These competencies are essential to remember when incorporating composing in your class. All children (and adults) feel most secure when they know exactly what is expected. You establish a sense of security through the use of clearly worded directions and consistent expectations. The transitions before and after composing activities must be planned very carefully so that valuable teaching time is not lost. As you plan your lesson, you should decide exactly what you will say in order to organize large numbers of children moving about the room. Your directions should be worded in such a way that every child understands exactly what to do. If you want them to be silent when they move to a group, you must tell them. If you want them to hold their instruments quietly, you must tell them. Specific and clear directions maximize the time for composing and learning.

COMPOSING WITH THE WHOLE CLASS

An excellent way to integrate the activities of the regular classroom with composing and creating music is to add sounds that will enhance the meaning of stories or poems the children are reading, writing, or acting out in their language arts classes. The teaching scripts in chapter 8 illustrate how to lead a musical activity that integrates different aspects of language arts with instrument exploration. (In chapter 8 you also read how to integrate science with music.)

Another exploration with sound involves having children make up simple accompaniments for songs they already know. You must organize this exploration by setting very specific parameters for the activity. If you want them to use pitched instruments, limit their choice of pitches to the tonic and dominant (pitches 1 and 5) of the key in which the song is written, and have them figure out which pitches sound best. If you want them to make up a nonpitched-percussion accompaniment, limit their choice of timbre and have only instruments of the desired timbre immediately available. No matter what the task, always allow children to work on their own for a few minutes to explore the sound possibilities of their chosen instruments and to reacquaint themselves with the correct ways to play the instruments. It is helpful to precede any playing activity with any special rules you may have developed for playing activities ("Do not use your instrument as a weapon or you will lose your turn!"). After this individual exploration time, you will need to guide the class in decision making based on careful and critical listening.

If you have read a poem with a repeated refrain, you can use this experience to create a composition with a similar form. Young children easily grasp the concept of binary form (AB) if you explain it as same/different. Words from the poem can be effective stimuli for children's sound explorations. Visual reinforcement of the stimulus helps all children to remember the task and is essential for special learners of many types. Instead of simply saying the words, write them on the board and then draw an icon for them as well.

A more elaborate process, taking much more time, is involved when you help children to turn a poem into a song. The song composition process may seem cumbersome, but it is an activity children love and is well worth the effort. As in the activities mentioned earlier in this section, the more you are able to limit their choices of sounds, the more easily they'll be able to create. You may wish to try the following process on your own, and you may also wish to ask your school music teacher for assistance in performing and recording the final product.

First, have the class read a poem together, and discuss various ways to make it sound different with their voices. When they have decided which way they like best, have them chant the poem several times as a class. Then try it with individual voices reading single lines but still using the agreed-upon contrasts and differences. This step could be one day's activity. The next time you work on your song, borrow a box of resonator bells from the music teacher. Then use the roots of IV–V–I chords in the key of C (IV–F; V–G; I–C). Have the class decide which patterns (the order of the bells as well as the long and short sounds to use) sound best to them while they say the poem. This could take a short or a long time, depending upon the individuals in the class.

The next time you work on your song, play the chosen accompaniment and have the class chant the poem over your playing. Then ask the class to sing what they have been chanting and tell them that you will expect to hear lots of different melodies when they do this. If you have them try the accompanied chant several times, those children with the stronger voices will prevail, and a melody, or even several different melodies, will emerge from the group chanting. Record these and have the entire class listen to them. You may want to use more than one version or parts of several versions. The class must be directed to make decisions based on what they hear, rather than on who made up a part. Song creation is an exciting activity in which the entire school takes great pride, and the class songs would make a great source for performance program material.

RECORDING THE PRODUCT AND USING PORTFOLIOS

Once your class has become involved in musical creation, you should consider the value of recording their products so they can be shared with parents or other classes. Many schools have demonstration nights or portfolio-sharing conferences where the students explain what they have learned. Including one or more recordings at these events will demonstrate another interesting facet of children's learning.

You can also use recordings to enhance the individual portfolios of your class members. As you may already know, a current trend in evaluation is to compile a portfolio of each student's work over the course of a grading period, an academic year, or even several years. Portfolio evaluation, derived from the type of evaluation done in visual art in which a collection of each student's work is compiled and surveyed, relies on the collection of several types of data to document student progress, rather than on a single test score. The wide variety of types of data included in portfolio evaluation make it an especially attractive way for both teachers and students to look at learning, for it requires students to reflect on and take ownership of their accomplishments as well as their difficulties. Portfolio evaluation offers all teachers a rich source of data on which to judge their students' progress.

Portfolios can include a wide variety of materials which document the student's learning, such as:

1. audiotapes of singing, individual and group compositions, small group or class performances;
2. written examples of student-created notation for individual or group compositions;
3. students' own reflections on musical experiences, both in and out of the music classroom; and
4. students' evaluations of their own learning.

Portfolios can be of four types, and they are classified by their function:[1]

1. *Presentation/product portfolios* are meant to be the culminating document of a student's learning at a particular level and serve as evidence that the student should be admitted to the next level, such as being promoted to the next grade.
2. *Product/performance portfolios* provide the teacher with a look at the same product from each child in a class or grade level at the same point. This type of portfolio may be used to assign grades or to sort students into groups based on ability or achievement.
3. *Program portfolios* are collections of the finest work of selected students from a grade level, school, or district. Program portfolios could be used by a teacher as supporting evidence for increasing funding for a classroom project, or as documentation of the teacher's success in the classroom.
4. *Process portfolios* are collections of an individual student's work that document the learning process the student is engaged in. Essential to process portfolios is the student's own commentary on the process. This commentary may take the form of written reflections, or it may be a tape-recorded conversation between the student and teacher in which the teacher asks the student about the portfolio.

Portfolio assessment is an exciting way to document each child's growth in learning, and many parents and schools expect this type of data collection. Of course, your task is to develop your own system of managing the large amounts of data required by the portfolio process.

NATIONAL STANDARDS FOR COMPOSITION

The National Standards for Arts Education include two Content Standards that apply to children's improvisation and composing.
Content Standard No. 3: Improvising melodies, variations, and accompaniments.
Achievement Standard:

Students:
1. Improvise "answers" in the same style to given rhythmic and melodic phrases
2. Improvise simple rhythmic and melodic ostinato accompaniments
3. Improvise simple rhythmic variations and simple melodic embellishments on familiar melodies

4. Improvise short songs and instrumental pieces using a variety of sound sources, including traditional sounds, nontraditional sounds available in the classroom, body sounds, and sounds produced by electronic means.

Content Standard No. 4: Composing and arranging music within specified guidelines.
Achievement Standard:

Students:

1. Create and arrange music to accompany readings or dramatizations
2. Create and arrange short songs and instrumental pieces within specified guideline
3. Use a variety of sound sources when composing

PLAYING RECORDER: HARMONY

Here are four rounds to practice and then play with your classmates.

Figure 12.1 Four Recorder Rounds

Alleluia, Amen

Traditional Round

1. 2.

Music Alone Shall Live
Canon

German Folk Song

Scotland's Burning

Traditional Round

Figure 12.1 *continued*

A Ram Sam Sam

Folk Song from Morocco

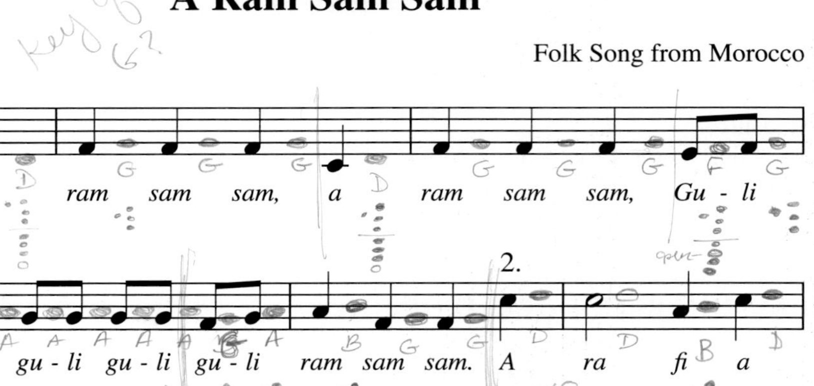

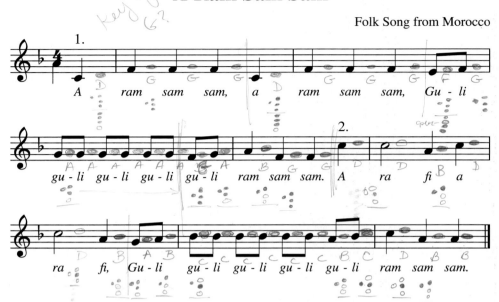

Another type of harmony is partner songs, described in chapter 4.

Figure 12.2 Partner Songs

All Night/Swing Low

Spirituals

The following song (figure 12.3) produces another type of harmony, called a canon.

Figure 12.3

The Water Is Wide
Canon

English Folk Song

Figure 12.4 Recorder Duets

We Wish You a Merry Christmas

English Carol

Figure 12.4 *continued*

Sweet Potatoes

Louisiana Folk Song

Soon as we all cook sweet po - ta - toes,
Sweet po - ta - toes, sweet po - ta - toes, Soon as we all
cook sweet po - ta - toes, Eat 'em while they're hot.

Figure 12.5 Duets from Sweet Pipes

Scarborough Fair

With motion English

Figure 12.5 *continued*

The Streets of Laredo

American

From Sonya Burakoff, *Duet Time.* Copyright © 1979 by Gerald and Sonya Burakoff. Reprinted by permission of Gerald and Sonya Burakoff.

J'ai Du Bon Tabac

French

Figure 12.5 *continued*

Danse de Hercules

Tielman Susato (d. 1561)

Figure 12.5 *continued*

Een kint gheboren in Bethlehem

Dutch (16th Century)

Danse de Hercules

Tielman Susato (d. 1561)

Figure 12.5 *continued*

Stowey (How Far Is It to Bethlehem?)
English

FURTHER PRACTICE

1. Using your elementary curriculum expertise from another class, develop a lesson plan from another area of the primary and/or intermediate curriculum that would incorporate composition. Use the lesson plan format followed in this chapter.
2. Create an original rap that you could use to help third-grade students memorize the multiplication tables.
3. Choose a social studies concept (such as the American Revolution or the Civil War) to teach to an intermediate grade level. Using the lesson plan format given in this chapter, create a lesson plan for writing a blues song that would let the students take on the role of someone involved in the situation and express their feelings about the situation. You may incorporate materials from chapter 11 in your lesson.

NOTES

[1]R. Miller. In New York State: Assessment and "A New Compact for Learning," *Special Research Interest Group in Measurement and Evaluation* 15, p. 2.

Life in the Classroom

13

TEACHER = COMMUNICATOR

Chapters 1 through 12 focused on developing your skills as a musician and showed you ways to extend the musical skills of the children in your classroom through activities that involve singing, listening, playing, moving, and creating. You have been invited to use your imagination and creativity to enhance the daily classroom life of your students by creating a wide variety of lessons that integrate music in the grade-level curriculum. You have learned how to teach songs, develop listening lessons, teach instrumental playing, plan movement lessons, and lead children in composition activities. Although these skills are essential in your future teaching career, they alone will not guarantee that you will be an effective teacher. You need to consider one other important aspect of teaching before you launch your career: communication.

It is time to refine your communication skills with a variety of constituencies, including students, fellow teachers, parents, and administrators. Communication entails listening, speaking, and writing, and the more effectively you are able to express yourself in these three modes, the better your message will be heard. Crucial to effective expression, however, is the thinking that happens prior to communicating.

This chapter contains materials meant to stimulate your thinking and to let you assume the role of teacher in a variety of situations that require professional judgment. These situations are all from the real world of teaching. This section contains eleven short case studies based on typical events in the careers of teachers. These case studies differ from the earlier case studies in this book in that *you* take the place of the protagonist in each scenario. Your task will include finding the problems in each case and proposing solutions based on what you know as a student, performer, and colleague. The experience you will gain from delving into these multilayered situations and discussing possible solutions is invaluable, and this course may be the last time you will ever have the opportunity to discuss situations such as these with teaching colleagues. One of the most valuable results of the task you are about to undertake is that you will gain a larger perspective on the wide variety of people's reactions and responses as your peers inform you about their reactions and solutions to the problems. Welcome to the world of life in the classroom!

TEACHER-STUDENT RELATIONS

CASE STUDY NO. 1

It is 8:45 A.M. and you are standing outside the door of your second-grade classroom, welcoming your class as they hurry to put their coats and backpacks away before the second bell. Before he enters the room, Danny stops at the door and hands you a note. "Thanks, Danny," you say as you open it and scan the contents. The note, written in Danny's scrawl, says, "Dear Ms. O'Brien, You never let me have a turn on the instruments yesterday. You said everyone could have a turn, and then you did not give me one. You are not a fair teacher. From Danny." The second bell rings, and you close the door and face the class. "Good morning, class."

Cooperative Questions for Discussion

1. What should you say next?
2. How does it feel to be challenged in this way?
3. With a partner, make a list of the possible ways you could approach Danny to discuss this problem.
4. With a partner, brainstorm as many ways as possible to keep track of tasks and assignments made to children in your class, including turns at playing instruments.

CASE STUDY NO. 2

For the last few days you've noticed that during transition times between activities in class, as well as while in line moving from place to place within the school, several of your fifth graders use what you consider foul language when speaking to their peers. Your school is not one of the "rough" schools you've heard about, so you are somewhat surprised by this. This afternoon at home time, while the class is packing up and putting their chairs on top of their desks, someone in the back of the room drops a chair and hollers, "OH (expletive)!"

Cooperative Questions for Discussion

1. What will you do next?
2. What can you say to the rest of the class to take them past this situation and leave school with a sense of closure?
3. Will you involve the principal? The child's parents?

TEACHER-TEACHER RELATIONS

CASE STUDY NO. 1

You and your first graders are having a great time dancing the hora, which you've used to end a social studies lesson on Israel. Suddenly there is loud banging on your door. While the children continue to dance, you rush to open the door. There you find the fifth-grade teacher from the next room, Jane Allen. "WE ARE TRYING TO TAKE A SPELLING TEST!" she snarls. "Why do you always have to make such a racket?"

Cooperative Questions for Discussion

1. What will you say next?
2. Think about the last time you were in a situation similar to this one. How did you feel? How did you resolve it? Discuss this with a partner.
3. Brainstorm a number of ways that you could avoid creating a situation like this one while still making music part of your classroom life.

CASE STUDY NO. 2

It is October of your first year of teaching third grade. You are the only first-year teacher hired this year, and you have found your peers to be friendly and helpful. One in particular, Dr. Susan Adams, has become somewhat of a mentor to you, and has offered you everything from classroom supplies from her private stash to advice on which of your students' parents are the most reliable volunteers. Dr. Adams has been especially complimentary about your musical classroom, and you have invited her third-grade class to join yours several times for musical activities, since Dr. Adams says that she "doesn't have a musical bone in her body."

After school today, Dr. Adams comes into your room and asks if you could take her class for "extra music" on a regular basis, as she knows how much her students love the activities you plan, "and they always fit the curriculum perfectly!" This catches you off guard, and you ask, "When did you have in mind?" She replies, "Tuesdays and Fridays, 1 to 1:30." You look at your schedule and realize that these two times are your only free periods on both of those days.

Cooperative Questions for Discussion

1. What should you say next?
2. With a partner, construct a list of the issues involved in this case. Then rank them in importance. Be prepared to share your list and rankings with the class.
3. Since this is a scheduling issue, should you involve the principal in this discussion?

TEACHER-PARENT RELATIONS

CASE STUDY NO. 1

It is late afternoon and you have one more parent phone call to make before you leave. Your principal has encouraged everyone on the staff to find as many positive moments to share with parents as possible, and you are really pleased that you can call Jessica's mother today and describe how she organized her composition group, kept them on task, and encouraged each of the other children in a positive and mature way. You are especially pleased at how gentle and supportive she was with one group member with ADHD who has difficulty in group work. All of the teachers in the school have been working on cooperative behaviors for several months, and you can tell from today's class that the children in your class have developed a warm and caring attitude toward each other. You dial the number and say, "Hi, is this Jessica's mother?" You explain who you are and describe the positive behaviors you observed today in your class. Her mother says, "Well, I just don't think we're talking about the same child here. My daughter never knows where her backpack is, or what she is supposed to do for homework. I sometimes wonder if she knows what day it is! She is the most irresponsible child I ever saw, and I don't know what to do with her."

Cooperative Questions for Discussion

1. What do you say next?
2. What other steps could you take to communicate with this parent?
3. What other faculty members should be made aware of this conversation?

CASE STUDY NO. 2

Mrs. Naji calls you and complains that her first grader is going around the house singing "Silent Night," which her child said you let them sing during "Free Choice" time in your class today. Mrs. Naji states that as a Muslim parent she does not think this song is appropriate for her child to learn in a public school. Your explanation that "Silent Night" is a traditional holiday song in this country and that most of the children in your class are not Muslim does not satisfy Mrs. Naji. She demands that you never let your class sing "Silent Night" again and ends the conversation by saying, "Your boss will hear about this."

Cooperative Questions for Discussion

1. What would you say next?
2. What would you tell your principal?
3. Would you continue to let your class sing this song, if someone chose it during "Free Choice"?

TEACHER-ADMINISTRATOR RELATIONS

CASE STUDY NO. 1

It is the third week of your first year of teaching, and you are sitting in the office of Ms. Brennan, your principal. She is meeting with you to discuss her report of her first observation of your teaching. (All first-year teachers in your district are observed eight times during their first year.) Ms. Brennan says, "I'm impressed with the rapport you've established with your class. You really have established yourself as a strong presence in your room, while at the same time you've got them all in the palm of your hand. Those children adore you, and that kind of atmosphere is tough to create, even for very experienced teachers. You should be very proud of that." You sit a little taller, smile appreciatively, and whisper, "Thanks." She continues, "I have a question for you, however. I've looked over your lesson plan book for the last few weeks, and I noticed that you do some sort of musical activity every day. This is really not necessary, since we already have a music teacher who sees the children once each week for 30 minutes. My big worry is that you are shortchanging the important content of the curriculum to make room for your musical activities. Music is great for kids, but it is not important."

Cooperative Questions for Discussion

1. What can you say to Ms. Brennan to convince her that you are capable of choosing course content appropriate for your students?
2. How does it feel to be challenged in such a way?
3. What, if anything, will you do differently in your teaching? You really want to get a good evaluation this year.

CASE STUDY NO. 2

It is March of your first year of teaching. You are meeting with your principal, Mr. Stone, to discuss your budget requests for the coming year. Mr. Stone says, "I think you've done a super job on this budget. You've covered all the important aspects, and you've kept well within the suggested guidelines. The only request I see on your list that does not belong there is number 12, the CD/tape player. That's a pretty big expense for something that you'll only use once or twice each year, don't you think? You need to see if the music teacher will let you borrow the one that sits in the music room."

Cooperative Questions for Discussion

1. What should you say next?
2. With a partner, make a list of all the compelling arguments you could present to Mr. Stone for having a CD/tape player in your room. Be prepared to share these with the class.
3. Make a "wish list" of all the musical equipment that you would like to have in your classroom. Estimate the cost of your items. Your instructor may provide you with catalogs to help you determine the exact cost. Compare your estimate with the actual cost. Be ready to discuss your results with the class.

Appendix

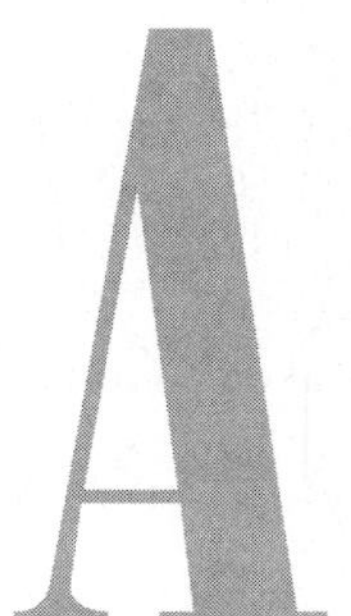

MUSIC FUNDAMENTALS REFERENCE

A. NOTES AND RESTS

Duration: The length of time assigned to a note or a rest.

Notes		*Rests*	
𝅝	*whole note*	𝄻	*whole rest*
𝅗𝅥	*half note*	𝄼	*half rest*
♩	*quarter note*	𝄽	*quarter rest*
♪	*eighth note*	𝄾	*eighth rest*
𝅘𝅥𝅯	*sixteenth note*	𝄿	*sixteenth rest*
𝅘𝅥𝅰	*thirty-second note*	𝅀	*thirty-second rest*

B. DURATION OF NOTES AND RESTS

The following are examples of the relative duration of note values (rest values are comparable):

Triplet: A 3-to-1 instead of a 2-to-1 relationship of note values:

Dotted notes and rests: A dot adds half the value to whatever note or rest it follows:

rests *Dotted notes* *Dotted rests*

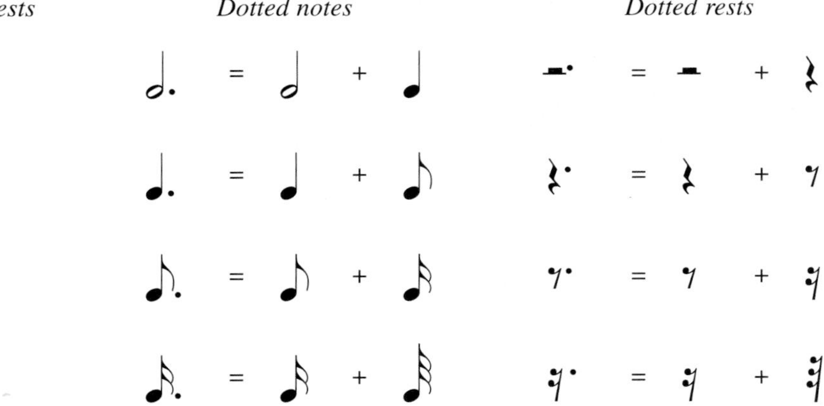

C. MAJOR AND MINOR SCALES

Major Scales Commonly Found in Songs

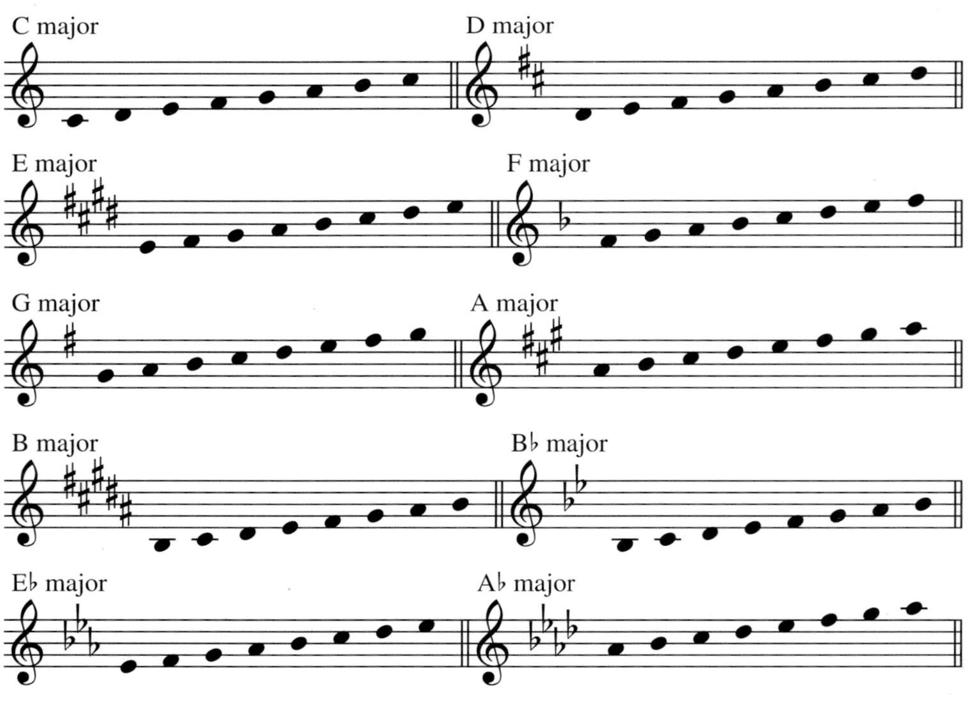

Harmonic Minor Scales Commonly Found in Songs

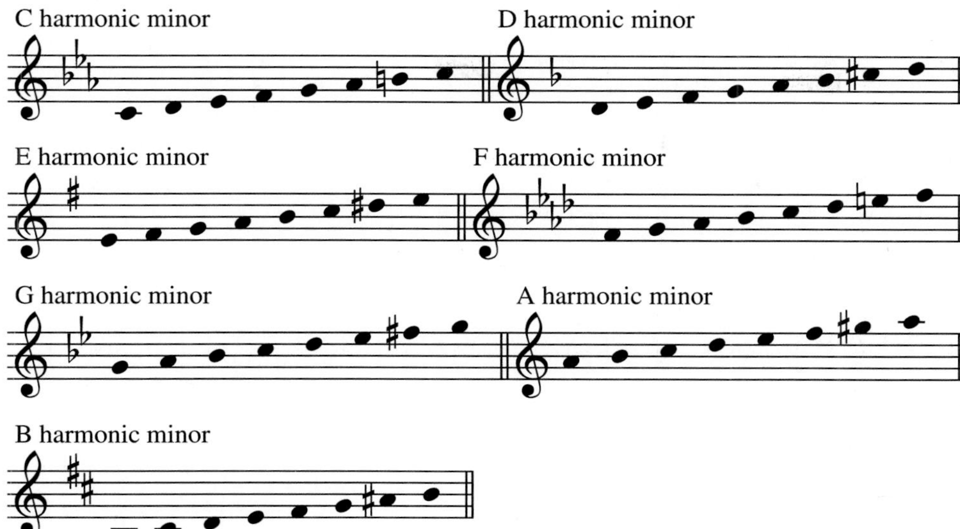

Appendix

GLOSSARY OF MUSICAL TERMS

Accidental (p. 232) A sign used in music notation to raise or lower a pitch one-half step: sharp, flat, or natural sign.
Accompaniment (p. 143) The musical background provided for an important part. Usually piano or instrumental support for a melody.
Aesthetic experience (p. 4) Responding with one's feelings when engaged in the experience of music.
Agogo bells (p. 222) A percussion instrument with two metal bells of different pitches, played by striking with a short metal rod.
Anacrusis (p. 26) An incomplete measure at the beginning of a piece, also known as a pickup.
Arpeggio (p. 344) A chord in which the notes are played not all at once but separately, moving from the lowest to the highest note.
Bar line (p. 18) A vertical line drawn on the staff that indicates the beginning and end of a measure.
Bass clef (p. 46) Also called the F clef; indicates that the fourth line of the staff is F. Music written after this clef is played by low-sounding instruments.
Beat (p. 12) The regular pulse felt in most music.
Binary (p. 159) A form of music with two contrasting sections (AB).
Blue notes (p. 341) The lowered third and sixth pitches of the scale that give blues songs their characteristic "mournful" sound.
Chord (p. 226) Four or more notes which are sounded at the same time.
Claves (p. 220) (kla′-vez) Short, thick wood sticks used as accompaniment in Latin American music.
Coda (p. 176) A section of a composition added as a conclusion.
Compound meter (p. 24) An arrangement of beats, each of which can be subdivided into three equal parts.
Crescendo (p. 40) Gradually getting louder.
Cut-off (p. 238) Conducting signal given to indicate when the performers should stop.
Decrescendo (p. 40) Gradually getting softer.
Diction (p. 148) Performing a song text in a manner that can be understood by the listener.
Djembe (p. 223) West African drum with a wooden body and skin head.
Dot (p. 19) When used after a note, a dot increases the original value of the note by one-half.
Double bar (p. 18) Two vertical bar lines placed on the staff that denote the end of a section or the end of a piece.
Duet (p. 150) A composition for two equal performers, with or without accompaniment.
Duple meter (p. 18) An arrangement of beats, each of which can be subdivided into two equal parts.
Duration (p. 11) The length of sound or silence in music.

Dynamics (p. 29, 40) The different degrees of loudness and softness of sound.
F clef (p. 46) *see* Bass clef
Fermata (p. 212) To hold the sound for an indefinite amount of time.
Flat (p. 230) Lowers the pitch one half-step (♭).
Form (p. 159) The structural organization of music.
G clef (p. 45) *see* Treble clef
Genre (p. 148) A type of music such as jazz or folk.
Gospel (p. 38) African American songs based on Biblical themes.
Guiro (p. 220) A hollow, wooden, grooved Latin American instrument in the shape of a fish, played by scraping it with a stick.
Half step (p. 229) The smallest interval on the keyboard. The distance from one black note to either of its adjacent white notes, and also between white notes E–F and B–C.
Harmony (p. 71) A simultaneous sounding of tones.
Homophonic (p. 178) A single melody with accompaniment.
Improvisation (p. 266) Free play with musical materials.
Interval (p. 143, 149) The difference in pitch between two tones.
Introduction (p. 176) An opening section of a musical composition.
Key signature (p. 232) The arrangement of sharps or flats at the beginning of each musical staff that indicates which notes are raised or lowered throughout the piece.
Ledger lines (p. 55) Short lines drawn above or below the staff on which higher or lower pitches can be written.
Lyrics (p. 342) The words of a song.
Major scale (p. 55) Seven successive tones in which the whole and half steps are arranged WWHWWWH.
Measure (p. 18) A group of beats between two bar lines.
Meter (p. 11) The grouping of beats separated by bar lines that remains consistent throughout a musical composition.
Meter signature (p. 18) Two numerals found at the beginning of a piece or a section. The top number denotes the number of beats in each measure; the bottom number identifies the basic beat.
Minor scale (p. 334) Seven successive tones in which the whole and half steps are arranged WHWWH(W+H)H.
Monophonic (p. 178) One-voiced musical texture.
Musical elements (p. 5) Melody, harmony, rhythm, dynamics, form, timbre, and tempo.
Natural sign (p. 230) The symbol that cancels the effects of a sharp or flat (♮).
Notehead (p. 19) The empty or filled-in circular part of a note.
Octave (p. 223) The distance or interval of an eighth between two pitches.
Orff instruments (p. 217) Barred percussion instruments developed by German composer Carl Orff (1895–1982), based on Javanese gamelan. Includes xylophones, metallophones, and glockenspiel.
Ostinato (p. 332) A repeated rhythmic, melodic, or harmonic pattern.
Partner songs (p. 126) Two or more songs with the same meter and chord structure that are sung simultaneously.
Pentatonic scale (p. 334) Five successive tones that use the following arrangement of whole and half steps: W(W+H)WW.
Pitch (p. 11) The relative highness or lowness of a tone, determined by the number of vibrations per second.
Plectra (p. 171) The quills used to pluck the strings on a harpsichord.
Polyphonic (p. 178) Many different independent voices moving in different melodies.
Preparatory beats The beats counted and conducted before the first beat of the piece.
Pulse (p. 11, 12) *see* Beat.
Rainstick (p. 221) A wooden or bamboo tube filled with small seeds that, when tipped, produces a rainlike sound.

Range (p. 29) The highest and lowest pitches of a melody, or the highest and lowest pitches that can be produced by a voice or instrument.
Refrain (p. 145) Repeated sections of a song that separate the verses.
Rhythm (p. 13) The combinations of durations of sound and silence in music.
Rhythm syllables (p. 11) An organized collection of sounds used to simplify introductory rhythm reading.
Rote song method (p. 104) A way of teaching a song through direct imitation, usually by sections.
Sharp (p. 230) Raises the pitch one half step (♯).
Simple meter (p. 24) An arrangement of beats, each of which can be subdivided into two equal parts.
Skip (p. 32, 143) An interval between two pitches larger than a second.
Staff (p. 55) Five parallel lines and the four spaces between them used to write musical notation.
Stem (p. 19) The vertical line attached to a notehead that helps to denote duration.
Step (p. 143) The distance between a note placed on a line or space and a note placed on the space or line adjacent to it.
Strophic A song form in which all the verses are sung to the same music.
Syncopation (p. 25) A deliberate upsetting of the stress in a measure or in the subdivision of a beat.
Tactus (p. 236) The up-down motion of the index finger showing the steady beat.
Temple blocks (p. 224) A set of five hollow, graduated wooden blocks mounted on a frame and struck with a wooden or rubber mallet.
Tempo (p. 12, 143) The rate of speed in music.
Ternary (p. 159) A form in music consisting of three sections, usually ABA.
Theme and variations (p. 176) A form with a musical idea and a number of modifications of the original idea.
Tie (p. 22) A curved line that connects two notes of the same pitch and unites them into a single sound lasting the length of both durations.
Timbre (p. 176) The distinctive quality of a played or sung tone.
Tonal memory (p. 84) The ability to remember a sequence of pitches and durations.
Tone color (p. 177) The distinctive quality of a played or sung tone; timbre.
Transpose (p. 232) Rewrite a musical composition in another key.
Treble clef (p. 45) Also called the G clef; indicates that the second line of the staff is G. Music written after this clef is played by high-sounding instruments.
Tremolo (p. 234) The quick, continued repetition of the same note on the resonator bells, used to create the effect of a note's being sustained.
Triad (p. 234) Three notes sounded at the same time.
Triple meter (p. 18) An arrangement of beats, each of which can be subdivided into three equal parts.
Triplet (p. 331, 28) A subdivision of a note in simple meter into three equal parts, indicated by a 3.
Verse A stanza of a poem; a section of a song separated by a repeated refrain.
Vibrato (p. 58) A slight fluctuation of pitch.
Whole song method (p. 124) A way of teaching an entire song by imitation.
Whole step (p. 229) An interval made up of two half steps. On the keyboard, the distance between C and D.

Appendix C

RECORDER FINGERINGS

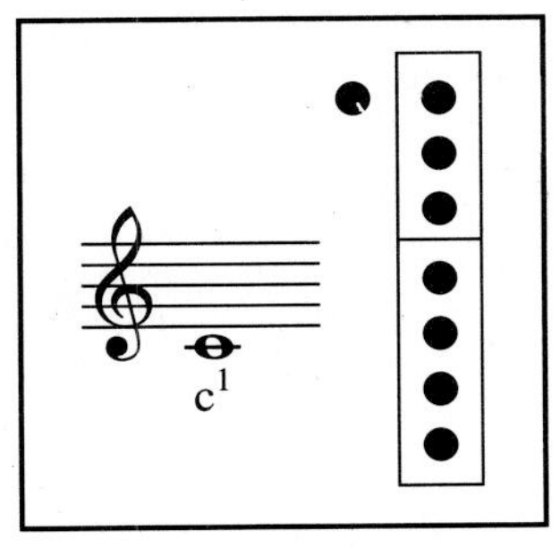

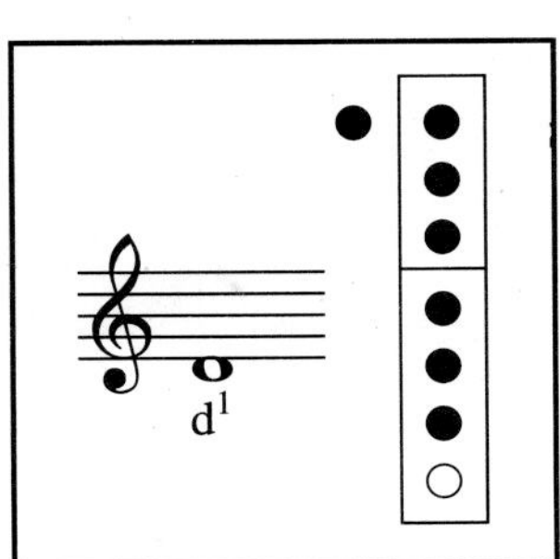

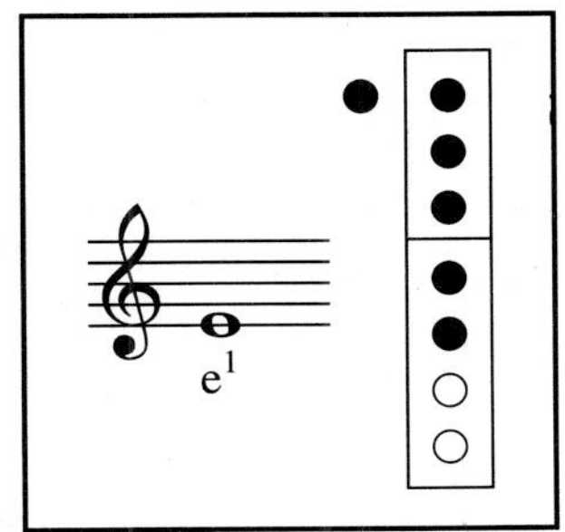

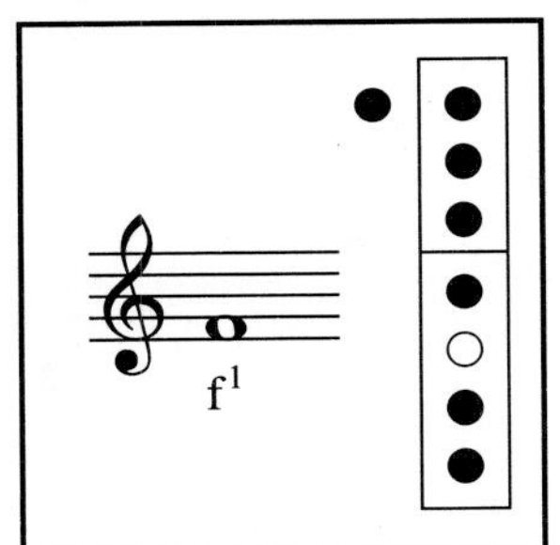

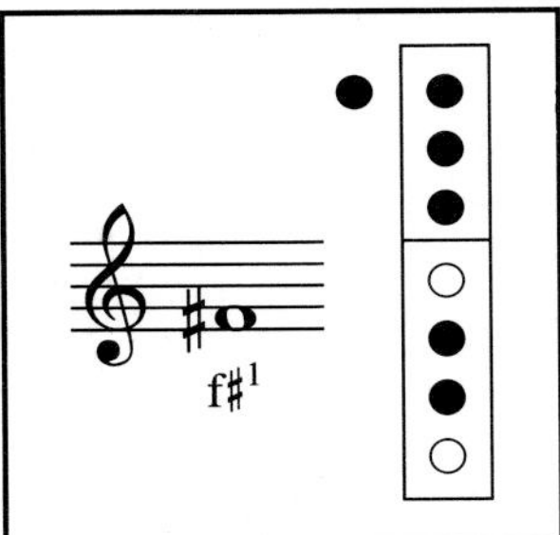

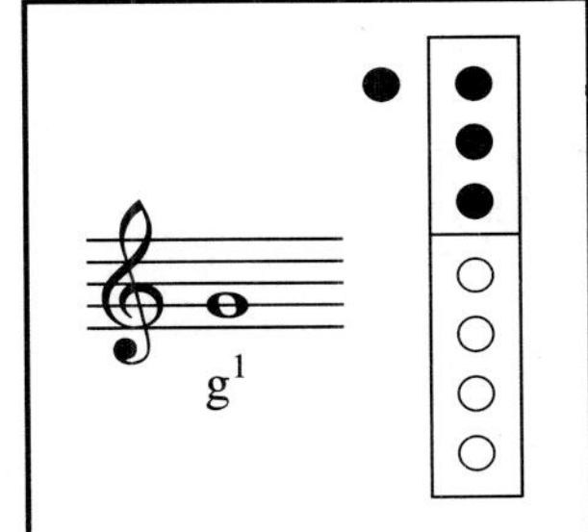

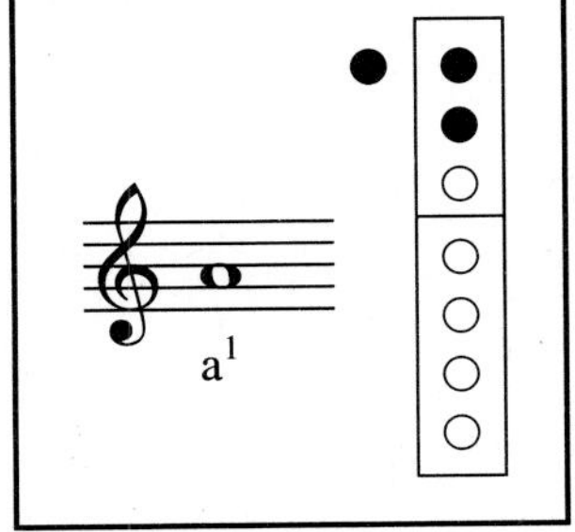

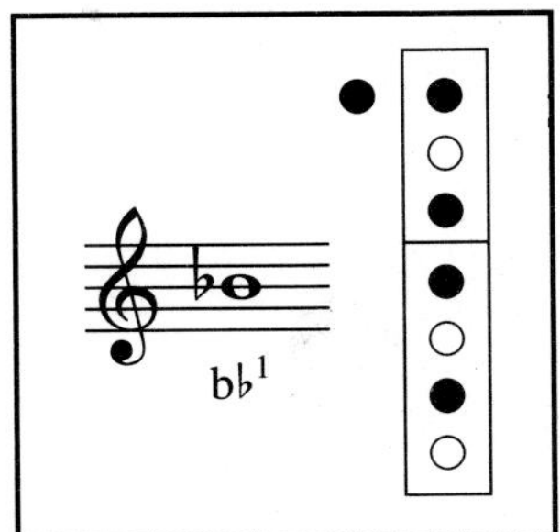

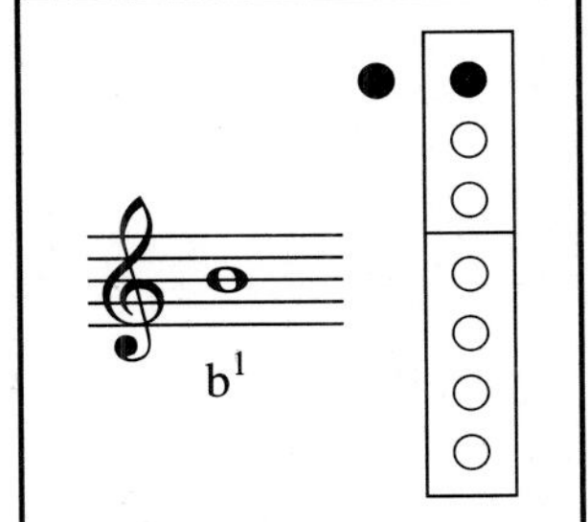

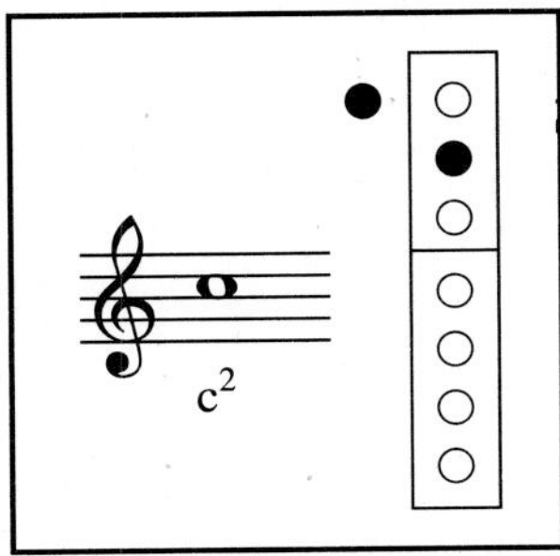

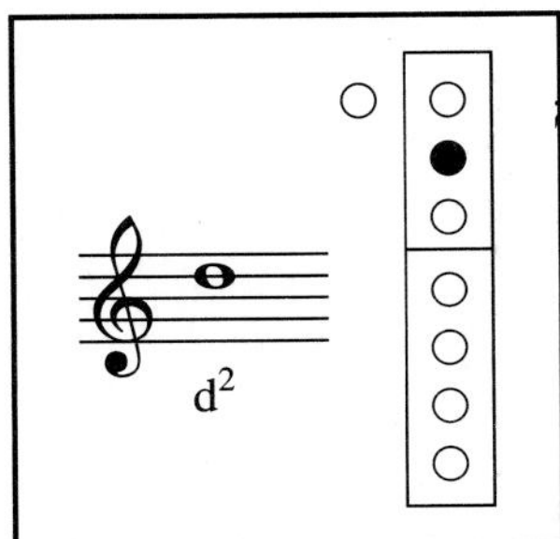

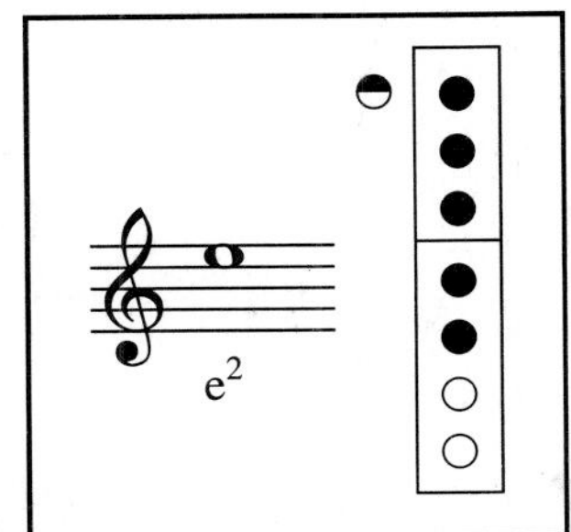

Appendix D

GUITAR CHORD FINGERINGS

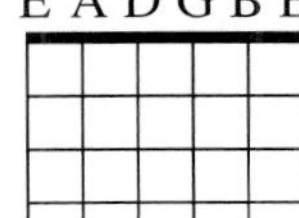

C

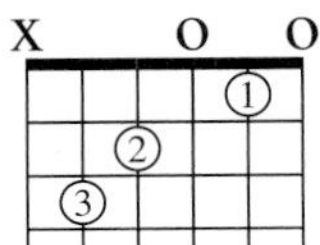

D

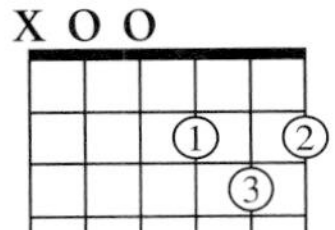

D7

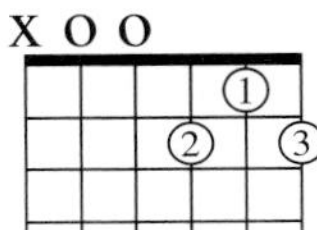

Dm

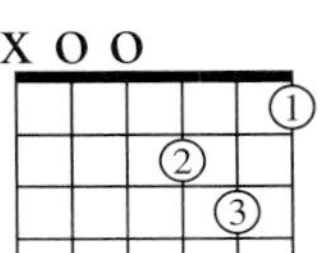

E

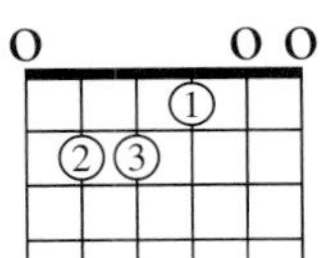

E7

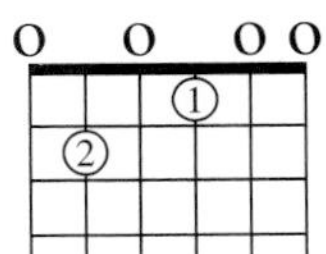

Em

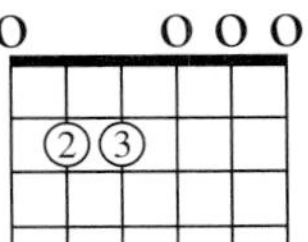

F

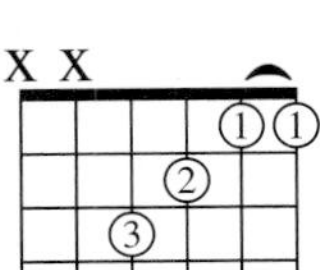

G

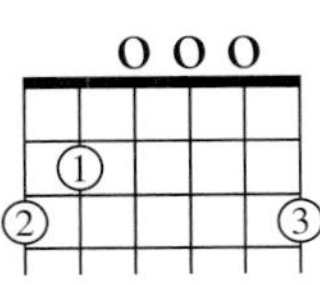

G7

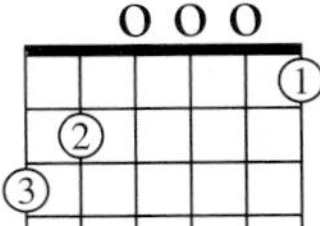

Easy Gm

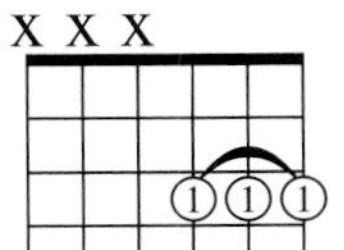

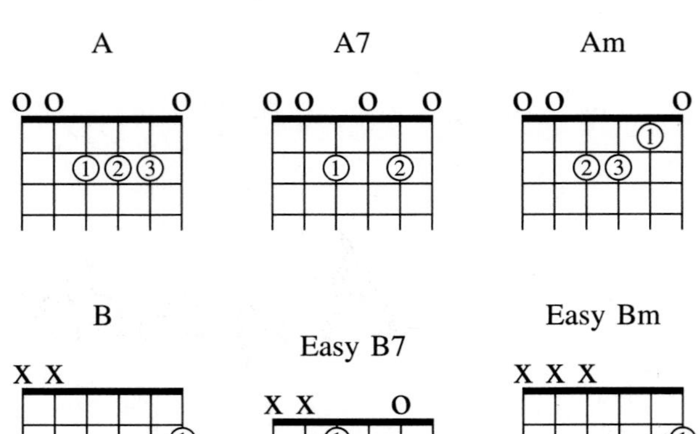

B

Easy B7

Easy Bm

Appendix

TAXONOMY OF MUSICAL CONCEPTS

RHYTHM

1. Awareness of beat and no beat
2. Beat subdivision (rhythm patterns)
3. Duration
4. Meter
5. Uneven beat subdivision (dotted, syncopated, fermata)

MELODY

1. Register
2. Direction
3. Contour
4. Duration
5. Phrases
6. Tonal centers
7. Intervals
8. Sequence

HARMONY

1. Presence/absence
2. Contrasts of texture (homophonic, polyphonic, monophonic)
3. Polyphonic (descants, canons, rounds)

TIMBRE

1. Difference between voices and instruments
2. Contrasts of high and low instruments
3. Contrasts of instrument families

FORM

1. Phrases
2. Song sections
3. Introduction, coda
4. AB, ABA
5. Rondo, theme and variations, fugue

MUSIC RESOURCES

SETS, BOOKS, AND TAPES

Conollo, Y., G. Cameron, and S. Singham. 1981. *Mango spice: Forty-four Caribbean folk songs.* London: A. C. Black. ISBN 0-7136-2107-9, Cassette ISBN 0-7136-2110-9.

East, H. 1989. *The singing sack: Twenty-eight song-stories from around the world.* London: A. C. Black. ISBN 0-7136-3115-5, Cassette ISBN 0-7136-56387.

George, L. A. 1987. *Teaching the music of six different cultures.* Danbury, Conn.: World Music.

Harvest song: Music from around the world inspired by working the land. 1995. Ellipsis Arts. Musical Expeditions CT 4040.

Jones, B. and B. Lomax Hawes. 1972. *Step it down: Games, plays, songs, and stories from the Afro-American heritage.* Athens, Ga.: University of Georgia Press.

Jones, B. 1988. *Step it down: Games for children.* Rounder Records C-8004.

Mattox, C. W. 1989. *Shake it to the one that you love the best: Play songs and lullabies from black musical traditions.* El Sobrante, Calif.: Warren-Mattox Productions.

CLASSICAL MUSIC VIDEOTAPES

Leonard Bernstein's Young People's Concerts with the New York Philharmonic. Distributed by Sony Classical.
Includes "What Is a Melody?," "The Sound of an Orchestra," "What Is Classical Music?" "What Makes Music Symphonic?" and "What Does Music Mean?"
The classic black-and-white music appreciation series from the 1960s.

Bach's Fight for Freedom
Handel's Last Chance
Liszt's Rhapsody
Strauss: The King of Three-Quarter Time. Distributed by Sony Classical.
Beethoven Lives Upstairs. Distributed by BMG.
Lively dramatizations of the lives of these five famous composers, written for today's young audiences.

Who's Afraid of Opera? An Introduction to the Joys of Opera for Children (and Adults, Too!), vols. 1–4. Distributed by Kulture International Films.
An introduction to opera hosted and performed by the Australian soprano Joan Sutherland.

MUSICAL VIDEOS INCLUDING OR ABOUT CHILDREN

Folk Dancing with Style, videotapes 1–4, taught by Sanna Longden; distributed by Folkstyle Productions. Available through website: www.FolkStyle.com; phone: 1-800-894-4378; or e-mail: sannamars@aol.com.
Folk-dance teacher Sanna Longden masterfully takes children through their paces in a wide variety of folk-dance styles from around the world.

Marsalis on Music (series): *Why Does Tap, Listening for Clues, Sousa to Satchmo,* and *Tackling the Green Monster.* Distributed by Sony Music.
Famed trumpeter Wynton Marsalis teaches music fundamentals to groups of children through performance and discussion.

Playing From the Heart. Distributed by Globalstage Productions, 1998. Phone: 1-888-324-5623; website: www.globalstage.net.
The centerpiece of this video is a play about the Scottish percussionist Evelyn Glennie (the performer on "El Dorado," track 29), who lost her hearing at the age of eight and went on to become the world's only percussionist to pursue a recital career. Concludes with an interview of the artist.

Sweet Honey in the Rock: Singing for Freedom. Distributed by Music for Little People, #5205. Phone: 1-800-346-4445.
An in-concert video of this five-woman African American a capella singing group, recorded during a family singalong concert at Glide Memorial Church in San Francisco.

Young Wonders. Distributed by the Metropolitan Opera Guild.
Forty-five fifth and sixth graders compose and perform an original opera with the help of the Metropolitan Opera Guild's education department.

G

CHILDREN'S BOOKS THAT ILLUSTRATE SONGS

PRIMARY SONGS

This Old Man. Illustrated by Carol Jones. Boston: Houghton Mifflin, 1990.
An illustrated version of the traditional counting song.

Oh Where, Oh Where Has My Little Dog Gone. Told and illustrated by Iza Trapani. Boston: Whispering Coyote Press, 1995.
An expanded version of the original rhyme.

The Itsy Bitsy Spider. Told and illustrated by Iza Trapani. Boston: Whispering Coyote Press, 1993.
An expanded version of the song.

The Cat Came Back. Illustrated by Bill Slavin. Morton Grove, Ill.: A. Whitman, 1992.
A persistent cat keeps coming back.

Over the River and through the Wood. By Lydia Maria Child; pictures by Nadine Bernard Westcott. New York: Harper Collins, 1992.
The illustrated lyrics of this traditional Thanksgiving song.

Six Little Ducks. Retold and illustrated by Chris Conover. New York: Crowell, 1976.
Illustrated lyrics of the song.

Hush Little Baby. Pictures by Jeanette Winter. New York: Pantheon Books, 1984.
An old lullaby in which the baby is promised a variety of presents.

EIEIO: The Story of Old MacDonald, Who Had a Farm. Pictures by Gus Clarke. New York: Lothrop, Lee, & Shepard Books, 1993.
In this version, Old MacDonald chooses a new profession when his farm gets too noisy.

Baby Beluga. By Raffi; illustrated by Ashley Wolff. New York: Crown, 1990.
The song about a little white whale is illustrated.

Shake My Sillies Out. By Raffi; illustrated by David Alexander. New York: Crown, 1987.
Illustrated song.

The Farmer in the Dell. Illustrated by Kathy Parkinson. Niles, Ill.: A. Whitman, 1988.
Illustrated version of the nursery rhyme.

The Man on the Flying Trapeze: The Circus Life of Emmett Kelly, Sr. By Robert Quackenbush. Philadelphia: Lippincott, 1975.
Circus experiences are related in verse.

Go Tell Aunt Rhody. Illustrated by Aliki. New York: Macmillan, 1986.
Illustrated version of the song describing the fate of Aunt Rhody's goose.

Fiddle-i-fee: A Farmyard Song for the Very Young. Adapted and illustrated by Melissa Sweet. Boston: Little, Brown, 1992.
A cumulative rhyme in which a parade forms when several farm animals join a boy and his wagon.

There's a Hole in the Bucket. Pictures by Nadine Bernard Westcott. New York: Harper & Row, 1990.
Illustrated version of a humorous folk song.

Wendy Watson's Frog Went A-Courtin. New York: Lothrop, Lee, & Shepard Books, 1990.
Folk song about the marriage of the frog and the mouse.

Animal Fair. Adapted and illustrated by Janet Stevens. New York: Holiday House, 1981.
A little boy is awakened by a friendly panda who takes him to the fair.

There Was an Old Lady Who Swallowed a Fly. Illustrated by Pam Adams. New York: Grosset & Dunlap, 1975.
Traditional song is illustrated.

INTERMEDIATE

Lift Every Voice and Sing. By James Weldon Johnson; illustrated by Jan Spivey Gilchrist. New York: Scholastic, 1995.
An illustrated version of the song that has come to be considered the African American national anthem.

Take Me Out to the Ballgame. By Maryann Kovalski. New York: Scholastic, 1993.
Lyrics of the familiar song with illustrations showing two baseball-mad girls with their grandmother enjoying the game.

Sweet Betsy from Pike. Adapted and illustrated by Roz Abisch and Boche Kaplan. New York: McCall, 1970.
Adapted from the ballad.

Yankee Doodle. By Gary Chalk. London and New York: Dorling Kindersley; distributed by Houghton Mifflin, Boston, 1993.
Original verses to song depict Boston Tea Party, Paul Revere's ride, and the Battle of Saratoga. Also includes traditional version of the song.

On Top of Spaghetti. By Tom Glazer; illustrated by Tom Garcia. Garden City, N.Y.: Doubleday, 1982.
Parody of "On Top of Old Smokey" tracing the wanderings of a meatball sneezed off a plate.

The Star Spangled Banner. Illustrated by Peter Spier. Garden City, N.Y.: Doubleday, 1973.
Illustrates verses and includes a history of the poem.

Appendix H

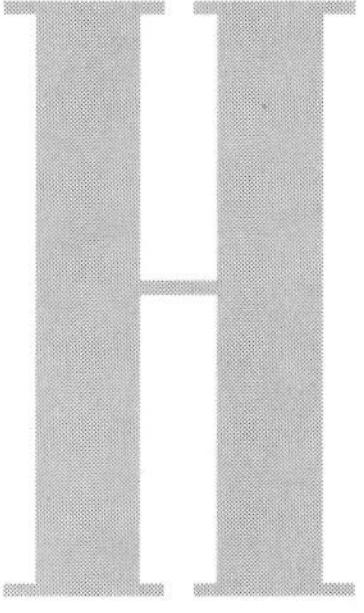

MUSIC CATALOG SUPPLIERS

Music for Little People
P.O. Box 14609
Redway, CA 95560
Phone: 1-800-346-4445
Specializes in recordings and videotapes for children.

Rhythm Band, Inc.
1212 East Lancaster
Fort Worth, TX 76101
Phone: 1-800-424-4724
Offers classroom instruments for teaching.

West Music
1208 Fifth Street
P.O. Box 5521
Coralville, IA 52241
Phone: 1-800-397-9378
Specializes in music teaching materials and classroom instruments.

Ladyslipper, Inc.
3205 Hillsborough Rd.
Durham, NC 27705
Phone: 1-800-634-6044
On-line catalog@www.ladyslipper.org
Specializes in recordings and songbooks of music by women.

Index